Principles of Speaking

Third Edition

Principles of Speaking

Third Edition

Kenneth G. Hance
Michigan State University (Emeritus)

David C. Ralph
Michigan State University

Milton J. Wiksell
University of Wisconsin – Milwaukee

Wadsworth Publishing Company, Inc.
Belmont, California

Designer: Gary Head

ISBN–0–534–003737

L. C. Cat. Card No. 74–81817

Printed in the United States of America

1 2 3 4 5 6 7 8 9 10 — 79 78 77 76 75

Illustration Credits:

United Feature Syndicate, Inc., for the Peanuts cartoons on pages 25, 34,
66, 75, 80, 92, 95, 98, 114, 128, 183, 213, 257, 274, 284, 291, 310, 319,
335, and 355.

Photographs: page 1 — © Howard Harrison 1970; page 31 — © Howard
Harrison 1970; page 125 — Vilms/Jerobaum, Inc.; page 271 — © Howard
Harrison 1971; page 325 — Powers/Jerobaum, Inc.

Preface

Principles of Speaking is written primarily for the beginning student in speech communication, whether he is an undergraduate college student or an adult who seeks to improve his skills in oral communication. Its content is related to everyday occasions, instead of strictly large-auditorium speeches; and it is developed upon the concept that most speaking opportunities arise out of particular occasions rather than out of free choices made by the speaker well in advance of the speaking situation.

The specific purposes of this book are (1) to develop attitudes toward speaking that pertain to the place of oral communication in everyday life and to the important ethical considerations that should underlie all speaking, (2) to develop tastes with respect to the purposes and standards of good speaking, and (3) to develop competence in the art of speaking.

The principles and methods set forth in this book represent a synthesis of what we believe to be the best materials of the rhetorical tradition as supplemented by the latest research and by the formulations of the field of communication. They represent, also, a synthesis of the materials the authors have developed and tested in their many years of experience with undergraduate students, with graduate students, and with persons in business and industry.

This book, organized on a functional plan, begins with an overall treatment of the art of speaking in respect to philosophy and to basic principles and methods (Part One). Attention is then directed to a body of principles and methods that pertain to all types of speaking (Parts Two and Three), after which attention is directed to specific types of speaking and speaking situations (Parts Four and Five). It is hoped that this plan combines the values of a deductive approach (with broad considerations presented in advance of specific matters) with those of an inductive approach (in which the development progresses from one set of principles and methods to another). It is hoped, also, that the approach in Chapters 1 and 2 will enable the student to proceed at once to the preparation and presentation of oral messages without having to wait until all principles and methods have been developed in detail.

Twelve years of teaching with this textbook, together with evaluations made by scores of teachers and by thousands of students, have indicated the need for this type of work and the validity of its general approach. This third edition, however, represents a number of general and specific areas and elements of departure from the first and second editions. In addition to several chapters having been completely rewritten and all others having been revised in a number of respects, substantial revisions are represented by the following features:

1.   The new edition continues the authors' attempts to broaden the concept of speaking and to step up our belief that the principles of oral communication apply to all "original" speaking for a purpose — not by eliminating or even deemphasizing the formal public speech but by giving added emphasis to less formal, informal, and interpersonal speaking. The book, in other words, is an introduction to *speaking*, not alone to a specific *form of speaking*.

2.   The new edition attempts to combine the best theory and principles from the traditions of both speech and communication; thus, we believe *Principles* will serve the student in classes in public speaking and in classes in human communication.

3.   *Principles*, Third, contains materials that reflect developments in theory and practice since 1969, including focus on nonverbal communication, a refocusing of attention from "choosing the subject" to one of "responding to the subject," and the inclusion of additional material (including a sample speech plan) on the inductive structure of the oral message.

4.   This edition has been updated with examples relevant to today's student of speaking, and it contains updated reference materials at the end of each chapter.

5.   Finally, the latest edition features a new format consisting of statements of principles followed by recommendations for implementing the principles in the practice of speaking. Thus, our readers have a choice of reasoning from the principles to their own specific applications of these principles or of accepting the conclusions and suggestions of the authors.

We remain grateful to those who offered suggestions on the previous editions and greatly appreciate the helpful comments made by teachers and students who used the second edition. We give our thanks, too, to our typists: Dena Brunsting, Ruth Langenbacher, LuAnn Love, and Edna Seeley.

Contents

Part Three   Preparing to Speak

Part Five   Related Speaking Situations

Dedicated to

Winifred Hance
Kathryn Ralph
Elizabeth Wiksell

Part One
An Introduction to Speaking

Part One describes what speaking is all about. Chapter 1 discusses the part it plays in modern society, the communication process, breakdowns in oral communication and some means of preventing them, and a basis for a code of ethics in speaking. Chapter 2 lays out—in seven steps—a simplified procedure for preparing, delivering, and evaluating the formal oral message, and applies it to informal, everyday communication.

1
A Rationale for Speaking

"I never give public speeches"

One way of describing democracy is as "government by talk." The very essence of democracy is communication between persons and between groups of persons—interchange of information and points of view *under all kinds of circumstances: informal and formal, unplanned and planned, small and large.* Since the days of Isocrates in Greece, the ideal society has been characterized as a "highly communicating society"—and the ideal citizen as both informed *and* articulate. *Oral communication* is, in fact, the very genius of democratic society—the kind of society in which most people would like to live.

Speech—the process of oral communication—is perhaps more essential to our effective functioning in a modern society than are our abilities to see and hear. Without speech, we must exist in almost total isolation; we can communicate virtually no thought, no wish, no need, no feeling to our fellowmen. (Although there is great potency in other methods of communication—the visual arts, music, written communication—oral communication gives rise to and supports a society's structure.)

The necessity for oral communication increases as the organization of the group—the society—increases in complexity and refinement. In the kind of society described as "government by talk," each person may have his say, which is the democratic way of life. Most of our social organizations—our families, our schools, our churches, and our residential communities—fall into the democratic category. This manner of living together places a high premium upon articulate expression on the part of every participant, whose personal effectiveness is in large part determined by his ability to express himself adequately. The ability of the individual member determines the success or failure of the work of the group as a whole.

Here *we are thinking of "speech" not solely as public speaking, as frequently conceived—that is, lengthy addresses delivered in formal situations. We are thinking, also, of the many communication situations we all experience daily in speak-*

ing to other persons for purposes that range from simple explanation to the securing of overt commitments. Although notes and audio-visual aids, platforms and lecterns, audiences, and the speaker's table constitute important elements of the business of making speeches, *they are not central to the basic process of speech as we are viewing it here.*

For purposes of our discussion, speech is simply the act of communicating with others orally — by means of words, with accompanying body action, or nonverbal communication. The situation may be very formal or quite informal; the relative formality of the situation — as well as the physical circumstances, the number of listeners, and the length of the discourse — is immaterial to this basic process. We are concerned with *talking for a purpose.*

Often we hear the comment "I never give public speeches" from persons who, in the course of a day, actually speak in connected discourses of a few minutes' duration to one or several other persons. Actually, they do give many "speeches" every day. During any week, a college student probably speaks in formal class recitations, presents oral reports, and expresses his ideas in meetings of one or more campus groups. Some of these situations are important and demanding. Any member of the community probably does a good deal of speaking — describing his activities, giving directions, passing on information, promoting his ideas, or expressing his views on a controversial subject.

Day in and day out, we are all very much speakers; and all of the principles and methods of speaking apply to our speaking situations quite as much as they do to those of lecturers, clergymen, and politicians.

Since we are all speakers, whether or not we think of ourselves as such, it is to our advantage to understand something of the process in which we are engaged — its nature, the causes of its failure and of its effectiveness, and how we can make it work best for us.

The Nature of the Communication Process

To understand the nature of speech communication, we must examine the process of *communication* in general. We should determine the separate elements of the communication process, observe their relationships, and attempt to discover where the process can go wrong and what we may do to make it work satisfactorily.

Let us do this by asking and answering five questions: (1) What is communication? (2) What are the important elements or variables? (3) What are the steps in the process of communication? (4) What are the more important kinds of breakdowns? (5) What are some means of preventing these breakdowns?

Definition of Communication

Communication may be defined as *the process of attempting to arouse meaning in the receiver that approximates the meaning in the source.* This process involves transmitting a message from the source to the receiver. Therefore, *effective* communication results when the substance of facts, judgments, or whatever else is in the mind of the person who is sending the message is perceived by the receiver just as the source intended. Another helpful definition states that communication is the process of attempting to share with another person, or other persons, one's knowledge, interests, attitudes, opinions, or ideals. Effective communication, therefore, is present when this information or these interests, attitudes, opinions, or ideals are actually shared.

Communication is a process with a purpose. It is effective when that purpose is realized; that is, when the source (the speaker) "gets through" to the receiver (the listener).[1]

Important Elements in the Communication Process

The important elements, or variables, used in our analysis of communication are (1) the _source_ (communicator, speaker, writer), (2) the _message_ (speech or article), (3) the _channel_ (medium or vehicle), (4) the _receiver_ (listener or reader), (5) the _effect_ (response, consequence, impact), and (6) the _feedback_ from the receiver to the original source.

Steps in the Communication Process

The process of communication involves, essentially, a flow from the source of the message through the channel to the receiver (in whom an effect is produced) and back to the original source as feedback. However, because not all of the implications and relationships of these steps may be apparent from this simple statement, let us analyze their nature more fully.

First, the _source_ wants to express himself— to share an experience, convey information, give directions, obtain agreement, or get something done.

Second, he "encodes" his idea into a *message* in the form of written or spoken language. The message is the essential thought of the communica-

---

[1] "Communication," as used here and generally throughout this book, implies: (1) *human* communication (between people, that is, and not including the kind of message a person receives from other living things or inanimate objects, such as the feelings aroused in him by a dilapidated house) and (2) *"conscious"* or "deliberate" communication. Sometimes, however, as in Chapter 5 on "Personal Proof," the authors speak of what may be regarded as "unconscious communication." The reader should make a careful distinction between the two.

tion process—the reason for communicating and the subject matter to be communicated.

Third, the message is transmitted through various *channels*—for instance, orthographic signs, graphic signs, light vibrations, air vibrations, electrical impulses, and electromagnetic waves.

Fourth, the *receiver* "decodes" or translates the message into the form of language that is meaningful (or, if the communication is faulty, meaningless) to him.

Fifth, the message produces an *effect* when the receiver reacts to it as he understands it.

Sixth, the receiver's reaction becomes, in turn, a message that may be picked up and interpreted by the original source. This *feedback,* as it is frequently called, is inevitable in nearly every communication situation—at least in every interpersonal communication situation. It ties together the beginning and ending of the original process and makes it truly continuous or circular. The speaker who understands the importance of feedback is aware of the necessity of watching his listeners and interpreting their reactions.

Breakdowns in Communication

The possibilities for breakdown in the intricate process of communication are numerous, and they can occur at several points.

Breakdowns may occur at the *source*. The communicator may (1) fail to have a clear conception of his purpose or main idea; (2) lack the proper information for the development of his main idea; (3) be deficient in organizing his materials and in thinking coherently and logically; (4) lack the vocabulary necessary for proper expression of his ideas; (5) "get in the way" of his message because he forgets, or is unaware of, those *personal* qualities that make for effective communication; (6) be unaware of all of the visible and audible symbols that make up his message; (7) have a faulty attitude concerning his function as a speaker; (8) have an inaccurate conception of the nature of the receiver or of the receiver's participation in the act of communication.

Similar breakdowns may occur within the *message.* (Of course, because the source is directly responsible for the message, there will be some overlapping between the breakdowns just described and those that follow.) The message may (1) lack a clear purpose or central idea; (2) suffer from poor organization, incoherence, or faulty logic; (3) be deficient in vocabulary and sentence structure; (4) not have sufficient interest or significance to hold attention; (5) be inadequately adapted to the receiver; (6) (if written) suffer from poor handwriting, typing, or printing.

Breakdowns may occur through the *channel:* (1) The sound waves may be adversely affected by distracting noises, distance, poor acoustics, and the like. (2) The light waves may be affected by distance or by distracting light waves. (3) Equipment, such as public address systems, radio, and television, may be mechanically defective.

Breakdowns may also occur in the *receiver*. The listener may (1) fail to "attend" (listen and observe)—physical presence is no guarantee of mental alertness; (2) be deficient in the faculty of hearing or sight, or both; (3) not understand the words and other symbols in the message; (4) be unduly prejudiced toward the message or the source; (5) be unfamiliar with the ideas presented by the source (and may, therefore, either find them meaningless or make inaccurate substitutions for them from the realm of his own experience).

Prevention of Communication Breakdowns

Necessarily, prescriptions for avoiding or preventing breakdowns in communication are subject to oversimplification or overlapping. However, ways of avoiding them can be learned, and the following are some brief suggestions.

First, the *source* has certain preventive means at his command. The speaker can (1) prepare his message adequately—giving consideration to its purpose, main ideas, details of content, organization, and development (this *is* possible even in highly informal and impromptu situations, requiring only some mental discipline and attention to the task at hand); (2) call on the resources of effective communication inherent in his own nature (competence, character, and goodwill), which will be described in Chapter 5; (3) diagnose and adapt to the communication situation—that is, the occasion and the audience; (4) understand the problems of reading and listening; (5) study the implications of feedback, and adapt accordingly.

Second, several preventive means are relevant to the *message*. It can have (1) a clear purpose and central idea, (2) careful organization and logical development, (3) proper word choice and sentence structure, (4) important ideas that interest the receiver and command his attention.

Third, breakdowns in the *channel* can be avoided by making it as "clear" as possible—free from distortions in light or sound waves—and paying proper attention to distance, lighting, sound equipment, and the like.

Fourth, breakdowns at the *receiver* can be prevented through efforts of both the source and the receiver. The source can do his or her part to assure effective communication by (1) understanding the role of the receiver in the communication process, (2) analyzing the nature of the receiver and the circumstances under which he will receive the message, and (3) making the necessary adaptations according to his understanding of the receiver and the situation. The receiver can do his or her part by (1) understanding his role and responsibilities in the communication process and (2) making himself a better listener through some of the methods available to him.

While these suggestions may seem to place too much emphasis upon separate and distinct elements of the process — thus making communication appear as a formidable task — the rewards of *successful* communication are well worth the attention paid, at least at this point, to its separate elements. Effective communication in virtually all situations *is* definitely possible and indisputably desirable, and the methods that lead to it may be clearly laid out before us.

The Nature of Good Speech

The foregoing analysis of the communication process suggests the qualities that characterize good communication of all types. The qualities of good communication are, of course, the qualities of *good speech*, which reflects a clear purpose and a central idea *and* a well-organized message. Even in casual conversation, a person is regarded more favorably if he speaks "for a reason" and speaks "with a point" and, also, if he does so "without rambling" incoherently. And in more formal discourse, even if impromptu, the composition should represent a plan characterized by organization and coherence. Further, this message is presented in clear, understandable, and compelling language, spoken with clarity and vigor, and is aimed toward a specific listener under a definite set of circumstances.

The message must also consist of good, solid content that meets all reasonable tests of accuracy and validity. In fact, we are assuming throughout this book that the speaker "has something to say" — that he "knows what he is talking about" and has made at least some preparation for speaking, whether it be in a formal or an informal situation. We are assuming, furthermore, that the speaker will constantly draw upon his general fund of knowledge and experience, that he will use the resources provided by courses other than the ones called "speech," and that he will make use of the methods of acquiring and handling materials set forth at several points in this book.

Let us make ourselves clear regarding the concept of subject-matter competence. While this book contains much material pertaining to the principles and methods of speaking, it does not presume to provide substance for the message. Such substance comes from everything that represents a liberal education, everything relevant to any subject a person might speak on. It can be found in encyclopedias and hundreds of other reference works, plus hundreds of thousands of books and other source materials — but not within the covers of a single textbook. As one educator has said, "There are two (complementary) types of education: Education *for* communication, and Education *in* communication. The former represents or embraces education in the subject-matter being communicated, and the latter embraces education in the principles and methods of effective communication of this subject-matter." This book assumes the means of achieving competence in the former; and it assists in providing resources for the latter.

Let us look at the standards of good speech in respect to the *composition* and *delivery* of oral messages. In this light, by composition we mean the *materials of the speech* and the *speaker's treatment of these materials;* and by delivery, we mean the *audible* and *visible* expressions of the message. (See the checklist of "Good Speaking" and "Poor Speaking.")

Good Speaking

Composition

Materials

1. *The subject matter is pertinent to the occasion and the listener.*

2. *The content of the speech is interesting.*

3. *The speech has abundant concrete examples—materials that create word pictures and definite situations.*

4. *The materials are varied.*

5. *The speech offers adequate support or proof of its lines of thought.*

6. *The amount of material is adapted to the time limits.*

7. *The language is precise and clear.*

8. *The ideas are worthwhile to the listener.*

9. *Feedback indicates that the ideas are adapted to the audience.*

Organization of Materials

1. *The opening remarks are attention-getting and pertinent.*

2. *The central idea and purpose are presented clearly.*

3. *The development of the ideas is logical, coherent, and easy to follow.*

4. *The conclusion is clear and emphatic.*

5. *Feedback indicates that the organization is adapted to the listener.*

Poor Speaking

Composition

Materials

1. *The subject matter is not pertinent (probably because of speaker's excessive subjectivity); he is not thinking of others, not adequately diagnosing the occasion and the audience.*

2. *The subject of the discourse is poorly chosen in relation to the listener's interests.*

3. *The discourse lacks materials that catch and hold attention.*

4. *The materials lack variety.*

5. *There is inadequate substance—lack of clarity or lack of support (proof).*

6. *There is too much (or too little) material for the time allowed.*

7. *The language is inexact and fuzzy.*

8. *The ideas seem unimportant to the listener.*

9. *Feedback indicates that ideas are not adapted to the audience.*

Organization of Materials

1. *The opening is abstract (too general and perhaps irrelevant).*

2. *The central idea and purpose are vague and indefinite.*

3. *The development is haphazard, incoherent, and difficult to follow.*

4. *The conclusion is too general and lacks punch.*

5. *Feedback indicates that the organization lacks adaptation to the listener.*

The failure of a speaker to communicate effectively—that is, his failure to measure up to the standards outlined in the lefthand column of the checklist (see inset)—means, of course, that something has gone wrong. However, because there are especially common and crucial instances of difficulties that may be responsible for the failure of a speech, we do more than merely list the failures; we analyze them in the righthand column.

At first glance, this table of suggestions, the *dos* and *don'ts* of effective

---

Good Speaking

Delivery

Audible Expression

1. The speaker talks clearly and distinctly.

2. The speaker adjusts his loudness to the communication situation.

3. The speaker maintains a good rate—neither too fast nor too slow.

4. The speaker adjusts the pitch of his voice to assure maximum directness.

5. The speaker's voice is lively and dynamic.

6. The speaker modulates his voice for variety and for emphasis of important ideas.

Visible Expression

1. The speaker makes a good approach and creates a good impression before he starts to speak.

2. The appearance of the speaker is pleasing and appropriate.

3. The posture of the speaker reveals alertness.

4. The speaker maintains eye contact (to "get over" to his audience and to detect feedback).

5. The speaker's facial expression gives evidence of friendliness and eagerness to communicate.

6. The speaker is lively, dynamic, and enthusiastic.

7. The speaker uses body activity to complement other means of communication.

Poor Speaking

Delivery

Audible Expression

1. The speaker's words are indistinct and fuzzy.

2. Loudness is inadequate—too little or too much.

3. Rate is inadequate—too fast or too slow.

4. Pitch sounds "indirect."

5. The voice is "lifeless," monotonous—shows insufficient enthusiasm.

6. Voice allows inadequate variety; a lack of stress on key ideas.

Visible Expression

1. Initial impression is poor.

2. The appearance is poor—not pleasing or appropriate.

3. The posture lacks tone.

4. Eye contact with the audience is poor (looking away, looking up, looking down).

5. The facial expression is poor; it lacks warmth and fails to help in communication.

6. Bearing and manner reveal little life.

7. Movement is meaningless or random—or absent.

speaking, may seem a formidable (perhaps artificial) list of standards. However, have we not consciously or unconsciously used some or all of these criteria when we have remarked that a certain speaker is "good" or "not good," "effective" or "ineffective"? This analysis of speech standards is doubly useful in that it (1) sets before us a goal toward which we can strive in our efforts to communicate effectively through oral discourse and (2) offers us a useful organization of criteria that we can keep in mind when we speak.

The rewards of understanding these criteria and translating them into practice are many. If we want to speak for a purpose—make our ideas clear, convince others of our way of thinking, show others that we are interested in them—we must know, among other things, how to communicate effectively.

The Ethics of Speech

If the spoken word did not influence the minds of men, we could practice speaking without regard to the ethical power of its methods and consequences. However, since we know that speech has a direct influence upon human behavior, any speaker has to assume a profound ethical responsibility for all that he says.

For these reasons, let us consider a code of ethics for speech communication—a platform of principles concerned with more than mere effectiveness or the securing of the intended results. Because at least four practices that are regarded by some persons as unethical are considered by others to be completely ethical, let us first deal with them to avoid misunderstanding and to clear the way for a discussion of "ethics in speech."

1. Contrary to some persons' beliefs, *the presentation of only one side of an issue* does not necessarily raise ethical questions. Every speaker has the right to present the best possible case for his or her thesis; and if he believes the best case to consist only of "favorable arguments," he is justified in offering only those arguments. (Even though some experimental evidence suggests that in some cases the "one-sided presentation" is less effective than the "two-sided," this has little, if anything, to do with the ethics of such a presentation.)[2]

2. Nor is *the use of emotional appeals*—in addition to those commonly described as "rational"—necessarily unethical. Many speakers emphasize emotional appeals; they are merely directing their attention to an important

---

[2] This point of view does not apply to *explanatory* messages and to *reports of the thinking of other persons*. In these circumstances, anything less than a full report would, of course, be unethical.

side of human nature. Although many of us may prefer to consider matters primarily in their rational aspects, this preference involves a judgment unrelated to ethics *per se.*

3. *Arranging ideas or arguments in a sequence designed to secure a desired effect* is also ethically valid. If the materials are honestly and fully presented and if no unwarranted conclusions are drawn from them, the only question that could arise is not one of ethics but of harmony or consistency with the principles of rhetoric, logic, and (in particular) psychology.

4. No ethical question is raised, similarly, when the speaker consciously makes full use of the *ethos* concept—the concept of the influence of the *person* of the speaker on the validity of his *message* (developed further in Chapter 5)—to present himself in a favorable light. Whether the speaker wishes it or not, the forces of ethos are operating constantly, and all of the elements of his personality—character, honor, competence, intelligence—are subjected to continual judgment as he presents his message. And if the presentation of himself is founded on fact, the conscious relationship of his person to the theme of his message is beyond ethical judgment.

A code of ethics for speech should be constructed, we believe, not from matters like those just reviewed, but from the values of the society in which we live—a society in which speaking plays a vital role. From the basic values of a democratic, or free, society, we can derive definite ethical standards for speaking.[3]

A democratic society is founded upon four essential values: (1) belief in the dignity and worth of the individual; (2) faith in equality of opportunity; (3) belief in freedom, subject to the restraints of laws made by established legal means; and (4) belief in special freedoms—of speech, of the press, of assembly—to enable the members of the society to acquire the knowledge that they need for making and testing decisions through discussion and debate.

On the basis of these essential values, we can establish certain minimum standards for the development of a code of ethics of speech. These standards, although especially relevant to speeches of advocacy, apply as well to explanatory discourse.

1. The speaker must be worthy of the respect that he or she wants from his listeners as he speaks. He must be well prepared. The theses and judgments that he believes to be valid must be the products of careful preparation and of thought based upon the highest principles of logic. *He must be worth listening to.*

2. He must present facts and opinions accurately, with care and respect for the raw materials of his discourse and for the foundations underlying his reasoning.

---

[3] For a more complete treatment of this concept, see "An Ethical Basis of Communication," by Karl R. Wallace, *The Speech Teacher,* Vol. 4 (January 1955), pp. 1–9. We acknowledge our indebtedness to Professor Wallace for this analysis.

3.   He must reveal the sources of his information. He must tell his listeners what persons, institutions, and motivations provide the background for his message, whether the sources be those of fact and opinion or those of inspiration (purposes, goals, values).

4.   He must welcome dissent. He must recognize not only the *existence* of other opinions, but also their *value* for testing his own judgments, even to the extent of taking the steps necessary to assure this testing.

In this chapter we have shared some thoughts about speech, and we have presented a rationale for the principles and methods to be developed in subsequent chapters. We have reminded ourselves of the universality of speaking; we have seen a few of the countless opportunities that arise for effective communication. We have analyzed the process of communication — how it is built up and where it can break down. We have examined the nature of good speech and the circumstances of failure in oral communication. Finally, we have established a code of ethics to serve as a guide in our efforts to communicate with our fellowmen, whether to provide them with information that we believe is essential to their welfare, or to demonstrate to them that our judgments are valid and worthy of belief and adoption.

Suggested Assignments

1.   Make an inventory of the number of oral communication situations in which you have participated as a speaker today. Include situations of all types: informal and formal; spontaneous and prepared. What types were they? What were their purposes?

2.   Make a similar inventory of the number of oral communication situations in which you have participated as a listener today. Include situations of all types — as in No. 1. What types were they? What were their purposes?

3.   How many "formal" prepared speeches have you presented during the past month? Year? What were the situations? What were the subjects?

4.   To how many "formal" prepared speeches (including lectures) have you listened during the past week? What were the situations? What were the subjects?

5.   If your recent experiences in oral communication (either as a speaker or as a listener) have been satisfactory, why so? In other words, what did you do, or what did any other speaker do, in content and delivery, that appeared to make the situation satisfactory?

6.   If any of these experiences has been unsatisfactory, why so?

7.   Evaluate a speaker in respect to the suggestions given in this chapter. How well does he "measure up"? How significant are any matters of which he does not meet the requirements set forth and discussed in this chapter?

8.   What do you think of the inclusion of a speaker's code of ethics in this chapter? Isn't an understanding of the process of communication enough? How much attention should be given to ethics in speaking?

9.   Analyze the four-point speaker's code of ethics that is presented in this chapter. Do you agree with it? If not, in what respects would you amend it? Why?

10.   According to this code, or your amendment of it, evaluate a speaker whom you have recently heard and seen. In what respects does he "measure up"? How significant are any matters of which he does not meet the requirements included in this code?

Suggested References

Andersen, Kenneth E., *Persuasion: Theory and Practice* (Boston: Allyn and Bacon, 1971). Chapter 16 (with Mary Andersen), "Ethics and Persuasion."

Bryant, Donald C., "Rhetoric: Its Functions and Its Scope," *Quarterly Journal of Speech*, Vol. 39 (December 1953), pp. 401–424.

Flynn, Lawrence J., "The Aristotelian Basis for the Ethics of Speaking," *The Speech Teacher*, Vol. 6 (September 1957), pp. 179–187.

Haiman, Franklyn S., "Democratic Ethics and the Hidden Persuaders," *Quarterly Journal of Speech*, Vol. 44 (December 1958), pp. 385–392.

Hance, Kenneth G., "The Character of the Beginning Course: Skills and/or Content," *The Speech Teacher*, Vol. 10 (September 1961), pp. 220–224.

Jensen, J. Vernon, "An Analysis of Recent Literature on Teaching Ethics in Public Address," *The Speech Teacher*, Vol. 8 (September 1959), pp. 219–228.

Johannesen, Richard L., in *Persuasion: Reception and Responsibility* by Charles U. Larson (Belmont, Calif.: Wadsworth Publishing Co., 1973). Chapter 9, "Perspectives on Ethics in Persuasion."

Minnick, Wayne C., *The Art of Persuasion*, 2nd ed. (Boston: Houghton Mifflin Co., 1968). Chapter 11, "The Ethics of Persuasion."

Nilsen, Thomas R., *Ethics of Speech Communication* (Indianapolis: Bobbs-Merrill Co., 1966).

Rivers, William L., and Wilbur Schramm, *Responsibility in Mass Communication*, Rev. ed. (New York: Harper & Row, 1969). Chapter 5, "Truth and Fairness."

Schramm, Wilbur, *Men, Messages, and Media* (New York: Harper & Row, 1973).

Thonssen, Lester, and A. Craig Baird, *Speech Criticism* (New York: Ronald Press Co., 1948). Chapter 18, "Toward a Philosophy of Rhetoric" — pp. 470–472: "Ethics."

Wallace, Karl R., "An Ethical Basis of Communication," *The Speech Teacher*, Vol. 4 (January 1955), pp. 1–9.

2
First Steps in Communicating Orally

"And how should I begin?"

This book aims to help you improve in your ability to communicate orally with other people. The principles of communication it employs (verbal and nonverbal) have been developed over thousands of years and, in recent times, have been tested and refined through scientific research. It is important for you to realize that the development or improvement of the skills of *communicating* will require a substantial effort over a considerable period of time — the principles of communicating effectively are neither few enough nor simple enough to learn overnight.

But your need to communicate will not wait while you master these pages — while you relate principles with practice. This very day, for example, you will deliver many, many messages: most of them probably brief; the great majority of them informal, without much time given to thinking about the message or its consequences; many of them unimportant and purposeless, but many of them vital to your moment-by-moment existence. True, you will probably be receivers much more often than sources of messages; but in a normal waking day you may give directions, inquire into the health of your neighbor, exchange quips concerning the latest activities on Capitol Hill, exert influence (or attempt to) upon your boss or a co-worker, explain why you failed to accomplish a certain task, discuss the apparent meaning of a passage with your teacher or with other students, cope with the wounded feelings of a young child, wriggle evasively out of a direct response to an embarrassing question, report on a project to your superior or a team of consultants, seek advice from a lawyer, wrestle with a group of other interested citizens over various solutions to a local problem, argue that pot smoking is no worse than getting drunk, achieve an understanding with your living companion concerning some philosophical point, and on and on.

Some of these messages will be "prepared," that is, thought about in advance; some will be off the cuff (and some regretted); some will be spoken in a dyad (a one-to-one conversation), some in a group; and some may be delivered to people who have gathered for the purpose of listening to your words. Messages will vary in length.

But they will all be messages and most of them will be oral (what many people call "speakin'"). And, what is especially significant to our purpose, they will all be based upon one set of communication principles, drawn from what we have been able to develop of communication theory. This book directs those principles to the comprehensive development of your skills as an oral communicator. This chapter offers an interim and brief look at the steps you will take in preparing and presenting a message.

Although some of these steps apply mainly to situations that call for a planned, carefully prepared message, most of them apply to the daily, informal messages that make up the bulk of our communication:

1. Decide the why and what of your message.
2. Analyze your receiver's potential response to your message.
3. Construct a basic, abbreviated plan for your message.
4. Discover, create, gather, interpret, and evaluate materials for your message.
5. Organize your message.
6. Deliver your message.
7. Evaluate your message.

Communicating for a purpose, as we have described it in Chapter 1, results from some kind of exigence[1] — a need, an event, a stimulus, a demand, a raison d'être, a cause, a situation. The process of communicating is, of course, much more involved than the simple list of steps (above) might suggest. However, this list is workable for the beginning speaker, and the order of the steps is probably the most workable order for him or her. As he attains the freedom that comes with experience and success, the communicator will learn (for both formal and informal occasions) to vary the order of preparation and the degree of emphasis upon the steps.

Step 1: Decide the Why and What of Your Message

Why are you communicating and what will you make known? These questions should pop into your mind the instant you feel the urge to open your mouth—at least in any situation where you are speaking for a purpose. The

---

[1] See Lloyd F. Bitzer, "The Rhetorical Situation," *Philosophy and Rhetoric*, Vol. 1 (January 1968), pp. 1–14.

questions are significant, urgent, whether your message is an almost in-stantaneous reply to a demand of your environment (an exigence) or whether it is a carefully prepared and rehearsed formal statement. Any further prep-aration, ranging from quick, unrehearsed decisions concerning the content of a brief message to extensive research for supporting evidence, depends upon the answers to the questions "Why am I communicating?" and "What do I want to say?"

First of all, as a beginning student of communication, you should deter-mine your *specific purpose* for speaking. Make a concise and accurate state-ment of what you want to accomplish—or, to put the matter in behavioral terms, state what you want your listeners to do or believe or understand. This is your *purpose sentence,* and you should refer to it throughout the preparation of your message so that you never lose track of why you are speaking.

If your message is a formal one, involving time and effort for prepara-tion, you should write down your purpose sentence at the top of the page on which you are planning your message. If the message is informal or must be presented quickly, with no time to set your thoughts on paper, "file" the purpose sentence in the front of your mind, where you can refer to it often and quickly as the message develops. In many instances you will actually use it in the presentation of your message—perhaps when you wish to declare what you are talking about; perhaps when you offer arguments or evidence in support of your purpose, or present key explanations of your purpose; perhaps at the conclusion, when you may wish to remind your listeners of the reasons for your speech.

Your purpose sentence, written down or not, should be as specific as you can make it: "The new federal regulations in the field of automotive safety are intended to reduce automotive accidents in three major ways."[2] "Extensive development of mass transportation between nearby metro-politan areas must be begun *now"* is an example of a specific purpose sen-tence for a message advocating a specific course of action. "The Beatles are gone—but never forgotten" does not sound terribly specific, but it may sum up precisely what you feel about hard rock music on radio.

Sometimes you feel a compulsion to originate a message—either as a reply to one that has just been aimed at you or as the result of some thinking on your part, and you may, therefore, want to ask yourself, "What is my *general purpose,* or goal, in speaking on this occasion?" Viewed from one perspective, the purpose of communication is affective—that is, you com-municate in order to affect the behavior of others. This motivation suggests at least three approaches to communicative situations: (1) You may want to advocate a change, or try to get your listeners to agree with your position on

---

[2] This sentence is probably *not* one you will say to your listeners, in an informal, un-rehearsed situation, until you have developed and presented the entire message. There is nothing more embarrassing than to promise your listeners three points and then be able to deliver only one or two of them!

a controversial subject (see Chapter 15). (2) You may want to explain something, or enlighten your listeners on a subject you think they should know more about (see Chapter 16). (3) You may want to amuse others (see Chapter 17). You may even want to do all these things in the same message.

Sometimes formal opportunities or exigences may occur calling for the delivery of a prepared message on a subject of your own choice; or you may be enrolled in a course in communication or public speaking where either you will be assigned a topic or subject area for investigation and oral report or you will be asked to choose your own topic. The following hints will apply to these situations, but they are also useful as study points for conversational or daily communication behavior:

Hints for the Beginning Student

1.   Choose a worthwhile subject. No one enjoys listening to someone talk about a subject that neither of them feels is important. Most listeners want to get something worth remembering, or at least worth thinking about, in return for making the effort to listen. Talk about ideas, issues, controversies, doubts, unresolved questions that affect our lives.

2.   Choose a subject your listeners will find interesting. Don't be afraid to be a little ambitious. Think about what your listeners like, what they do, how they feel. If they can identify their own interests in your talk, it is a safe bet they will enjoy it.

3.   Choose a subject in which you are interested. Your listeners will seldom care any more about a topic than you do. You will find that your best speaking in any situation — formal speech making or coffee-break conversation — happens when you stick to subjects that interest you and fit your beliefs. Even though your interests can never be identical with those of your listeners, people gathered in one group usually have many things in common — that is why they are there. If your interests are very different from theirs, they may just

be uninformed about your particular subject, and you may kindle their interest.

4.   Choose a topic you understand. If you don't understand it, you can hardly expect your listeners to. As you become more experienced in speaking to people, you will find yourself tackling subjects you know little about and discovering new ideas and viewpoints. But as a beginner, talk about something you know.

5.   Choose that aspect of the assigned topic that you understand best or believe in most. If the subject under consideration is "Peace," you might choose to show how "Peace Begins in the Heart of an Individual."

6.   Choose that aspect you think will be most enjoyable or most useful to your listeners. Don't try to cover the whole subject in a few minutes.

7.   After your topic is chosen and limited, analyze your listeners' probable reactions. Will they be interested or bored, receptive or hostile, apathetic? If it seems unlikely that your subject will receive some kind of positive reaction, now is the time to choose a new one.

Step 2: Analyze Your Receiver's Potential Response to Your Message

In Chapter 1 we discovered that the receiver is as much a part of the communication process as is the source. In fact, in many—if not most—daily communication exchanges (interpersonal communication, for instance), speaker and listener exchange and share roles so frequently that a spy in the corner often could not distinguish between the two. It follows, then, that the speaker should give as much consideration to his audience as he does to what he is saying; and the time, place, and conditions under which he speaks deserve no less careful thought.

Analysis of (and adaptation to) the receiver's potential response takes place throughout the life of the particular communication event, beginning at the moment of the exigence or the decision to create a message is made, and continuing throughout the preparation, during the actual presentation, and certainly during whatever evaluation circumstances permit.

Significant decisions are made during the analysis and adaptation phases of your message preparation and delivery. You may elect to plunge ahead with your original ideas and message structure, to modify them, to alter language, to change your basic mode of communication (from directly persuasive to explanatory, for example), or even to abandon the message altogether.

It is most important to remember that listener analysis and adaptation are not restricted to formal messages prepared in advance. In almost any communication situation, verbal and nonverbal cues will be given off by your receiver, cues that will help you to discover (1) whether you're getting the message across, (2) whether you are convincing your hearer (or whether he is accepting your explanation), or (3) when he wants to respond or present a message of his own.

Moreover, adapting your message to improve its chance of getting across is not necessarily evil or tricky or unethical—unless you deliberately choose to become so. Understanding between two human beings through communication is the first step toward consensus, whether consensus means that you have persuaded the other to your views or that the two of you can agree to respect each other's beliefs.

While the following hints are intended primarily for the speaker who has some time *in advance of the presentation* to analyze and adapt to his listener and to the occasion of the message, careful study will show you that some of them can fit even the most informal and spontaneous communication situations. (Analyzing and adapting to the listener is discussed more thoroughly in Chapter 4.)

Hints for the Beginning Student

1.   Note the physical conditions of the place in which you will communicate and adjust your method of presentation accordingly. Is the room large? Speak loudly. Small? Use ordinary conversational volume. Will you be speaking from a stage or platform, in an office, or in a family living room? Whatever conditions are present in the room—shape, size, and so on—take note of them and adapt accordingly.

2.   Learn the purpose of the meeting. If the audience is coming to hear <u>you</u> speak, prepare your message with this in mind. If the meeting is more a round-table discussion, a seminar, or a committee meeting, prepare your message with an eye to contributing what you can to the meeting's intent.

3.   Learn as much as you can about the people you will communicate with. In most impromptu, everyday speaking situations, you probably already know something about your listeners from having worked and/or talked with them; and conscious adaptation will sometimes be unnecessary; it will have become

almost automatic. However, when you are presenting a prepared speech or are speaking to strangers, it will help you to know in advance the sex and age groups of the listeners, their occupations and life styles, their education, interests. It will help you to know something about their political or religious affiliations, cultural inclinations, and views on current controversial issues. These things help reveal the personalities, attitudes, beliefs, and behaviors of your listeners, and they assist you in deciding what kinds of language and ideas you'll need to use to get your messages across most effectively. When you prepare your message, spend a little time finding out about your audience; when you communicate without specific preparation, give these items a little thought before you open your mouth—and throughout the duration of your communication. Chances are you know your listeners better than you think you do and can speak to <u>them</u> (and, most importantly, <u>with</u> them), not just hear yourself speak.

Step 3: Construct a Basic, Abbreviated Plan for Your Message

If your message is to be spontaneous, informal, or otherwise unshaped for specific circumstances, you will, of course, not plan it out in advance. However, lack of opportunity for planning does not excuse the communicator from communicating as clear and effective a message as possible. You should, therefore, even in the brief time it takes to clear your throat, shuffle your feet, or otherwise signify your intention of communicating—think out a basic plan of what you intend to say and the order of your main points.

As we shall demonstrate in Step 5, it is convenient to think of a prepared message as consisting of four parts: *purpose sentence, introduction, body*, and *conclusion*. Even in an impromptu, interpersonal message, it is usually possible to ask yourself, "What do I want to say? Why?" The answers to those questions constitute your purpose sentence. You also will probably have time to ask, "Shall I hit the matter directly or work up to it slowly and indirectly?" The answer to this question produces the basic structure of your message—the direct approach we call "deductive" and the indirect approach "inductive"—and it also tells you something about your introduction and your conclusion. (Remember that all of this is going through your head in a split second, or while you are blowing your nose or lighting a cigarette or otherwise stalling for a little time!)

For example, if your message is to be short and direct, you may want no introduction other than some word or nonverbal sign to assure the attention of your listener. But, because you did launch into your main point first, you may wish to say it again at the end of your message (conclusion), to make sure your receiver remembers it. On the other hand, an indirect message usually demands a beginning that will capture the listener's attention and a general theme that will lead into your "gut" point. And in this case, the statement of the main point may also be the end or conclusion of the message.

Obviously, many interpersonal messages and others of the off-the-cuff variety (and that accounts for most of our communication) fail to get through because the communicator either didn't understand or ignored the principle of order or structure—after all, if we can't follow the message, we can't understand it.

Hints for constructing a plan are found in Step 5. With a little study, they can be adapted and abbreviated to fit the message that cannot wait for formal planning. And by the way, what better procedure for the composer of the formal message to follow than to include Step 3 in *his* preparation, as well? You cannot really wait until you have gathered up all the material for your formal speech to start thinking about how you intend to order it. So you, too, should compose a basic, abbreviated plan for your message, early in your preparation stage. (Chapters 10 and 11 will detail all these matters for you.)

Step 4: Discover, Create, Gather, Interpret, and Evaluate Materials for Your Message

The stuff of which talk is made—the materials of speaking—can be classified as three kinds: *personal proof* (to raise or maintain our credibility with our listeners), *materials of development* (to carry the sense of our message), and *materials of experience* (to help our listeners associate our experience with their experiences). (These are developed in detail in Chapters 5, 6, and 7.) As situations and audiences differ, they demand different uses of and emphases on the materials; and even within one speaking situation, you may have to change your emphasis from time to time as you analyze your listeners. Some of these materials are just waiting for you to find and use them. Others you must create with your own reasoning abilities and imagination. Or you must put old wine in a new skin — that is, put together materials from an outside source into your own patterns. Of course, the more time you have to prepare, the greater use you can make of these materials; but persistent and careful study will enable you to employ them even in informal, impromptu, and interpersonal speaking situations (which is just another way of saying that the more attention we pay to what is going on around us, the more effective we become in the art of communication).

Hints for the Beginning Student

1.   *Use personal proof. Try to show your listeners that you are interested in them, that you know your subject, that you really* want *to share your ideas with them. The* you *in speaking will work wonders in putting your message across.*

2.   *Use materials of development. Your listeners will not "get" your message unless you back up your statements with evidence and reasoning, and make clear to them points they may not understand immediately.*

3.   *Use experience and sensory materials. Help your listeners feel what you feel, experience (vicariously) what you have experienced, and become as interested in your talk as you are. Use words and phrases that appeal to the* "doors of perception" — the senses — *and your listeners will feel actively engaged in your talk.*

4.   *As you gather materials, consider how much you know about your subject and how much more you need to know to accomplish your speaking purpose.*

5.   *Talk with other people who have information about your topic.*

6.   *Learn about your subject by first-hand observation.*

7.   *Read as much as you can on your subject. Make good use of libraries, and exploit any other research facilities you can.*

8.   *Record all your findings accurately and clearly so that they will be available as you prepare your speech.*

Step 5: Organize Your Message

Now that you have all the basic parts of your message — the materials — you will want to make some sense of them; that is, you will want to put them together, in outline form, according to a speech plan. But first, you will have to decide how you will start and in what direction you will develop your message. Normally, the most useful plan is one that has four parts: the *purpose sentence,* the *introduction,* the *body* of the message, and the *conclusion.*

When circumstances demand a carefully prepared speech, you should organize your materials into a form that will show what you are going to say, how you will say it, what you will emphasize, and in what order you will present the points of your message. There is no substitute for a thorough job of organization, using an outline. Without an outline, it is extremely difficult to present your message step by step in coherent and understandable development; instead, you may find yourself punctuating your presentation with apologies and excuses for not having said something earlier, for having said something prematurely, and for other evidences of carelessness and disorganized thinking.

In impromptu discourse, too, you will discover that by learning the principles of outlining and organization you will do a better job of speaking without conscious and deliberate preparation.

Hints for the Beginning Student

1.   *Suppose you wish to develop your plan according to your* specific purpose. *Let's say that you want to tell about the history of acupuncture. You might start with the ancient Chinese; next show how the outside world responded to this technique down the years, and then bring the history up to date with attitudes and developments following the recognition of Red China.*

2.   *Suppose you wish to set up your plan according to your* general *purpose. In speaking to inform, for example, you might start with some fundamental background material and then develop toward more complex and detailed material.*

3.   *For first attempts at formal oral communication, use as simple a plan as possible, such as the chronological plan for speaking of the history of a movement. It may be more effective to combine a chronological plan with one that shows cause-and-effect relationships, but save the more complicated plans for later, when you have had more experience.*

4.   *First prepare your purpose sentence (placing it in the plan at the point where you want to tell the purpose of your speech); then prepare the body, the conclusion, and, finally, the intro-*

duction. (Since the introduction introduces the message, you cannot logically prepare it until you know what the message is all about!)

5.   *Follow the instructions for outlining given in Chapter 10. Don't take shortcuts; you may forget your original intention if you do. Chapter 11 will explain the process of organization in detail.*

6.   *Remember that outlining and organizing are different — outlining gives form and order to the plan.*

7.   *An outline that shows part-to-whole relationships is best for speaking to inform, at least for the beginner. Speaking to advocate requires an outline that shows reasons and evidence (proof) in support of your main contentions.*

8.   *An outline can be made of words, simple phrases, or complete sentences, depending on its purpose. Each form has its advantages and limitations. Your instructor will tell you what he wants (but if he doesn't, take a look at Chapter 10 for some help).*

9.   *The outline is useful both in preparation and in presentation of your formal message. It is the product of your thinking and a reminder of what you thought.*

Step 6: Deliver Your Message

In most communication situations, which do not permit much advance preparation, Step 6 will follow immediately after Step 3, in which you constructed a brief mental plan of the message to be delivered. In other communication situations, however, you have had an opportunity to prepare — that is, to acquire information and to design arguments or explanations that add strength to the message (Step 4); and you have organized all this material into a speech plan, employing one or more forms of the outline (Step 5). Whether prepared or unprepared, however, your moment of truth has arrived: No preparation, little preparation, much preparation — you have no message, you have no oral communication until you open your mouth and breathe life into the thoughts in your head or the words on your paper.

This brief discussion concerning delivery and the detailed treatment in Chapter 14 are designed primarily for the more complicated forms of oral communication, the prepared speech or talk (it follows that the more complicated the communication situation is, the more complex and detailed are the principles of delivery involved). *However, and this is important, the basic principles of delivery are the same for all oral communication, and by studying and mastering the principles of formal delivery of speeches, you will learn the necessary principles of delivery for informal, everyday communication. With experience and thought it will be simple for you to abstract those principles that apply to the communication situation in which you find yourself.*

Suggestions about *what to do* to present your message cover four problem areas associated with delivery: (1) the modes of delivery, (2) conversational quality in speaking, (3) stage fright, and (4) language.

The Modes of Delivery   There are four modes, or methods, of delivering a talk: *impromptu, extemporaneous, reading a manuscript,* and *memorizing the speech.* These methods will be discussed at length in Chapter 14; here we will concentrate on the first two, impromptu and extemporaneous, because they are most frequently used.

By far the most frequent mode of oral communication is the *impromptu.* This method is the one you use to tell a stranger how to find the post office, to report on the progress of a project in business, to tell a younger brother and his friends how to play chess, and to rap with friends about the current political situation. Except for those concerned with deliberate preparation, the steps we have outlined so far apply to impromptu speaking in the sense of mentally running through them in the brief moment before you speak. Some of the preparation can be accomplished during communication. You can recall certain bits of information and knowledge or improve upon your organization as you go along; one idea will call to mind a related idea that may be important. Experience in more formal speaking will help you become familiar with the steps of preparation; and they will eventually become almost automatic in your handling of daily communication encounters.

In most situations in which you will be expected to present a *prepared* talk, the *extemporaneous* method will be well received because it seems most natural to your listener and offers you greater freedom for development and flexibility. Extemporaneous speeches are not memorized word for word; after careful preparation, the speaker, frequently using brief notes to remind himself of the emphasis and order of his ideas, just talks to his listeners. If your first classroom exercise is to be an extemporaneous speech, don't try to memorize it, thinking that you can later learn extemporaneous speaking as you become more proficient. Since the requirements of contemporary communication situations (and of your speech or communication teacher) will force you sooner or later to make the decision to talk from notes instead of from memory or manuscript, you might as well do it right away.

Conversational Quality in Formal Speaking   One of the best ways to approach speaking to a group is to think of the situation as an *expanded conversation*. Depending on your listeners, certain adaptations will be necessary in language and manner, because conversation is often filled with irrelevant materials and private language is usually somewhat disorganized. However, conversations are ordinarily marked by enthusiasm, animation, excitement, and naturalness; and it is these qualities that can be carried over into the speaking situations discussed here. This principle was illustrated well by James A. Winans, one of the foremost teachers of speaking:

> Here comes a man who has seen a great race, or has been in a battle, or perhaps is excited about his new invention, or on fire with enthusiasm for a cause. He begins to talk with a friend on the street. Others join them, five, ten, twenty, a hundred. Interest grows. He lifts his voice that all may hear; but the crowd wishes to hear and see the speaker better. "Get up on this truck!" they cry; and he mounts the truck and goes on with his story or his plea.
>
> A private conversation has become a public speech; but under the circumstances imagined it is thought of only as a conversation, an enlarged conversation. It does not seem abnormal, but quite the natural thing.
>
> When does the converser become a speech-maker? When ten persons gather? Fifty? Or is it when he gets on the truck? There is, of course, no point at which we can say the change has taken place. There is no change in the nature or the spirit of the act; it is essentially the same throughout, a conversation adapted as the speaker proceeds to the growing number of his hearers. . . .
>
> I wish you to see that speech-making, even in the most public place, is a normal act which calls for no strange, artificial methods, but only for an extension and development of the most familiar act, conversation.[3]

---

[3] James A. Winans, *Speech-Making* (New York: Appleton-Century-Crofts, 1938), pp. 11–12. Copyright, 1938, D. Appleton-Century Company, Inc. Reprinted by permission of Appleton-Century-Crofts, Inc.

Conversational quality, of course, does not mean slipshod grammar, sloppy diction, confused thinking, or addled organization. It does mean that the speaker can add to his speaking in public the freedom, the relative informality, the friendliness, the sincerity, and the honesty of conversation.

Stage Fright Almost everyone is nervous before speaking in a formal setting. Even in impromptu situations, you may find that your hands are shaking a little, the room is suddenly too warm, and you are at a loss for words — for a moment. Sometimes your palms itch or you get a slight feeling of nausea. On the other hand, you may experience none of these symptoms or only one or two of them, or possibly nothing but a little self-conscious nervousness. These feelings — commonly called stage fright — may stay with you throughout life, every time you encounter a situation that demands some sort of connected discourse, but you can learn to live with them and still be able to communicate effectively.

Perhaps the knowledge that this tension is good rather than harmful will help to dispel some of the discomfort of stage fright. A football coach who walks into the locker room just before a game to find his players relaxed and contented is likely to have a fit. They are *supposed* to be a little nervous; in order to play well, they must be keyed up. Likewise, the speaker who is a little keyed up will speak more effectively — unless his nervousness is so great that he cannot move his lips or finds his throat too dry to make a sound. In any case, stage fright is a perfectly natural phenomenon. Nature has provided us with the kind of energy we need to meet challenging situations; the skillful speaker can exploit the nervous energy that nature provides.

Moreover, it should help you to know that your listeners perceive much less nervousness than you are experiencing. If, however, you find that your nervousness makes you unable to speak clearly and keep track of your ideas, you must give some attention to curbing it. Here are some suggestions that should help establish the confidence you need in order to overcome excessive nervousness.

Choose a topic in which you are interested. When you are vitally interested, your mind will be full of ideas about your subject and you won't have much time to think about yourself. (Stage fright stems from excessive self-consciousness.) Even when you've had little option in selecting the subject, keep your attention on your ideas and the listeners instead of on yourself. Use materials that will sustain the listeners' interest, and you will be more interested in the talk, too.

Prepare thoroughly.   When you are excessively nervous, you risk forgetting something. Don't let this frighten you; simply prepare enough material beforehand so that even if you forget part of it, you will be able to keep your listeners with you. Find out more than you need to know; a frequent cause of stage fright is the fear that you don't have enough to say.

Beware of attempting to memorize your speech.   Nothing promotes stage fright so quickly as trying to memorize a speech that is supposed to be extemporaneous. You can't fake it, unless you are a real pro. And if you fill your mind with fear of being exposed as a fake, instead of filling your mind with your subject, you deserve all the stage fright you will inevitably have.

Relax.   There *are* ways to relax, and they can be learned. Two of the simplest are: (1) Take a few deep, long breaths just before you rise to face your listeners. (2) Take your time in getting ready to speak—look at your listeners, smile at them, appreciate them, discover that they, like you, are human beings. Take a moment to get set to speak. No one's in a hurry.

In recent years a new technique for reducing anxiety in speaking, "systematic desensitization," has been developed and is being used in a number of colleges and universities with considerable success. The procedure is not difficult to learn, under proper supervision, and you should take advantage of this opportunity to learn relaxation while communicating, if a school near you offers it.[4]

Channel nervous energy into movement and gestures.   Walk around; use the chalkboard; demonstrate objects; even arrange your notes. At first you may be a little stiff with these actions and gestures; but, if you let yourself do what feels natural and right, these bits of nonverbal communication behavior will help you to put your message across and to use energy that might otherwise manifest itself in quaking knees and trembling hands. After all, you probably use your face, hands, and body when you communicate informally with another person—why not let these natural actions become a part of your more formal messages?

Language   Obviously, language is what you use to express your ideas and feelings, for the most part. Therefore, you should take the trouble, whenever you communicate orally, to use the kind of language that you believe will best convey your message to your listeners. The situation will determine the degree of formality that is appropriate for the occasion. For your first formal

---

[4] You or your communication-speech instructor may wish to read a description of SD and the results of experimental work in this area in James C. McCroskey, David C. Ralph, and James E. Barrick, "The Effect of Systematic Desensitization on Speech Anxiety," *The Speech Teacher*, Vol. 19 (January 1970), pp. 32–36.

attempts at oral communication, the best and safest suggestion is to concentrate upon maintaining clarity and precision. Vague phrasing usually leads to greater complications than precise phrasing does, even though precision seems to take more effort at first.

Hints for the Beginning Student

1.   How does an extemporaneous speech grow from accumulated ideas into spoken words? The fact is, preparing to speak extemporaneously begins with Step 1 and continues through Step 7. If you will regard planning, outlining, organizing, and practicing your speech as steps in the speaking *process, you will find that, by the time you are required to speak, you will be ready. As you plan, you are really deciding upon and committing to memory the basic order of your remarks. As you outline and organize, you are preparing and memorizing the key points of your speech. As you practice, you are* not *practicing to remember individual words but to remember thought sequences, to find transitions from one idea to another, and to improve the clarity of your thinking. If you do this and compose a new and shorter set of notes each time you practice, you will discover that your speech is ready and that you can deliver it with little worry about words and little or no reference to notes. This is an effective way to learn to speak, and countless speech teachers around the country will testify that* it really works.

2.   Use audio-visual aids with your prepared speeches; they will help put your message across, arouse and maintain your listeners' interest, and use up some excess energy that might otherwise come out as stage fright.

3.   The visible impression you make on your listeners is part of your presentation. Be sure your appearance and posture will earn their respect.

4.   Body movement, gestures, and facial expression can contribute a lot to your listeners' understanding and acceptance of your message. A smile or slight laugh before a humorous comment, for example, will let them know what's coming — but don't "lead" the laughter!

5.   Pay close attention to articulation, pronunciation, and loudness; your listeners do not want to work harder than they have to in order to figure out what you're saying. Speak more loudly — and articulate more carefully — in a large room than in a small one.

6.   Vary the pitch of your voice to keep it from tiring the listeners. A monotonous voice always seems to be talking about a boring idea.

7.   Vary your rate of speaking according to the size of the audience and the acoustics of the room, the emphasis you wish to make, and the complexity of your ideas. Slow down a little for ideas that are new, particularly important, or difficult to understand.

A world-renowned concert pianist was strolling around the neighborhood of Carnegie Hall one evening, so the story goes, to relax a bit before his performance. An eager young man approached him, obviously in a hurry, and asked, "Pardon me, sir, I'm a stranger to New York. Can you tell me how to get to Carnegie Hall?" The pianist's answer: "Practice, my boy, practice."

The same advice applies to successful formal oral communication. If you want to get your message across as effectively as you can, you must practice. Moreover, the more attention you can give to practicing speeches, the better your informal communication will be—but here are a few more hints.

Hints for Practicing Your Formal Message

1.   *Allow enough time to practice your message thoroughly. Don't put it off until the last minute and dash into the room jotting the last item on the end of your speech plan.*

2.   *Practice the entire message. Sometimes you will be tempted to neglect the conclusion, thinking that it is bound to "come off" well because the rest of the speech leads up to it; more often than not, however, your conclusion will fall flat unless you have given it the same care and attention as the introduction and the body.*

3.   *Practice your message aloud. Most beginning speakers have no idea how they sound; practicing will give you a chance to listen to yourself. Later on, you may practice silently; or you may want to continue to practice aloud because it lets you adjust the sound of your voice in advance.*

4.   *Find your own best means and your own best place for practicing. This is a matter of personal preference; what seems best for one communicator may not work out for another. Try this method for practicing extemporaneous talks. First, find some privacy: shut*

yourself into a room alone or go down by the river or out behind your dorm or house. Take your plan with you. Then simply start talking about your subject as if your listeners were there. As you talk, jot a few notes on your plan—like "Need to say more here," or "Belaboring the obvious." Remember, you are trying only to learn what your ideas are and in what order they fall as you practice. You are not trying to decide on exact words; the words of your message, except for specialized terms, are conceived at the moment of delivery. Each time you practice, try to reduce your dependence on the speech plan and try to cut down on the notes. In this way you will develop the ability to speak extempore and lessen your dependence on notes. For the actual speaking appearance, leave your speech plan behind; use only a very few note cards, and type your notes in all caps, triple spaced.

5.   *Do not practice your message too many times. It is possible to wear out your interest in it; and if you do, your audience will sense—and share—your boredom. Practice until you know it well, and no more.*

Step 7: Evaluate Your Message

The advantages of learning something about the effect that your oral communication has upon the person or persons with whom you are communicating are obvious. We most often communicate for a purpose, and whatever the purpose is, it is more likely to be achieved if we can receive and accurately interpret feedback from our message.

Most well-known speakers try to evaluate their public speaking during delivery and afterward. Many have this evaluation done for them by competent critics, and often elaborate polls and other devices are employed to ascertain listener reaction. Experienced speakers recognize what every beginning speaker and every communicator should come to know: that only through evaluation can one learn to improve his speaking.

Hints for the Beginning Student

1. Use the checklist for successful-unsuccessful speaking found in Chapter 1 (page 8) as a guide for your self-evaluation and for learning common listener reactions. Some of these will apply primarily to formal speaking, but many are designed for everyday communication.

2. Make an effort to evaluate listener reactions <u>while you are speaking</u>. Try to learn which ideas, words, sentences, and movements achieve the effects you want and which ones do not. Study audience feedback — the way the audience reveals its reactions often provides a reliable guide to evaluation. Try to discover the meanings of facial expressions, yawns, and body movements, because these reveal reactions to what you are saying. And <u>you can improve your message while you are communicating it.</u>

3. If you are about to give a prepared speech and a tape recorder is available, record your message — <u>before</u> you present
it, if possible. In this way you can find weaknesses and correct them ahead of time. Listening to your taped speech after the event is perhaps the best way <u>to</u> assimilate the criticism you have received.*

4. If you are in a speech-communication class in which students communicate messages under some direction, you will be fortunate enough to receive the evaluations of your instructor and sometimes of your fellow students. They have the advantage of being able to concentrate on all the aspects of your performance while you are talking. If, by some chance, they do not offer actual appraisal, ask for it.

5. Finally, never avoid criticism and evaluation; this is what you paid your money for. Ask for evaluation, take it in good grace, and then evaluate the evaluation. Do not be depressed when the criticism reveals your faults. Use it to become a better communicator.

If this statement of first steps in communicating is simple and easy for you to grasp, you are quite ready to move on to the next chapter. If, on the other hand, you are appalled by the seeming complexity of the process of speaking, take time to reread this chapter carefully. Prepare all of the suggested assignments, even though your instructor may not require them of you. But don't panic. In a very few weeks you will come to look upon this "first steps" chapter with a superior smile. With experience in speaking, assistance from your instructor, and a careful reading of the remainder of the text, you will improve in your ability to communicate—"First Steps in Communicating Orally" will then be useful to you only as a review of what you have learned.

Suggested Assignments

1.   Divide the class into groups of three to five persons. Each group will decide upon a subject of mutual interest, such as attitudes held toward current economic, social, ecological, or political problems; vocational ambitions; possible group projects for the benefit of underprivileged persons in the community. The groups will then discuss their chosen subjects—among themselves, with the instructor listening in, or before the entire class. Try to follow as many of the "First Steps" as you think are applicable to this informal communication and to your impromptu delivery.

2.   Try a similar set of meetings, only this time let all the groups have a day or two for preparation before they hold their "formal" meeting. Study the steps in communicating and try to make them work for you as you communicate extemporaneously.

3.   Select a basic idea from a speech published in *Vital Speeches* or a similar publication. Explain briefly to the class what the speaker had to say concerning the particular idea and then express your *own* judgment concerning his conclusions.

4.   Prepare a two- or three-minute speech on the subject that appeals to you most at the moment. Prepare a plan of the speech in outline form, using complete sentences. Include an introduction, purpose sentence, body, and conclusion. Study the plan carefully. Practice your speech, following the suggestions in this chapter. Be careful not to memorize your speech. From your plan prepare a short set of notes (not more than a few words on one small card). When your turn comes to speak, walk to the front of the room and talk with your hearers about your subject. Concentrate on what you are saying and what they seem to be thinking about it. Forget everything else.

5.   Listen carefully to a speech delivered live or on television or radio. Is the speaker, in your judgment, using conversational quality? Try to answer *Yes* or *No*. If he is, list ten instances to help prove your contention. If he is not, suggest ten changes that would add conversational quality to his speech.

6.   Tape-record your speech before you present it in class. How did it sound? Be honest. Try to put yourself in the place of your listeners. What can you do, *now*, to improve your speech before you deliver it?

7.   Make a list of ten questions you would like to ask the members of your class about themselves. Compose your questions carefully, on the assumption that the answers will provide you with all the information you will have about your audience when you make your first formal classroom speech. With your instructor's permission, ask the class to take a few minutes to answer the questions. Compile, summarize, and interpret their answers; and use the results as a guide in the preparation of your first speech. Turn in your raw data and summary sheet, along with your speech plan, after you have spoken.

Part Two
Preparing for Speaking

Part Two discusses the circumstances surrounding the message — the occasions upon which you choose to speak or are compelled to speak (Chapter 3); and the receivers of your message, the people to whom you talk (Chapter 4). It also details — in Chapters 5, 6, 7 — the materials of speaking available to you and the materials you can create — the materials that make up your message.

These important concepts may be studied before you begin to prepare your messages, or they may be combined with a comprehensive treatment of the steps in message preparation, found in Part Three.

3
Understanding and Adapting to the Occasion

"What's it all about?"

Your speech classroom may be a very different place from the college dining hall where you eat lunch. The classroom provides a reasonably quiet, well-lighted area where fellow students will sit patiently and listen to carefully prepared messages on "corruption in government" and "the general decline of public and private morals." They listen because they are interested or because they sympathize with your plight, or because they have to listen as part of their grade in the course.

You have had adequate time to think of what you wanted to say, to develop a plan of speaking, to research the library for information, to confirm the accuracy and timeliness of your ideas with friends and experts. You can choose the words you want (sometimes even rehearse certain phrases before the speech), produce appropriate changes in loudness and pitch, and even take a chance on bringing off some subtleties—a classic allusion, if it's appropriate, or some planned humor. The occasion calls, in short, for a performance, a performance in which you are the chief honcho, the ringmaster, the *person in charge*.

Not so in the dining room. Here there are dozens, perhaps hundreds, of busy people, eating and talking and banging dishes, coming and going, intent upon a myriad of activities. Suppose you are still interested in "corruption in government"—you point your fork at your lunch companion and launch into your message. You must speak loudly; he cannot hear. You try it again; he interrupts. His attention (and yours) is caught by a pretty girl hurrying by. A third person stops to chat and cuts into your argument; she tells you that you're wrong; you've got your facts on backwards. A slice of conversation about where gas could be bought for a penny cheaper drifting across from the next table catches your attention briefly, and suddenly you cannot remember either your own point or your interrupter's. You become irritated. You resume, speaking more slowly, more loudly, reaching with your voice for the authority you hoped your message would convey. You simplify the arrangement, begin to omit complex ideas, drop a point that now seems a little silly, maybe even wrong. You lean across the table, gesturing harshly with your hands, your face screwed up into wrinkles— you grab the paper napkin and draw a model of how orders are passed down from cabinet secretary to undersecretary to bureau chief. In the process of revising the argument, you realize that dessert is finished and that your companion's chair is scraping away from the table.

In short, although what you say in the classroom speech may be *essentially* the same as what you are saying in informal discourse, the preparation and presentation of the message must be different because the occasion is different. If you want to improve your speaking, you must be aware that the occasion frequently demands important adjustments in content, arrangement, and delivery; indeed, the occasion may even dictate the content of the message—it may be the cause of the message—it may demand the message. Moreover, you may sometimes have to adapt to the physical setting, or, when possible, adapt the physical setting to your speaking.

The Immediate Circumstances
of the Occasion

The first question a communicator should ask himself is, "Why do I intend to speak?"—or "Why am I invited to speak?" if the occasion is a formal one and preparation time is allowed. A close study of the circumstances of the more formal occasion should provide principles that may be employed in the less formal or impromptu speaking occasion as well.

The answers to the "why" question and such subordinate questions as "How long is my talk to be?" and "How formal is this meeting?" will determine, to a large extent, the approach we will use as speakers. We should know whether we were invited to speak because of our point of view on a certain subject (which in itself imposes a definite limitation) or because of our general reputation as a person and a speaker (in which case we have fewer limitations on choice of subject and approach). We should also know whether we were invited because we were the only person who would say *Yes.*

Second, as the communicator, we should find out whether we are to be the main speaker of the program or only one of several speakers. We should know who proposed our name and under what circumstances. We must know the theme of the program, the reason for the meeting, and whether we are expected to present all or only part of the message of the program.

It is very important for the speaker to understand that every meeting of every group has a *purpose.* In the first place, the group itself was organized for

a purpose; in the second place, the particular meeting to which we have been invited also has a specific purpose. For example, the Parent-Teacher Association was formed to provide for communication between the parents and teachers of the schoolchildren so that the children would benefit, through PTA efforts, from an improved educational system. A school principal invited to speak at a PTA meeting would know the purpose of the PTA and therefore would have some idea what its members might want to know more about. Naturally, because the parents are interested in all efforts supportive of the educational program, the principal might offer a speech entitled "School Board Services You Never Heard Of." The occasion—a meeting in which the local PTA planned to inform its members about agencies affecting their child in the classroom—determined almost exclusively the subject of the principal's speech and also his approach: he explained to the PTA that the excellence of the school system is in large part the result of the hard work of the school board—an area they probably were not aware of.

In addition, the principal found in this occasion an opportunity to speak on a subject he wanted parents to know about. This is often the case: By relating it to the purpose of the meeting, the speaker can talk on a subject he considers very important. On some occasions, by making the subject *appear* to be related, we can find an audience for ideas we burn to express. But let us beware! Either we must keep relating our ideas to the purpose of the meeting throughout our talk or we must capture attention with the force of our ideas. Otherwise, our efforts will be regarded as a sham.

The process of adapting to the occasion, then, may begin with a careful analysis of its demands: the reason for the meeting, the reason for the speaker's invitation, the kind of approach the assemblage warrants, and the like. With certain adaptations, all of the principles that relate to utilizing the occasion can be applied to every situation that involves *speaking for a purpose*, whether it is to persuade our lunch partner that corruption in government must be stopped or to discuss with an advertising manager the possibilities of marketing a new product. Obviously, the more preparation time the communicator is allowed, the more steps he or she can take to analyze the occasion and adapt to it; but skilled speakers, those who are aware of the importance of the occasion to their communication, will seize even the slightest opportunity to size up the situation and make whatever adaptation they can in the brief moments before they begin to speak, as well as during the communication itself.

The Physical Setting

The physical setting in which a communicator works often contributes considerably to the success or failure of his attempt to get his message across. The example at the beginning of this chapter—the conversation at lunch—illustrates but one of the ways in which the physical setting influences a speech: the differences between speaking in a classroom and speaking in a public setting. However, there are other conditions in the physical setting that also affect communication, although not in so obvious and extreme a way. The essential thing is for us, whenever possible, to investigate the conditions *before* we present our message.

For purposes of this discussion, let us assume a relatively formal speaking situation, for which the speaker is usually prepared well in advance; but the informal communicator, even the spur-of-the-moment talker, should at least take a quick look around and attempt to adapt to the physical setting.

The Hall or Room

Every speaker is limited by space. Even an outdoor appearance is limited by the size of the audience, the boundaries of sight and sound, and objects like trees and buildings. However, communicators commonly speak in limited and enclosed areas, ranging in size from a small room to an auditorium or hall. The size and dimensions of the area will in many ways determine the speaker's method and style of delivery.

Most obvious, of course, is the way the *size of the room* influences the speaker's voice. Naturally, in a large hall without amplification, we must speak more loudly than we would in a small classroom or office. Not only must we adjust loudness, but in the larger area we must also speak more slowly and with sharper articulation; each gesture—all body movement, in fact—should be more pronounced. The size of the room influences the language of the message as well. In a small room, words and phrases, relationships among ideas, and intonations and implications can be more subtle and intimate than would be possible in a large hall. (However, this influence exists primarily because the size of the room corresponds to the size of the audience, and this factor is discussed in the section on the audience as part of the occasion.)

The *dimensions of the room*—or more accurately, the relation of width to depth—are also significant, especially as they affect the speaker's movement before the audience. Confronted with a long, narrow hall, we will find our lateral movement restricted by the narrowness of the platform, and we will find it necessary to project our voice to a great distance. On the other hand, a wide platform in a relatively shallow auditorium—a situation characteristic of some theaters and college lecture halls—may free the speaker from the worry about projection but, instead, necessitate quite a bit of lateral movement, at least of our eyes and head, to avoid losing contact with the people sitting at the extreme right and left.

In some speaking situations, the dimensions of the room can cause quite a problem. A difficult situation was met by Dr. Margaret Mead, the noted anthropologist, when she spoke in a dormitory multipurpose room on the Michigan State University campus. Dr. Mead spoke from the middle of a room so wide and so shallow that she could not clearly see the extreme ends. In addition, several dozen members of the audience were seated in a lounge opening off the main room. The persons in the lounge could barely see the speaker, and she could not see them at all. She could maintain eye contact with not more than one third of her audience.

Fully realizing the situation, Dr. Mead began by telling a story of her experiences in England during World War II. Her audiences there frequently consisted of workers who were on their lunch-hour break. As she put it, with only thirty-five minutes in which to eat, these workers were determined to eat, regardless of who might speak or what she might have to say. She was accustomed, as most speakers are, to direct contact with her audience, and she often brought into her speech techniques intended to establish good physical rapport.

Frustrated by her lunch-hour audiences with whom she knew she could never achieve such contact, she pretended that she was speaking over the radio, putting her efforts to maintain attention solely into the content of her material and into her voice, forsaking eye contact, gestures, and other visual effects. After she became used to the idea, Dr. Mead told her MSU listeners in the wide and shallow hall, it worked for her. Therefore, she said to them, she would use the same techniques in this situation. "Relax," she instructed them. "Don't try to look at me. Don't strain your eyes. Relax and pretend you are listening to me over the radio."

They did, and it worked. Dr. Mead's message was carried to her audience by the importance of what she had to say, the way she organized her thoughts, the language she used, and the quality and variety of her voice. What does Dr. Mead's experience say to us?—Physical dimensions of the place in which we are to speak may force us to make adaptations to the "normal" principles of speaking.

Acoustics

For all that we presumably know about the science of acoustics, we still have with us halls and rooms that present problems in hearing. Whenever possible, a speaker should test the room in which he is to talk. Every good singer does this, or has it done for him, so that he may know how to adjust his loudness, tone, and articulation. The speaker must also realize that there may be "dead" spots here and there in the room or an echo, and that sometimes outside interferences—like hissing radiators, basketball games next door, or a building under construction—may plague him.

While correcting such adverse conditions is not in the speaker's domain, it is up to us as speakers to determine, in advance, whether unfavorable conditions exist and, if they do, how we can adapt to them. If there are only a few listeners, we can direct them, either through the chairman or in our opening remarks, to sit in the section of the room where the sound is best. We can also slow down our rate of speaking, pronounce our words with unusual care, and increase our loudness. We should study the faces before us carefully to learn whether we are being heard. We can enlist further cooperation of our listeners by telling them of our earnest desire to speak so they all can hear us.

Fortunately, in situations where there are only a few listeners, the room will be too small to present any severe acoustical problems. Most speaking situations are of this nature—for example, the hasty hallway conference of an executive and a few sales representatives on the way to lunch, or the small graduate seminar. Generally, acoustical problems are associated with large halls and therefore with more formal occasions for speaking.

The most important thing for the speaker to know, of course, is that rooms and halls present different problems, and we should be aware of them so that we can investigate and adapt to them as much as possible.

The Stage or Platform

The presence or absence of a stage or platform affects the presentation of an oral message. Usually, the more formal the situation is, the more suitable the platform is, formal speech situations often demanding that the speaker be set apart and raised above his listeners. Informal situations, on the other hand, often require that the speaker make his presentation at the same level as his listeners because of rapport established by physical proximity. Ideally, the nature of the speech and the occasion should dictate what kind of platform, if any, should be used; however, since the physical setting is often more or less fixed, the speaker must adapt his presentation to inflexible circumstances.

The size of the audience often determines whether a platform will be used. Usually, a small group requires no platform; communicators may want not only to stand on a physical level with the listeners but to circulate among them as well. In the give-and-take of a question-and-answer session, this procedure often helps the listeners to feel more like taking part. Larger audiences, of course, require the speaker's using a platform simply because without it he cannot adequately be seen and heard. If visual materials are to be used with the speech, a platform is sometimes helpful, although seldom necessary. Visual materials are frequently used in small meetings, such as sales conferences, management councils, and Sunday School classes, where there are only a few people seated in a semicircle or around a table, and where a platform not only would be unnecessary but also might get in the way of the presentation.

Occasionally we may find ourselves facing an audience from a formal theater stage, regardless of our preferences. When we have a formal message to deliver to a large audience or when we want to use visual aids like chalk-boards and charts, we will probably welcome the opportunity to speak from a stage. Sometimes, however, a speaker wants to be closer to his listeners, wants to establish a kind of rapport that is difficult to achieve from a stage. In such circumstances, it is best to have the curtains closed and to speak from the edge of the stage or, if the audience is not too large, even from the floor directly in front of the stage.

Lighting and Heating

As communicators, we often forget that improper lighting and heating are frequently responsible for poor audience-speaker rapport and that the speaker usually has some control over these conditions.

Small audiences are usually most comfortable in a temperature of about seventy degrees; large audiences, about sixty-five. While proper adjustment of the heating is usually managed by the host group or the chairman of the program, the speaker should arrive in good time to check the adjustment and, if necessary, should request that the heat be turned up or down as his judgment dictates. A large audience or any audience in crowded quarters will generate enough heat to affect room temperature. The speaker should bear in mind that listeners who must stamp their feet to keep from freezing will probably be more alert than those who must fight to stay awake in an over-heated room!

The communicator usually has less control over lighting arrangements. In a classroom or a small meeting room, he may have no control except for the choice between lights on and lights off. However, in such situations, usually the small size of the audience, the informality of the occasion, and the closeness of the listeners to the speaker remove any worry about proper lighting. On the other hand, with a large audience in a large hall or audi-torium — where there may be a stage designed for theatrical productions — lighting can create monumental problems.

Footlights, for example, prevent the speaker from establishing eye con-tact with his listeners: He just can't see them; instead, he sees only a vast area of blackness. One speech teacher told of problems he encountered in addressing an audience in a theater where the footlights were turned on. Try as he might, he could not see his listeners out there in the blackness. Finally, in desperation he stepped over the footlights and landed — on a projection of the apron (fortunately he did not fall into the front row). He delivered the remainder of his talk teetering on the edge of the stage, but at least he could *see* his audience. Since not all of us can hope to be as fortu-nate as this man — who did not fall — the best advice for most speakers is to have the footlights turned off.

Other lights intended for theatrical use, including arc lights and beam spots, are generally undesirable in speaking situations. For, besides making it impossible for the speaker to see his listeners, they subject him to intense direct light that can make him look sick, since, unlike an actor on stage, he is not wearing theatrical makeup.

Generally, the easiest solution to improper lighting effects on a theater stage is to call for the "work lights" and nothing else. These ordinary high wattage lights are sufficient to light the stage and the speaker. Sometimes a low-powered spotlight is helpful, especially if the speaker has visual materials to present; and side spots are acceptable, though hardly ideal. In general, however, the speaker should avoid any lighting that hurts his contact with the audience or shows him up "in poor light."

The Speaker's Stand

The decision to use a speaker's stand should depend on the wishes of the speaker and the demands of the situation. The instructor in a speech class may insist, as a training situation, that his students have the experience of speaking with and without a stand. Many instructors and textbooks claim that a speaker's stand is only a crutch and that the speaker should get along without it. Many others admit to its usefulness but give detailed instructions on how to use it—instructions that the speaker is expected to remember even though he is supposedly concentrating on what he is saying.

The situation will often require a stand or table. A speaker with a sheaf of notes or some display materials cannot be expected to hold them in his hands throughout his speech. Suppose, for example, he wants to explain the workings of the stock market to a group of potential investors who know little or nothing about it. The communicator may wish, first, to give them a few definitions and then explain the workings of the exchange, followed by a brief discussion of the market reports in the daily paper. For this presentation, he will need fairly complete notes and perhaps a few copies of a newspaper to show the audience. The speaker's stand will be very useful for him at this time. Later, however, he will probably leave it, circulate among the audience, perhaps pass some material around. There are many such occasions on which the speaker uses the stand not as a crutch but as an aid to his presentation.

When we want to use a stand or when the situation calls for one, we should know how to use it properly. Perhaps the one rule we should keep in mind is this: *Dominate the speaker's stand; don't let it dominate you.* In effect, this rule means that the speaker is free to take a position that is comfortable to him and pleasing to his audience, that he may vary from this position when he feels like it, that he may even lean on the stand if he wishes (if the occasion is informal); but he should never allow the stand to become so important that the audience can confuse it with the speaker. In short: The stand should be used as an aid to the speaker and not as a prop to hold him up.

There will be occasions when we definitely need a stand and none will be available. Sometimes a small table will suffice, although we will have difficulty seeing our notes unless we are farsighted. Sometimes a large dictionary placed on top of the table will raise the notes to the proper level. Winston Churchill advised this solution to the problem:

> Rather a good way of dealing with notes at a dinner is to take a tumbler and put a finger bowl on top of it, then put a plate on top of the finger bowl and put the notes on top of the plate, but one has to be very careful not to knock it all over, as once happened to me . . . ."[1]

When such devices are the only solution, it would seem best to hold the notes in our hand.

Speaking Aids

In most speaking situations, we may depend on our own unamplified voice to carry to the audience. On occasion, however, it becomes necessary to use a public-address system — when we are speaking in a large hall, where noises or disturbances are going on, when speeches are taped for later use, or when we are broadcasting to another hall or room by means of radio or television. In any of these situations, we will have to use a microphone or microphones; for television, we must adapt to one or more television cameras as well as audio paraphernalia. (See Chapter 18 for a discussion of microphone technique.)

Physical Interference

It may be that you, as a beginning speaker, have never been exposed to overt noise or other interference with your speaking. You have still to experience the confusion of people wandering in and out of the room in which you are speaking, interrupting the concentration of your audience, sometimes standing and talking at the back of the hall (especially at conventions and other gatherings where strict order is not the rule of the day). These problems may be overcome, at least in part, by making an appeal to your audience for cooperation. You may enlist the aid of the chairman and ushers to keep the traffic down. The best results, however, will be gained by excellent speaking. A really good communicator rarely has to beg favors of his listeners; they will listen because they want to listen.

Such disturbances as kitchen noises, waiters clearing tables, and use of the bar in the rear of the room may be most readily resolved by anticipating these interferences and arranging with your hosts to prevent them. Here, too, effective communication will do much to alleviate these conditions.

Outside noises are more difficult to handle, because persons in charge of the program or conference usually have little or no control over them. Every college teacher has experienced the discomfort of attempting to lecture on a

---

[1] Quoted from a letter in *A King's Story: The Memoirs of the Duke of Windsor* (New York: G. P. Putnam's Sons, 1947), p. 137.

difficult subject while just outside the window a gardener is mowing the lawn or a workman is breaking up the sidewalk with a pneumatic drill or an unwitting undergraduate is blowing a trumpet.

Sometimes the most sensible thing to do is to ignore the interruptions, or possibly to try to locate another room. At other times a frank appeal for attention will seem in order. Perhaps the best course is for the speaker to exert maximum effort to hold the attention of his audience by the excellence of his ideas, the importance of his subject, the use of visual aids, and the best delivery at his command.

The Audience as Part of the Occasion

The audience is not only a group of individuals; it is also a physical entity having the two properties of size (number of listeners) and arrangement in a room. The *number of listeners* influences the speaker's approach, loudness, gestures, and choice of language. Generally, the larger the audience is, the more formal is the approach, the greater is the loudness, the more overt is the nonverbal action, and the more formal is the choice of language.

However, let us agree that these principles—like all the principles set down in this book—are neither final nor rigid rules. A speaker using a public-address system will not need to raise his voice and may be able to introduce a degree of informality into his manner. A plant foreman in conference with his immediate superior may choose and pronounce his words more carefully and more formally for his audience of only one person than he does when he addresses the larger audience of the workers under his supervision. He will probably make a conscious effort to improve his sentence structure and style. Similarly, a humorist speaking to entertain an after-dinner group of a hundred men might very well choose simpler and more earthy language than he would use when talking with his family around the dinner table at home. Generally, however, the speaker can go by the principle that a larger audience requires greater formality.

The *arrangement of the audience* may require specific adaptations, too. An informal semicircle of listeners requires that the speaker stand or sit close and speak intimately to them. His voice should be nearly conversational in tone; he should, usually, try to avoid being a lecturer. College professors frequently have classes ranging in size from the seminar, which consists of only a few members, to the large lecture group composed of hundreds of students. Sometimes it is difficult to remember which adaptation is appropriate to which group, and the members of the seminar often complain of being shouted at, while the students in the lecture hall have difficulty hearing the professor's whisper. If your professor shouts at you in a small class meeting or seems to be muttering something under his breath in the middle of a lecture, possibly he has temporarily forgotten which audience he is addressing.

Adapting to the Chairman

Being introduced by a chairman[2] is a well-established tradition in formal speaking, and every speaker should be prepared to handle the difficulties that may arise in a chairman's introduction. Chairing a meeting is an honor frequently bestowed upon a leading citizen of the community who may not be fully aware of all the duties and responsibilities of the office; and he or she may, with all good intentions, do grave disservice to the speaker. Basically, the chairman's duty is to prepare the audience to receive the speaker and to prepare the speaker to meet the audience. Sometimes the chairman will seize the opportunity to display his erudition or to curry the favor of the audience by intimating his long-established friendship with the speaker (a little of this may serve as an attention-getter and may help establish personal proof for the speaker, but let the speaker beware of too much!); sometimes he will be too timid or too shy to give as complete an introduction as he should. Because of these possibilities, the speaker who wishes to retain command of the speaking situation should be able to fill in what the chairman has left out and to correct his errors when he has said too much.

One of the best ways to avoid the possibility of a faulty introduction is to get in touch with the chairman before the program and acquaint him or her with yourself and your intentions, suggest what he should or should not say about you and your speech, and give him a background of personal data. It is also a good idea to include such information as the correct pronunciation of your name, your occupation, possibly the title of your message, your experience as a speaker and as a competent authority on the subject of your speech. Sometimes an amusing personal story about you will help the chairman get into the introduction (but know your chairman's abilities as a storyteller before you trust him with this technique!).

Even after you have taken these precautions, you must be prepared to cope with an inadequate or, worse, an overexuberant introduction. Both kinds can be damaging to the rapport that the speaker hopes to establish with the audience, and both can be corrected in much the same way. The short, stumbling introduction will not give an accurate picture of the speaker; the long-winded one may tire the audience. The best way to correct both is to thank the chairman, then swing into your speech with an attention-getting story, a startling statement, or some other device calculated to wake up the audience and focus its attention on you and your message.

Many of you have undoubtedly sat in the audience and watched a speaker wriggling uncomfortably while the chairman introduced him as the

---

[2] For information concerning speaker-chairman relationships from the point of view of the chairman (or chairperson), see Chapter 19. (*Note:* Because usage of the term "chairperson" is not yet widespread, the term "chairman" will be used here, with the understanding that women very often serve as chairmen.)

world's greatest, the foremost authority, and the pride of the community; this exuberant and extravagant praise is often the most difficult kind of introduction to correct. One of the classic rejoinders is that offered by the speaker who, after sitting through an excruciatingly long and extravagant presentation, rose from his chair, smiled at the chairman, and said, "I don't know who's going to speak—but with all that praise, I can hardly wait to hear him." This kind of opening might be considered in poor taste and might antagonize the chairman; but the principle remains clear: The speaker must take steps to establish the rapport with his listeners that a faulty introduction may have cost him.

Once the chairman has concluded his or her introduction, it is wise to try to get him off the platform—as politely as possible. There are few distractions that can destroy the audience's attention so easily as the bored figure of the chairman sitting idly behind the speaker, tapping his fingers, staring off into space, crossing and uncrossing his legs. He will be far happier, and so will you and the audience, if you can suggest to him—before the program, if possible—that he might enjoy the speech more if he were to sit with the audience. When this is impossible, the following technique has worked successfully on numerous occasions: Unless the chairman is some world figure or a person of great prestige, thank him personally for his introduction and gently steer him toward the stairs. Chances are he will gratefully accept the hint and go take a seat in the audience.

Another undesirable situation you may encounter as a speaker is finding that not only the chairman but all of the distinguished guests and other speakers of the program are lined up in a row behind you. Since they will not be able to see or hear you well, they may whisper, pass notes, gaze around, and give other indications of boredom. The best way out of this problem is to avoid it altogether—by making arrangements for the guests to sit in the first row of the audience. When such arrangements are impossible, the next best thing is to try to include these people in your audience by acknowledging them as you begin to speak and turning to them frequently throughout the speech.

A United States senator, noted for his quickness of wit and shortness of temper, was confronted by this kind of situation. On the platform behind him were the governor and the lieutenant governor of his state, other members of the state government, and several congressmen. The senator noticed after a while that these people were not paying him much attention. Indeed, the governor was signaling the lieutenant governor past several other members of the party. Soon the senator walked over to the extreme downstage right area of the platform and, scarcely pausing in his speech, turned suddenly to the platform party and said, "You agree with this point, do you not, Governor?" There was an agonizing silence, while the governor gulped and turned brick red. He had not, of course, heard a word of the speech, and was incapable of replying. After a moment the senator resumed his speech, but from then on, whenever the attention of the platform party seemed to be lagging, all he had to do was to turn his head in the direction of the party as he spoke, and they snapped to attention.

A good chairman and courteous guests can help to make a speaking occasion successful and even memorable, but the speaker should be on his guard to keep the audience's attention on himself and his speech. He should prepare the chairman in advance and exercise care to see that the entire party is properly seated and properly controlled.

We have looked at the principles of adapting to the occasion largely as they relate to the more obvious factors associated with formal speech delivery or presentation. However, we also must often adapt the *language* and *organization* of our speech — and sometimes even the *ideas* of the message, the core material of the speech — to the specific occasion. For a specific occasion we may have to remove ideas that are unsuitable or that might work against our purpose. Again, these suggestions are not limited to formal speaking but may be adapted for use in informal or spontaneous communication occasions.

In summary, then, we must remind ourselves that the effective speaker first analyzes the occasion of his speech — the immediate circumstances, the physical setting, the audience as a unit, and the chairman and other people on the platform — and adapts himself and his message to the several factors in each of these elements of the occasion. Even more important than analyzing and adapting to the occasion, however, are analyzing and adapting to the *audience* — that group of individuals who have opinions, prejudices, beliefs, feelings, purposes, tastes, and varying levels of education, to whom the speaker must get his message across. (The audience is the subject of the next chapter.)

Suggested Assignments

1.   In the next few days, you will undoubtedly find yourself in a speech situation — a formal lecture, a political meeting, or a lunch-hour discussion — in which someone will be *speaking for a purpose.* Study the occasion in detail. Note the size of the audience. How many listeners arrived after the speaking started? Were there outside noises? Other distractions? Note also the lighting and heating. Did these conditions affect the comfort of the group? Note every condition that was potentially damaging to effective communication. What attempt did the speaker make to compensate for these conditions?

2.   Read the introduction to the speeches in Paul M. Angle's *By These Words* (Skokie, Ill.: Rand McNally & Co., 1954). These introductions frequently contain a brief description of the occasion of the speech. Summarize the elements you believe were important to the speaker; you may find them applicable to both formal and informal, prepared and impromptu speaking situations.

3.   Describe, according to the analysis presented in this chapter, the elements of the occasion of your latest attempt to communicate a message to someone orally. Which of these elements helped your efforts? Which may have hindered your efforts and what did you do to compensate?

4.   From any available collection of published speeches, choose a speech to read and analyze. See whether you can determine what the occasion might have been like from the subject, the arrangement of the speech, the use of reasoning and evidence, the language, and the nature of the illustrations used to develop various points. Write a short paper in which you analyze the occasion as you imagine it.

5.   Even though you may feel that the "occasions" of your classroom speeches are static, make careful observations of what happens during the next round of speeches — study the immediate circumstances; the physical setting (the room itself, the acoustics, the location of the speakers, lighting and heating conditions, the presence or absence of a speaker's stand, inside and outside interferences); the location and number of listeners; and the activities of the student chairman. True, you may not be able to change any of these factors, but what can you do to change your own approach to your speech? Make a list of adaptations to the classroom that you can make during your next speech. Then, try them on for size — make a determined effort to adapt to the occasion.

6.   For your next speech (which will be fully prepared, according to the principles you have learned thus far) have the man or woman sitting next to you in class act as your chairman. You will tell him about the subject of your speech (in some detail), but he will not tell you anything about the introduction he will prepare to present you to the audience. As part of his introduction, he will set the stage — create an occasion for your speech. Your instructor will criticize both your partner's introduction and your speech and will point out the effect of the introduction on the success of your speech. He will evaluate your attempts to adapt to your partner's introduction of yc·1 in the introduction of your speech. In a short paper, honestly criticize your own speech in terms of what happened to you as a result of the introduction and the occasion.

Suggested References

Baird, A. Craig, Franklin H. Knower, and Samuel L. Becker, *General Speech Communication*, 4th ed. (New York: McGraw-Hill Book Co., 1971). Chapter 6, "The Audience and the Occasion."

Fausti, Remo P., and Edward L. McGlone, *Understanding Oral Communication* (Menlo Park, Calif.: Cummings Publishing Co., 1972). Section 3, "The Settings of Oral Communication."

Monroe, Alan H., and Douglas Ehninger, *Principles and Types of Speech Communication*, 7th ed. (Glenview, Ill.: Scott, Foresman and Co., 1974). Chapter 8, "Analyzing the Audience and Occasion."

St. Onge, Keith R., *Creative Speech* (Belmont, Calif.: Wadsworth Publishing Co., 1964). Chapter 13, "The Occasion."

4
Analyzing and Adapting to the Listener

"How can I reach them?"

When you turned that magic age and had completed your driver's training, the climactic moment came when you felt you were ready to take the family car out on your own—with no parent as passenger. The problem, for many of you, was Dad—good old conservative, favorite-chair, six-o'clock-news, car-keys-in-pocket Dad. How to get the keys? How to get permission to take the car out alone? How to convince Dad that you were really a responsible driver?

Well, most of you accomplished the job; by some means or another, you persuaded Dad that you ought to have the car. How did you do it? Think back a few years. What magical, mysterious means of communication did you employ? Did you subtly turn the television set to the right channel at 5:59? Did you enlist the support of another member of the family? Did you produce a set of B or better six-weeks grades? Did you mope around the house looking bored, or imply that you were unattractive to the opposite sex? Did you produce statistics from the National Safety Council pertaining to the excellent safety record earned by teens who had passed a driver's education course? Did you demand the car in a peremptory tone? Did you steal the keys? Or did you give up and soon forget how to drive?

If your method of operation was somewhere between violence and inactivity, you made use of some form of persuasion, probably mainly oral. You also did two other things: You analyzed your audience of one; and, having decided what approach was most likely to work, you adapted your presentation to the audience you had analyzed.

Analysis of and adaptation to the listener are necessary in all forms of effective human communication. Furthermore, audience analysis and adaptation are at the very core of the communication process—you choose or react to a subject with your audience in mind, you gather material to affect that audience, if there's time for preparation, you compose your message for your audience, you present your communication to your audience, and when the job is completed, your audience judges you (good old Dad says, "Yes, you may have the car" or "No, you may not").

Consider a third point in connection with the struggle for the family car: Not only was there a demonstrable need for analysis of and adaptation to the listener (audience), but also *you made that analysis and that adaptation.* By the time you have fought your way through high school and into college, you have made a great many speeches—formal and informal, prepared and unprepared, long and short, recognized and unrecognized—and you have learned a great deal about human nature and how to influence your human fellows.

Thus it is not a new, untried, hypothetical concept that we are contemplating, but the results of thousands of years of individual efforts at speech making. It then becomes clear that the first step in understanding audience analysis and adaptation is to recognize that what we have learned to do without conscious preparation in day-by-day living we must learn to apply in the formal and informal speaking situations that confront us as adults.

However, we must acknowledge that, while we perform listener analysis and adaptation as a daily part of our communicative lives, we really know very little about this phenomenon; that is, how one human attunes himself to the ideas, feelings, and reactions of another. This chapter, then, has five ways of examining the problem: (1) by stressing the need for analysis and adaptation in oral communication, (2) by aiming to increase our understanding of the listener, (3) by demonstrating the materials of speaking that are available for adaptation, (4) by pointing out the difficulties of analysis and adaptation, and finally (5) by weighing a plan for "instant" analysis and adaptation—not a panacea, not a formula in the mathematical sense, but some suggestions that can be useful in preparing a message, no matter whether there are ten seconds or ten minutes or ten hours to do it in.

The Need for Listener Analysis and Adaptation

Classical writers analyzed the speaking situation by its *parts:* the speaker, the speech, the occasion, and the audience. Contemporary scholars make use of a communication *model,* consisting, for example, of the source, the message, the channel, and the receiver. Whatever terminology we use in analysis of the speaking situation, it is clear that *there is no speaking situation without an audience.*

The communicator who presents his or her message without considering the audience has little chance of getting it across. Therefore, the wise speaker will want to know as much about his audience as he can, so that he can adapt his materials—and himself—to the people with whom he wants to communicate.

Effective speakers study their audiences before they deliver formal speeches; the most effective speakers study their audiences, if possible, even before they prepare their speeches. Realizing that their ideas are not always the ideas of their listeners, they try to put themselves in the listeners' shoes, and then, without necessarily compromising their points of view, try to state their message in words that will elicit maximum agreement and understanding.

In January 1961, President Kennedy took the oath of office with full realization that there was a tremendous job to be done. He wanted to indicate his awareness of the size of the job in his inaugural address; but he wanted to do so without seeming overcritical of the previous administration, because, for one thing, he knew that he would need the support of Republicans and Democrats and all other Americans. He did not, for example, say:

> The job to be done is a big job, and we have wasted a lot of time complaining about our many problems. We have wasted a lot of time doing nothing. It is time we started.

He managed to get the true idea of his message across without saying bluntly, "It is about time we did something":

> All this will not be finished in the first one hundred days. Nor will it be finished in the first one thousand days, nor in the life of this Administration, nor even perhaps in our lifetime on this planet. But let us begin.

". . . Let us begin." Few listeners could refuse to accept that proposal. It contained no criticism of parties or personalities; it was necessary to get the support of parties and persons, despite some differences of beliefs. Rather, the new President phrased what he had to say in terms acceptable to all, without sacrificing any of the meaning.

At the opposite extreme are the many communicators—business persons, politicians, teachers, labor leaders, students, committee members, conferees—who, formally and informally, express only what *they* want their listeners to believe, without considering what their listeners believe and want, or the ways in which one listener or set of listeners differs from another. Suppose, for example, you have just told a group of friends your views concerning the worldwide energy shortage and the implications this shortage may have for our peculiar American life-style. It was a very successful statement, and your listeners indicated complete agreement with your point of view. One of these is the daughter of a local fuel oil distributor, and at dinner she mentions your "speech" to her father. As program chairman for the Fuel Oil Distributors Association (FODA), it just happens that he is desperate for a speaker for next Tuesday's noon meeting. He asks you to prepare a speech on your topic, and you (foolishly) agree.

If you simply go to the meeting and communicate the same ideas in the same way you did for your friends, you are in big trouble. You are about to lose your hero's crown, and your credibility, and your self-confidence.

Aside from the problems of translating informal remarks into a formal speech —and these are serious enough—you have not analyzed your *new* audience. You will label the oil distributors as reactionary, and they will call you subversive (at best). Furthermore, scratch one friend.

What will be the difficulty? Is your topic different? No, certainly not. Have you suddenly lost your ability to communicate? The words surely make sense. The message and the source are about as they were in last week's informal discussion. That is exactly the trouble. You are the same; so is the speech. But *the audience is different!* The fuel oil distributors are not young, nor adaptive. Their bones are old and cold; they don't regard wearing thick socks and an extra sweater as a slightly adventurous challenge to nature. Besides, *they make their living out of selling oil—lots and lots of oil.*

At the same time, you can see that your message is not entirely inappropriate for the new occasion and that fuel oil distributors are not selfish and blind to the problems and challenges of the energy crisis. But your speech must be reworked and altered considerably—and this can be done only after you have discovered some of the experiences, desires, and interests of your *new* audience.

In this discussion of the need for audience analysis and adaptation, we should not overlook two important considerations: (1) Not only are *audiences* (defined here as collections of individuals gathered together to make up cohesive groups) different one from another in their beliefs and their responses, but also individuals within a given audience may vary widely in their attitudes and behaviors toward the communicator and his message and in their knowledge of the issues being discussed. (2) While the communicator who has time to prepare his message obviously has more time to study his listeners and thus greater opportunity to adapt to them, the informal speaker, who must rise to the occasion and present his message with no advance planning, needs to know all he can about listeners in general and about the principles and art of analyzing and adapting to an audience, so that he can make all possible adjustments to his listeners, quickly and almost automatically. Moreover, interpersonal communication, wherein the roles of source and receiver are shared fully, requires that each member of the communication team make maximum adaptation to the beliefs, needs, and demands of the other.

The Audience as Listeners

What is a listener? What are audiences? Who are the people to whom we must address our messages, who must be considered from the first moment of speech preparation to the last moment of the post-speech evaluation? To begin with, obviously, listeners are human beings, not machines. They are unpredictable, unlike machines, which can be programmed to respond in certain ways to certain stimuli. A reasonably complete description of the people we talk to would require several tomes in psychology and sociology. Baird and Knower, however, have given us a revealing description of our listeners:

> We inherit certain physiological characteristics and abilities. These characteristics identify us with the animal kingdom. We have biological needs or drives. We learn more or less conventional ways of satisfying those needs. We have many sensations, feelings, emotions, and cognitive reactions. We acquire habits, some good, some bad. We develop complicated mental processes, memory, thought, language, curiosity, imagination, judgment, knowledge, and if we are fortunate perhaps a bit of wisdom. We develop tastes, preferences, interests, find preferred foods, friends, work, and relaxation. We mature, accept responsibilities, cooperate, and exercise some freedoms. We develop self-awareness, pride, a sense of values, a realization of the dignity of man—all of which helps us rise above our animal nature. We experience insights and relations and create art and beauty for our enjoyment. We seek to survive but also to contribute to the common good and the betterment of our world. Our world is orderly and as human machines we like this because it enables us to carry on our lives with an economy of energy. We resist changes or any stimulus which creates discord in our lives, yet we seek variety within this unity. Everything doesn't happen at once, but piecemeal. Now we are concerned with this aspect of our lives, now with that. While all men are doing most of these things each is an individual. In our culture we value both commonality and individuality. Differences and conflicts create tension and struggle within ourselves or between ourselves and others. Dissonance is unpleasant and we seek ways of achieving or returning to a state of harmony.[1]

Thus, we see that the objects of our messages, the people we "give speeches to," or, far better, the people with whom we communicate, are at one and the same time predictable and unpredictable. Human behavior, in short, runs the gamut from the random to the set, and *these variations are to be expected in every audience and within every individual in every audience in every speaking situation that we are likely to encounter.* Nor are the listeners the only variable in the problem of analysis and adaptation; for, as we must adapt *to* someone, we must also have something to adapt *with*.

Later in this chapter we shall deal more precisely with the listener, and in the three chapters to follow we shall consider in detail the materials which the speaker has available to him. It is important at this point, however, to present, if only in a general way, the materials of speaking that the speaker must consider in the process of analyzing and adapting to the audience.

---

[1] A. Craig Baird and Franklin H. Knower, *General Speech: An Introduction,* 3rd ed. (New York: McGraw-Hill Book Co., 1963), pp. 106–107.

Materials to Be Adapted —
The Materials of Speaking

The materials—the stuff—of speaking consist of the subject matter itself (see Chapter 8, "Responding to and Selecting the Subject") and the various supporting, clarifying, impressing, and entertaining materials that modify, expand, and focus upon the subject. Materials of speaking are the elements of the communicative process that make up the message; without them there can be no message at all. They appear in the message mainly as words, which translate the thought of the source into communicative impulses that can be picked up by the receiver and integrated into his own life system; and the communicator chooses to employ words that he hopes will activate a response in the receiver consistent with his own concept of his subject or message. Materials of speaking are not limited to spoken language—body action, gestures, facial expressions, and audio-visual materials also fit the description—but language is the main conveyor.

Most rhetoricians agree that, generally, the speaker has available to him three broad categories of materials: oldtimers have called them heart, head, and belly materials; that is, the materials (1) that affect the credibility of the speaker, (2) that seem most closely associated with the reasoning process, and (3) that help the listener "see into the speaker" and associate the spoken ideas with his own experience. Taken all together, we shall call these *materials of speaking*; or, separated into their workable if somewhat arbitrary parts, *materials of personal proof, materials of development,* and *materials of experience.*

Materials of Personal Proof

Available to us are materials of speaking that are intended to maintain or increase our credibility as a speaker.[2] The need for source credibility is never absent from speaking of any type, but the less acceptable our message is to our listeners at the outset or the less acceptable *we* are to our audience, the greater use we must make of materials of personal proof.

Although there are materials that can be classified primarily as personal proof, the major impact of personal proof comes from the way we employ or adapt materials of the other two categories. For example, it may be a fact that you are a college senior and have had more than three years' experience in observing campus policy toward distribution of student-written literature. If you say to your listeners, "I am a senior and I know the university has changed its distribution policy three times since I have been here," you think you are making a statement of fact. This "fact," a material of develop-

---

[2] For a detailed treatment of this category, see Chapter 5.

ment, is perhaps logically unassailable. But, pause a moment before you speak. What are the relevant conditions under which you are going to speak? You are the only senior in the class, you have referred to your senior status previously, and a freshman has just concluded a speech in which he complained that seniors at this campus "know it all." Perhaps your credibility is at stake, just a little. So, you omit the direct statement you had in mind and say, instead, "We freshmen were told, in our first weeks on campus, that only the offical daily campus paper could be delivered to our rooms; the next year they allowed three issues of a literary magazine; and last year, you'll remember, our houses were flooded with papers and magazines and other student-written stuff."

Just a small example, granted—not earthshaking, and not even guaranteed to put your message across. However, it could be that you reduced the antagonism toward your senior status a little, you made your point in a little more detail, and maybe the audience listened a little more intently.

In a more serious situation, materials of personal proof can make the difference between acceptance and nonacceptance of your message by the listener; and these materials exist not only in themselves, but also in the way you adapt them to your audience, in the way you interweave them with the other materials of your speech. Nonverbal cues are also significant forms of the materials of personal proof—if you look or act like a snotty senior when you're attempting to influence freshmen, you'll be perceived as a snotty senior, no matter how carefully you may have constructed the verbal part of your message.

Materials of Development

This major group of materials[3] available to the communicator includes observed and derived phenomena and the interpretations or relationships among these phenomena. Perhaps the two most commonly understood materials of development are what we call facts (such as statistics and statements that are commonly believed or can be substantiated) and the basic forms of argument and explanation used to relate these facts to each other and to establish conclusions based on them. These materials are often called supporting materials, because they lend support to the argument or explanation made in a speech.

However, in addition to reasoning and evidence, there are other means of support that add to the logical structure of a message. Factually based examples, narratives, and quotations are developmental. Repetition, restatement, and comparison and contrast, which are matters more of composition than of logical development, are sometimes used as materials of development.

---

[3] For a detailed treatment of this category, see Chapter 6.

Materials of Experience

If you have ever sold candy to raise money for your high school band uniforms or to help equip a playground or to help put yourself through school, you know that in addition to convincing the housewife that you are a genuine student, of decent background, and serious about your product and your objective; and in addition to presenting accurate and relevant data about your product and your reasons for selling it, something else is needed: You must get the prospect's attention and maintain it throughout your sales talk. Frequently, you must overcome hostility by planting in the mind of the receiver a favorable notion about your product or about your goal or about the institution you represent. And, almost always, you must contact whatever latent interest your receiver may possess in the candy you have to sell, or candy in general; in the band uniforms you are helping to buy, or in the band uniform she wore in high school some years ago—and stimulate that interest by relating it to your own product, your own situation. Materials of experience,[4] frequently called sensory materials, attempt to liven up a message, to re-create in the listener's mind an experience similar to the one you are discussing, and to appeal to the senses (as well as to the sense) of the listener.

A canny student in an eleven-o'clock speech class made good use of materials of experience recently when, speaking on the problem of world hunger, she said, "Suppose that always, every moment of your day and night, every day, three hundred and sixty-five days a year, you were always as hungry as you are right now." A groan, half of amusement, half of irritation, rose from the students in the class, and they sat up straighter and looked at the speaker.

Materials of experience do not "prove the case," they may have little effect upon the reaction of the listener to the speaker as a person, but they will often hold attention and open the door to understanding and to acceptance.

Let us bear in mind that these categories of the materials of speaking are labels that we use to make our job of analysis and adaptation a little more successful. No one can neatly pigeonhole all available materials of speaking; there are always exceptions, materials that seem to belong equally in one, two, or all three categories. Although communicating has become more a science than it once was, it still is an art. We can use these categories as helpful guides in selecting materials that will accomplish our purpose in speaking, and we can recognize their differences and their different functions without falling into the trap of attempting to make absolutes.

---

[4] For a detailed treatment of this category, see Chapter 7.

The Difficulties of Audience Analysis and Adaptation

In his *Art of Persuasion*, Minnick defines audience analysis as "the applica-tion of all that is known about human behavior in general to a specific audience in order to anticipate or evaluate its response to a particular persuasive communication."[5] The sources of the difficulties are implicit in his excellent definition. We speculate or theorize a great deal about human behavior; it can be said that we "know" quite a bit in general. Much informa-tion is available to us from psychology, rhetoric, and communication theory. Some of it we think we know; other knowledge is theoretical, with no more than a beginning made by researchers in attempts to verify what we suspect. This plethora of information, then, we are expected to use in adapting to any specific set of listeners. Much adaptation is to be done before we speak *(if there is time)*; we are supposed to achieve more during the presentation; and, finally, after the speech, we are supposed to analyze our own analysis and improve our listener adaptation for our next communication event.

Impossible, we might conclude, except for one thing: *The evidence strongly indicates that the speaker who, using his best knowledge of people, makes a strong attempt to adapt what he wants to say to the listener as he has analyzed him, is more successful than the one who does not make the effort.* Therefore, with some misgivings, we set out to do the impossible, realizing that our efforts will not often be crowned with success but that just making the attempt will increase our chances of success.

A speaker may have a few minutes each night for a few weeks to prepare a major speech, or four hours of intensive work before talking the next morn-ing, or the five minutes it takes him to reach the boss's office before making his defense, or the time it takes to cough twice before attacking an idea that he has just heard and that strikes him as ridiculous. What do analysis of and adaptation to the audience mean to him?

Some professional students of audience analysis and adaptation talk about polarizing the audience, as Woolbert did in his 1916 monograph.[6] Others maintain that the speaker must identify with his listeners. Still others refer to correcting an imbalance between individuals or within the listener. In different ways, these theories are attempting to describe the re-lationship between the source and the receiver of the message and to fathom the deep-seated cultural patterns that underlie this complex relationship. We find ourselves asking, "What response do I seek from my audience mem-bers? What behavioral changes am I attempting to bring about? What do I want my listener to do, to say, to think? How do I want him to react?" And,

---

[5] Wayne C. Minnick, *The Art of Persuasion*, 2nd ed. (Boston: Houghton Mifflin Co., 1968), p. 253.

[6] Charles H. Woolbert, "The Audience," *Psychological Monographs* (June 1916), pp. 37–54.

further, "How will he respond to my ideas, to me, if I present my message this way? That way? If I am just my 'natural' self? If I give it to him straight? If I reveal this bias, that prejudice? If I go into detail here? If I use a story there?"

In a practical sense, we ask, and answer, questions like these at three stages in the preparation and presentation of a message: *before* the message is delivered (prior analysis), *during* delivery, and *after* the speaking situation is ended (post analysis).[7] Analyzing and adapting to listeners is a lifelong process: Throughout our lives as speakers, those of us who want to be successful communicators—that is, who want acceptance of our messages—will devote attention to our listeners, to the means of adapting we have at our disposal, and to the results of our labors.

Audience Feedback

Audiences, then, must be analyzed. This analysis is possible partly because of what we know of human behavior from psychology and related sciences, and partly because we know that communication is a two-way or circular process. Clearly enough, the speaker "sends" a message to his audience; but the audience not only receives the message—it also *reacts* to the message. We discover something of how an audience is reacting through feedback.[8]

Most audiences feed back their reactions indirectly. Relatively few speakers need fear a barrage of overripe tomatoes; and most of us need not anticipate wildly cheering, foot-stamping crowds every time we speak. Nonetheless, there are very definite, if subtle, signs of approval or disapproval, boredom or interest. The listeners inform us through their nonverbal communication—silences, smiles, changes of expression, body position, yawns and gasps—whether we are getting our message across and what they think of it.

Elaborate devices have been designed for measuring audience feedback. Perhaps the most familiar are the kinds used for the various television rating polls—Nielsen, for instance. For gauging smaller speech situations, feedback can be obtained by means of the *audience analyzer,* a device that requires the listeners to push buttons registering red lights for disapproval or green lights for approval of the speech. Questionnaires and depth interviews have been employed in efforts to discover what makes audiences tick. None of these devices will help us when we are trying to convince a client across a luncheon table or to explain the technique of tooth-brushing to a five-year-old. We cannot trap our audience in a tangle of wires and flashing lights or pass out questionnaires or have interviewers circulating. We must make our own

---

[7] See Minnick, Chapter 10, "Overcoming Obstacles—Strategy and Audience Analysis."

[8] The term "feedback" is used in this context with a source or speaker orientation.

judgments about the reactions of our listeners—before, during, and after speaking. Thus it is necessary to give thought to a simple and accurate set of suggestions for analyzing audiences.

The Process of Audience Adaptation and Analysis

Speaker experience and communication research over many hundreds of years have provided us with a collection, of some utilitarian value, of items to look for in analyzing listeners before, during, and after a speech. As guides, they are not all scientifically founded, they don't always work, but they are workable. Both skilled and beginning speakers can make use of them as we struggle with the task of adapting what we want to say to those to whom we want to say it.

Four notes of caution are in order here: (1) We would do well to restudy the previous chapter, "Understanding and Adapting to the Occasion," since adaptation to the audience also means adaptation to the occasion of the speech. (2) Every audience, every speech situation, is different; therefore,

A Checklist for Analysis

1. *Study your subject in the light of the probable reaction to it. This suggestion may seem to be circular, since the "probable reaction" is what you are trying to identify; actually, however, it is a helpful beginning. If you have taken the time to research your subject thoroughly, you may know what attitudes people typically hold toward it, or you may be able to make a shrewd, temporary guess, pending further investigation. Moreover, if you are speaking on one side of a controversial topic, remember that it is controversial only because there are a certain number of people who disagree with that position, and your own reaction will probably be shared by a good part of your audience.*

2. *Find out your previous reputation with this group. Many listeners develop an attitude toward an idea from their attitude toward the speaker who pre-sents the idea. Do your listeners know you, your name, your profession, your general reputation? Are they likely to have a definite opinion about the profession, party, or organization you represent? If they know you in some way, try to determine what the connection is. If they do not know you, you will tend to be, at the start of your speech, in a sort of neutral position: you should have no enemies, but neither will you have partisan support.*

3. *Study the place where you are to speak. (The details of the analysis of this factor can be found in Chapter 3.) Often, the degree to which you can polarize your listeners into an audience may be heavily influenced by the size, shape, location, and decor of the room or hall in which you are to speak, as well as by the relationship of the size and location of the audience to the size and shape*

every suggestion on the checklist (see inset) will have to be adapted to individual circumstances. (3) Although the suggestions in the checklist are intended primarily for the use of the speaker who is able to plan in advance, even the impromptu communicator, in the brief moment he has for thought, should analyze his audience as well as he can. (4) Amid all this attention to audience analysis, we must never lose sight that we are often proposing to influence people's minds; that this is a highly dangerous task at best and downright evil at worst; that we must be as sure as we can be that our objective is both ethical and useful; and that we must observe rules of fair play and decency no matter how right we think we are.

From Checklist to Analysis

Finally, after utilizing the checklist to the best of our ability, we should try to sum up all of the clues it has given us. For our next speaking effort, let us apply this process not only to the preparation of our speech but also just before and during the delivery. In impromptu situations, of course, where little or no preparation is involved, there may still be a brief moment before we speak during which we can glance at our listeners and consider as many of the elements of this analysis as we can take in.

---

of the room.* In a formal situation there is really little you can do to alter existing conditions, but you can be aware of the problems inherent in the place in which you are to speak, and you can compensate for them through other forms of audience adaptation. Possibly you are to speak in the only available place, but it is equally possible that the arrangement committee simply gave no thought to this matter, beyond merely providing a place. On the positive side, the size of the room may indicate how much of a drawing card you are expected to be; the location and prestige of the hall may indicate your own prestige. If you are speaking to a professor in his office or to

a group of suburban housewives gathered in a living room, the place again deserves your consideration and analysis. Are many interruptions likely? Is the room comfortable? Is there a lot of noise outside that makes hearing you difficult? The questions about location and place apply as well to the small room and the informal or impromptu speaking situation as to the lecture hall and the formal speech.

4. Know the purpose of your speech. Sometimes the title of the speech or the theme of the program does not indicate the real purpose of the message. There may be an unexpressed purpose; suppose, for example, as a class assignment you give a talk describing the churches in your city; you may have the hidden purpose of stimulating church attendance, although you do not mention it explicitly. You may also have a hidden purpose

---

* A dissenting view of the importance of audience proximity is offered in Gordon L. Thomas and David C. Ralph, "A Study of the Effect of Audience Proximity on Persuasion," *Speech Monographs*, Vol. 26 (November 1959), pp. 300–307.

When we have summed up all the facts and feelings that we might know about our listeners—including the checklist (inset) and *our own*—let's ask ourselves: "Now that I hope I know my audience, how different are they from me? Are we cut from the same mold? Do we believe the same things, hold to the same ideas? Are they my kind of people? Am I their kind of people?" The purpose of asking such questions is to find out how much we will have to change our normal or habitual way of speaking (and thinking). It is nonsense to assume that being natural will always bring our efforts to a successful end; our listeners may not like us that way. We know very well that our friends speak one way when they talk about their dates last Saturday night and quite another way when they answer the economics professor's questions about gross national product. Our business associate is bound to be one kind of speaker on the golf course and another in the sales conference.

This doesn't mean that we must play a role or be affected when we speak; we are, rather, recognizing a phenomenon that almost inevitably occurs when people are confronted with different speaking situations. Probably without conscious effort, we do alter our language, our voice, our thoughts, and our manner in conversations with different people. If this adaptation occurs in impromptu speaking situations, there is no reason why it should not occur as easily in more formal situations that require a

---

Checklist (cont'd)

without realizing it. You should know your true purpose for certain, for an unexpressed purpose will surely affect your speaking and audience acceptance of what you say.

5.   Know the purpose of the gathering. You should discover this purpose before you prepare your message. The members of the audience may have come expressly to hear you speak or they may have come for another reason, and their attitudes toward you will likely be different in each case. Certainly one of the most embarrassing experiences you can have as a speaker is to prepare a feature speech and arrive at the meeting to discover that another person will be the featured speaker. Even so, you should be able to analyze the situation quickly and adapt what you have to say to the unexpected developments.

In analyzing the following items, you would do well to get the help of the chairman of the program, by submitting a list of questions to him covering the items of your checklist.

6.   Try to find out the occupations of your listeners. Audiences often consist of people with a common vocation. You may address an audience composed entirely of doctors or members of a labor union or teachers or typists or juvenile delinquents. Or your listeners may be all employees of one company. On the other hand, many audiences consist of people whose jobs are so varied that this element of the analysis will reveal little about the audience as a whole. However, what a person does for a living is often a reliable guide to his values, his orientation toward problems, his sense of humor. A line from a play of Aristophanes prepared speech. However, we must be careful — it is unwise to sound like a company president (if one is not) when we are addressing a group of union members. It is worse yet to sound like a company president trying to sound like a union member. Audiences do not like fakes; they don't like a speaker who plays a role with them.

Although our speech or our remarks are finished, our analysis of the communication situation is not, for, in most cases, no matter how poorly we may have done, there will be another chance, somewhere, sometime. We had better take advantage of every opportunity to learn from our past mistakes. If ours is a classroom speech, we will probably receive some form of evaluation or criticism — from our instructor, orally or in writing or both; from our classmates, in a formal critique period or informally after class. Let's never treat such criticism lightly; this is what we paid our money for. The experience of speaking in a public speaking classroom is greatly enhanced when we learn where we went right and where we went wrong.

When we give a speech on the outside, we can accept the usual platitudes from the chairman and the group leader graciously; then try to analyze our mistakes with our listeners in two ways: by talking with those we feel will level with us and, when we get home, by taking a few minutes to think through the listener reactions as we perceived them.

---

might appeal to one person, a cartoon from the Chicago Tribune *to another, a quip from a television comedy to another.*

7. Find out what you can about the previous social conditioning of your listeners. Such factors as education, social class, and economic status are important in determining their reactions to you and to what you say. Information about social conditioning will influence, among other things, your selection of evidence and illustrative materials, the organization of your message, and even the main points you're trying to make.*

* Beware of lumping all your listeners together simply because they belong to the same formal organization. The local Parent-Teacher Association, for example, may seem to be the epitome of a structured group, all of whose members are concerned equally and in the same direction with improving education for their children. However, a brief study of the PTA in Lansing, Michigan, revealed that one group consisted primarily of college graduates in the middle-income bracket, while another

8.   Learn about the strongly held attitudes and beliefs of your listeners. How do they feel about religion? What are their attitudes toward American involvement in foreign wars, the preservation of our natural environment, air pollution? Are they Democrats or Republicans? How do they feel about honesty in government? the continuing energy crisis? exploration of space? young people? old people? the morality of the present generation? You can't determine every belief held by every listener, and perhaps only a few beliefs and attitudes

group across town was drawn primarily from families of union members who work in the industrial district, and a third group operated in a depressed area, where there was often considerable unemployment and where English was frequently a second language. If you were to speak on one subject — say, "The Advantages of Higher Education for Your Children" — you would have to make a different speech for each of these groups, although they belong to the same organization.

From Analysis to Adaptation

It is impossible, actually, to separate analysis from adaptation; ways of adjusting keep popping up whenever we talk about gauging the audience. Let us now, however, concentrate on the very practical problem of utilizing what we have learned about our listener to make our message more acceptable to him. We must bear in mind, throughout the process of audience adaptation, that our purpose is *not* to distort the message, to compromise our ideas, to backwater, or otherwise to chicken out of the responsibility which we have accepted. Rather, our job is to try to overcome the obstacles that prior prejudices and other circumstances have placed in the way of communication between us and our listener—in other words, to adapt both ourselves and the way we handle our messages to our listeners and to help the listeners adapt to us and to our messages.

Audience analysis and adaptation are lifetime endeavors; students of communication and other scholars in the fields of human behavior are constantly doing research in efforts to understand better what makes us tick. The selected bibliography at the end of this chapter will suggest the magnitude of this task. But the speaker who must speak now—this moment or tomorrow or next week—must have at hand some practical suggestions for

---

Checklist (cont'd)

are relevant to what you want to talk about. But to ignore a strongly held belief and then to stumble upon it with an ill-chosen example can be fatal to the success of a message.

9. *Try to learn something of your listeners' behavioral patterns. Your views on gun laws must be articulated quite differently for the first-grade teacher who takes her students to the local arboretum and the automobile worker who longs for the opening of deer season. A man who loves to garden may respond to figurative analogies and illustrations about Mother Nature, whereas the man who has paved his yard and spends his time reading books on naval history may not. Pre-knowledge about hobbies and interests may provide a way of securing a common ground with your listeners, as well as reveal a lot about their attitudes. If you appeal to what other persons consider impor-*

tant interests, you are certainly not hurting your relationship with them. (This approach, of course, is pretty well limited to use with fairly homogeneous groups. If a group of listeners have common behavioral patterns, you can make use of this circumstance in your message; but by overstressing their commonality, you will only diminish their individual response.)

10. *Find out what your listeners read. This, again, may be a difficult task. If your audience has its own meeting place, try to arrive early and look around. You may find a reading room or library or perhaps a few magazines on the chairs and tables or a rack in a corner with some publications and periodicals in it. If you find horror comics, you have some idea of your listeners' tastes and thoughts. Likewise, if you find The New Yorker, Time, or Playboy, each of*

audience adaptation that are brief and to the point. The suggestions below do not pretend to promise a sure-fire formula for audience adaptation, but they are the results of the experience of many speakers and researchers. The real work of adapting to a given listener or set of listeners must be performed by each of us, and we must learn to adapt these suggestions to the unique audience problems we will face.

Adaptation and Audience Classification

Experienced speakers have found that classifying audiences into a few basic types helps them adapt; and the information that we used in audience analysis will provide us with data for classifying our listeners. Speech theorists and psychologists have classified audiences according to their purposes for assembling, the size of the audience, the formality of the situation, and so on. Perhaps most useful to our viewpoint is a classification that indicates how the speaker must adapt to the behavior, attitudes, interests, beliefs, educa-

these will tell something about the character and personality of your listeners. Your judgments derived from the magazines will, of course, be far from infallible; but reading material does provide clues for adapting your presentation.

11. Find out about the predominant physical characteristics of your audience. Sometimes your speaking must be adapted to variations in audiences' age, sex, and health. A talk on "Adult Participation in Sports" would hardly go over big at a convalescent home. Your entertaining speech on "Politicians and How They Get That Way" might be humorous to a group of male county commissioners but might provoke anger from a women's liberation group struggling to stimulate more female participation in politics.

12. Study the nonverbal cues exhibited by your listeners. You should carefully study your listeners before you begin and as you speak, because their manners and their physical activity reveal a good deal about their reactions. One of the reasons for maintaining eye contact with members of the audience is to gauge the extent of their interest or apathy by the way they sit in the chairs or the way they move around. If they look puzzled, they probably are puzzled, and you know that you are not getting your message through. If they wriggle, cough, or drop things, you can be sure you do not have their attention. If they look bored by a startling statement, it may mean that you have misjudged their probable reactions. Most listeners let you know how well you are communicating with them, even though they may be unaware that they are doing so; good poker players, it is said, rely on unconscious cues—and a good speaker does no less.

tion, and knowledge of the listeners — in short, a classification based upon audience analysis, and utilizing the materials of speaking available to the speaker.

Because we have found that the most important determinants of the listener's reaction to the message are his attitudes and behaviors toward the *subject* and the *speaker*, together with the information he possesses about the subject and the speaker, our audience classification will stress these two factors. Of course, the purpose of the speaker will influence such a classification; data relevant for persuasion may sometimes be useless for speaking to inform or speaking to entertain, and vice versa. But the basic attitudes and the amount of information possessed by the listener are paramount, regardless of the purpose of the speaker and the speech.

Classification by Listener Attitudes

A classification of audiences that is useful and practical for beginning speakers postulates five types, according to the listeners' attitudes: *neutral, friendly, apathetic, hostile,* and *mixed.*

The Neutral Audience   We describe the neutral audience as basically rational or objective. It tends to be open-minded toward the speaker and his ideas; the listeners have not yet made up their minds on the issues at hand, and they want from the speaker reasoning and evidence that will help them decide. To this audience, reasoning and evidence are usually more persuasive than high pressure and emotional appeals.

Theoretically, the speaker is often confronted with a neutral audience; city councils, state legislatures, Congress, board of directors' meetings, juries, and task-oriented committees — all try to base their decisions on evidence and reasoning, on facts and figures, on rational materials. However, although most of us like to think of ourselves as objective, rational thinkers, we are apt to let unconscious motives influence our standards of rationality. We think we are being entirely objective about an issue when actually our previous conditioning about such things as ethics, religion, and politics makes it impossible for us even to know whether we are being objective or not.

For example, the television debates of the 1960 presidential campaign were designed to convince an audience of rational listeners — a neutral audience — to vote one way or another. The appeals necessarily had to be primarily rational. Yet possibly 90 percent of the voters watching these debates could not be classified as neutral; a study by the Survey Research Center shows that only about 10 percent of the electorate is actually independent — the rest having varying degrees of party affiliation and sympathy.[9]

The neutral audience is intellectually honest; it seeks the truth; it asks

---

[9] Murray S. Stedman, Jr., "The Problem of the Independent Voter," *Current History* (August 1956), pp. 96–99.

the speaker to present his materials and then, in a sense, to stand aside and let the listeners make up their own minds. When we are confronted with this all-too-rare kind of audience, our approach is essentially the "didactic method," in which we make greatest use, obviously, of *materials of development*. We give our audience facts, figures, testimony, examples, explanations, and the best reasoning of which we are capable. *Personal proof* is also important, for it is imperative that we indicate belief in ourself and in our message. If we do not, our audience can hardly be expected to believe or understand or react favorably. We will also make some use of *materials of experience* with a neutral audience, for we must maintain interest and hold people's attention in all forms of speaking; however, this type of audience will require less emphasis on such materials than other types will.

The Friendly Audience   This is an audience that is already convinced of the speaker's proposition or has a favorable view toward his subject—and its members probably like him as well as his ideas. Persuasive speaking with listeners who are friendly is not primarily a matter of getting them to reach a conclusion or change their minds; the usual purpose is to persuade them to *act* on what they already believe. In informative or entertaining speaking, "action" of some kind is also the goal—there is already present a "set" toward the speaker and his ideas.

A competent speaker urging support for a campus blood drive is aware of this audience set in his favor. Most people believe that giving blood is a good thing; for instance, a good supply of blood for emergencies must be maintained, giving blood when we are able will make some available for us or someone we love when an emergency occurs. We know, also, that it is not really painful to give blood, that only a fraction of a day's time is required, and that it is "morally right and economically sound." But, believing in giving blood and driving two miles, entering a strange, hospital-like atmosphere, rolling up our sleeves, and letting a nurse or doctor puncture us are two very different things. A show of hands of those who believe in giving blood would be impressive; quite a number of hands would be raised to indicate some knowledge of the process of giving blood; but a show of hands of those who are willing to give blood now, this very day, would often prove disappointing.

The speaker in this kind of situation has to rely on something other than evidence and reasoning, since his listeners don't need to be convinced of his point of view. His job is to get them to make a commitment—to realize emotionally what they believe intellectually. For these persons, whose beliefs are not so vital, intense, or urgent as to motivate action, we will need to use the "impressive method"; that is, we will work to impress upon our hearers the urgency of the matter and the necessity for their positive action. We will clothe our ideas with compelling and passionate phrases so as to make our listeners *want* to do something about their beliefs. *Materials of experience* are our most effective weapon here, materials that help our audience to see, to hear, to smell, to taste, and to touch the substance of our belief. And, simply because our speech is labeled "informative" or "entertaining," rather than "advocative or persuasive," let us not abandon use of *materials of experience,* for our listeners in these cases, too, must be made constantly aware of the need for close attention to and emotional involvement with the content of our message.

Personal proof is of great importance when speaking to a friendly audience, for these receivers must not think that we are attempting to destroy their reasoning processes (as indeed we are not); they must understand that *we* believe so passionately in our subject that we want to share this belief with them.

If we should neglect *materials of development,* we would have nothing but demagoguery; our speech would be "full of sound and fury, signifying nothing." We should use sufficient materials of development to assure that the speech makes logical sense and that the audience is reminded of the facts of the case. However, there is no need to detail reasons our listeners already know, to belabor the obvious, and to insist upon restating the stand that they share with us. On the other hand, even listeners who want to behave as we do may want new reasons for doing so, or new explanations of concepts. In this context at least, while it is unnecessary to repeat what the listener already knows and believes, adding to his knowledge and beliefs will improve our message.

The Apathetic Audience   An audience is apathetic when it just doesn't care one way or the other about our subject. The apathetic audience is neither friendly nor hostile, neither in agreement with nor opposed to the speaker's ideas. If apathetic listeners have opinions about the subject under discussion, they don't care enough to express them. In the more formal speech situation, they have assembled, perhaps under pressure, perhaps by indifferent choice, perhaps to avoid twinges of conscience; in our more common and less formal daily encounters, our listeners may hear us out merely to be polite, without having any interest in what we have to say.

Many audiences should be classified under this heading, probably far more than most speakers realize: service club audiences, lecture audiences, church congregations. A speaker invited to address a meeting of the Business Women's Club may think that the talk he has prepared will have the women sitting on the edges of their seats in rapt attention — only to discover, from the yawning faces and busy fidgeting, that evidently most of the listeners came only out of a sense of obligation. When the communicator knows enough about his or her audience to expect this kind of apathy, he is wise to start his talk and maintain it with attention-getting devices. His first job is not to persuade or inform but to arouse interest in his subject and himself. Even a hostile attitude on the part of the audience at least shows interest; and when apathy is destroyed, the first obstacle to agreement is overcome.

With the apathetic audience, as with the friendly one, we must arouse in our hearers the desire to listen, but the task is more difficult here. For the friendly audience is "with us," whereas the apathetic audience has no fixed attitude at all. Here we must pour on the *materials of experience,* and we must also be prepared to use *materials of development,* but in an unusual way. *Application* is the key. Materials of development must be presented in a sensory manner; instead of using straight facts or statistics, we must clothe them in interesting and attention-getting garb.

Moreover, once we have obtained full attention, we must be ready to cope with it. For an apathetic audience that has lost its apathy may become friendly, hostile, objective, or mixed in its attitudes. When a change in attitude becomes apparent, we must be prepared to take one of several courses: *If the audience members become neutral,* to present materials of development; *if they become friendly,* to continue the motivation; and *if they become hostile,* to shift to a strong use of personal proof. And if they are split into many camps—as they may well be—we must evaluate as best we can and speak so that our message will appeal (hopefully) to most if not all.

The Hostile Audience   Well-known speakers frequently find themselves facing audiences that are opposed to their ideas or hostile to them personally; this is, naturally, one of the penalties of having a reputation of any kind. Most speakers, however, and most people in everyday speaking situations, do not have to contend with the perils of fame or notoriety; when the listeners are hostile, it is usually because the speaker is supporting a position that his listeners oppose.

We may make our request for a raise in pay or for a higher grade on an examination to a listener who may be strongly opposed to our point of view, although he may think the world of us personally. Likewise, anything we say about subjects on which there are numerous points of view—from movies to sex—is likely to be greeted, sometimes, with hostility. The effective speaker recognizes the possibility of hostility, tries to understand its source, and, with understanding, learns how to deal with it.

When confronted with hostility, many people try to persuade their listeners by becoming more argumentative—by leveling blasts of either "ironclad logic" or highly charged emotional appeals. This approach usually increases the listeners' hostility, confirms their original beliefs, and leaves them deaf to any argument about the subject from any source.

The speaker confronted with a hostile audience should do her best not to hammer away at the hostility but to reduce it in a way that shows understanding of and respect for the listeners' ideas. One way of reducing antagonism is by focusing attention on matters about which audience and speaker are in agreement. Most subjects of controversy have related ideas about which there is little disagreement, or at least little disagreement within one audience in one speaking situation. The speaker will be wise to commence by emphasizing these areas of agreement and establishing a

common ground on which to meet the listener. In this way, the audience can come to feel a respect for the speaker, and the speaker will have a launching pad from which to talk directly and logically about her subject.

Hostile listeners have closed their minds to us and our ideas. They may appear to be listening — they may think they are listening — but our ideas are not getting through, at least not in the way we intend them to. Our mission is to cool down that hostility by helping the hearers accept us as a person of good character and goodwill, who has their best interests at heart and wants only a full, fair, and favorable hearing. Here we must use the "method of conciliation," and this requires *personal proof* as a means of establishing common ground and other bases for further discussion. Until our audience thinks well of us, we may not successfully continue with the reasoning and evidence or explanation that will form the heart of the speech (*materials of development*). Sometimes, indeed, a speaker finds her audience so opposed to her ideas that she fills her speech entirely with generalities or specificities of another sort. She may be forced to introduce her real thoughts through indirection or suggestion (see Chapter 7). Furthermore, *materials of experience* must be used with great care. When an audience is extremely hostile, it tends to regard narrations, descriptions, figures of speech, and the use of appeals as tricks to confuse the listener. There may be an even greater aversion to humor. Thus we must be very careful with these materials, proceeding cautiously so that we can shift our tactics if they seem to be fanning the hostility.

Personal proof has been found to be the most effective material of speaking in reducing hostility. The televised remarks of Muhammad Ali, after his heavyweight championship fight with Zora Folley, are a case in point. The twenty or so viewers with whom we watched the fight responded favorably to Muhammad Ali's praise of his opponent's abilities as a fighter. They nodded approvingly as the champion assured Folley's wife that Folley was not badly hurt. When Muhammad Ali told his opponent's children that they should be very proud of their father, several of the viewers made such remarks as "He's all right"; "Cassius is really with it"; "He's not the smart aleck he used to be." Yet, to a man, these viewers had expressed opposition to Muhammad Ali before the fight began; they had made unfavorable remarks about him during the bout. After the post-fight speech, not a single voice was raised in opposition.

The Mixed Audience In many—perhaps most—cases, the speaker will be confronted with an audience whose overall attitude toward his or her subject cannot be placed in a single classification. Some listeners may be objective; some may favor the speaker's position; some may not care one way or another; others may be actively opposed. Attitudes toward the speaker as a person may vary within a given audience. Various degrees of hostility or partisanship may be present, and some listeners may like the speaker but oppose his position. To complicate the picture further, a given listener may experience ambivalence within himself concerning both the speaker and his message. He may like the speaker one moment, dislike him the next; he may support one idea, oppose another.

The members of a family having a house built may feel differently about the ideas their architect suggests; he may have to convince each of them of a reasonable compromise between having a fashionable showplace in which to entertain, a practical dwelling for raising the children, and a sufficiently private place for getting away from it all. Speaking in such a situation—wherein several attitudes must be met and dealt with—requires combinations of the several methods of adapting to receptiveness, hostility, and neutrality, in order to make a maximum appeal to the listeners. Our task is to provide materials for all members of our audience to accept. While we placate those who oppose us, we must not forget to give credit to our loyal supporters. The intellectuals must have our reasoning to chew upon, and those who are bored must be given interesting and provocative materials to digest.

Classification by Listener Knowledge

In addition to their attitudes and behaviors toward a message and toward the individual presenting the message, listeners also possess (or lack) knowledge about our subject—as our analysis of them may frequently reveal. We cannot rest content with adapting to listener attitude; we must also adapt our message and sometimes even ourselves to their sophistication with regard to our subject. For convenience and ease in making adaptations in the relatively brief time that we have, let us consider listener knowledge in three areas: the well-informed audience, the generally informed audience, and the uninformed audience.

The Well-Informed Audience On occasion, we will speak to people who already know a great deal about our subject. Sometimes this can be an unfortunate situation, for the well-informed audience may know all it needs or wants to know; on the other hand, it may be able to profit from new material and from our singular point of view. If our audience is well informed, we can surely avoid explaining anything that needs no explanation. We won't waste our efforts on discussing the whole subject; we will concentrate instead on particular aspects that may show where our point of view or our information is new or different from what our listeners already know. We will give details about new information, or cover a segment of the subject that we feel our listeners should understand or appreciate better.

A history professor was asked recently to speak before a high school history class on the Turner thesis concerning the role of the frontier in American history. Upon inquiry, he discovered that most of the students were well informed on the subject. Because his audience knew quite a bit about the Turner thesis itself, he decided to spend little time on basic explanation and to concentrate more on pointing out to his audience how such social hypotheses can change the world as much as scientific hypotheses.

The well-informed listener probably will have little respect for the speaker who knows less about the subject than he. As speakers, in addition to *being* extremely well informed on the subject at hand, *we must also employ throughout our speech techniques intended to convey the impression, subtly and modestly, that we are well informed.* Of course, we should continue to do our best to arouse and maintain the interest and attention of the audience.

Thus, when we find an audience well informed on the subject we intend to talk about, we must make judicious use of *materials of development*, concentrating on new materials or on new applications of familiar materials. Our *personal proof* must be high, for there may be an initial tendency by our listeners to feel that they've been through all this stuff before. They must be convinced, early in the speech, that we have something worthwhile to offer them. *Materials of experience*, used to arouse attention, to focus attention upon new ideas, and to relate the familiar to the unfamiliar, will help to overcome initial lack of interest in the speaker and his subject.

The Generally Informed Audience   This audience usually knows enough about the speaker's subject to have at least a rudimentary understanding of it. Most of the speeches given in a college speech class are delivered to this kind of audience; there is usually a wide area of subjects about which there is some general knowledge, and the job of the speaker is to provide further information, usually covering details about which our audience has little knowledge. For example, an explanation of the workings of a credit union to members of a college faculty or employees of a business concern would be presented to an audience of listeners who know that the credit union exists and that they can invest in or borrow from it (possibly many of them have already done so). However, they may not have a full understanding about the rules, the rates of interest, and the services of the credit union; and the speaker's task is to fill them in on some of the finer points.

With a generally informed audience, we can choose a broad or a narrow approach; that is, we may elect to discuss our entire subject, filling in gaps of knowledge for our listeners, or we may decide to reserve that general knowledge as background for a foray into some specific aspect of the subject. We have considerable latitude in our choice of *materials of development*, depending upon the goals we select. We must be certain that we are as well informed on the subject as possible, because the generally informed audience is likely to be comprised of listeners who believe they know more than they actually know, and such as these tend to be contemptuous of a speaker who appears to be ignorant. However, adequate demonstration of our knowledge may require detailed explanations and technical terms that could be over our listeners' heads — an undesirable situation. The best approach is to keep the talk simple but respectful, without either talking down or assuming too much knowledge on the part of the listeners.

It can be argued that the less informed the audience is, the more we must employ *materials of experience*, in order to sustain interest and lead the listener to a greater understanding of our point of view. These materials — attention factors, appeals, description and narration, for example — will be needed to hold the listeners' attention and to help lead them from their previous knowledge to the new knowledge we feel they must have.

The Uninformed Audience   Although speaking to an audience that knows as much about our subject as we do may be a trying experience, an audience that is uninformed may prove even more difficult. Let us take the plight of the twelve-year-old trying to explain to his six-year-old brother and his friends some of the fine points of baseball; for example, what to do if you are leading off second base and the ball is hit back to the pitcher and you're not sure whether the pitcher caught it or trapped it. This youngster's little brother has probably been allowed to join in a baseball game with his brother and other older boys, but most of his friends have not been so fortunate. They don't know the terms peculiar to baseball or how to hold the bat, let alone how to pitch or catch. The older boy may soon become discouraged by the necessity of explaining so many things he takes for granted. He discovers that he must reduce all that he knows about baseball to the simplest terms in order to reach the comprehension of his eager but ignorant listeners.

In most situations of this nature, simplicity of *materials of development* is the answer. We start with the most basic information; it is not so important to establish our personal authority on the subject as it is to keep the attention of our listeners. We must be careful not to appear to be talking down, however. The uninformed listener will appreciate our willingness to present basic, fundamental material, but he will resent the idea that we think he is stupid or incapable of learning.

Moreover, the less informed the audience members are, the greater must be that portion of the speech devoted to *materials of experience*, for an uninformed audience must be constantly stimulated to *want* to learn, and concepts must be made interesting through the devices of this kind of material. (Even the well-informed audience does not permit the speaker simply to lay out his information without concern for attention-holding materials.)

The Mixed Audience   As with the audience whose members vary in their attitudes toward us and our subject, so it is with the audience whose members are mixed in their knowledge. For these audiences, we must vary the amount, placement, and sophistication of the materials of speaking. The *amount of information* to be given, the *degree of difficulty* of the explanation, the amount of material the audience is willing to accept *secondhand,* and the application of information to the specific needs of the audience — all these will try our patience and skill when we face a mixed audience. Always *personal proof,* always some *materials of experience,* but how much? how often? when? — these are the questions you must answer. Now you can feel some empathy with a twelve-year-old and his problems of explaining baseball, or you will feel it when you select for your classroom speech a subject that meets with a mixed audience.

Analyzing and adapting to an audience is a complex and difficult process. It is quite possible to follow the checklists and methods suggested here and still go wrong. However, most analyses based on these principles will be effective, because the principles have been derived from the work of rhetorical and communication scholars, from the results of experimental research in human behavior, and from the experiences of effective speakers in varied speaking situations. They will work for you if you remember that you can affect your listeners best by finding out what they usually want to hear, and then telling them your message in terms they are generally used to hearing. No method of analysis is foolproof; but you can communicate more easily with someone you "know" than you can with a stranger.

If this perusal of audience adaptation causes you to believe that speaking is a difficult process, we can only say that effective speaking most certainly is. Problems met in speaking are not like those of simple arithmetic; there are no answers in the back of the book to confirm your analyses. Audiences are made up of people who are far more complex and unpredictable than our simple analysis has suggested.

The message you intend to deliver must be colored and shaped by the kind of person you are. It is equally important that you give weight to the setting of the speech — the situation in which you will operate — and realize that you are speaking to real people, with all the fears, loves, hates, puzzlements, uncertainties, and pressures that you yourself suffer from. The real speech — the speech that will affect the hearers — must be composed in the complicated real-life situation in which we live and then be delivered to the real people whom we face.

Suggested Assignments

1. Put your checklist (as well as what you've read in this chapter about adapting to your listeners) to work in the next informal oral communication situation you encounter. See how much analysis and adaptation you can manage, while keeping your attention on the conversation. Try the same procedures while acting as listener-critic, instead of participant. Jot down your own evaluation of your efforts as soon as possible after the communication event. How well did you do? Notice any difference in your confidence as a communicator? any difference in the results of your participation? Did you pick up any ideas for improving your communication in informal or formal speaking situations?

2. Study the speech plans and speaker's notes of the latest speech you have delivered. What assumptions do you now think you made about your audience? Do you think you consciously analyzed your audience in any way? To what extent? In what ways? What were your conclusions? If you did not make a deliberate effort to understand your audience, what do your speech plans and notes reveal about any unplanned analysis you think you made?

3. Consider the topic you have chosen (or the one assigned) for your next speech. First, make some guesses concerning the probable reaction to your subject by each member of your class or group. Next, make up a questionnaire, using the checklist in this chapter, and obtain as much information about your audience as you can. Try to classify your audience, using the labels suggested in this chapter. Then announce your speech topic to the class. Finally, ask each member of your class to indicate his attitude toward your subject. Compare your original guess with the results of your survey and each of these with the poll you took of your classmates. How did you come out?

4. Assume that you are to speak on the topic "The Role of the State Legislature in Higher Education" to each of the audiences listed below. Analyze each audience, as best you can, and indicate how you think each might respond to your speech.

a. Members of the legislature of your state

b. Members of your college class in public speaking

c. The Parent-Teacher Association of your high school

d. The local Lions Club

e. A group of high school seniors in the lower third of their graduating class

f. Members of the faculty of the speech-communication department of your college or university

g. Members of the largest union local in your town or city

h. A convention of the National Association of Manufacturers

5. When you make your next speech, observe as carefully as you can all the signs of feedback from your audience. Ask a friend to sit near you, facing the audience, and note down all the feedback he can. How many different kinds of feedback did you observe? Interpret these signs as best you can. Compare your list with that of your friend.

6. Tell your listeners about the operation of some device, institution, or process with which they, in a general way, are already quite familiar. Assume that your listeners agree with you that knowledge of the process is a good thing to have; assume, however, that their very familiarity with the idea will tend to lessen the impact of the

speech upon them. Try to associate the ideas in your talk with some of the basic "feelings" in your audience, and attempt to motivate your audience to listen to your explanation.

7.   Choose a subject about which you believe most of the members of your class will care little but in which you think you can interest them. Prepare an introduction to your speech in which you arrest their attention and acquaint them with your basic purpose in speaking. Then, prepare a speech plan or several speech plans that will make you ready to speak to them regardless of the attitude they will take toward your subject. Deliver your introduction. Make an immediate analysis of your listeners' reactions. How many are neutral? hostile? friendly? still apathetic? Adapt quickly to these reactions and deliver the remainder of your speech, doing your utmost to influence as many of your receivers as you can.

8.   Find a subject in which you strongly believe but which you feel the majority of your listeners will oppose. First, outline your topic in a straightforward manner, as though you were speaking to an objective audience. Then develop a speech plan that you think will enable you to obtain a fair hearing from your audience. You may wish to survey your audience's reactions in the manner described in Assignment 7.

9.   Choose a subject that you know is controversial and that will meet with a mixed reaction from your audience. Prepare your speech as carefully as you can, doing your utmost to excite the interest of those who already believe as you do, to present evidence and reasoning that will convince those who are on the fence, to stir up those who are apathetic toward you or your topic, and to get through to those who have closed their minds against you. This is a difficult assignment, and you will not be altogether happy with the results, no matter how fine a job you do.

Suggested References

Bem, Daryl S., *Beliefs, Attitudes, and Human Affairs* (Monterey, Calif.: Brooks/Cole Publishing Co., 1970).

Bettinghaus, Erwin P., *Persuasive Communication,* 2nd ed. (New York: Holt, Rinehart and Winston, 1973).

Clevenger, Theodore, Jr., *Audience Analysis* (Indianapolis: Bobbs-Merrill Co., 1966).

Larson, Charles U., *Persuasion: Reception and Responsibility* (Belmont, Calif.: Wadsworth Publishing Co., 1973).

Miller, Gerald R., and Michael Burgoon, *New Techniques of Persuasion* (New York: Harper & Row, 1973).

Minnick, Wayne C., *The Art of Persuasion,* 2nd ed. (Boston: Houghton Mifflin Co., 1968).

Shrope, Wayne Austin, *Experiences in Communication* (New York: Harcourt Brace Jovanovich, 1974). Chapter 11, "Improving as a Sender."

Wagner, Richard V., and John S. Sherwood, *The Study of Attitude Change* (Monterey, Calif.: Brooks/Cole Publishing Co., 1969).

Winans, James A., *Speech-Making* (New York: Appleton-Century-Crofts, 1938). Chapter 2, "Conversing with an Audience."

5
Materials of Speaking: Personal Proof

"He knows what he's talking about"

After the speaker had folded his notes and stepped down from the outdoor wooden platform, the audience rose from scattered benches and positions on the grass, stretching, gathering up belongings, and comparing impressions. Some of the comments were: "Being so friendly really made his speech"; "Yes, I liked him, but I think he spoke in generalities because he really didn't have much to say"; "But don't forget, he has a good reputation in this field, and I'll bet he knows what he's talking about."

We have all heard comments like these following a speech, but what are these listeners really talking about? Not the qualities of the speech per se —certainly, none of the comments deals basically with content, logic, development of ideas, or adaptation to the listener. Rather, they are referring to *personal proof (the person of the speaker)* and its effects on the perceived merits of the composition or verbal message.

The ancient Greeks knew, and all students of speaking since that time have known, that the *ethos* — the person of the speaker — is fully as important to the success or failure of communication as are logic, evidence, and development. Furthermore, research has shown that personal appearance, personality, character, age, competence, and related personal attributes or traits *do* affect the success of all efforts to communicate.

For instance, on a legal question we are likely to accept the advice of a lawyer more readily than that of an English teacher because we presume that the lawyer's training and experience lend a credibility to his judgments. They tend to create a good *ethos* — an image of attributes, qualities, or elements that are regarded as good or desirable. Because the speaker's *ethos* is so important to his getting his message across, we should learn what it is, what elements make it up, what makes the listener react to it, and how it affects the principles of speaking.

The Nature of Personal Proof

Personal proof is the kind of proof—or the element that lends credibility to the message—*that arises from the person of the speaker*. It influences the total speaking situation; it affects the listener's point of view and his attitude toward the speaker; and therefore, it also affects the amount of information the listener receives. This element is often called *source credibility*. (While the concepts of *personal proof* and *source credibility* are not exactly the same, the differences are negligible; and the terms will be used interchangeably here.)

The Elements of Personal Proof

In the fourth century B.C., Aristotle presented one of the first systematic analyses of personal proof. Since then, scholars have quite generally considered good personal proof to consist of three elements: *competence, good character, and goodwill.*[1] These attributes are generally regarded as *aids* to the speaker; likewise, the lack of one or all of them is a *deterrent* to effective communication. Personal proof, therefore, can either enhance or destroy the credibility of the speaker's message, depending upon whether he possesses or lacks these three elements.

Competence, as it relates to personal proof, is the quality that grows out of a combination of mental ability, intelligence, know-how, understanding, experience with the subject, and knowledge. Listeners tend to believe that a speaker is competent when they can say, "He knows what he's talking about."

Good character is measured by honesty, integrity, sincerity, fairness, and similar qualities that meet the standards of the listeners. Of a speaker who exhibits this quality, listeners are likely to say, "She is honest, fair, and really believes what she says."

Goodwill shows itself in friendliness, likableness, warmth, rapport, interest, concern, eagerness to be of help, and a spirit of being "in" with the audience. The listener may say of the speaker who exhibits this quality, "I like him; he is warm, friendly, concerned, and interested in me."

In short, the speaker with a *good ethos* conveys the impression of knowing what he's talking about; of being honest and sincere; and of being friendly, congenial, and likable.

Awareness of these three elements will no doubt help us to be more effective speakers. However, with this awareness we run the risk of as-

---

[1] While it is true that some scholars refer to slightly different elements and analyze them differently at some points, they basically agree that personal proof is an important factor in the communication process.

suming that creating the *impression* that we possess these attributes is what matters—whether or not we really do. This raises an ethical question: If we agree that it is enough merely to create an impression, are we condoning chicanery and subterfuge? Actually, there may be no ethical problem at all—*if we believe that good impressions cannot be created unless the qualities of these impressions are actually present.* Therefore, let's deal here with the question of methodology: How does a speaker give evidence to his listeners that he really does possess competence, good character, and goodwill?

The first and most obvious answer is that we should strive to possess in the highest degree the attributes of a good ethos. We should use our native intelligence, act with some sense, and do all that we can to prepare ourselves to speak with authority on the subject at hand. In short, we should be worth listening to; we should *be* competent. Also, we should strive to be honest, sincere, straightforward, and conscientious. We should *be* persons of good character. Finally, we should strive to be friendly, cooperative, warm, and interested in other people. We should *be* persons of goodwill.

However, there is more to being a speaker with good ethos than striving to possess these qualities. Ideally, we should have nothing in our past that will create in the listener's mind a poor image of what we are, and we should do nothing in the immediate communication situation that will destroy a good image or create a poor one. If we are to be effective speakers, we should, of course, live our lives in a manner that bespeaks competence, good character, and goodwill. Anything less will erect significant obstacles to our success in the communication situation—at least in those circumstances wherein source credibility is a decisive factor. While, to be sure, there *are* persons who have enjoyed success in many speech situations who have lived lives that fall short of ideal, these persons are the exceptions; and their success is likely to be short-lived.

Besides, there are methods by which we may seek to convince our listeners of our personal credibility—methods that can be discovered through a careful analysis of the speaking situation and of the sources of listeners' impressions of the speaker. A study of these methods is important to every speaker, because—although we may be oblivious of it—we may not be letting our audience see our best qualities.

It is certainly more than a coincidence or an accident that one of the most renowned and effective speakers of this century, Franklin D. Roosevelt, usually prefaced his messages with subtle and effective statements about the reasons for his competence with a certain subject, with evidence of his character, and with testimony of his goodwill toward the American people (his primary audience). Examination of almost any of his speeches will reveal his sure touch in creating impressions and making his audience aware of his real qualities. For example, in one of his most famous and most frequently quoted speeches—the 1944 political campaign speech to the International Brotherhood of Teamsters, Chauffeurs, Warehousemen, and Helpers of America—he began:

> Well, here we are together again—after four years—and what years they have been! I am actually four years older—which seems to annoy some people. In fact, millions of us are more than eleven years older than when we started to clear up the mess that was dumped in our laps in 1933.

Another reference to himself in the opening portion of the message occurred in his last public speech, the famous report to Congress on the Yalta Conference—one of the very few times when he made public reference to his physical disability:

> I hope that you will pardon me for an unusual posture of sitting down during the presentation of what I want to say, but I know that you will realize it makes it a lot easier for me in not having to carry about ten pounds of steel around on the bottom of my legs and also because of the fact that I have just completed a 14,000 mile trip.
> First of all, I want to say that it is good to be home. It has been a long journey, and I hope you will also agree that it has been, so far, a fruitful one.

This method of establishing personal proof is not used to create false impressions; rather, it is a way by which a speaker can reveal his or her true nature. A speaker who is unaware of these methods may be hiding his light under a bushel because he does not understand what happens in the communication situation.

Sources of Listeners' Impressions

Sources External to the Composition (The Verbal Message)

There are at least four readily discernible *sources of impressions* in this category: (1) previous reputation; (2) advance notices; (3) introduction by the chairman (in a formal situation); and (4) visible-audible presentation of the message. Although some of these sources appear to be relevant only to a formal speech situation, most of them have a potential bearing on the image of the speaker in any situation.

Previous Reputation The reputation the speaker brings to the communication situation is very important. His past behavior should demonstrate that he is a person of competence, good character, and goodwill; and his actions should cause the listeners to associate him with ideas, causes, convictions, and statements suggesting that what he will have to say will be worth hearing. His past actions are sets of facts that he carries with him everywhere; they are part of the record. Because *reputation* is a source of impression that lies outside the verbal message and the immediate communication situation, there is nothing that the speaker can do to alter it at the time of his speech. But he can bring to bear certain impressions from within the message that will aid his cause in respect to his reputation (discussed in the section on "Sources within the Composition.")

Advance Notices This source of impression, obviously, is associated with formal speaking situations. Advance notices are press notices, announcements, comments, and publicity that herald the event. One form of advance notice may be an exchange of letters in the public press. The late John Foster Dulles, for example, was invited to give a university commencement address. Before his arrival, the campus newspaper published a crossfire of letters discussing virtually every trait of his character. Quite naturally, the controversy that resulted from this exchange had an influence upon the audience's reception of the Secretary of State and his message: Some persons saw him as a man with "good" personal proof; others saw him in quite a different light. For some, the letters to the editors were the only source material available before the actual speaking situation even though, as Secretary of State, Mr. Dulles was presumably well known to millions of United States citizens.

Because the speaker has little or no direct influence over this kind of advance notice, the best we can do to assure a good image is to conduct ourselves so that these notices will be favorable — recognizing, of course, those areas of public opinion where controversy is inevitable and where conduct is based (and judged) upon valid differences in judgment. We can also provide the persons in charge of the speaking situation with material that accurately and honestly reflects credit upon us. Finally, we may make certain adaptations to advance notices in our speech (discussed later in this chapter in the section on "Sources within the Composition").

Introduction by the Chairman This source of impressions, too, is limited to formal speech situations. While the chairman's introduction presumably will attempt to present the speaker in a favorable light, it may, either through errors in fact or emphasis or the omission of significant information, do more harm than good to the speaker's image. Recently, for example, a chairman inadvertently introduced a speaker as the dean of a school of speech in a university when, actually, the speaker was the head of a division within the school.

Probably the most that the speaker can do to influence this source of impression is to provide the chairman with accurate biographical information. Hopefully, this will reduce the likelihood of error in his introductory remarks. Also, he can make *diplomatic* corrections and adaptations to an erroneous introduction when he presents his message—diplomatic in order not to hurt the chairman's feelings and/or to call unnecessary attention to his mistake. (In the example above, the speaker made a very diplomatic, somewhat lighthearted statement, saying in effect, "I appreciate your very kind compliment concerning my position in the school of speech—it would be nice if I were to be the dean, but I assure you that we have a most capable man in that position.")

The Audible-Visible Expression of the Verbal Message   Both experience and research demonstrate conclusively that "delivery" is fully as important for what it reveals about the speaker himself as for what it contributes to the communication of the verbal message. Delivery covers not only the actual presentation of the message but the speaker's conduct before, during, and after the use of the audible and visible codes. If we slouch, yawn, and daydream during another person's speech (to use an example from a somewhat formal speaking situation), we are not going to impress the audience as a speaker of competence, good character, and goodwill—no matter how good our verbal message may be.

The speaker may do much to create a good image of himself. Again in respect to the more formal speaking situation, if our posture and conduct, our manner of walking to the rostrum or platform and of walking away from it, and our attitude while seated during the speeches of other persons all bespeak an awareness of decorum, propriety, respect, and understanding, we will be providing the audience with evidence of good ethos.

An even more important influence on the listeners' impressions of personal proof is the actual "audible-visual expression of the message." Lack of volume or of inflection, or too much of either, creates an impression that the speaker is uncertain or timid. A monotonous tone or a wooden, singsong rhythm suggests that we don't really care about our listeners or their opinion of us—or our opinion of them.

Thus, the total act of the delivery of the message—from the moment we arrive and await the time to present our speech until the audience leaves the auditorium (to refer to circumstances in a somewhat formal situation), as well as in the actual presentation of the message—must be pervaded with those elements and qualities that suggest competence, good character, and goodwill. We must be able to suggest through posture, bearing, appearance, voice, and contact with our listeners that our speech is worthy of the best attention and has the highest possible level of credibility. (The methods of delivery will be discussed in Chapter 14.)

Sources within the Composition

Within the verbal message (the speech composition) are sources of impressions, over which the speaker has some control, that can be classified in two categories: (1) direct statements made by the speaker about himself or about other persons; (2) implications and inferences arising from what the speaker does and does not do with the verbal elements of the message.

Direct Statements Made by the Speaker   Daniel Webster opened his speech to the jury in the Knapp-White murder case with the words, "I am little accustomed, gentlemen, to the part which I am now attempting to perform. Hardly more than once or twice has it happened to me to be concerned on the side of the government in any criminal prosecution whatever, and never, until the present occasion, in any case affecting life. But I very much regret that it should have been thought necessary to suggest to you that I am brought here to 'hurry you against the law and beyond the evidence.'" Alexander Hamilton, in urging the State of New York to adopt the new Constitution of the United States, concluded his speech with several paragraphs about his character, his reputation, and his personal relationship to the issue. Recently, a speaker opened his address with the words, "If you think that there is tension up here — that I am nervous — you are correct. I am so much concerned about the issue at hand that I can hardly hide my tension." Each of these persons — Webster, Hamilton, and the nervous speaker — presented an effective speech; each of them also either opened or closed his message with direct statements about himself. (Note that each direct statement "said something" about the man — *good personal proof.*)

Effective speakers, in addition, employ direct statements not only about themselves but also about their supporters, their opponents, and the supporters of their opponents. Political debaters, for example, invariably make direct references not only to one another's *competence* (the question of experience in government, for instance), *character* (consistency or inconsistency of positions on issues), and *goodwill* (interest in, or concern for, the welfare of the citizenry); they cover their own supporters and their opponents' supporters as well.

What, in essence, was each of these speakers doing? He was operating on the assumption that direct references to himself and to persons associated with him — whether in agreement or opposition — would enhance his ethos and strengthen his case. Experience and research validate this assumption.

If such statements are misused, they can defeat a speaker's purpose rather than serve it. There are both advantages and disadvantages in the use of personal references. Whether we should speak directly about ourselves or about any other person is a matter of judgment. If we believe that our competence, our motives, and our attitude toward our listeners need to be spelled out, we will be wise to put them in. On the other hand,

©1967 *United Feature Syndicate, Inc.*

we can defeat our purpose if we go too far and ignore the principles of decorum and good taste by talking too much about ourselves or extolling our virtues. When such temptation arises, the speaker should ask himself two questions: Should I use a personal reference at all? If so, what kind?

The use of such references is not limited to opening and closing remarks; they may be helpful at any point in the speech. Before we decide to use a personal reference, we should consider what effect it will have at that particular place in the speech. As for the kind of reference to use, we should consider how we can most easily comment on our (or another person's) competence, character, and goodwill without violating the boundaries of good taste, without suggesting egotism, or without causing offense. In short, we should recognize the value of this source of personal proof and at the same time use discretion about the frequency, placement, and phrasing of personal references.

Implications and Inferences   A speaker in a university lecture series recently gave an address on a subject of considerable controversy. The address was characterized by questionable evidence, somewhat superficial reasoning, disjointed organization, and a language style constructed of ambiguous terms, phrases, and sentences. Several of the listeners, on their way out of the auditorium, questioned *his knowledge of the subject* and also *his respect for his audience*. They remarked that he was "obviously careless" and that he treated them rather shabbily by presenting such an ill-prepared speech. Their discontent was focused not only on the speaker's message but on his ethos—his character, competence, and goodwill. And it is important to note that this discontent was based largely on *his workmanship in preparing the speech*.

Implications and inferences can arise from the quality of the workmanship of the composition (the verbal message), and these affect the listener's impressions of the speaker as a person. The way the speech is put together suggests a great deal about the speaker's competence, character, and goodwill. For purposes of analysis here, let us consider six possible sources of these impressions: (1) choice of subject; (2) choice of lines of thought; (3) choice of evidence; (4) the reasoning process; (5) arrangement of the materials; and (6) style, or language. We can examine each of these sources in respect to its effect upon personal proof.

Choice of Subject   Because our choice of subject (or our choice of approach or emphasis concerning an assigned subject) reveals a great deal about our ethos, we should take pains to select a subject that not only has captured our interest or struck us as important but also will be appropriate to the occasion and to the audience (relevant, in other words, to the circumstances of the communication situation). Those of us who neglect these criteria risk giving the impression that we have a narrow background and education, that we are attempting to pawn off an old speech, or that we don't care about the listener's needs and interests. On the other hand, the speaker who keeps the occasion and the listeners carefully in mind—and adapts to them in "what he talks about"—should find himself held in esteem as far as this problem is concerned. This does not mean that we should not speak upon our convictions or present our point of view upon an issue. Rather, it means simply that we need to consider such factors as *relevance, attention, and interest* in order to be effective.

Choice of Lines of Thought   The way a speaker chooses to develop his subject—what points he chooses to emphasize, what points he decides to expand, what relationships he tries to establish—reveals much about him as a person. The lines of development, as well as the choice of subject, must be suited to all elements of the situation.

Let us consider a specific example of the operation of this principle. The convocation committee of a college received a glowing report on a speech (subject: "The International Situation") presented to a Rotary Club in a nearby city. On the basis of this report, which praised the speaker's topic, development, and delivery, the committee invited the speaker to address a convocation. He presented the same speech. The development and delivery were of the same high quality as on the previous occasion. However, it soon became obvious that this audience—this time—did not think so well of him, for although the lines of development of his speech had been fresh and original to the Rotarians, they were stale and repetitious to the students, who had been hearing the same thing day after day in their classes in history, international relations, and political science. The speaker seemed to ignore the experience, knowledge, and interests of his listeners; and he paid the price by establishing a faulty ethos in their estimation.

Choice of Evidence and Source of Evidence   The evidence (the facts and opinions used by the speaker to support his thesis) and the source of this evidence also provide a reflection of the speaker as a person. When we rely on facts and opinions that are irrelevant, inaccurate, or prejudiced, we are likely to be thought of as one who has these same attributes. Similarly, if the source of our evidence is perceived as incompetent or unreliable or prejudiced, our ethos is likely to be adversely affected. Not only would our composition be unconvincing; we, too, as a person, would be undermined by weak evidence. Listeners frequently base their whole judgment of a speaker on their impressions of the strength and relevance of his supporting materials.

Evidence must be selected in accordance with the most rigorous tests of logical adequacy and psychological acceptability (to be discussed in Chapters 6 and 7). We should ask ourselves whether there is *enough* evidence to support a contention, whether that evidence is logically sound, and whether it is appropriate to the attitudes, biases, and feelings of our listeners.

The Reasoning Process   A speaker who has the habit of making hasty generalizations or of seeing strong cause and effect where little exists, will have each element of his ethos called into question. The listeners are likely to think him stupid or uninformed; or they may think that he is trying to deceive them for his own ends — all of which will leave no doubt in their minds about his attitude toward them. Actually, we may have the most honorable of intentions and may even be an authority, but the entire structure of our ethos can be shattered by a "hasty generalization," a poor analogy, or a non sequitur that is detected — and pondered upon — by our listeners. (Chapter 6 discusses in detail the principles and methods of reasoning, and has some tests that the speaker can apply to each of his inferences.)

Arrangement of Materials   The speaker's ethos is called into question when he violates the principles of good organization (arrangement) — especially when he finds it necessary to offer explanations and apologies like "I should have mentioned this earlier, but . . ." and "The thought just occurred to me; I neglected to include it where it should have appeared" and other statements that indicate poor organization. The audience will inevitably doubt our competence in such circumstances, and probably our character as well, because we will seem not to know our subject, not to have prepared with care and responsibility, or not to be competent in making on-the-spot adaptations according to principles of coherence.

We speak most effectively when we organize our material according to the *logical analysis* of our subject — which is dictated by natural sequences associated with chronology, causation, comparative and contrasting associations — and according to the *psychological acceptability* of this analysis in respect to the listener's attitudes, interests, biases, and knowledge. While at first thought the former (logical analysis) may appear to be not only the preferred consideration but the *only* consideration, psychological acceptability is vitally important also if the communication is to be satisfactory.

(Chapter 11 considers the *speech plan,* or means of organizing the message, more fully.)

Style — Language   Winston Churchill promised the British people in 1940 that he would work for them and worry for them — if necessary, even die for them; but he said that he expected every man, woman, and child in Britain would do his duty. However, he never used those words. He made his promise concisely, humbly, and dramatically with the words "I have nothing to offer but blood, toil, tears, and sweat." His choice of words and his arrangement of them in the speech composition revealed to the world that he was a man of deep feelings, convictions, responsibility, and ability —

or, in terms of our discussion, a man of competence, good character, and goodwill.

Listeners receive their impressions of us in at least some measure from the quality of our language style. The words that we use, our grammar and sentence structure, represent opportunities for us either to create or to destroy a good ethos. The wise speaker will utilize these resources to the full by consulting authoritative works on English diction and usage. (Style will be discussed further in Chapter 12.)

Some Implications for the Remaining Chapters

The subject of personal proof encompasses all of the elements of the communication situation, both those within and those external to the speech composition itself. Everything in a speech situation is a potential means of gauging the dimensions of the speaker's ethos; every source of listener impressions contributes to the image of the speaker. Because of the all-pervading nature of personal proof, we would do well to consider the following chapters in the light of their relevance to our own ethos. The chapter on "Delivery" will be helpful in considering certain elements outside the speech composition. The chapters on "Materials of Development," "Materials of Experience," "Organization," and "Style" will be helpful in controlling sources of impressions within the composition. Along with the preceding chapters on "Adapting to the Audience and the Occasion," the chapter on "Selecting the Subject" will be helpful in almost every respect in the attempt to create a good, strong ethos.

Suggested Assignments

1.   How valid is the statement "Who you are speaks so loudly that I cannot hear what you say"? What are the implications of this statement for the oral communicator?

2.   Make an inventory of the oral communication situations in which you have participated today, and determine the impact of the speaker's ethos (or personal proof) in each case.

3.   In the light of your experiences in speaking, how would you reply to the statement "It is *what the speaker says* that is important; *who he is* is only an incidental matter"?

4.   After reflecting upon your experiences in speaking and upon your responses to assignments 1, 2, and 3, how do you react to the point of view and to the topics of this chapter? If you disagree, in what respects? Why?

5.   Interview a few of your associates regarding their attitude toward the importance of a speaker's personal proof (ethos) in speaking. Do they tend to agree or disagree with the point of view of this chapter? If they disagree, in what respects and why?

6. Evaluate a speaker's personal proof in all the factors of composition discussed in this chapter. How significant are any of the points upon which he fails to measure up?

7. Evaluate a speaker's personal proof in all the factors of delivery discussed in this chapter. How significant are any of the points upon which he fails to measure up?

8. Select a specific speaker-listener situation that you can use for a piece of research. On the basis of your own responses and those of some of your fellow-listeners, determine, as best you can, (a) the results or effects of the speaker's communication effort with respect to the subject of the message; (b) the listeners' reactions to "the speaker as a person"; (c) what relationship appears to exist between the results noted in (a) and the evaluations noted in (b). In the light of your findings, what conclusions can you make regarding the content of this chapter?

9. How would you reply to the statement "A person either does or does not have the qualities of competence, good character, and goodwill; there is nothing that he can do about it—nothing can be done to make people think that he is what he is not"?

10. How would you reply to the statement "Not only is the statement in assignment 9 true, but it is *unethical* to try to do anything to improve one's personal proof other than actually to *be* more competent, to *be* of better character, and to *be* of more goodwill"?

Suggested References

Adams, John Quincy, *Lectures on Rhetoric and Oratory* (Cambridge: Hilliard and Metcalf, 1810). Lecture XV, "Intellectual and Moral Qualities of an Orator."

Andersen, Kenneth E., and Theodore Clevenger, Jr., "A Summary of Experimental Work in Ethos," *Speech Monographs*, Vol. 30 (1963), pp. 59–78.

Bettinghaus, Erwin P., *Persuasive Communication*, 2nd ed. (New York: Holt, Rinehart and Winston, 1973). Chapter 5, "The Influence of the Communicator."

Cooper, Lane, *The Rhetoric of Aristotle* (New York: Appleton-Century-Crofts, 1932). Pp. 8–9, 91–92.

Freeley, Austin J., *Argumentation and Debate: Rational Decision Making*, 3rd ed. (Belmont, Calif.: Wadsworth Publishing Co., 1971). Chapter 18, "The Speaker as a Person."

Johannesen, Richard L., in *Persuasion: Reception and Responsibility* by Charles U. Larson (Belmont, Calif.: Wadsworth Publishing Co., 1973). Chapter 9, "Perspectives on Ethics in Persuasion."

Minnick, Wayne C., *The Art of Persuasion*, 2nd ed. (Boston: Houghton Mifflin Co., 1968). Pp. 161–177.

Sattler, William M., "Conceptions of Ethos in Ancient Rhetoric," *Speech Monographs*, Vol. 14 (1947), pp. 55–65.

Thonssen, Lester, and A. Craig Baird, *Speech Criticism* (New York: Ronald Press Co., 1948). Chapter 13, "The Character of the Speaker."

Wallace, Karl R., "An Ethical Basis of Communication," *The Speech Teacher*, Vol. 4 (January 1955), pp. 1–9.

6
Materials of
Speaking: Development

"The solid 'stuff' of the speech"

How many times have we listened to a speech and said something like: "It was poorly developed. The subject was O.K.; the main points were clear enough, but the *materials* were thin. The speaker seemed to be just stating a series of assertions, with nothing to support them—no examples, no statements from authorities, no real 'proof.'" Unfortunately, we do have to conclude these things about some spoken messages—because some speakers do not develop their speeches adequately. But this predicament does not have to be.

The development of a subject after it has been selected, narrowed, and analyzed constitutes an important part of the work of speaking. There are several classifications of material that we can use for this development—materials that are essential to the construction of a clear, convincing, and interesting message.

Materials Common to All Speaking

Materials Found and Used by the Speaker

Several kinds of materials of development exist in fact and have only to be found and used by the speaker: (1) examples of phenomena; (2) narratives; (3) statistics; and (4) quotations.

Examples   These are instances and illustrations that we may use to support, clarify, or lend interest to a point we wish to make.

Instances are allusions or references to specific cases; *they are not fully developed descriptions and do not include details.* They are, rather, references to or citations of facts and experiences.

> The successes of Hannibal in Italy and of Sherman in Georgia suggest
> the practicality of having alternative objectives in a military campaign.

In this use of the instance, the speaker merely referred to the success of the two generals in order to support his point—"... the practicality of having alternative objectives ..."—He included no development or description of the reference.

Illustrations are instances that are developed (perhaps fully or perhaps schematically). The speaker above could have expanded the instance of the successes of Hannibal and Sherman into a full *illustration* by offering details of some of their campaigns.

> The successes of Hannibal in Italy and of Sherman in Georgia suggest the practicality of having alternative objectives in a military campaign. When Hannibal came down from the Alps into the northern part of the Italian peninsula, he maintained a high degree of mobility so that he could decide, at the last minute, whether to attack this legion in the field or lay siege to that town on the river or retreat into a valley and lay a trap for the pursuing Romans. Sherman, likewise, stormed through the South of the United States with the same kind of mobility, the same kind of last-minute decisions made possible by keeping alternative objectives in view. He himself never knew until the last minute whether he was going to attack one town or another; instead, he waited, he kept as many possibilities open to his army as he could, and he let the movements of the Confederate Army determine which of the alternatives he would pursue.

Narratives and Stories   The *narrative* consists of a set of real or fictional details told as a story and used to clarify or prove a point. It differs from the example in that its details are arranged in a specific sequence (usually chronological) and its events are unfolded according to a plot or scheme that leads to a climax. When the narrative sustains interest and explicates or supports the main point under consideration, it is a good and effective material of development.[1]

Just as the example may appear as an instance or as a full illustration, so we may also use the *narrative* in either the short-reference form or the fully developed story form. Following is an example of the shorter form:

> Some of you may have heard about what happened to CBS newsman, Daniel Schorr, who wrote a series of articles critical of the Administration. He suffered damaging effects of extensive surveillance by the FBI and other governmental agencies—effects bordering upon intimidation.

In the expanded form, the narrative offers a complete set of details that are arranged in a sequence which gives the story a plot. For example, Senator Sam J. Ervin, Jr., presented the following narrative:

---

[1] The narrative may also be used in the setting of materials of experience because it lends interest, color, and appeal to the composition. (See Chapter 7 for a treatment of the narrative as a material of experience.)

Some of you may have heard about what happened to CBS newsman, Daniel Schorr. After a series of articles critical of the Administration, Mr. Schorr woke up one morning to find himself the object of a full-scale FBI investigation. On the specious grounds that Mr. Schorr was being considered for "possible federal employment," the White House had ordered a thorough investigation of Daniel Schorr, his past and present associations, activities, employment, and the like. Friends, acquaintances, colleagues, employers, and former employers were telephoned and interviewed by FBI agents, who asked about Mr. Schorr's character and patriotism, as well as his fitness for a position in the Executive Branch.

When I heard about what had happened to Mr. Schorr, I sought to find out from the White House just what high-level executive position purported to justify this apparently punitive surveillance of a newsman known to be critical of Administration policies and programs. First the White House replied that Daniel Schorr was "being considered for a job that is presently filled." A few days later the White House announced that Daniel Schorr was being considered for a new position which "has not been filled." In the end he was never offered any job by the Administration. The White House finally lamely announced that Daniel Schorr's name had been "dropped from consideration" and that the FBI investigation had been "terminated in the early stages." According to the White House, the preliminary surveillance report, which was "entirely favorable," had been "subsequently destroyed." But the damage had already been done.

Daniel Schorr described the damaging effects of such surveillance on a news reporter in this way. . . .[2]

Statistics   These are sets of figures compiled to present data concerning phenomena, trends, or activities of people. Like examples and narratives, they have only to be found and used by the speaker. An example: "According to the 1960 U. S. Census, there were 38 cities with a population in excess of 300,000, whereas the 1970 Census records 48 cities with more than 300,000 inhabitants."

Of course, *statistics* are valuable only to the extent that they are clear, meaningful, accurate, and relevant.

Quotations   By definition, a quotation is "a passage referred to, repeated, or adduced." In speaking, we may use the words of somebody else to illustrate, support, or expand a point. We may quote from *literary materials* (verse or prose) or from the *testimony* of other persons (statements of *fact* or of *opinion*).

From the vast records of human feelings and experiences — biography, poetry, drama, newspapers, and other literary materials — we can draw materials to make what we have to say stronger or clearer. For example, President John H. Fischer, Teachers College, Columbia University, made

---

[2] "Justice, The Constitution, and Privacy," *Vital Speeches of the Day* (September 1, 1973), p. 679.

good use of a passage in Carl Sandburg's poetry as he brought to a conclusion an address entitled "Education and the Democratic Dilemma":

> Our task, our institutional, professional, and personal task, can be
> put briefly and simply: It is to clarify the principles we really mean to live
> by in the schools and then to live by them.
> Carl Sandburg, in his poem, "The People, Yes," compressed in beauty
> what I have taken many more words to suggest:
>
> "I am credulous about the destiny of man
> And I believe more than I can ever prove
> Of the future of the human race
> And the importance of illusions,
> The value of great expectations."
>
> For all the complexity that plagues the issues we have thought about
> tonight, what we do and the final judgment on the way we do it will ulti-
> mately be determined by the character and the expectations on which we
> habitually act.[3]

The value and the power of any literary material quoted in a speech
depend upon its relevance to the point of the message and upon its strength
in saying something—with grace, felicity, and a sense of the poetic or the
dramatic—that could not be said as aptly in the speaker's own words.

We use *testimony of fact* when we quote another person concerning historical fact. For instance, in discussing some of the problems in the communication industry, especially those related to its financial aspects, a
speaker quoted Schramm's *Responsibility in Mass Communication* as follows:

> It is harder to enter the communication industry than it used to be. It
> used to be possible to start a newspaper in New York City, one hundred
> years ago, with 15,000 dollars of capital. Now it would take 5 million dollars
> of risk capital to compete successfully with large dailies, and even then the
> chances of succeeding would be less than even. Marshall Field dropped a
> sum that must have been in the millions on *PM* and the *Chicago Sun* before
> accepting failure.[4]

By using testimony of facts, we can turn to somebody who has observed
phenomena, conducted an experiment, or in some other way had access to a
body of factual material. We can quote relevant statements made by this
person to clarify or develop our composition.

We may support or illustrate our point with *opinion testimony*, which is

---

[3] *Vital Speeches of the Day* (May 15, 1973), p. 470. The lines from the poem, "The People,
Yes," are reprinted from *The People, Yes* by Carl Sandburg by permission of Harcourt Brace
Jovanovich, Inc. (Literary materials may also be considered as "Materials of Experience." See
Chapter 7.)

[4] Wilbur Schramm, *Responsibility in Mass Communication* (New York: Harper & Row, 1957),
p. 29.

quoting another person's interpretation, value judgment, conviction, or other expression of opinion. A pertinent example of the use of this material of development by a college student is seen in a speech entitled "Modern Science: Man's Salvation or His Doom" presented by Kenneth Vaux.

After submitting his views about one of the points in his discourse, Mr. Vaux said, in effect, "You wish, I am sure, to know what an older, more experienced person has to say about this issue. Indeed, you are probably asking: 'Does any person of renown support your thesis?' I refer you to the judgment of one of our greatest religious-social leaders—one of the most articulate spokesmen of our generation—Dr. Harry Emerson Fosdick." He then invoked the opinion (judgment) of Dr. Fosdick:

> I sat in the study of Dr. Harry Emerson Fosdick. At eighty-two years of age he was still one of the brilliant and sensitive leaders of American Christianity. There was a sense of urgency in the old man's eyes as we shared our thoughts of the world that science has given us. As our talk drew to a close, Dr. Fosdick said with great sincerity, "Ken . . . the longer I live, the more I realize what a realistic man Jesus of Nazareth was. His teaching that "he who takes the sword will perish by the sword" is very vital to our own day—only today the sword has become the nuclear bomb."[5]

The effectiveness of opinion testimony depends primarily upon the *qualification of the person* whose opinion is quoted. The wise speaker will quote authors whose experience and intellectual competence (attainment) enable them to provide "expert" conclusions, judgments, and interpretations concerning events or human motivation. The value of the particular quotation we select depends upon the relevance of the opinion to the matter at hand as well as upon the author's comparative competence, reliability, and freedom from prejudice. Of course we must identify our quotations for our listeners, just as we do in written materials for our readers.

Materials Created by the Speaker

In addition to the materials of development that we gather from other sources, there are materials we can *create* by our own artistry. For the most part, we create these materials by *doing something new* with what we find—by arranging and relating the materials in ways that strengthen and support our main points.

Let us consider four types of this kind of material: (1) repetition; (2) restatement; (3) comparison; and (4) contrast.

Repetition   This is saying, in the same words, something that has just been said. It helps to make a point stronger and drives it home with more cer-

---

[5] *Winning Orations of the Interstate Oratorical Association.* Reprinted by permission of the Interstate Oratorical Association.

tainty. The value of repetition is that it gives the listener a chance to absorb and remember the idea—in just the same way that we might reread a particularly important passage in a book. It also lends emphasis. Usually, two impacts are stronger than one, in speech as well as in war and advertising; the second blow reinforces the first.

One kind of repetition is merely a *repetition of a complete thought:*

> We must restrict A-bomb production and provide for international inspection or we face inevitable annihilation. I repeat: We must restrict A-bomb production and provide for international inspection or we face inevitable annihilation.

Or, as Patrick Henry is reported to have said:

> The war is inevitable—and let it come. I repeat, sir, let it come.

Another kind of repetition uses a *key word or phrase* to begin every sentence or paragraph. This device often has high emotive force, as it did in Martin Luther King, Jr.'s famous speech, in 1963, at the Lincoln Memorial in Washington, D. C. Repetition and refrain were an integral part of the speech:

> So I say to you, my friends, that even though we must face the difficulties of today and tomorrow, I still have a dream. It is a dream deeply rooted in the American dream that one day this nation will rise up and live out the true meaning of its creed—we hold these truths to be self-evident, that all men are created equal.
>
> I have a dream that one day on the red hills of Georgia, sons of former slaves and sons of former slave-owners will be able to sit down together at the table of brotherhood.
>
> I have a dream that one day, even the state of Mississippi, a state sweltering with the heat of injustice, sweltering with the heat of oppression, will be transformed into an oasis of freedom and justice.
>
> I have a dream . . .

There are, however, definite limitations on the use of *repetition.* They include the danger of losing the listener's attention through monotony—lack of variety, dullness, and lack of forward movement of thought—and the danger of weakening the impact by deadening the listener's sensitivity, unless the repetition is used very selectively.

Restatement   This may be defined as "repetition in different words." The speaker says something that he has just said, but he uses different words the second time in order to clarify, expand, or develop the message in terms the listener may understand more clearly.

We use restatement frequently in our ordinary, day-to-day discourse as well as in more formal speaking. We might hear a friend say, after attending a concert, "I don't think the conductor was very good; I mean his interpretation of the work wasn't quite up to the standards that I'm used to." Almost everything in our daily conversation that we preface with the words "I mean" is an instance of restatement.

The value of restatement is essentially the same as that of repetition: It provides, with its second impact, reinforcement, clarity, and emphasis. The weaknesses of restatement are also the same as those of repetition, with the possible exception that there is not so great a danger of monotony because some variety is provided through differences in phraseology.

Comparison   This consists of setting forth points of similarity between two or more persons, events, or things. As a resource in explanatory speaking, it is a way of using the *known* to make the *unknown* understandable. As a resource in persuasive speaking, it is a way of making something new acceptable by relating it to something that we already find acceptable. (This method of using similarities is explored further in the section called "Reasoning from Analogy," later in this chapter.)

Comparison may be used in a speech of explanation as follows:

> The city is laid out in a half-circle, with the main streets moving outward from the City Hall Square, just as the spokes of a wheel move out from the hub.

In discussing problems of education, a speaker made effective use of comparison:

> Our colleges can no longer be the Coney Islands of education where too many of our young people enroll to have fun and end up by being pushed around. Without purposeful air, many college students go today from one course to another, and, finally, after flunking out of school, return home with only the papier-mâché toys, the kewpie dolls, and the garish pillow tops of education to give mute evidence of wasted energy and money.
>
> The automobile industry offers an interesting counterpart in productive thinking to meet today's problems. From the time Henry Ford put the nation on wheels with the Model T, cars have become increasingly longer, wider, more powerful, with more extras and with higher price tags. No end seemed in sight, until an about face was made in the revolutionary decision to develop the small, compact car. In the same manner, with the same functional expediency employed in the new thinking in autos, revised programs in education must provide for our needs in a manner we can afford.[6]

In both explanatory and persuasive speaking, we should be sure that the thing we compare something with is well known to our listener; we should also be sure that we make our comparisons with something that is demonstrably true, something that we can back up with evidence should any doubts as to the validity of our comparison arise.

---

[6] *Winning Orations of the Interstate Oratorical Association.* Reprinted by permission of the Interstate Oratorical Association.

Contrast   This is similar to comparison, except that it consists of pointing out differences (instead of similarities) between two or more persons, events, or things. It employs the principle of identifying the unknown by means of the known, achieving this by telling what the unknown is *not*.

We use contrast frequently in daily conversation. A student who is describing a new coed in his lecture hall might be heard to say, "Well, she's more the Ali McGraw type than the Raquel Welch type, if you know what I mean." Another example occurred as an oral explanation:

> Perhaps I can help you visualize the new married-student apartments to be built next spring. In contrast to those built a year ago, which have walls largely of steel panels, these will have walls of brick; also, whereas the present buildings have no outside projections, the new ones will have private balconies.

In attempting to persuade, the speaker may, for instance, strengthen his position regarding the United Nations with the following contrast:

> The United Nations certainly has more to recommend it than did the old League of Nations. For one thing, it has the United States as a member, whereas the League of Nations had to get along without the membership or the support of the United States.

As with comparison, we should be certain that the elements of contrast are *known to the listener* and *demonstrably true*.

Materials and Procedures of Reasoning and the Argumentative Process

Other materials of development are those used in connection with *evidence* and *reasoning*, and they appear most frequently and most effectively in advocacy. Although these materials have their greatest value in *advocacy*, they are also frequently useful in the process of *explanation*. Many of these materials are similar to examples, statistics, comparisons, and quotations, but they change their character through their function in the argumentative process.[7]

The Nature, Sources, and Uses of Evidence

Evidence may be defined as facts and opinions used as the basis of reasoning. *Facts* are cases, statistics, and physical objects — phenomena that are observed, described, classified, reported, and presented. *Opinions* are points of view — interpretations and evaluations of facts — held by persons other than the person doing the reasoning (for our purposes, the speaker).

Evidence can be further classified as (1) written and unwritten, (2) direct and circumstantial, (3) real and personal, and so on. However, let us stick with fact and opinion as the two categories of materials that constitute the basis of reasoning.

The sources of evidence are two: the reasoner himself and other persons. Facts can result from the reasoner's own observations or through reports and testimonies of the observations of other persons, while opinions, when used as evidence, come only from other persons.

Because facts and opinions are the raw materials of reasoning, they are necessarily part of the raw materials of speaking. Just as a good final product requires good raw materials, so a good message cannot be created without *good evidence* — as to both logical and psychological adequacy. The tests of logical adequacy are based as exclusively as possible on objective, impersonal factors; the tests of psychological adequacy, on the feelings, attitudes, and prejudices of the audience (see the inset, page 94).

The Nature of Reasoning

Reasoning may be defined as the *process of inferring conclusions from evidence or from other conclusions.* In the first instance (inferring from evidence), reasoning consists of using facts and opinions to reach a conclusion beyond that embodied in the evidence itself. For example, take the facts:

> When Dr. Jones used closed-circuit television to teach his class in accounting, he found that the students "learned 15 percent more than under the nontelevision method."
>
> When Dr. Smith used closed-circuit television to teach his class in journalism, he found that the students "learned 12 percent more than under the nontelevision method."
>
> When Professor White used closed-circuit television to teach his class in the physical sciences, he found that the students "learned 14 percent more than under the nontelevision method."

---

[7] The analysis presented here is necessarily somewhat brief; a textbook devoted to argumentation would offer a longer and more detailed discussion. Nevertheless, the analysis in this section will provide a set of useful concepts that should be adequate for the beginning speaker.

From these facts we can reason that, when professors use closed-circuit television in their classrooms, they can probably expect a 12 to 15 percent "improvement in learning." (While this may not necessarily be *good* reasoning, as later tests will indicate, it *is* reasoning.)

In the second instance (inferring from other conclusions), reasoning consists of joining two or more ideas or propositions to form a new idea. For example, we can reason that because our university is very much like XYZ University, and since a certain plan of registration has proved to be efficient at XYZ University, therefore, that plan will prove to be efficient here. (Again, this may not necessarily be *good* reasoning, according to later tests, but it *is* reasoning.)

Tests of Logical Adequacy

1. Is the evidence clear? (To be of value, evidence must be free from ambiguity and from the danger of being misinterpreted.)

2. Is the evidence consistent internally? (Evidence will be worthless if it has contradictions within itself.)

3. Is the evidence consistent with other known evidence? (If it is, the speaker can find other evidence to strengthen his point; if not, the new evidence must be stronger than the known evidence.)

4. Is the evidence relevant to the matter at hand? (Sometimes we can cite evidence that may seem to prove our point, but it may actually be concerned with a different subject.)

5. Is the source of the evidence competent? (Does the person who presents the testimony possess the physical faculties and the mental capacity to make him a competent source of facts and opinions?)

6. Is the source of the evidence free from prejudice? (Is this person sufficiently objective or disinterested to make him a source that we can regard as fair and unbiased?)

7. Is the source of the evidence reliable? (Is he free from habits of superficial observation, irresponsible assertion, and inconsistent behavior?)

Tests of Psychological Adequacy

1. Is the evidence in harmony with the beliefs of the listeners? (This test does not mean to imply that the speaker should restrict his evidence to what will please his listeners or confirm what may be erroneous beliefs; rather, it suggests that the speaker should expect some resistance to evidence that does not coincide with the attitudes, values, and personal beliefs of the listeners; and he should take this resistance into consideration when he selects and presents his evidence.)

2. Is the source of the evidence a person whom the listeners are willing to accept? (While the source may measure up in competence, freedom from prejudice, and reliability, some resistance may be encountered if he does not measure up in social position, party affiliation, profession, and the like. The speaker should consider these factors as he makes choices.)

Types and Tests of Reasoning

Let us briefly consider the basic types of reasoning and the forms in which they are put to use.

Reasoning from Example   Reasoning from example may be defined as the *process of inferring conclusions from specific instances, cases, illustrations, or examples.* This kind of reasoning was employed in the reference to the experiences of Professors Jones, Smith, and White with closed-circuit television. In this reference we had three specific instances (cases), and we proceeded to infer a general conclusion from them.

The most important tests of reasoning from example are these:

1. Are there enough examples?
2. Are the examples typical?
3. Are any negative examples adequately accounted for?

We can now apply these tests to our illustration about the use of closed-circuit television. The first test raises the question of whether three cases are enough to support our conclusion. Perhaps we should have five cases, or ten or a hundred. (Although there is no precise answer concerning "how many are enough," common sense would probably dictate that there should be at least three or four and, also, that ten or a hundred would greatly strengthen our argument, though their use in a speech would be both cumbersome and unnecessary.)

The second question asks whether Professors Jones, Smith, and White (and their classes) are typical—that is, whether the subject matter, the methods, and the students are sufficiently like other subject matter, methods, and students to be considered representative, or whether they are unique. If they can be considered typical, our conclusion is justified.

The third question asks whether any professors have tried closed-circuit television and found it unsatisfactory for learning, and, if so, whether the dissatisfaction could be explained away (because of mechanical difficulties, or the complexity of the subject matter, or faulty methods) and whether the number of negative experiences is significant in comparison with the number of satisfactory experiences.

Reasoning by Analogy   Reasoning by analogy may be defined as the *process of making a comparison between two cases that are similar in many respects and then inferring that they are similar in further respects.*

By way of illustration, we can reason that because Professor Brown's teaching situation is similar to Professor Jones's and because Professor Jones has found closed-circuit television to be satisfactory, Professor Brown would also find closed-circuit television satisfactory.

Because this type of reasoning is valid only under certain conditions, we should apply tests such as the following to make sure that the relationship is analogous.

1.   Are there any points of similarity?

2.   Do the points of similarity outweigh (not necessarily outnumber) the points of difference?

3.   Are the points of difference adequately explained?

Turning again to our example of closed-circuit television as used by Professor Jones, we apply these tests by asking, first, whether Professors Jones and Brown and their teaching situations are similar in any respects (such as personality, ability, teaching style, subject matter, and physical conditions); second, whether these points of similarity are more significant than any noticeable differences (perhaps locations of classrooms, time of day, number of students); and third, whether these differences can be shown to be comparatively insignificant—that is, whether the *number of students* can be shown to have less influence on the success of instruction than *ability,* for example.

Reasoning from Cause   Reasoning from cause may be defined as the *process of inferring that a certain phenomenon (a cause) has produced another phenomenon (an effect);* or, conversely, *that a certain phenomenon (an effect) is the result of another phenomenon (a cause).* The former process is called *cause-to-effect* reasoning; the latter, *effect-to-cause.*

If we say, "The introduction of a set of visual aids will increase interest and comprehension on the part of our listeners," we are implying that the visual aids will be a *cause* producing the *effect* of increased interest and comprehension. On the other hand, if we say, "The increased interest and comprehension that we noticed during this speech were the result of the use of visual aids," we are implying that the *effect* of increased interest and comprehension was *caused* by the use of visual aids.

Again, there are tests for the validity of this kind of reasoning:

1.   Is the cause relevant to the effect?

2.   Is the cause adequate to produce the effect?

3.   Is there a probability that no other effect may result from this particular cause (in cause-to-effect reasoning)? Is there a probability that no other cause operated to produce this effect (in effect-to-cause reasoning)?

Applying the first test to our example of the use of visual aids while speaking, we ask, "Is there a definite relationship between *comprehension* and *visual aids?*" If we must answer No, then our reasoning is no more valid than the reasoning behind the old superstition that breaking a mirror causes seven years of bad luck.

The second test raises the question, "Is the use of visual aids a strong enough device to have produced the increased interest and comprehension?"

The third test asks, in cause-to-effect reasoning, "Are increased interest and comprehension the only effects that the use of visual aids could have produced? Or could there have been less interest and comprehension? Or an effect of a different kind?" And, in effect-to-cause reasoning, the third test asks, "Could the increased interest and comprehension have been the *result* of some *cause* other than the use of visual aids?"

Reasoning from Sign   Reasoning from sign may be defined as the *process of inferring associations between two phenomena that are not causally related.* This kind of reasoning assumes that the presence of one thing (an *attribute*) indicates the presence of another (the *substance*), or that the absence of one indicates the absence of the other. Like reasoning from cause, reasoning from sign works both ways: we can say that the presence or the absence of the *attribute* indicates the presence or the absence of the *substance;* or that where there is the *substance,* there also is the *attribute.*

When we say that this room must contain a chalkboard because this room is a classroom — or, conversely, that this room must be a classroom because it contains a chalkboard — we are reasoning from sign. In the first instance, we are reasoning from *substance* ("This room is a classroom . . .") to *attribute* (". . . therefore it must contain a chalkboard."). In the second instance, we are reasoning from *attribute* ("There is the chalkboard . . .") to *substance* (". . . therefore, it must be a classroom.").

We can test sign reasoning as follows:

1. Is the substance (or attribute) identified accurately?
2. Is the attribute inherent in the substance (or, does the substance always have that attribute)?

To return to our illustrations, we apply the tests by asking first whether we have accurately identified the room as a classroom (and not a lounge, a reading room, or a nursery), and second whether a chalkboard is an inherent attribute of a classroom. Conversely, for attribute-to-substance reasoning, we ask first whether this object, with chalk in the troughs, is really a chalkboard (and not a bulletin board or an abstract mural), and second whether chalkboards are found always and only in classrooms.

Naturally, the strongest validity that we can expect here is merely a high degree of probability since chalkboards can be found in many kinds of rooms, and not every classroom has a chalkboard.

The Structure of Reasoning

In addition to analyzing reasoning in the light of example, analogy, cause, and sign—a method concerned with thought relationships—we can also analyze its *structure*. (We are presenting it for the record as well as for the purpose of relating our discussion to the historical-traditional patterns which emphasize the well-known patterns of *inductive* and *deductive* reasoning.)

Reasoning is used in argumentative discourse for two basic purposes: (1) to develop a conclusion immediately from facts and (2) to develop a conclusion from other conclusions or propositions. Historically, the term *inductive reasoning* has been (and still is) used to designate reasoning that proceeds from the specific to the general (as in 1 in the preceding sentence); and the term *deductive reasoning* designates reasoning that proceeds from the general to the specific (as in 2 in the preceding sentence).

Induction   Inductive reasoning is the *process of drawing inferences from facts, evidence, and experience.* It is the means by which we make generalizations or formulate conclusions about phenomena that we see, hear, or perceive in any way.

In our illustration of the three professors using closed-circuit television for teaching purposes, we reasoned from three specific instances (Dr. Jones found a 15 percent gain, Dr. Smith found a 12 percent gain, and Professor White found a 14 percent gain) to the general conclusion: Closed-circuit television seemingly provides a "gain in learning in the 12 to 15 percent range." This illustration, by the way, employed at least two types of reasoning: reasoning from example (the three cases led us to a conclusion) and reasoning from sign (where there was the *substance*—a professor using television—there was also the *attribute*—gain in learning). Perhaps, too, a third type was present: reasoning from cause—if it is inferred that the increase in learning was caused by the use of closed-circuit television.

Regardless of the *types* of reasoning we employ, when we proceed from facts, experiences, specific instances, and so on, to statements based upon these facts, we are reasoning inductively. One of the clearest illustrations of inductive reasoning was offered by Thomas Henry Huxley, the renowned British scientist of the last century, in an essay entitled "The Method of Scientific Investigation" (from *Darwiniana*):

A very trivial circumstance will serve to exemplify this. Suppose you go into a fruiterer's shop, wanting an apple, — you take up one, and, on biting it, you find it is sour; you look at it, and see that it is hard and green. You take up another one, and that too is hard, green, and sour. The shopman offers you a third; but, before biting it, you examine it, and find that it is hard and green, and you immediately say that you will not have it, as it must be sour, like those that you have already tried.

In this illustration, Huxley shows us how we may, from the specific instances of testing apples that are hard and green, draw the general conclusion *that all hard and green apples are sour apples.*

Deduction   Deductive reasoning is the reverse of inductive in that it proceeds from the general principle to the specific instance. It works by going *from one proposition to a second proposition and then to a third proposition (the conclusion) that is the necessary (or logical) result of the first pair.* Sometimes deductive reasoning draws the propositions it uses from the conclusions obtained through inductive reasoning. In Huxley's illustration about the apples, we reasoned that all apples that are hard and green are also sour (a conclusion reached by induction). We could reason further from this conclusion so that, the next time we are offered a hard, green apple, we will refuse it because we are confident that it will be sour. The pattern of reasoning is as follows:

1. All hard and green apples are sour.
2. This apple is hard and green.
3. Therefore, this apple is sour.

This kind of deduction is often called a *categorical syllogism*, because the first (and major) step in the deduction refers to a whole category or class of things: *all* hard and green apples.

There are other forms of deductive reasoning, two of which—the *hypothetical syllogism* and the *disjunctive syllogism*—are of immediate concern to the principles of speaking.

In the *hypothetical syllogism*, the first proposition presents an "if" clause (*antecedent*) followed by a "then" clause (*consequent*), which is supposed to be a necessary result of the "if" clause. The second proposition says something about the first—either affirming the "if" clause or denying the "then" clause. The conclusion is then a statement that follows necessarily from the first two propositions. If the second proposition affirms the antecedent ("if" clause), then the conclusion affirms the consequent ("then" clause); if, on the other hand, the second proposition denies the consequent, then the conclusion denies the antecedent. Let us look at two examples of the hypothetical syllogism:

1. If teachers know nothing, then students can't learn.

2. Teachers know nothing. (The antecedent is affirmed.)

3. Therefore, students can't learn. (The consequent is affirmed.)

1. If women were rational beings, then we could convince them.

2. We can't convince them. (The consequent is denied.)

3. Therefore, women are not rational beings. (The antecedent is denied.)[8]

In the *disjunctive syllogism,* the first proposition presents an "either-or" statement; the second proposition affirms or denies one of the alternatives of the first proposition; and the conclusion affirms the other alternative if the first alternative is denied, or it denies the other alternative if the first is affirmed.

Of course, the disjunctive syllogism is invalid if we say "*Either* this or that" when *both* this *and* that are possible. We can use this kind of syllogism only when the alternatives are mutually exclusive—that is, only when the two alternatives cannot exist at the same time. The first proposition must also include all possibilities; we cannot say "Either this or that" when the truth is "Either this or that or thus or so."

An example of the disjunctive syllogism may help to clarify:

1. I must either find a car pool or move closer to the campus.

2. I cannot find a car pool.

3. Therefore, I must move closer to the campus.

While this concept of the structure of reasoning has served as the basic model since the days of Aristotle (fourth century B.C.), attention has recently been directed to an alternative method—the Toulmin model, named after its originator, Stephen Toulmin. In essence, this describes the basic steps in reasoning as follows: an argument consists of *movement* from acceptable *data,* through a *warrant,* to a *claim.* (Data correspond to materials of fact or opinion; warrant represents a supporting argument; and claim constitutes the conclusion.) For example, a person may reason or "argue" as follows:

> Ninety of one hundred Honors College graduates have found its program to be excellent preparation for graduate school (data); these experiences are symptomatic of probable future successes (warrant); the Honors College program will, in the future, serve our students well in planning to enter graduate school (claim).

In addition to the three elements of *data, warrant,* and *claim,* three subsidiary elements are also presented as means of describing the structure of

---

[8] The authors hastily (but firmly) deny any charge of male chauvinism that may result from the use of this *hypothetical* example of a hypothetical syllogism.

reasoning: *backing, qualifier,* and *rebuttal.* (*Backing:* additional support for the *warrant; Qualifier:* the degree of probability associated with the *warrant; Rebuttal:* material modifying the *claim* — refuting, discounting, and so on.)

The essential nature of the "Toulmin Model" has been graphically presented by Freeley in his *Argumentation and Debate.* The argument that "The Supreme Court has made socially harmful decisions" is structured as follows. (Note the basic elements of *data, warrant,* and *claim,* together with the additional elements of *backing, qualifier,* and *rebuttal.*)[9]

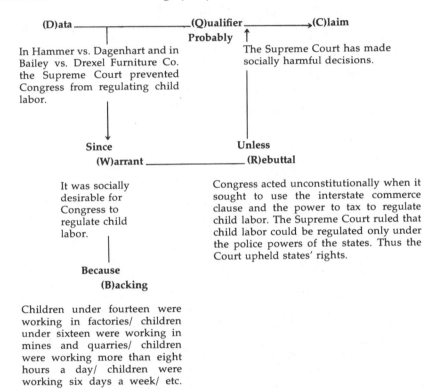

(D)ata	(Q)ualifier	(C)laim
In Hammer vs. Dagenhart and in Bailey vs. Drexel Furniture Co. the Supreme Court prevented Congress from regulating child labor.	Probably	The Supreme Court has made socially harmful decisions.

Since

(W)arrant _____ **(R)ebuttal**

Unless

| It was socially desirable for Congress to regulate child labor. | Congress acted unconstitutionally when it sought to use the interstate commerce clause and the power to tax to regulate child labor. The Supreme Court ruled that child labor could be regulated only under the police powers of the states. Thus the Court upheld states' rights. |

Because

(B)acking

Children under fourteen were working in factories/ children under sixteen were working in mines and quarries/ children were working more than eight hours a day/ children were working six days a week/ etc.

Common Uses of the Materials of Development in Speaking

In our survey of the several kinds of materials of development, we have considered how these materials function in the principal kinds of speaking situations. However, a brief summary at this point may help to recall their uses.

---

[9] For a more detailed discussion of the Toulmin model, see Austin J. Freeley, *Argumentation and Debate: Rational Decision Making,* 3rd ed. (Belmont, Calif.: Wadsworth Publishing Co., 1971). The example is reprinted here by permission. © 1971 Wadsworth Publishing Company, Inc.

In an Explanatory Message

When we try to explain a subject — to make it clear and understandable — we can make use of the following materials:

1. *Examples* and *narratives* provide concrete references and illustrations, which help to clarify and add interest to the composition.

2. *Statistics* enable us to present and compare data succinctly and often in graphic form.

3. *Quotations* provide us with information that we may not be able to get from our own experiences, and with the phraseology that may be more effective than our own.

4. *Repetition* and *restatement* give us the opportunity to emphasize a point and to allow the listener to "look back" as a reader does.

5. *Comparison* and *contrast* help us to explain new ideas through references, direct or indirect, to older or more familiar ideas.

In a Message of Advocacy

When we try to argue the merits of a proposition in order to secure its acceptance, these materials will help in the following ways:

1. *Examples* and *narratives* provide concrete references to cases that presumably prove the truth of our contention.

2. *Statistics* provide tangible and graphic data on which to base our claims.

3. *Quotations* are useful for drawing on the authority of persons whose word the listeners may accept more readily than they would the speaker's.

4. *Repetition* and *restatement* again provide emphasis of important points.

5. *Comparison* and *contrast* serve to make a new idea acceptable through association with an idea the listeners already accept.

6. *Evidence* and *reasoning* support our statements. It is only in the processes of reasoning that we establish relations among our materials and arrive at conclusions. Without evidence and reasoning, our messages would be mere unsupported statements of our own thoughts; and they would not be very convincing.

Suggested Assignments

1. Think of an oral message (a "speech") which appears to you to be deficient in its development — which appears to be thin or weak in its attempt to develop or reinforce the major subject or theme. Ask yourself: (a) why does this appear to be thin, even though the subject itself is clear and the organization of the message is satisfactory; (b) specifically, *what is lacking* — what materials do you want added?

2. Analyze an oral message (a speech composition) as to its use of specific instances, illustrations, narration, and quoted matter. Comment upon the nature of these materials of development and upon their value in the composition.

3. Analyze an oral message in respect to the use of repetition and restatement. What are the values of these materials of development in this composition?

4. Analyze an oral message in respect to factual evidence and opinion evidence. Identify at least two specimens of each, and evaluate in terms of the appropriate tests considered in this chapter.

5. Perform the operation as in assignment 4 with an argumentative editorial and also with an advertisement that contains argumentative material.

6. Prepare a speech of explanation upon a subject of your choice. Develop this subject by means of one or more examples (instances and/or illustrations), by means of one or more narratives, and by means of statistics. Also, use repetition and restatement, as well as comparison and contrast.

7. Prepare a speech of advocacy upon a proposition of your choice. Select one point or argument subsidiary to this proposition, and develop it by means of at least two pieces of factual evidence and at least two pieces of opinion evidence.

8. Analyze a speech as to its use of (a) reasoning from example and (b) reasoning from analogy. Identify all specimens of these types of reasoning, and evaluate them according to the appropriate tests considered in this chapter.

9. Perform the operation as in assignment 8 for reasoning from causal relationships and for reasoning from sign.

10. Prepare a speech of advocacy upon a proposition of your choice. Develop it by using the necessary evidence (as in assignment 7) and by using at least one piece of reasoning from example, one piece of reasoning from analogy, one piece of reasoning from causal relationships, and one piece of reasoning from sign.

Suggested References

Ehninger, Douglas, *Influence, Belief, Argument* (Glenview, Ill.: Scott, Foresman and Co., 1974).

Freeley, Austin J., *Argumentation and Debate: Rational Decision Making*, 3rd ed. (Belmont, Calif.: Wadsworth Publishing Co., 1971). Chapter 6, "Evidence"; Chapter 8, "Reasoning"; Chapter 9, "The Structure of Reasoning."

Kahane, Howard, *Logic and Contemporary Rhetoric* (Belmont, Calif.: Wadsworth Publishing Co., 1971).

McBurney, James H., and Glen E. Mills, *Argumentation and Debate: Techniques of a Free Society*, 2nd ed. (New York: The Macmillan Co., 1964). Chapter 7, "Evidence"; Chapter 8, "Kinds of Argument"; Chapter 9, "The Structure of Argument"; Chapter 10, "Explanation as Argument."

Minnick, Wayne C., *The Art of Persuasion*, 2nd ed. (Boston: Houghton Mifflin Co., 1968). Chapter 5, "Confirming Hypotheses: Cognitive Support."

Newman, Robert P., and Dale Newman, *Evidence* (Boston: Houghton Mifflin Co., 1969).

Thonssen, Lester, and A. Craig Baird, *Speech Criticism* (New York: Ronald Press Co., 1948). Chapter 11, "The Integrity of Ideas" (Proofs).

7
Materials of Speaking: Experience

"Rarely is anything we do determined by reason alone"

In this chapter we shall introduce those materials that are aimed primarily at helping the listener to re-create in his consciousness experiences similar to those that the speaker has in his consciousness. Materials of experience do not concentrate upon facts and statistics or upon the reasoning process; rather, they are designed to appeal primarily to the listener's basic motives, his sensory experiences and memories of them, and his needs, hopes, fears, and desires. These materials are used to make the message more real to the listener and to sustain his interest.

Many speakers believe that if they take the care to develop their messages with the most painstaking use of reasoning and evidence, their listeners will understand and believe what they are saying. Unfortunately, this is not so. The exclusive use of reason to determine human behavior is a fine and noble ideal to those who have faith in its efficacy and justice; but rarely is anything we do determined by reason alone. Most of our activity finds its source in more basic physical and social needs: in hunger, thirst, sex, sleep, and warmth; in acceptance, companionship, and recognition.

Some of the more obvious manifestations of the way these needs influence our behavior are easy to see. Religious organizations establish missions for hungry men because they believe that a man will often respond to their ideas more readily after his empty stomach has been filled. A shampoo manufacturer relies more upon descriptions of the soft, shiny, beautiful hair that results from application of his product than he does upon the fact that it removes dirt from hair.

Social stimuli also have a strong effect on our behavior because many of our responses are conditioned by the environment in which we live and grow. From infancy we learn to conform to certain behavioral expectations. Because we learn that it is wrong to steal, we are moved by the promise of a man running for a political office when he says he'll put an end to graft. Because we learn to respect intellectual achievement, we save our money for education. Because we learn to enjoy the company of other people, we respond to advertisements that warn us not to "offend."

It is through appeals of this nature—to the listener's senses, needs, and drives—that we as speakers can often sustain interest, reduce hostility, and put an end to apathy on the part of the listener. This kind of appeal makes the listener want to hear what we have to say next. We can help him or her experience what we have experienced or we can recall his own experiences in such a way as to make him empathize with our message.

As we explore the materials of experience that we shall be using in our oral messages, as well as some of the principles of speaking and some of the devices of speaking that most frequently include materials of experience, we should understand that there is not always mutual exclusivity among the materials of speaking: A device, a technique, or a material may serve in one context as an aid to personal proof, in another as a component of a key part of the message. What may be used in one instance to help the listener feel an emotion may be used in another to assist the speaker in proving his point. In general, it is the *use* or *intent* of the material that allows us to classify it as to type. These are all elements of the process of communication, and just as examining the separate systems that make up an automobile—the electrical system, the transmission, the motor, and so on—will help us understand the automobile as a whole, so should this analysis of the materials of speaking help us understand the process of communication as a whole.

Some Examples of Materials of Experience

Narration

Suppose you were trying to tell your listeners that everyone, no matter how insignificant he may seem, can perform some useful function in our society. You could speak for half an hour, casting about for evidence to support your assertions, explaining your ideas step by logical step. However, you could get the same message across in two minutes if you were to tell your listeners the Aesop fable of the lion and the mouse.[1] You remember the story: The lion saves the mouse from a trap. The mouse, naturally, is grateful, and he offers to help the lion if he ever needs help. Of this, of course, the lion is skeptical and contemptuous; he merely laughs at the mouse. One day the lion falls into a trap and the mouse comes along and finds him tied to a tree. The mouse, true to his word, chews the rope and frees the lion.

Most readers are familiar enough with this story to be able to repeat it any time they may be asked; yet, in all probability they read the paragraph

---

[1] For a discussion of narration as it is used to clarify or prove a point, see Chapter 6, pp. 86–87.

above with some interest. Stories, examples, anecdotes, fables, and other types of narratives will almost always be followed with some interest and are often useful for getting the listener to feel what the speaker wants him to feel.

Description

Description is another form in which we can employ materials of experience to good advantage. Especially if we have learned something of the art of oral reading, we can use description to create a mood that may help to persuade our audience or make our ideas clearer. Sometimes—especially when we read silently—we are tempted to skip passages of description because we feel that they add nothing to the content or progress of the story; however, these passages were put in for definite reasons, one of which is to create a mood that will serve the author's (or speaker's) purpose. Notice how the sensory details of the description of Theodore Roosevelt's "The Man with the Muck-Rake" tend to evoke a note of despair, of futility:

> In Bunyan's "Pilgrim's Progress" you may recall the description of the Man with the Muck-Rake, the man who could look no way but downward, with the muck-rake in his hand; who was offered a celestial crown for his muck-rake, but who would neither look up nor regard the crown he was offered, but continued to rake to himself the filth of the floor.
> In "Pilgrim's Progress" the Man with the Muck-Rake is set forth as the example of him whose vision is fixed on carnal instead of spiritual things. Yet he also typifies the man who in this life consistently refuses to see aught that is lofty, and fixes his eyes with solemn intentness only on that which is vile and debasing.

Of course not all speakers—especially in extemporaneous and impromptu speeches—can be expected to take such care to create the effect that this description creates or to use words as well as this orator does; but the principle remains the same: Description can help to put the listener in a certain frame of mind—as well as help to sustain his interest. The following description of a storm at sea is from an actual student speech. Observe how the speaker gives us an idea of what sea storms are—not with facts and figures about the height of the waves or the velocity of the wind or the roll of the ship, but with sensory detail:

> First, there is an intangible dread, as you stand on the bridge of your ship gazing at the dark, still water. You raise your head and sniff, and there is the smell of rain in the air—yes, rain, and something else, something ominous, something terrible, something as inexplicable as the feeling you get when you stand at the top of a high building and look down, a sort of bottomless feeling of dread.
> You look around you, and over on the horizon, looming up in ever-swelling proportions, is a black, ugly, unwashed blanket, sweeping over

the sky. There are holes in that blanket, and through the holes, flashing light as though from a crack in a door. The ship begins to quake under you. There is a curious rhythm in its shaking, a surging like that of a sidewalk under a drunken man.

Suddenly, the storm bursts upon you with a roar. Gone is the solitude, gone your easy contemplation of life at sea. Instead, a black void rushes out of nowhere and crushes you in its embrace. The wind rises to a shrill whistle and threatens to smash you against the deck. The water crashes into your face, and you come up gasping, fearfully awaiting that bully's hand to slap you under again.

The ship is rocking now, pitching forward and backward, sun-fishing, staggering down to the right, up to the left, like an angry bronc suddenly released from his chute. This is no poet's drama, no artist's conception. This is real, nature at her rawest, driving with all her forces to squash you beneath the weight and strength of her omnipotence. This is storm at sea.

Figures of Speech

The cliché "to lay an egg," old and worn as it is, manages to convey the idea of achieving absolute zero much more lucidly than does the simple statement "a total failure." Even the oldest clichés are of *some* value in a speaking situation because figurative language lends a certain brightness and spice to communication that ordinary direct statement does not. Original figures of speech have the further advantage of revealing imagination and insight on the part of the speaker; they serve not only to enliven the speech but also to enhance the speaker's personal proof.

Massing of Detail

The massing of detail is a device we can call upon to make our audiences feel or experience the conditions we are describing. This device often combines evidence or facts (materials of development) with description and a certain tautness or tension, which makes a mass of details far more effective than a simple list of factual material. John Hersey's *Hiroshima* contains such a massing of detail in the opening lines:

> At exactly fifteen minutes past eight in the morning, on August 6, 1945, Japanese time, at the moment when the atomic bomb flashed above Hiroshima, Miss Toshiko Sasaki, a clerk in the personnel department of the East Asia Tin Works, had just sat down at her place in the plant office and was turning her head to speak to the girl at the next desk. At that same moment, Dr. Masakasu Fujii was settling down crosslegged to read the Osaka *Asahi* on the porch of his private hospital, overhanging one of the seven deltaic rivers which divide Hiroshima; Mrs. Hatsuyo Nakamura, a tailor's widow, stood by the window of her kitchen, watching a neighbor tearing down his house because it lay in the path of an air-raid-defense fire lane; Father Wilhelm Kleinsorge, a German Priest of the Society of

Jesus, reclined in his underwear on a cot on the top floor of his order's three-story mission house, reading a Jesuit magazine, *Stimmen der Zeit*; Dr. Terufumi Sasaki, a young member of the surgical staff of the city's large, modern Red Cross Hospital, walked along one of the hospital's corridors with a blood specimen for a Wassermann test in his hand; and the Reverend Mr. Kiyoshi Tanimoto, pastor of the Hiroshima Methodist Church, paused at the door of a rich man's house in Koi, the city's western suburb, and prepared to unload a handcart full of things he had evacuated from town . . .[2]

Audio-Visual Aids

Listeners frequently do not respond to words as readily or as intensely as they do to other stimuli that they can see or hear or even smell, touch, and taste—even if the words are the most vivid and emotional words in the language. One of the students in a class in speaking had some difficulty convincing his listeners that it's fun to eat hot dogs—especially at ten o'clock in the morning—until he had his assistant wheel in a portable grill and cook the hot dogs while the speaker delivered his message. After the speech, the hot dogs were passed among the audience; there was not one vote of dissent. (Audio-visual aids are discussed at greater length in Chapter 13).

Message Structure

Message structure is discussed in detail in Chapter 11. Here we simply note that patterns of organization, in addition to their effect on the sense of a message, may be used to stimulate a listener's attention, to recall half-forgotten experiences, and to appeal to the listener's wants and desires.

Message Appeals

Since the beginning of historical times, man has been interested in the study of man, what makes him tick, why he behaves (or misbehaves) as he does.[3] One of the important reasons for his interest has been the desire of man to influence man, to persuade him. Plato saw man largely as a product of his environment, while Aristotle observed in man innate qualities which, in turn, influenced his environment. Down through the years, philosophers

---

[2] John Hersey, *Hiroshima* (New York: Alfred A. Knopf, 1946), pp. 3–4. Reprinted by permission.

[3] For an interesting discussion of historical approaches to the study of man's behavior, see Winston L. Brembeck and William S. Howell, *Persuasion: A Means of Social Control* (Englewood Cliffs, N. J.: Prentice-Hall, 1952), Chapter 4, "The Search for the Sources of Persuasion."

and theorists have viewed man as more or less susceptible to the persuasion of others, by means of appeals to his basic drives and needs. Some, like Plato, saw these needs as developing out of the physical and social milieu in which man finds himself; others, like Aristotle, believed that behavior patterns were basic and fixed in man. With the impact of behavioral science upon communication in the early years of the twentieth century, systematized lists of behavioral traits began to appear in textbooks in speech.

Perhaps the most famous of these early lists is that published by Phillips[4] in 1908. His set of impelling motives still finds its place in contemporary literature. In recent years, however, we have come to understand that a person cannot be categorized so precisely; we cannot predict with certainty that a particular stimulus will produce a particular reaction.

Among the earliest users of what we have come to call *message appeals* were the advertisers. Brembeck and Howell write that the "earliest advertisement on record, written on a sheet of papyrus paper from Thebes and advocating the return of a runaway slave, is dated about 3000 B.C. . . ."[5] Modern advertisers, at least according to Vance Packard, have refined the study of motivation and the techniques of using motives appeals:

> The way these persuaders—who often refer to themselves goodnaturedly as "symbol manipulators"—see us in the quiet of their interoffice memos, trade journals, and shop talk is frequently far less flattering, if more interesting. Typically they see us as bundles of daydreams, misty hidden yearnings, guilt complexes, irrational emotional blockages. We annoy them with our seemingly senseless quirks, but we please them with our growing docility in responding to their manipulation of symbols that stir us to action. They have found the supporting evidence for this view persuasive enough to encourage them to turn to depth channels on a large scale in their efforts to influence our behavior.[6]

For many years, speakers, like advertisers, have known that needs and drives play a large part in determining what the listener will accept and believe and what he will reject. The speaker, too, can make use of appeals to influence his listeners. Like the advertiser, he may indirectly suggest that adoption of his ideas will lead to satisfaction of certain needs and drives; he may take advantage of the tendencies of some of his listeners to react to fear appeals by providing these stimuli in his speaking and then suggesting that the fear thereby aroused can be reduced through adoption of his ideas.

As we have learned from the behavioral sciences and in spite of the "all or nothing" beliefs of some advertisers, there is no magical formula for

---

[4] Arthur E. Phillips, *Effective Speaking* (Chicago: The Newton Co., 1908), p. 48.

[5] Brembeck and Howell, p. 46.

[6] Vance Packard, *The Hidden Persuaders* (New York: David McKay Co., 1957), p. 4. Copyright 1957 by Vance Packard. Courtesy of David McKay Company, Inc.

influencing the listener. We cannot truly categorize a human being and predict his behavior. We can, however, by employing materials of experience through appeals, often assist the listener to re-create in his consciousness something akin to the feelings we, as the source of the message, have created in ours.

However effective these methods may be, they do pose a question of ethics. Is it right to appeal to human feelings to persuade people to act or to help them to understand something fully? Is it ethical to appeal to basic motives to secure decisions that should, traditionally, be rooted in reason? The question has no absolute answer. Most of us will agree that we have a right to try to persuade others — by peaceful means — yet each of us also feels that he has certain limits, although perhaps not yet adequately defined or properly tested, beyond which he will not go no matter how intensely he feels he must persuade.

Yet, in a democratic society, where force generally is not employed as a tool of information or persuasion, we must employ other means to cut through ignorance, apathy, and antipathy, if we believe that our causes and our ideas are worthwhile. There is a tradition of the use of appeals in speaking that is as old as the art of speaking itself; and recent and current studies in message appeals have extended the utility of this means of persuasion in all forms of communication.

Contemplation of the following categories of message appeals can serve as a springboard for our individual study and ethical consideration.

Appeals to Preservation

Nearly every human being wants to preserve his own life and health, and the lives of those dear to him. Modern American families spend a goodly portion of their income on trips to the doctor, health insurance, prescriptions, drugs and nostrums, self-improvement books and records, athletic equipment, and a myriad other items that, taken together, are intended to preserve physical, mental, and emotional health. This tendency to work at preserving life ranges from a parent's desperate attempts to rescue his child from a burning bedroom to a young mother's interest in a child-study group; from a middle-aged woman's periodic checkup trips to the family doctor to her husband's swallowing the latest television-promoted remedy for sinus trouble or stomach distress or sleeplessness.

When we consider the vast amount of attention that people pay to human preservation, we can see how valuable it would be to relate our proposal — in speaking situations where this is possible — to the safety and welfare of our listeners. A tire manufacturer would hardly refuse to spend money to advertise the safety of his tires, although he might also want to emphasize their durability and economy. For the same reason, your explanation of your plan to spray the small swampy area in the neighborhood would be far more persuasive to your neighbor if you pointed out the danger of mosquitoes to the health of the children. Your argument, as a student, for a new chemistry lab would point out the risks and dangers of working in the old lab.

Appeals to Pride

Except for an occasional hermit or a monk or a person grown weary of the ways of the world, most of us have a deep desire to look well in the public eye. Because we want our children to be proud of us, we strain our backs playing baseball on the corner lot. Because we want our neighbors to think we are reasonably well off, we buy a new car before we need one. Because we want our fellow employees to respect us, we take on added responsibility. Much of this pride has beneficial results; many of our finest works and deeds are the result, at least in part, of pride. On the other hand, pride in the sense of vanity can move us to do foolish things, like spending money from the food budget on new clothes that we really don't need, or claiming to be better informed on a subject than we really are.

Experienced communicators recognize pride as a strong motive, and they know how to appeal to it in their attempts to achieve their ends. A speaker advocating the construction of a new school in River City will point out not only that the new school will help raise educational standards in the community, produce better educated children and increase their earning power as adults, and promote the welfare of the nation and world as a whole; but also that the new school will be known all over the state for its advanced educational ideas, the citizens will be known for their up-to-date attitudes, and River City will be the Athens of the Prairie. These are definitely appeals to pride. If we can relate our ideas to the pride of our listeners, we may be able to strengthen the appeal of our cause.

Appeals to Altruism

Another strong set of appeals that speakers use is related to the desire apparent in many people to do good without thought of reward or recognition.

Unlikely as this desire may seem to be, it is real, genuine, and at times stronger than any other. Angry men and women have been known to contain their anger and forget enmity to work together to save a church or to ease a problem involving the children of the neighborhood. Residents in another neighborhood agreed to the loss of several inches of their property to obtain a boundary solution fair to all.

Some of our most inspiring speaking is filled with appeals to altruism, as, for example, in every message about supporting CARE or the United Fund (or United Crusade). A speaker who can relate his message to altruism may well achieve his ends.

Appeals to Conformity and Change

Most of us, most of the time, appear to want things left about as they are. We resent changes in our institutions, in our manner of living, in our ways of thinking. Sometimes this resistance to change helps us to preserve the things in life we value most dearly; sometimes it stands in the way of progress. Recently, the citizens of a large city refused to convert an old but well-liked park into a parking lot, despite the obvious need for more parking facilities. In another city opposition to slum clearance projects stemmed in part from the tendency to conform, to maintain the status quo, and to prefer the known to the unfamiliar.

On the other hand, we also seem to have a desire for change; nearly everybody stands for progress if it does not interfere with his own way of life. Most of us will accept change if we can be shown how it will benefit us, and we will resist it if more successful efforts are made to show us how change will do us more harm than good. In any case, the tendencies of resistance to change and desire for change both seem to be based upon self-centered wishes, and the speaker who knows this can often make his persuasion more effective by making use of his knowledge.

Appeals to Sex

Appeals to sex bombard us on television every day. Television commercials rarely show bald men applying roll-on deodorants or obese women opening refrigerator doors. The heroes of both the plays and the commercials are usually men whose virility, if nothing else about them, is unquestionable; and the heroines are unquestionably feminine. Since audiences are definitely—although usually unconsciously—affected in many ways by the speaker's appeal to sex, we have—as speakers—both an opportunity to influence and a responsibility not to take unfair advantage of impressionable listeners.

Appeals to Pugnacity

Our social environment tends to develop within many of us a desire to compete, a love of a fight for its own sake, as well as an admiration for fighters. Although many people did not sympathize with his goals, they found themselves forced to admire John L. Lewis, leader of the mineworkers, as he struggled, worked, and fought for his men during the 1930s and 1940s. Some businessmen, for example, would curse Mr. Lewis and then add, with obvious reluctance, "But you've got to admire the old son-of-a-gun—he's a fighter—wish we had more like him on our side." More recently, political leaders like Harry S. Truman and Lyndon B. Johnson have elicited respect, even admiration, while simultaneously arousing negative reactions in those who did not approve of their political ideas.

Pugnacity is not limited to competition between men and men, women and women, men and women; it extends into the realm of ideas. In 1844, the war-minded shouted "Fifty-four Forty or Fight"; in our own century we fought "to make the world safe for Democracy." Down the years Christians have sung "Onward Christian Soldiers."

Today we shout slogans for and against young people who would alter our society; we rail against political "enemies"; and every fall our football stadiums ring with threats and imprecations that are reminiscent of the ancient Romans rooting for the Christians and the lions.

Young people often express their need for pugnacity in violent physical activity. We put on the gloves and box, not really to hurt the other boy — he may be our best friend — but because we just want to fight. We play football in T-shirts in the field behind the house, and return oozing with mud and crippled with bruises. We join the debate team to sling verbal abuse at one another. We throw ourselves almost hysterically into queen contests and pushcart derbies. We participate in wild, psychedelic musical events.

For older people, pugnacity is often vicarious. We no longer want actually to fight, but we enjoy watching conflicts. So we sponsor Little League; attend ball games or sit clutching pennants while two teams slug it out on television; we attend political conventions, board meetings, city council meetings, in part to see the show.

As speakers, we can appeal to the tendency within many of our listeners to be pugnacious and attempt to direct it toward the end or purpose we have in speaking. "Turn the rascals out" is the cry of one political speaker toward the politicians of the other party. "Let's go down to that school board! Let's fight those bureaucrats! Let's get that traffic light installed!"

Arousing listeners to action by appealing to pugnacity is certainly acceptable under the right circumstances; but if we tend to overdramatize in speaking, the results can be more physical than intellectual. Therefore, when we appeal to our listener's pugnacity, we should exercise caution, for this kind of speaking at its best comes close to stepping over the line between persuasion and coercion; at its worst, it can result in violent action.

Appeals to Curiosity

The speaker who must persuade can make use of the desire within us to learn, to explore, to seek out the new and different, to discover. When we were young, many of us took apart the family alarm clock just to see what made it run. As adults, we may continue this interest in mechanical things or we may satisfy our curiosity by analyzing difficult logical concepts or running down the sources of obscure comments and quotations in the library.

As speakers, we may appeal to curiosity by introducing into our speeches

rhetorical questions, wherein we ask the audience questions that we, not they, are expected to answer. We use narratives that build up to a climax; we hold back the point of our speech, hoping to create suspense and a little mystery in the minds of our receivers.

Fear Appeals

In recent years, considerable attention has been paid to the persuasive power in employing appeals to fears—fear about getting cancer, dying in automobile wrecks, having a heart attack. Consequently, messages advocating medical checkups, the use of seat belts, and proper diet have been loaded with fear appeals. The results appear to be inconclusive; while fear appeals seem to work sometimes, at other times they tend to focus the receiver's attention more on the fear than on the proposed solution. The personal proof of the communicator may be a factor in their success or failure, as also may be the perceived importance of the topic; that is, there is some indication that when the personal proof of the communicator is high, high fear appeals tend to be successful. Evidence also supports the thesis that high fear appeals work when the receiver has high concern for the message.

Perhaps the best position we can take at this time is that offered by Bettinghaus, who suggests that unless the speaker knows his audience well enough to believe that his personal proof is high or that his topic is considered important, it is better to avoid using high levels of fear appeal.[7]

Reward Appeals

Politicians have thrived for years in the belief that reward appeals influence the voters, and certainly experimental research tends to support the notion that the promise of monetary reward does influence attitude change. "What's in it for me?" is a question audiences tend to ask—or at least so speakers believe—and one of the most fundamental principles of audience adaptation is that the speaker's goals must be demonstrated as equally beneficial to the

---

[7] Erwin P. Bettinghaus, *Persuasive Communication*, 2nd ed. (New York: Holt, Rinehart and Winston, 1973), p. 159.

listeners. What communicator would advocate higher taxes without pointing out the benefits to those who must pay them? And the speaker who makes private remarks to members of his own organization, concerning the advantages to them of some course of action, is in deep trouble if his speech becomes public—and there is no benefit for the public in the proposed action.

Gaining and Maintaining Attention

Materials of experience are especially valuable in helping to arrest and to maintain the attention of the listener in the speaking situation. It has long been recognized that while the art of holding the listener's attention— together with the materials of speaking necessary to accomplish this—is not the most important aspect of speaking, the source's meaning cannot be aroused in the receiver unless he attends to the message. Indeed, William James wrote many years ago that what holds attention determines action. We know that this statement is not literally true, of course, but it is important because it attests to the necessity of arresting and holding attention and especially because it emphasizes that *the communicator must gain his listener's attention first,* before he presents the heart of his message.

Minnick has defined attention, from the point of view of the listener or receiver:

> Attention is the process of selecting a particular stimulus of the many available in one's perceptual field and clearing one's sensory channels of competing information so that the selected stimulus is passed with minimal interference into the central nervous system.[8]

Turning this definition around, then, and looking at it from the speaker's point of view, we can say that arousing attention consists of leading our listeners to select the particular stimulus we (the speaker) want them to select and, through use of materials of experience such as those presented here, helping them to clear their sensory channels of competing information so that the selected stimulus is passed with minimal interference into their central nervous systems.

Because attention is a process of selecting, the speaker should be well aware of competing stimuli. Listeners are distracted not only by outside disturbances, such as a passerby whistling in a hallway, an air hammer across the street, and birds singing outside the window, but also by their inner thoughts and worries, such as the baby left at home with the sitter,

---

[8] Wayne C. Minnick, *The Art of Persuasion,* 2nd ed. (Boston: Houghton Mifflin Co., 1968), p. 53. Chapter 3 is an excellent statement of the principles of attention.

an unpaid bill, a moral conflict, an uncomfortable stomach, and the remark overheard in the hallway. The careful speaker knows that, except in rare instances, he is in competition with many such interferences, and he will address himself to the task of overcoming them by offering alternatives that will arrest his listener's attention even more strongly: (1) himself, (2) his subject, and (3) his presentation of that subject.

We have all listened to speakers who exhausted their whole stock of interesting material in their opening statements. Such a speaker typically begins with "A funny thing happened to me on the way . . ." and proceeds to tell an amusing story, evidently thinking that this one device is worth fifteen minutes of our attention to the rest of his dull material.

The effective speaker, on the other hand, knows that attention is fleeting and that he must work to keep it. He too may start his speaking with an amusing incident, but he will continue to amuse or illustrate or describe or use colorful, moving language to assure that his listeners remain interested

---

Techniques of Composition

1. Organize your message in an interesting manner. Consider a plan other than one with a simple one-two-three approach. Read the chapters on developing the speech plan. While the simplest plan may be best for your logical development, try modifying it if the basic material of the message is not in itself sufficiently interesting to hold the audience's attention.

2. Employ materials of development — facts, statistics, opinions, and good reasoning — that are germane to the basic message and actually develop it for the listener. Remember that a speech without materials of experience may bore people, but a speech without good use of materials of development will not convey what you want them to learn or think or do — and so it is useless.

3. Start with a reference to what was said immediately before you speak. If you are giving a prepared speech, you can refer to the chairman's introductory remarks; perhaps, if he is a close friend, even trying a little humor at his

expense. In impromptu and daily-discourse situations, make some sort of transitional remark to help tie the conversation together.

4. Use a significant, meaningful opening statement or, if appropriate, begin with your purpose sentence — expressed dramatically, if possible. Rephrase it one or more times during your talk. Use a quotation (from a play, a famous speech, a poem, an essay, or a work of fiction) when you think it will embody a point you wish to make in language more effective than your own. To keep the audience's attention, try repeating your main idea in the same form you chose to begin your talk. Winston Churchill aptly summed up this device when he observed, "If you have an important point to make . . . don't try to be subtle or clever. Use a pile driver. Hit the point once. Then come back and hit it again. Then hit it a third time — a tremendous whack."*

* *A King's Story: The Memoirs of the Duke of Windsor* (New York: G. P. Putnam's Sons, 1947) p. 137.

in what he is saying. He employs materials of experience all the while he is speaking. The impromptu speaker should pay as close attention to this matter as the speaker who has a chance to prepare; he can make use of his wit, if he is quick enough, and he can relate his views to current events or illustrate his points with references to plays, films, songs, places, and ideas familiar to all of his listeners. He can spread these materials of experience throughout his talk, without trying to burden the listener with more content than he can absorb at one time.

Beginning speakers need to learn some of the basic techniques for getting and keeping the attention of their listeners. The first step is to speak, whenever we have the choice, about something interesting and worthwhile. The next is to develop a number of techniques and devices to help us hold attention. Such techniques — see the insets — have to be learned and practiced; it is only when they become part of our individual style that they really succeed.

---

5.   Level a barrage of facts or questions at the listener. "Do you want to know why your test grades are so low?" asks the teacher. "Are you interested in the average scores of the class that took the exam just ahead of you? Do you want to know how to do better next time?" Such rhetorical questions are intended not to elicit a response but to arrest the listeners' attention and focus it on the speaker and his answers. Two warnings about use of rhetorical questions: (1) Make your questions meaningful and germane to the subject, so that the listeners (curiosity aroused) will want the questions answered. (2) Answer the questions you raise. Listeners tend, with good reason, to be irritated with the communicator who arouses their curiosity and then fails to satisfy it. (A series of startling statements will accomplish the same results. It will force the audience to pay attention at the same time that it presents important factual materials.)

6.   Use narrative material. "Did you hear the story about . . . ?" usually gets immediate attention. "Terribly trite beginning," says the critic of this device. Probably quite true, but watch your listeners straighten up and pay attention. This device is useful not only in the beginning of the speech but also at other times when your listeners' attention is noticeably flagging.

7.   Try a little humor. Humor in the hands of an experienced speaker or raconteur is extremely effective for getting and holding attention. For the beginner, humor is admittedly a chancy thing, and it seldom comes off well when the speaker feels ill at ease. However, if your audience is sympathetic — and if you have a little daring — try some humor; even the attempt will provide a little relief from the heavier content of your message. And you never know how it will work for you until you try it.

Suggestion and the Use of Materials of Experience

Suggestion, stated simply, is an attempt to arouse an idea in the mind of the listener without directly referring to it, at least at first. Suggestion is not ordinarily a preferred method of speaking, but it is sometimes forced upon the speaker because of the inability or unwillingness of the audience to accept or even listen to your point directly. If, for example, the board members of the company you work for have resisted the idea of door-to-door selling, which you believe is the best way of assuring sales of the company's product, it will do you little good to introduce your position directly and argue for it. In the first place, your listeners will have closed their minds to the subject; in the second, even if your argument sounds valid to them, their firm stand against it in the past will make it impossible for them to lose face by accepting it now.

Your problem is to let the idea become theirs, to introduce it in such a manner that they will not recognize it as yours, or if they do, they will still be able to claim it as their own. There are many methods of accomplishing this objective. For example, you may wish to use the device of implication

---

Techniques of Delivery

1.   *Approach the platform, if there is one, deliberately. It is nearly always wise to pause for a moment before you speak. Look at your audience with interest; then smile (if your subject permits). Do not start speaking until you are thoroughly ready. This approach produces a dramatic effect that doesn't happen when you rush to the platform or start speaking without taking a moment to collect your thoughts and establish contact with your audience.*

2.   *Make a sudden dramatic gesture. One professor used to begin his lectures by thrusting his hands down to the table top or smacking a hand against the blackboard; sometimes he would empty his briefcase onto the table and*

rummage through the mess to find the example he wanted to use. This device can be corny if it is overused; but with discretion it can be a good way to gain attention.

3.   *Use expressive language. Dull, monotonous language will encourage attention to wander; but words that are exciting, dramatic, and full of sensory impressions, used in sentences and paragraphs that reveal a bit of insight into the art of English composition, will keep people from daydreaming. "There are more race riots and demonstrations this summer of 1966 than any previous year in the history of the civil rights movement," said a speaker in a beginning public speaking course; and this is*

by listing all the ways in which your competitors sell their products, noting the relatively low sales in each case and then asking your colleagues for their ideas. If you have properly listed and disposed of all possibilities except door-to-door selling, the chances are that some bright young executive will come up with your preferred *modus operandi.*

You will now have to swallow your pride and thank him for his suggestion, keeping to yourself the knowledge that you have saved the company; but if it is saved, you have accomplished your purpose. You can only hope that an astute boss will soon catch on to what you are doing and suitably reward you.

Or you may introduce your point differently. You may discuss an analogous problem, say, that of persuading people in your neighborhood to vote. You may mention that party headquarters receives few visitors, that literature is rarely read, that telephone calls seem remote and do not produce many votes, but that when your party workers knock on doors, the voting rate in your district goes up 25 percent.

If suggestion is so effective, why don't more people use it? Actually, many more speakers do than we might expect. The apostle Paul might have called the Athenians heathen, but he chose to tell them, "Men of Athens, I perceive that in every way you are very religious. For as I passed along, and observed the objects of your worship, I found also an altar with this

---

not a bad statement, from the point of view of holding an audience's attention. U. S. News & World Report put it: "Riots, battles, power marches—it's still a hot summer,"* and had the speaker used this phrase he probably would have jerked his listeners up to attention more quickly.

4. Begin speaking with one extreme or the other in volume. This is an old device that almost never fails. A loud beginning will attract the listeners' attention; once you have it, you can lower your voice to normal. An extremely quiet, barely audible beginning will make your listeners put forth effort to hear you—you will notice waves of

silence sweep over the room. Once you are reasonably sure you have the audience's attention, you can raise your voice to its normal loudness.

5. Ask the listeners to do something together, in unison. Shortly after World War II, the Korean War, and Viet Nam, teachers often began their classes by asking, "Will the veterans please raise their hands?" Because many of the students were veterans, there was quite a bit of movement in unison, and everyone in the class paid attention. Similar devices: asking the listeners to reply to a question, having them stand up and stretch, and—one that will arouse attention when other means fail—even having them change their seats to another part of the room.

---

* August 15, 1966, p. 36.

inscription, 'To an unknown God.' What therefore you worship as unknown, this I proclaim to you.'"[9]

Winston Churchill, in his famous speech to the American Congress shortly after the attack on Pearl Harbor, might have exclaimed, "Come on, forget the Japs; we've got to lick the Jerries first," but he chose to suggest that the Japanese were fools to dare to attack so mighty a nation, implying that we could deal with them when we got around to it.

These speakers did not sacrifice their goals; but they did modify their approaches in order to allay suspicion, to open up minds, to prepare people to receive the truth.

It is true that many people do not use suggestion intentionally. Many of us have been brought up to believe that if we have an idea, we should express it forcefully and logically, and if the audience is intelligent, the idea will be accepted. In other words, let the chips fall where they may. This theory is fine, as long as the audience *is* thinking intelligently (assuming, of course, that we have done our part). However, what happens when the audience has been prejudiced to the point that it will not accept our ideas, not even listen to them? Then reasoning and evidence will not secure us a hearing, and our efforts will be in vain.

Furthermore, many speakers do not use suggestion because they don't understand that it is possible to speak openly on one level while introducing a subject marginally through suggestion. If this expression of the method seems sinister and somewhat dishonest, you may not wish to use suggestion. However, you will have to consider two points: (1) you should in any event be prepared to do battle against suggestion when it is used against you; and (2) if the audience is prevented by blindness, ignorance, or predisposition from grasping your ideas, or if it has been turned against you by other speakers, there may be no other way for you to operate than to employ suggestion or some other subtle method of persuasion.

Suggestion operates hand in hand with appeals as a method of persuasion. For example, a speaker (salesman) may make use of his knowledge of his listeners' motivations by appealing to their pride in order to sell them an expensive brand of watch. When this technique becomes so obvious that customers no longer respond to it, the salesman may shift ground slightly: the cheap watch is a fine one, very adequate for most people; indeed, only those who are really leaders in their community or important to their businesses need buy the expensive watch. Here suggestion is operating, for the potential customer is being told—without being told—that if he is an important person he should have the expensive watch or—even more insidiously—if he wants to be important, then he should buy the expensive watch.

---

[9] Acts 17:22–23, *Revised Standard Version of the Holy Bible,* copyright 1946 and 1952 by the Division of Christian Education of the National Council of Churches.

Types of Suggestion

Suggestion has been categorized in a number of ways by psychologists and rhetoricians. Of special concern to our discussion are positive and negative suggestion and intentional and unintentional suggestion.

Positive suggestion is suggestion intentionally or unintentionally employed by the speaker to show himself in a good light, to intimate that he is a man to be admired and trusted or that his idea or product is one the listener ought to accept. The car salesman who tosses you his keys and says, "Here, take a spin. Try her out yourself, you'll like her," is using positive suggestion—suggestion that his car will stand your scrutiny, that he is an honest man, and that he trusts you.

Negative suggestion should rarely be employed deliberately, for it implies that you are ineffective, weak, and vacillating, and have little confidence in your own ideas. The car salesman who follows you around, wipes your child's fingerprints off his car, and hovers over your shoulder while you drive is suggesting that his car will not stand up under the strain of you and your family, that his product is weak, and that he cannot trust you. Many speakers use negative suggestion unwittingly; let us watch out for it in our own speaking.

To sum up, positive suggestion is good, insofar as it helps us to be successful persuaders; negative suggestion rarely, if ever, aids us.

While we have control in speaking over much of the use of suggestion (*intentional*)—that is, we can elect to be direct or indirect—some suggestion is impossible to prevent (*unintentional*). The way we walk, the spirit (or lack of it) with which we present our points, the interest (or lack of interest) we evince in our listeners, the care with which we select our materials of speaking—all these suggest to our listeners attitudes they will develop toward us and our subject, whether we will it or not. The surest way we can avoid unintentional negative suggestion is to choose a subject in which we are truly interested or to develop a sincere interest in the subject upon which we must speak, and then do our best to put that subject across to our audience. Anything less will redound against us in the minds of our receivers.

The use of intentional suggestion in speaking, like the use of many of the other devices for getting ideas across, is controversial. It is certainly used extensively and it often works. In the hands of a person of good character, it may often persuade us to do what we ought to do and would have done anyway, had we not fallen prey to contrary persuasion at a previous time. In the case of an expository speech, suggestion may be used to give an audience understanding of a subject or process to which it otherwise might not pay heed.

Use of Suggestion

The practice of suggestion is by no means limited to persuasive speaking. Learning is also frequently resisted by audiences, as those of us who teach know only too well; and you may find it necessary to utilize some of the principles and methods of suggestion when you are speaking to inform. Suggestion may be brought to bear in the speaking situation in four ways:

1. *Your Choice and Organization of Ideas*   By choosing this idea, rejecting that one, placing this one in a prominent place in your speech, relegating that one to an unimportant treatment, you assuredly suggest to your listener what is important, what he can easily understand, and what attitudes you expect him to take toward your ideas.

2. *The Way You Word Your Ideas*   "Domicile" implies, to most of us at least, a house; but "home" indicates fireside and comfort, dog at your feet, your favorite music playing, and peace and contentment.

3. *The Manner in Which You Speak*   You can call a girl a liar with one voice, and she laughs with you at the joke; change your tone slightly and she may strike you. "May I help you, Madame?" with a tired, irritated pitch will make you leave the store; the same phrase spoken with confidence and friendliness may tip your mind to buy the product you were only considering.

4. *The Way You Reveal Yourself as a Person*   We have all had the experience of working for a person for whom we would do anything—stay late, sweep out, accept a postponed paycheck. Another person rubs us the wrong way so strongly that we begrudge anything we do for him even when we are hired to do it.

One-Sided versus Two-Sided Messages

It is hard to decide which is more persuasive, a message that presents only the side of the issue we advocate or a message that presents our side plus the arguments for the other side. (It may be argued that the use of two-sided messages is a form of suggestion—of indirect persuasion, but the results of this form of suggestion are still open to question.)

There is some evidence that two-sided messages are more effective with better-educated listeners, and with listeners who are initially opposed to a position than with listeners who already support the position. For many speakers, too, a question of ethics arises—is it fair *not* to inform our hearers of the evidence contrary to our position? On the other hand, is it fair to use an apparent objectivity—presenting both sides of the coin—when we really believe such a device will aid our own cause? (See Chapter 1, page 10.)

A Word about Self-Persuasion

The materials of speaking are useful not only to the communicator but also to the receiver of the message—not simply as materials with which he is to be persuaded or made to understand but as materials he can use to help him persuade himself, or understand. A communicator does not inoculate his listeners—he opens doors of understanding, he encourages us to think for ourselves, he offers us choices, he asks us to evaluate his position and then to make up our own minds. If he does not do these things, in the long run he is unlikely to become an effective communicator and, worse, he is unlikely to become an ethical communicator.

With this chapter we have completed our discussion of the "stuff" of speaking, the materials with which the speaker works as he prepares his speech. Throughout the remainder of this book, as you study topics for speeches, outlining and organization, style, delivery, and the types of speaking, you will find, of course, frequent references to these materials. You will want to return to Chapters 5, 6, and 7 from time to time, however, to refresh your memory of principles and methods discussed in them.

Suggested Assignments

1.   Look around you and take notice of the colors and textures of the clothes the others in the room are wearing. Listen carefully to the various sounds in the room and outside: people breathing, the shuffling of papers, a car taking off. What does the air smell like? Observe as many of the sensory stimuli that make up your immediate environment as you can. Jot your impressions on a piece of paper, without following any system of organization unless one comes naturally. Later on, try to organize these impressions into a coherent message. After a week has passed, read what you have written and discover whether your message conveys a sense of the reality of the environment.

2.   Read "Fern Hill" by Dylan Thomas, making mental notes as you go along of the number of sensory impressions in this poem. How well does the poet succeed in communicating—through references to colors, light, temperatures—the vigor of his pastoral youth?

3.   The next time you speak to someone in an informal setting, try to make use of the observations you made in the first two exercises by giving your listeners a rich supply of sensory images. Put these images in the forms suggested in this chapter—tell a story, use figures of speech and so on, and try to use some message appeals.

4.   Choose a subject about which you are vitally concerned. Develop a speech that consists entirely of narration and description—in other words, tell a story that illustrates your point of view concerning the subject chosen. Do not moralize; do not prepare an introduction or conclusion. Make your story, with description, do the entire job.

5.   Prepare a speech in which you take a stand for or against a policy of our present national administration. (You may substitute a policy of your state or local government, if you wish.) Pile up as much evidence as you can and arrange your evidence so that each piece seems more powerful, more persuasive, than the one before. See whether you can make your message persuasive, not only through the use of the evidence itself, but also through the arrangement of the evidence.

6.   Choose a subject in which you strongly believe. See how many attention-arresting devices you can work into your speech, from beginning to end; yet do not lose sight of the message. Use as many appeals as you can, along with your reasoning and evidence, in an effort to convince your audience.

7. Prepare a three-minute introduction to a speech on any subject you choose. Just for the experience, cram your introduction as full of attention-arresting devices as you can. Don't worry, this one time, about overloading your speech. Make your own evaluation of your speech. Were you able to sustain the interest of your listeners throughout the introduction? Were you able to focus their attention upon your message?

8. Go to hear a speaker in your community, if possible someone who is speaking on a political or other controversial theme. Make a careful list of the speaker's attempts to adapt to his audience. Include notes on his or her use of appeals, attention-arresting devices, suggestion, description, narration, figures of speech, massing of detail, and audio-visual aids. From the point of view of your own particular bias, do you think he was successful? Why or why not?

9. Choose a subject in which you strongly believe, but one to which you believe the majority of your listeners will be opposed. Develop your subject indirectly, using suggestion. (You may wish to refer to Chapter 11 for appropriate speech plans to use.) Do not state your purpose sentence in this speech. See how close you can come to informing your listeners of your true purpose without actually doing so.

10. Select a speech by Franklin D. Roosevelt, Eleanor Roosevelt, Adlai Stevenson, John Kennedy, Martin Luther King, Jr., or Gerald Ford. Analyze the speech carefully, making notes of the speaker's use of materials of experience, attention-arresting devices, message appeals, and suggestion. Study your list to learn which of these techniques you can use in your own speaking.

Suggested References

Bem, Daryl J., *Beliefs, Attitudes, and Human Affairs* (Monterey, Calif.: Brooks/Cole Publishing Co., 1970).

Bettinghaus, Erwin P., *Persuasive Communication*, 2nd ed. (New York: Holt, Rinehart and Winston, 1973). Chapter 3, "Persuasibility and Personality"; Chapter 7, "Structuring Messages and Appeals."

Cohen, Arthur R. *Attitude Change and Social Influence* (New York: Basic Books, 1964). Chapter 4, "Personality Predispositions and Persuasive Communications."

Doob, Leonard W., *Propaganda: Its Psychology and Technique* (New York: Holt, Rinehart and Winston, 1935). Chapter 5, "Suggestion, Prestige, and Social Change."

Miller, Gerald R., and Michael Burgoon, *New Techniques of Persuasion* (New York: Harper & Row, 1973). Chapter 4, "Counterattitudinal Advocacy as a Persuasive Technique: Theoretical Interpretations"; Chapter 5, "Counterattitudinal Advocacy as a Persuasive Technique: Research Findings."

Minnick, Wayne C., *The Art of Persuasion*, 2nd ed. (Boston: Houghton Mifflin Co., 1968). Chapter 3, "Attention—The Tuning Process"; Chapter 8, "Confirming Hypotheses—Motivational Support."

Phillips, Arthur E., *Effective Speaking* (Chicago: The Newton Co., 1908). Chapter 5, "Action and the Impelling Motives."

Part Three
Preparing to Speak

Part Three is a comprehensive discussion of the steps in oral message preparation: responding to or selecting your subject (Chapter 8), collecting the materials for your message (Chapter 9), using the outline as the chief tool (Chapter 10) for organizing your message (Chapter 11), considering the language and style of your message (Chapter 12), using audio-visual aids to strengthen your message (Chapter 13), and delivering your message (Chapter 14).

These chapters should be studied in conjunction with those in Part Two, which are concerned with your listener and the content of your message.

8
Responding to and Selecting the Subject

"One idea will seem better than another"

Most speaking topics or subjects (outside of public speaking courses) are chosen for us, not by us. They are assigned by teachers, chairmen, parents, supervisors and, more often than not, by circumstances. Ordinarily they arise out of an exigence, an occasion, a crisis, out of a need for speaking. Sometimes we initiate the communication; sometimes we respond to a message or a series of messages; sometimes our message is interspersed between the messages of others. In all these cases, however, as well as when we have free choice of our subject, there are principles we can learn and procedures we can follow that will make our task somewhat easier and a good deal more successful.

Moreover, the problem of responding to a subject (or selecting it) is equally significant whether the speech occasion is formal or informal, whether the speaker has a month to prepare his message and unlimited resource materials at his disposal, or a few seconds after the exigence arises to collect his thoughts. Whatever the circumstances, you, as the message-builder, are still responsible for the effective handling of the problem, testing the specific choice, narrowing it down, keeping it relevant to the listeners' needs, and making it consistent with your objectives.

An Inspirational Approach to the Subject

Success is rarely accidental. Usually, it is the result of a painstaking approach to a problem. It is obvious that when you have been given a speech assignment or a free choice of a subject (and after you have considered your listeners and the occasion), your first impulse *should* be aimed at searching immediately for an appropriate topic.

Speakers differ in their preparation habits; some begin with *intrapersonal communication,* or "talking with themselves" — thinking, reflecting, or even repeating something in order to learn. Others begin by *brainstorming,* which involves a free association of ideas during which we pile up many alternative ideas. The creative process of brainstorming requires an open mind and the practice of jotting down on a piece of paper every idea that comes to mind, no matter when or under what circumstances. After you have a substantial list, you can carefully weed out the ideas that are entirely unsuitable. During this analysis period some wild idea may be chosen and subsequently prove to have been an extremely wise choice. These four procedures are recommended:

1. Suspend criticism of ideas in order that the flow of ideas will continue.
2. Welcome wild ideas; record any seemingly impractical idea.
3. Permit a large quantity of ideas to occur; they can be pared down later.
4. Improve some idea by modifying or adapting it in some way.

Brainstorming is a useful technique in communication whether you use it alone or within a group, in which case people stimulate ideation in one another.

You may, however, decide to consider some other, more systematic method of selecting a topic than these, and certainly a more rational approach is recommended for responding to a subject or exigence originating apart from you.

A Rational Approach to the Subject

Authorities offer various approaches. The one described here has these four separate stages: (1) preparation, (2) incubation, (3) inspiration, and (4) evaluation.

Preparation for Responding to or Selecting Your Subject

To generate ideas for speech topics, our minds should turn to the basic material out of which ideas can be formed. This basic material is "experience," by far the richest resource we have.

Personal Experience   The speaker's dynamic pool of material is to be found in his lifetime of experiences. This means that all of our relations with people — in family, jobs, school, community life, recreation, travel — speak loudly to us and help determine our viewpoint. In this category may be

found hopes, ambitions, dreams, and desires; grudges and aversions; prejudices and convictions. Many communicators do not take advantage of these experiences because they fear to bring them out into the open. In failing to do this, they miss many good topics.

Allowing our personal feelings, thoughts, and beliefs to influence our choice of a subject, or our adaptation of a subject, will give the stamp of personality, or individual identity, so essential in communication. When Erich Fromm, author of *The Art of Loving* and other widely read books, spoke to an overflow audience at Michigan State University, he made the point that the individual must stop using double-talk, or speaking knowingly about concepts in which he has no real belief. Fromm maintained that man uses conviction based on personal experience to save himself in our industrial society. Many speeches have been made successful with this personal touch, even though doing so often requires courage and conviction. For example, one student speaker, although the disclosure may have embarrassed him, dared to talk about his experience under the care of a psychiatrist.

In this regard some of our outstanding leaders have been known to take many more risks than do followers. When the late Senator Robert Taft was personally distressed by some particular problem, he did not fear to speak out even though it endangered his political fortune.[1] The late Senator Everett M. Dirksen said that it doesn't matter what or who you are, you should follow through your ideas and express yourself even after discouragement and reverses, permitting these to be the incentive. Psychologist Carl Rogers believes that young people are becoming more aware of, and more expressive of, persistent inner feelings they have about themselves and the human species—and, moreover, that it is unhealthy to bottle up these impulses.

The advantages of speaking about important personal experiences and revealing our own feelings are many: We will be more original; we can say what we honestly think and believe; and we will be more highly motivated to communicate than if we depend entirely on other people's ideas. Our speaking will probably become warm, direct, spontaneous, and possibly more forceful; and our voices will reveal our enthusiasm for our ideas. This

---

[1] John F. Kennedy, *Profiles in Courage* (New York: Harper & Row, 1955), pp. 211–216.

movement toward openness should result in increased trust in ourselves and a more genuine sharing with listeners.

Reading   Constant, careful reading of contemporary material can foster potent ideas about current affairs, and all sorts of knowledge can be obtained through reading other works as well. Thomas A. Edison was a good example of an eclectic reader. More than just a purely original and spontaneously creative improvisor, Edison was a man who studied vast quantities of printed materials in science, astronomy, biology, mechanics, music, physics, and political economy in order to form a background of ideas.[2]

The effective speaker makes a practice of reading the daily newspapers, which report late developments in almost every field of thought and provide editorials written by prominent writers in the contemporary scene. Magazines offer a more extensive review of current affairs, and books provide even more detailed analyses of subjects. Almost all of the reading we do will contribute essential source materials for speech topics, both those imposed upon us and those we select.

Listening   Daniel Webster once said that by listening to intelligent men he had learned more than from reading books. We can follow his lead, keeping in mind that educated men don't have a corner on ideas, and listen to people in all walks of life and in every kind of situation and circumstance — conventions, coffee conversations, workshops, institutes, church meetings, workbench confabs.

Listening to radio and television broadcasts of news, debates, and discussions will likewise stimulate thought and keep us informed on subjects of current interest. What are politicians, military personnel, and scientists discussing about war, peace, food, clothing, and foreign policy? Do we agree with their views?

It has been said that nothing interests people more than themselves and their problems, and ways to deal with them. Some speakers feel that we can become brilliant conversationalists if we communicate with people about problems that concern them. The subjects that ordinary people want and need to discuss are fairly reliable indications of current social and educational problems; the topics picked up from active listening will surely reflect these interests and give us an opportunity to discover our own feelings about many subjects.[3]

Some speakers tend to view speaking as one-way communication — a means by which *we* alone do the persuading to action. Even in speech classes, we are apt to think about giving messages rather than listening to them. We miss opportunities for taking issue with a previous speaker or for de-

---

[2] George S. Bryan, *Edison: The Man and His Work* (New York: Garden City Publishing Co., 1926), p. 281.

[3] See Eleanor Craig, *P.S. You're Not Listening* (New York: Richard Baron, 1972), pp. 47–48.

veloping some particular ideas in a speech that have aroused us to action. The secret of effective communication lies in its *interpersonal* treatment, an interchange of talk and listening in face-to-face situations. Bill Moyers, former Deputy Director of the Peace Corps, found this to be true when in the summer of 1970 he traveled 13,000 miles through America to listen to the good and the bad, and then published these illuminating comments into a nationwide bestseller, *Listening to America.*

The grapevine, which flourishes both positively and negatively, should not be ignored as a source for careful listening. What is it generating in your dormitory, club, society, home, or church? If we disagree with or distrust one of these rumors, we can do our listeners a service by choosing that story as a topic, learning the facts of the situation, and bringing this problem out in the open.

This source of ideas (what others say) is often lost to us to some degree because we do not listen actively. Why not? Possibly because:

1.   We think we already know the full implications of the idea.

2.   We find the message too difficult or too abstract to grasp.

3.   We look at the source and concentrate on what we see, rather than on what we hear.

4.   We are preoccupied with our own emotional problems.

5.   We are fearful lest the source convince us of the truth of a situation we don't want to admit.

6.   We dislike to transfer a leadership role of speaking to a subordinate's role of listening.

7.   We are impatient with the speaker's slowness in making his point.

8.   We are preoccupied with our own work.

9.   We tend to be more interested in ourselves than in other people.

10.   We dislike the other person.

Wendell Johnson adds the warning that a Mr. A talking to a Mr. B is a deceptively simple act, which we take for granted to a tragic degree. He brands us a noisy lot who should spend much more time listening to unheeded words.[4]

How can we listen more productively for key ideas in order to obtain topics for speeches? There are some definite steps we can take:

1.   Try to develop a positive attitude about listening.

2.   Make an effort to be open-minded.

3.   Ask questions.

---

[4] Wendell Johnson, "The Fateful Process of Mr. A Talking to Mr. B," *Harvard Business Review*, Vol. 31 (January–February 1953), p. 50.

4. Use words such as "I see," "uh-huh," and "that's interesting" to encourage added ideas.

5. For clarification, restate ideas not understood.

According to Nichols and Lewis,[5] we must do more than just absorb the literal content in various ways:

1. Try to anticipate what someone will say by asking yourself: "What is the person attempting to say?" (Every time you guess correctly the retention of the point is reinforced.)

2. Try to identify and determine how points are supported. It helps if you ask yourself: "What are his major points?" "Are they fairly and reasonably supported with illustrations and facts?" Think more about the principles than just the facts, for too much attention paid to facts may cause you to lose the idea behind them.

3. Attempt to review each point covered as these ideas are brought to a close.

4. Try to listen between the lines—this means listening for hidden feelings and trying to figure out what an apparently simple remark really means. It also means (a) getting in touch with the other person's connotations, or feelings associated with words, (b) sensing his prejudices and his frames of references and, (c) responding to his nonverbal communication (the way he uses his eyes, his voice, his gestures, his mannerisms, and what he does not say). These signals are without doubt as important as, if not more important than, the thought expressed.

As important as guidelines for listening are for the speaker who is looking for a subject upon which to speak, they are vital for the person who is hearing a message to which he knows he must reply—listening and "getting it straight" are the first prerequisites for the communicator whose own message is both called up and structured by the preceding oral message.

Observing   The late E. C. Uihlein, executive and philanthropist, disciplined himself particularly in the power of observation. To develop the same skill in his sons, he would ask them after each visit to a new building to write a 5,000-word essay on what they had seen. They became so skilled in observation that they could visit a building or an event and notice hundreds of details, dimensions, arrangements, and elements that most people would overlook. Obviously, the capacity to observe varies with the individual; but since it can in general contribute to clearer impressions, we can keep it in mind as a readily available source of ideas.

In our concern with human problems, we will be better informed speakers if we go look at existing conditions before talking about them. In adding

---

[5] See Ralph Nichols and Thomas Lewis, *Listening and Speaking* (Dubuque, Iowa: Wm. C. Brown Co., 1963), pp. 60–65.

to our knowledge, firsthand observations will provide or strengthen our personal convictions, perhaps to the point of our working to correct certain social evils.

We can begin by attending political rallies on our campus, lectures, student demonstrations; by visiting jails, substandard living areas, various governmental agencies, council meetings; by paying attention to what people do, how they react to lectures, films, and social events. In all probability these observations of people functioning in their various worlds will provoke strong feelings and personal convictions, and they will immensely facilitate our locating and adapting subjects for speaking.

Personal experiences, reading, listening, and observing all provide a rich storehouse of raw materials, a background from which we can formulate and identify the things that interest us and our listeners most. This basis, however, is only preparation — the first stage in the systematic responding to or selecting of a topic.

Incubation of Ideas

After you have tentatively chosen a subject, or decided upon the nature of your response to an exigence, there will be a period during which one idea will seem better than any other; then another will seem more important than the first, or unexpected developments will produce a third topic. It will thus be difficult to decide which one topic or approach is the best. Creative effort will be slow, laborious; you will have to suspend judgment, consider other possibilities, and weigh the relative merits of each topic or approach until one seems to come to the fore and stand out above the others because you feel it is more important or your listeners will find it more interesting or there is more material available on it to verify your own judgments. Whatever idea you finally decide to speak about, your speech will be more successful when your choice has resulted from a period of *incubation* — that is, a warming up to your ideas.

Inspiration of Ideas

While preparation (personal experiences, reading, listening, and observing) and incubation *may* lead directly to your final choice of topic, or your final response to an exigence, frequently they serve to generate additional ideas, sometimes even unrelated to the original tentative choice.[6] As your imaginative activity continues, relate your thoughts to the kind of speaking assignment you are to undertake, avoiding fixed ideas and emotional patterns, for flux is what encourages inspirational activity.

As in the incubation stage, there may be a period of indecision during which one topic briefly seems better than another. Creative effort is slow

---

[6] Osborn defined such association of unrelated ideas as "imagination." See Alex F. Osborn, *Applied Imagination* (New York: Charles Scribner's Sons, 1957), p. 110.

and laborious. It may be helpful now to vary your scene of work or activity — socialize with people or seek some form of recreation or entertainment.[7]

If you are fortunate, an idea may suddenly occur as you are driving your car, talking with others, or walking down the street. Sometimes, inspiration comes as a result of preparation; sometimes, for seemingly no reason at all; but in any case a topic has suggested itself, and before it escapes you, set it down on paper. Your inspiration or idea, however, is still only in a tentative stage, not the final one. An inspired choice of topic left alone will not always make for a successful speech.

Evaluation of the Topic or the Proposed Response

From the Receiver's Perspective   Studies have indicated that, while we may have the best intentions, we may still be inaccurate in evaluating people's interests; speakers often fail to satisfy their listeners. The reason seems to be that groups differ in their interests. For example, one group rated, in order of preference, water pollution, auto safety legislation, and keeping America beautiful; while a similar group indicated, in order of preference, rolling back food prices, cutting the income tax, and increased retirement benefits. For the communicator who has a relatively free choice of subject, the Problem Census is one answer to this predicament, according to Professor Lawrence Borosage of Michigan State University. He suggests that the *real* problems and concerns of a particular group can be ascertained. The following are some of the steps he uses in the Problem Census:

1.   Pass out blank pieces of paper or cards to your group.
2.   Ask each person to write a list of his or her major problems.
3.   Emphasize that names do not need to be signed on the cards.
4.   Collect the cards to make a listing on the blackboard or to use for your own personal analysis.
5.   Note, in order of preference, which problems are of most concern to the group; and perhaps you will find that your original choice is high on this list, needs modification, or should be discarded in favor of another problem you had considered.

We will often speak to highly critical listeners who will become apathetic and bored if we fail to consider their interests. To ignore the receiver when we are conducting our pretopic selection evaluation may even invite failure; and as a result, our next speech may cause us increased apprehension. However, the sure-fire topic that survives such evaluation can help us attain success, a strong feeling of commitment, and added self-confidence.

---

[7] Keith R. St. Onge, *Creative Speech* (Belmont, Calif: Wadsworth Publishing Co., 1964), p. 32.

From the Source's Perspective If you have doubts about your topic, if you're wondering whether your proposed response is the right one, you can first examine your own attitudes toward the subject:

1. Am I really concerned about this subject?

2. Am I qualified to talk on this subject?

3. Do I have an original contribution to make, or will it be a rehash of someone else's speech, article, or editorial?

4. Is the subject timely, or is it old and tired?

5. Will I offend my listeners by talking on this subject? (Sometimes circumstances may compel us to speak on an unpopular topic; see Chapter 7 on the use of suggestion with a hostile audience).

6. Does my response or choice of topic reflect the concerns I have for my listeners and the behavioral changes I expect from them?

Then, if you feel satisfied in this regard, you can be fairly certain you have an excellent starting point. If you have used the systematic stages of preparation, incubation, inspiration, and evaluation, you will have chosen a topic or decided upon a response through careful thought and study. You can now proceed with conviction and with some assurance that the topic is worth all the effort you've put into it.

There remains now the matter of deciding how much you will say and what your specific purposes will be.

Suggested Subjects for Speeches

Personal Experiences

1. *Summer job*
2. *Ecology and you*
3. *Building a tool shed*
4. *Problems on school playgrounds*
5. *School admission tests*
6. *What physical fitness means*
7. *Why self-assertion is important*
8. *Changing habits*
9. *Overcoming bad manners*
10. *Borrowing money*
11. *The American student abroad*
12. *Living on natural foods*
13. *Bicycling cross-country*
14. *Working with autistic children*
15. *A religious experience*
16. *Backpacking*
17. *Making a TV appearance*
18. *Men as elementary schoolteachers*
19. *Coed dormitory living*
20. *Leaving home*
21. *Postponing college*
22. *Making dropping out pay*
23. *Living in a commune*
24. *Learning through a mistake*
25. *Teaching kids to swim*

Narrowing the Subject

Most subjects must be narrowed to a limited area of thought to fit into the time allotted and to conform to the attention span and the listening abilities of our receivers. This is true whether we are originating a message or responding to an exigence. Generally speaking, to do justice to a subject that covers a broad field — property taxes, education, defense expenditures, air pollution, wire tapping, honesty in government, energy resources — would require more time than a single speaking session permits.

The contrast between a broad and a restricted topic is illustrated by the methods of students A and B giving hypothetical eight-minute speeches on "space exploration." In the first case, student A thoughtlessly assumes that such a speech can embrace the whole field or a large part of it. Therefore, he reviews the familiar details of recent space history, including Sputnik, the competition in space exploration between the United States and the USSR, and types of space vehicles that have been developed. The chances are good that his speech will meet with apathy and boredom, and student A will feel a sense of failure. Why so? Because he cut too wide a swath to accomplish anything beyond scratching the surface of his topic.

Student B, a more experienced speaker, does not plunge into the process of communicating but assumes responsibility for choosing a worthwhile topic. Realizing that a "once over lightly" treatment would have little value for his group, he senses the importance of carefully breaking the subject

The Home, Family, and Health

1.	*Family round table*	14.	*Fencing out the neighbor*
2.	*Our senior citizens*	15.	*Values of praise*
3.	*Marriage by contract*	16.	*Budget your time*
4.	*Family therapy*	17.	*Vitamin C and the common cold*
5.	*Abortion*	18.	*Marijuana*
6.	*Divorce*	19.	*Smoking and health*
7.	*Family arguments*	20.	*Alcohol and health*
8.	*The family pet*	21.	*Food and health*
9.	*Planning a career*	22.	*Birth control*
10.	*Hydroponic gardening*	23.	*The family doctor*
11.	*The market places*	24.	*Designing a house for a handicapped person*
12.	*Avoiding accidents in the home*		
13.	*Recreation at home*	25.	*Privacy*

"space exploration" down into a number of possible areas, choosing the one of greatest interest and use to his listeners and himself, and proceeding to present a detailed treatment of it. To illustrate, he might restrict his speech to an explanation of the physical conditioning of astronauts.

Groups can also be surveyed in advance to determine their preferences in topic focus. Prior to the presentation, officers of a business organization were asked to "please indicate the area of communication you would like the speaker to focus on." The results gave priority to (1) how to discipline employees, (2) how to communicate changes in policies, (3) how to listen, (4) how to overcome communication barriers, and (5) how to interview effectively.

The speaker who uses a narrowed focus will have a much better opportunity to kindle thought and interest during the time allotted him. By dealing with a central idea, his speech can be shaped into a meaningful pattern of thought and serve as a valuable experience to listeners.

The restricted topic also gives a speaker adequate opportunity to keep his message "on the beam." It acts as a safeguard against the tendency to digress, to be vague, or to speak without a purpose. Suppose, for purposes of clarification, we set forth these possibilities for the narrowing down of subjects:

General	Narrowed	Narrowed Further
Cost of living	Food prices	Planning your purchase
Poverty	Slums	Providing jobs for unemployed
Health	Hospitals	Training of nurses

Suggested Subjects (cont'd)

Education, Culture, and Athletics

1. Busing students
2. Elective schooling
3. The local art museum
4. Speed reading
5. Graduate work
6. The honor system
7. Vocational training
8. Academic freedom
9. Funding private schools
10. Educating the handicapped
11. School dropouts
12. Religion in schools
13. The alternative school
14. Improving motion pictures
15. The little theatre
16. News broadcasting
17. Jazz
18. Building a music library
19. Handcrafts
20. The demise of manners
21. The creative approach
22. Television and terrorism
23. Black history
24. Improving athletics
25. The professional athlete

Each of these subjects could be narrowed still further; on the general subject of poverty, for instance, you could relate your talk to your particular city.

Knowing why you want to speak on one aspect of a general subject rather than another is an important part of the narrowing process. For this undertaking, you need to determine your purposes, both general and specific. In the majority of cases, the specific purpose will be determined by the events or the occasion out of which your speech arises.

The General Purpose

While it is difficult to classify speeches as purely informative, advocative, or entertaining in nature, talks in these categories have somewhat different general purposes. For example, a person who gives a talk about poisonous snakes normally intends to present facts or explain the situation without advocacy; a citizen who wants to provoke action for impending legislation speaks to advocate; while at an annual banquet the after-dinner speaker strives to entertain his audience.

Any speech can be a combination of these three general types, and this often occurs. In classroom speech assignments, however, the instructor frequently requires a speech aimed at one general purpose or another in order to emphasize particular rhetorical principles and techniques.

Knowing the general purpose of your speech should give you a clue to the nature of the materials of speaking you will need. Briefly, if you chose to inform your class about urban noises, you would need to construct an explanatory treatment of the causes, extent, and types of such noises. If you

---

Economic Conditions

1. *The economy bargain basement*
2. *Starting a small business*
3. *The flight to the suburbs*
4. *Guaranteed annual wage*
5. *Paid vacations*
6. *Job training*
7. *Urban renewal*
8. *Relocating workers*
9. *No-fault car insurance*
10. *Rebuilding old houses*
11. *Airports of tomorrow*
12. *Electric cars*
13. *Mass transportation*
14. *Investing in the stock market*
15. *City planning*
16. *Government subsidies*
17. *Advertising*
18. *Moonlighting*
19. *Unemployment compensation*
20. *The small car market*
21. *Shorter work week*
22. *Women's liberation*
23. *The energy crisis*
24. *Inflation*
25. *Making passenger trains pay*

wish to advocate doing away with excess urban noises, you would need to develop materials that would justify your viewpoint. Lastly, if you wish to entertain, you could develop a topic called "Up Your Decibels," which would be a funny commentary on city noises. The various speech types will be explained in much more detail in Chapters 15, 16, and 17; and the various materials of speaking have been described in Chapters 5, 6, and 7.

The Specific Purpose — The Purpose Sentence

Once the general purpose has been determined, you are ready to choose a specific point of view and a definite goal or purpose. Unless the listeners have confidence in the value of your purpose, apathy and negative feelings can arise. Many speakers overlook this point in the preparation of a talk and end up presenting messages having no aim whatsoever; they are just a statement of facts and events. Effective speakers clearly state their objectives to their listeners not once but at periodic intervals. Listeners who are made aware of goals and given reasons for doing something are more likely to learn quickly or alter their behavior in the direction the persuader wishes.[8]

Your message needs a goal statement to clarify your purpose for speaking. If you bring all the resources now at your disposal to bear on this goal, the message has a chance of getting through. There are speakers who excite listeners, but when the end of the message comes, the listeners are asking "What did he say?" or "What does he want us to do?" Though this "com-

---

[8] For exceptions to this general conclusion, see Chapters 4 and 7.

Suggested Subjects (cont'd)

Social, Political, and Scientific Problems

1. Racism	14. Need for prison reform
2. Pesticides	15. A free press
3. Unidentified flying objects	16. Breakdowns in justice
4. The inner city	17. Radioactive fallout
5. Victimless crimes	18. De facto segregation
6. Police control	19. Wiretapping
7. Reducing red tape	20. Obtaining weather data
8. Progress in civil rights	21. New sources for water
9. Restructuring political campaigning	22. Black power
10. Criminal behavior	23. The Mexican-American
11. Acupuncture	24. The American Indian
12. Deep sea exploration	25. Honesty in government
13. Improving local government	

munication strategy"[9] of clarifying your purpose seems simple and easy, it involves consideration of various factors and depends upon a careful analysis of both the occasion and the audience as described in Chapters 3 and 4.

Let us ask ourselves these questions in focusing upon a specific purpose:

1. What is the point of my message?
2. Why do I want to talk about this point?
3. Whom does this goal concern?
4. Can my listener(s) understand my purpose?
5. Can they be led to accept it?

To apply the guidelines for pinning down the specific purpose, let us evaluate the following statement, which could possibly be the basis of the specific purpose of some speech.

> In the time allotted me, I intend to refer to numerous exciting implications relative to our past and future plans in interplanetary travel and space exploration.

Such an unwieldy statement would, of course, be difficult for the speaker to state and for the listener to comprehend. Just as important is that it may be virtually meaningless to the speaker himself as he prepares his message! A

---

[9] See Theodore Clevenger, Jr., *Audience Analysis* (Indianapolis: Bobbs-Merrill Co., 1966), pp. 24–25.

International Problems

1. *Food shortage in Asia*
2. *The foreign car threat*
3. *The Common Market*
4. *NATO*
5. *Oil in the Middle East*
6. *Shipping surpluses abroad*
7. *Cultural exchanges*
8. *The Peace Corps*
9. *Sharing scientific knowledge*
10. *Peace in our time*
11. *Improving international goodwill*
12. *Latin-American aid*
13. *Helping satellite countries*
14. *The United Nations*
15. *Immigration control*
16. *The new Africa*
17. *Cuba today*
18. *Red China today*
19. *International control of nuclear weapons*
20. *Population growth*
21. *Spy rings*
22. *Potential outer space agreements*
23. *The future of Israel*
24. *Oil supplies in the Middle East*
25. *Brotherhood in practice*

good purpose sentence should (1) be phrased as a declarative sentence; (2) state the purpose of the message in specific, concrete terms, free from ambiguities; and (3) be as concise as possible, yet include the major divisions of the speech.

To illustrate how a specific purpose may be chosen and stated according to these three principles, let us take the unwieldy statement concerning space travel and rework it into a specific *purpose sentence*. For the speech to inform, we might say:

> This talk will discuss U. S. plans for interplanetary exploration during the next fifty years.

For a speech of advocacy, the purpose sentence might read:

> The admittedly high cost of U. S. plans for interplanetary exploration is fully justified.

For a speech of entertainment, we might phrase it this way:

> Earth monsters will meet space monsters as the U. S. moves into interplanetary exploration.

To be effective, specific purposes can be stated and presented in various ways depending upon circumstances. Note these methods:

1. You can concentrate your efforts on a clear-cut declaration of intent by announcing your specific purpose after you have finished your introductory remarks. This procedure is necessary when the material is complex, and it can be effective when the purpose sentence is clarified by restatement as the speech progresses. (See the "Deductive Speech Plan" in Chapter 11.)

2. You may state the purpose sentence near the end of a message when you have presented sufficient detail to lead to the specific purpose as an inevitable conclusion. In many instances, such as speaking before hostile listeners, this procedure will be effective. The specific purpose can be made known by some such statement as this: "From the materials I have presented to you, it seems clear that we should plan interplanetary exploration." (See the "Inductive Speech Plan" in Chapter 11.)

3. You may refrain from stating your specific purpose, even though it has been formulated in your own mind. Use this method not as an evasive device but rather as a tactful way of dealing with a delicate matter that may easily cause offense or be misunderstood. Misunderstanding can occur in this case, but with careful organization, accurate language, and appropriate nonverbal communication, you can usually make known a specific purpose that is implied but not stated. (See the section on "Suggestion," Chapter 7. The relationship between the use and placement of the purpose sentence and the organization of the speech plan will be explained in detail in Chapter 11.)

In summary, the consideration of the subject for a speech you must make, or the choice of a subject for a speech you opt to make, is an important function in speech preparation. When the decision is a good one—the general aim and specific purpose clear in mind—your chances of obtaining the desired response should be much improved.

Perhaps some of the suggested subjects (see insets) may be useful to you; perhaps some of them will stimulate other topics of your own.

Suggested Assignments

1. Use brainstorming techniques in your home, dormitory, or class. Note how many ideas you obtained for the solution to a problem.

2. Survey your classmates concerning major problems they are facing. Use the results in determining future topics for your speeches.

3. Listen to the speeches delivered in your class; choose one you feel compelled to respond to. Prepare and deliver your response.

4. Perform the same exercise as in assignment 3 above, but make your response immediately, without preparation.

5. Select five general topics having current appeal. Narrow each down to a specific purpose sentence as was done in this chapter.

6. Find a topic of particular concern to people of your own major field of interest. From this topic, phrase purpose sentences for informative, advocative, and entertaining speeches.

7. List five local organizations and two possible topics you would recommend for a speech on a specific occasion to each of the organizations.

8. Assuming you are chairman of a program planning committee of a local organization, write a brief report relative to speakers you would select for specific occasions and the topics you would suggest in each instance.

9. Listen to two speakers who are visiting your campus or city. Are you moved to reply to their speeches? Prepare your responses for delivery in your speech-communication class or any other place you can find an audience.

Suggested References

Barker, Larry L., *Listening Behavior* (Englewood Cliffs, N. J.: Prentice-Hall, 1971). Chapter 5, "Improving Your Listening Behavior."

Bem, Daryl J., *Beliefs, Attitudes, and Human Affairs* (Belmont, Calif.: Wadsworth Publishing Co., 1970). Chapter 2, "The Cognitive Foundations of Beliefs."

Brown, D. W. F., *Putting Minds to Work* (New York: John Wiley & Sons, 1972). Chapter 5, "Concept Formation."

Johnson, David, *Reaching Out* (Englewood Cliffs, N. J.: Prentice-Hall, 1972). Chapter 2, "Self-Disclosure."

Kendall, H. B., and Charles Stewart (eds.), *On Speech and Speakers* (New York: Holt, Rinehart and Winston, 1968). Part 4, "Do We Know How to Listen?" by Ralph G. Nichols.

Osborn, Alex F., *Applied Imagination,* Rev. ed. (New York: Charles Scribner's Sons, 1963). Chapter 5, "Ways by Which Creativity Can Be Developed."

St. Onge, Keith R., *Creative Speech* (Belmont, Calif.: Wadsworth Publishing Co., 1964). Chapter 1, "Ideas in Theory."

Shrope, W. A., *Experiences in Communication* (New York: Harcourt Brace Jovanovich, 1974). Chapter 2, "Communicating Yourself."

Thompson, Wayne N., *Quantitative Research in Public Address and Communication* (New York: Random House, 1967). Chapter 6, "The Teaching of Public Speaking."

Thonssen, Lester, and William Finkel, *Ideas That Matter: A Source Book for Speakers* (New York, Ronald Press Co., 1961). Appendix A, "Guide to Major Ideas in the Selections."

9
Collecting Materials

"But where can I find some materials?"

When Daniel Webster was asked how long it took him to prepare his remarks on one occasion, he said that he had been collecting ideas for those remarks for a period of forty years. Obviously, the best way to gather materials for effective speaking is to follow the example of those who devote a substantial part of their lives in preparing and delivering messages— political leaders, ministers, business leaders, and teachers. These men and women are constantly collecting materials for speaking, because they have conditioned themselves to think of every idea they hear, every fact they encounter, every principle they develop as possibly useful stuff for some future message—and they often discipline themselves to record these materials in a systematic manner.

William Henry David (Alfalfa Bill) Murray, a pioneer leader in the development of the State of Oklahoma and that state's governor during the early 1930s, reported that his method of speech preparation was to read and think about many subjects, whether or not he ever intended to use them in speeches. Murray developed the ability to construct an entire two-hour speech in his mind without making or preparing any notes. Because he viewed everything that crossed his mind as potential speech material, in ten minutes he could "think up" a two-hour speech.[1]

Needless to say, Governor Murray's method would be beyond the great majority of us who do not possess his fantastic memory; but we too are surrounded by a vast storehouse of materials, and it is essential that we make intelligent choices from these materials and use them to good effect in preparing our messages.

A note of caution is in order: As we discuss the various sources of materials for speeches, we must realize that our listeners want to hear *us* speak

---

[1] Interview with former Governor Murray, Tishomingo, Oklahoma, July 14, 1952. Reported in "The Public Speaking of William H. (Alfalfa Bill) Murray," by David C. Ralph, unpublished Ph.D. thesis, Northwestern University, 1953, p. 453.

and learn how *we* handle the topic which has chosen us. They are not interested in our rehashing ideas of others from a magazine article but in our collecting relevant, suitable, and timely materials that will develop *our* particular and unique ideas. This means that we must concentrate upon these resources within our reach: (1) observation and personal experiences, (2) interviewing, (3) correspondence and questionnaires, (4) the telephone, (5) general reading, and (6) libraries and other collection agencies.

Observation and Personal Experiences

Observation—the apprehension of relationships between ourselves and the physical objects that surround us—can give us intense personal ideas and feelings for use in speeches. People tend to accept the word of the man who claims, "I saw it." His having experienced something personally lends to his statements a credibility that may not be produced by other forms of support. Dr. Albert Schweitzer, acclaimed as one of the leading figures of this century, said that one of the greatest mistakes people make is to go through life with closed eyes, not noticing opportunities to observe both little and big things. Such scrutiny includes taking notice of colors, sounds, smells, activity, details of the surroundings—which, when skillfully reported, help the listener to relive our experience.

The value of observing cannot be overstressed. Suppose, for example, a river has flooded a large region. We will find many investigators, including perhaps the President of the United States himself, visiting and observing the extent of damage. On-the-spot observation is a basic principle behind the format of television news coverage: the anchor man switches to the scene of the news, where it can be viewed and described firsthand. By the same principle, when we want to speak on a phase of institutional change, we offer some clear and convincing testimony after observing a particular institution that surely needs repair or improvement.

Observation, however, is a two-edged sword. It can be a very partial, personal activity, and it can also be far from accurate—in both viewing and reporting aspects. If you ask five persons to describe in detail an unusual event of which they have been eyewitnesses, you will probably receive five quite different accounts. Even a trained or experienced observer is less accurate than a wide-range camera in reporting the chain of events of some happening. Furthermore, trained observers who are deeply involved in what they view can give vastly different interpretations from those of an observer who remains detached and uninvolved.

Still another factor inherent in observation is the effect of the observer's presence. For example, when parents visit school classrooms, they can hardly expect to observe normal behavior of the children (or even of the teacher). A primary concern, then, in making an observation, is to remain as inconspicuous as possible.

It is easy in communicating to offer snap judgments and first impressions about people and events. In observing, a reliable principle to follow is to check our interpretations by further observations.

Guidelines for Successful Observing

1. Strive to be as unobtrusive as possible.

2. While observing, jot down notes as clearly and coherently as you can to reduce faulty recall.

3. Check your impressions with by-standers who see the same event.

4. Compare your impressions with news reports (newspapers, radio, television) regarding the event.

5. Attempt to remain emotionally detached as you observe.

6. Note actions that indicate what seems to occur within people, rather than merely observing their more obvious behavior.

7. Report these personal observations with utmost concern for accuracy, thereby tending to avoid exaggeration, excessive dramatization, or other incorrect reporting.

Interviewing

One of the oldest and perhaps most fruitful means of securing information is the interview. The best-known form of interviewing on today's scene is probably the pre-election political poll or survey of attitudes toward aspiring candidates for high office. In addition, interviews are successfully used in industrial, educational, and other fields.

The interview is a more effective way of collecting materials than is observation because it gives the person an opportunity (1) to see and to discuss with people what has occurred, (2) to question people about their reactions to an event, (3) to talk with more than one person and, by comparing viewpoints, perhaps arrive at a more realistic impression, (4) to seek clarification if there is confusion and to obtain amplification when there is insufficient information, and (5) to state openly that he has talked with experts, to say, "Here's what X and Y told me, and I agree"; by so doing, he is more likely to be considered credible and a valuable source of information.

While there are many advantages to the interview, some suggestions for avoiding trouble are needed. In our haste to select data, we must avoid choosing only those that fit our viewpoints while neglecting to probe into contrary data. The good interviewer has no fear of truth and should carefully note various pitfalls he might encounter during this process, such as: (1) On matters of age, religion, and income, inaccuracies may be reported. For example, people have a tendency to round off their ages, especially as they grow older; the census shows many more people who report their age as 50, 55, and 60 than there are people who admit to 52, 53, and 63. (2) An unfriendly tone of voice or the use of effusive language by the interviewer can cause resentment and evasiveness in the replies. (3) If an interviewer gives his own opinion, responses can be influenced by it. (4) Respondents give incomplete answers when insufficient time has been allowed for their reply. (5) Overly friendly interviewers may cause the respondent to withhold his true feelings in order to maintain a cordial relationship. (6) The interviewer's status may persuade respondents to modify their views. (7) No competent interviewer attempts to trap people. To avoid suspicion, encourage trust and willingness to impart frank information by using a low-key approach and noncommital transitions as does Elizabeth Drew, Washington editor of the *Atlantic Magazine,* who interviews many of our leading government officials on the Public Broadcasting Network.

Guidelines for Good Interviewing

1. *Use an interview guide that affords you a space for an answer after each question.*

2. *Be sure the question is worth asking; know what you want to achieve.*

3. *Ask such probing questions as are needed to clarify intent or meaning. ("Why is that?" "Why do you feel this way?")*

4. *Avoid asking questions that are too personal in nature.*

5. *Rephrase a question in different words if the meaning isn't understood.*

6. *Have an attitude and use a tone of voice that will encourage an informal atmosphere.*

7. *Avoid suggesting answers to questions; however, try to reflect what is said—"So you feel you're not getting paid enough?"*

8. *Refrain from giving your own opinions or disagreeing during question periods; rather, say "Uh-huh," "I see," or "That's interesting."*

9. *Phrase your questions so that a yes or no is possible; but provide for other likely replies in order to obtain understanding.*

10. *To obtain added information, use follow-up questions after the answers.*

You probably can anticipate some apprehension or suspicion regarding your motives for wanting information, particularly on delicate matters. Other barriers may arise unexpectedly during the face-to-face meeting. Thus it is a good idea to take these precautions:

1. *Call the person concerned for an appointment. Tell him who you are and why you are seeking information.*

2. *Be on time. Promptness indicates courtesy and respect.*

With these general suggestions for interviewing in mind, let us consider some applications to our speech topics. Obviously, the best way to obtain information is to interview people who are directly involved with our subjects. A message on the plight of American Indians may be incomplete without the opinions of both Indians and government officials concerned with Indian affairs. A speech on conditions in nursing homes would be more illuminating if we were to report the opinions of patients as well as staff members.

The "patterned interview" is a helpful device to insure that, through the use of a checklist, we don't forget essential questions. Although some people believe that preplanned questions hamper the free flow of ideas, planning certain questions will keep the interview from bogging down in repetition, vagueness, and digression. The interviewer should test his questions beforehand to make sure they make sense and to elicit only productive answers that will contribute to accuracy. For example, the question "How many TV shows do you watch?" may be answered without much preciseness. But if the question is rephrased as "Will you tell me the names of all the TV shows you view?" the answer in respect to the number of TV shows should be more specific.

---

3. Ask permission if you wish to tape-record the interview.

4. Attempt to converse in a private place, away from interruptions by people and telephones.

5. Offer to keep his or her views anonymous if that is desired.

6. Treat your interviewee as an equal (don't talk down to her).

7. Be a patient, friendly, and uninterrupting listener, and show interest in the ideas expressed.

8. Allow enough time. Too often, important points are missed when ideas are cut short.

9. Avoid argument and advice, and delay judgments until you have received sufficient information from the interviews.

10. Determine whether there are any elements of self-interest that might

color the replies or make them less objective.

11. Realize that vocal inflections may be clues as vital as the views expressed.

12. Read between the lines to get the full meaning, but don't read into answers meanings that aren't really there.

13. Take note of what is not said (this in itself may be revealing).

14. Discuss the person's attitude and why he takes the position he does.

15. Seek to determine the validity of the person's statements by learning the sources of his views.

16. Encourage the person to discuss the situation as he sees it. Let him do most of the talking.

17. Request permission to quote or use the name of the interviewee.

18. Express thanks for the interview.

Should we take notes during the interview? Because we can remember only a small part of what we hear, it is unquestionably better to write notes than to trust to memory. Naturally, we should jot our notes down as carefully as possible. In some cases it will be possible to record the entire interview on tape, if we can get the necessary apparatus and if the person interviewed will permit it. Tape-recorded interviews have several advantages; we can be certain of complete accuracy in quoting; we can have a more conversational interview because there's no note-taking; and we can play portions of the tape during our talk.

Planning and conducting interviews is a challenging task, and no simple formula can make it easy. The value of the information obtained during the interview depends, to a considerable extent, upon the way in which we plan and ask our questions, upon the confidence, informality, frankness, and respect developed during the interview, and upon our interpretation of the information received.

Correspondence and Questionnaires

If you find it difficult to conduct a personal interview, you may be able to get the information you want through correspondence. Even though you must sacrifice the personal insight that face-to-face interviewing allows, you can still obtain a great deal of information from letters and questionnaires. The principal advantage of writing is that it saves the interviewer's time and allows the respondent to complete the questionnaire or answer the letter at his own convenience.

However, there are disadvantages in written instruments as fact-finding tools. First, people often dislike taking the time to provide the requested information. Second, the answers to various questions may not yield the exact kind of information we are seeking. Third, the answers may be careless, incomplete, or hard to interpret.

Nevertheless, there are many ways of making written inquiries worthy of attracting useful responses. In our correspondence, a statement of the reason for our request and some form of personal appeal informally written will usually motivate a personal response. Short sentences and paragraphs are read more easily and are less likely to be ignored than long ones. Questions should be but few in number, brief, and to the point; numbering them sometimes helps to avoid confusion and repetition. Requests for information should be addressed to a specific person by name, and not to an "occupant," senator, or chairman; a stamped, self-addressed envelope should be included for replies, and mail should be sent first class.

If we want to obtain raw data that will provide our listeners with percentages of *yes* and *no* responses (as in the case of the sampling of public opinion by the Gallup Poll), we will formulate a simple questionnaire for our respondents. If we tell them that they need not sign the questionnaires, we can expect frank replies—an up-to-the-moment indication of how some people feel about our problem.

Guidelines for Good Questionnaires

1. Plan, in outline form, the information to be covered.

2. Arrange appropriate questions in logical order under each heading in the plan.

3. Plan as few questions as possible; lengthy surveys are likely to be disregarded.

4. Phrase the questions so clearly that they stand little chance of misinterpretation.

5. After each question, leave possibilities for more than <u>yes</u> or <u>no</u> answers. Label these possibilities. (In addition to <u>yes</u> and <u>no</u>, provide space for "seldom," "occasionally," and "frequently.")

6. Allow ample space at the end of the survey for the respondent to interject additional remarks.

7. Pretest your questions by conducting dry runs to determine any weaknesses.

While it is conceded that you ordinarily will not consider using written inquiries and surveys for classroom speeches because of the time they take, you might consider letters and/or a survey for your final speech; certainly, correspondence and questionnaires will be of great assistance in obtaining data for talks outside of the classroom.

Using the Telephone

The telephone is so basic to the giving and receiving of information that we are prone to take it for granted. However, if we think of it as a separate and special means of locating key people, we will usually be rewarded by getting information from those who are especially knowledgable and who might be difficult to contact otherwise. In some universities we will also find a "telephone dial access library" whereby certain valuable information on tape can be obtained. On occasion, information can be procured from Tele-lectures.[2]

---

[2] Tele-lecture apparatus can amplify telephone communication so that it can be heard by larger groups. By using this device, a speaker from a distant point can share his knowledge with listeners by telephone.

In spite of its values, however, telephone, tape communication, and/or Tele-lectures have some quite obvious disadvantages: (1) People cannot see each other—a communication barrier. (Some persons refuse to discuss business on the telephone because they can't see the face of the person at the other end and determine his reaction to what they say. While this is changing with the advent of televised telephone conversations, we still cannot secure the total responses to be found in face-to-face dialogue.) (2) Telephone inquiries and commentary, as such, may produce negative responses because they may be sought at inconvenient times. Despite such shortcomings, however, countless inquiries must be made by telephone because of its unquestionable convenience.

Before we use the telephone to seek information, we should (1) decide what we are going to ask, (2) write each question in brief form, and (3) leave ample room for jotting down answers.

Guidelines for Effective Telephone Interviewing

1.   Place the call yourself and identify yourself at once.

2.   If the person is not free to talk, leave your number or inquire when you may call again.

3.   Be ready to proceed when the person answers your call.

4.   Briefly give the purpose of your call.

5.   Try to convey an attractive image, using a pleasing tone of voice. (For more detailed information on voice quality, see Chapter 14 on "Delivery.")

6.   Avoid both abruptness and effusiveness. Be alert, distinct, and expressive.

7.   Show your alertness and interest by listening carefully so that repetition is unnecessary.

8.   Use simple language.

9.   Be natural and friendly as you speak.

10.   Thank your interviewee for his information and permit him to hang up first.

If your telephone interviewee finds it necessary to return your call, keep these additional tips in mind:

1.   Answer the telephone yourself if possible to avoid giving the caller the impression of the "Who's calling?" run-around.

2.   Identify yourself at once by saying, "John Jones speaking."

3.   Greet the caller pleasantly.

4.   Use the caller's name several times and try to visualize him as you converse.

5.   Avoid constant interruption of his train of thought.

6.   Review some of the details of the telephone call if necessary.

7.   Thank the person for returning your call and for his cooperation in your survey.

Reading

We can collect relevant materials by consulting published works as well as by observing, listening, interviewing, and telephoning.

In books and magazines we will find any number of facts and other evidence to support our statements; examples, stories, and illustrations to enhance our talk; and opinions and quotations to confirm our views. Effective speakers read as much as they can in many fields of thought: humanities, science, politics, education, and social sciences. They realize that a general background of worthwhile reading provides them with a personal and social perspective not to be had from any other source. All of the reading we do gives us some general information that will doubtless influence our speaking.

Guidelines for Effective Reading

1. Be a purposeful reader—look for magazines, books, and documents relating to your topic.

2. Examine the preface of a book to determine the author's purpose.

3. Skim the table of contents and index for relevant material.

4. Be alert for key ideas that are emphasized by major and subordinate headings.

5. Use various rates of speed as you read, depending upon the relevance of the material to your topic. When you find a pertinent idea, read it slowly

and carefully to try to comprehend the author's intent and meaning.

6. Note the most important words.

7. Try to determine the meaning of a sentence by observing how the words are used.

8. Refer to the dictionary when you don't understand a significant word.

9. Make special note of the important sentences. If you own the book, underline these thoughts.

10. Read the summary at the end of the chapter to see which ideas the author regards as important.

People have learned that information from the present as well as from the past has value for them. In gathering specific materials for your immediate speaking situation, you will do well to read some recent publications. These sources will keep you up to date on developments in the fields of your interest and the subjects of your talks. For example, a student speaker who always reads the morning newspaper while eating breakfast discovered that the headlines were concerned with the subject of the speech he was to give that day. He brought the paper to class and displayed the headlines with considerable timeliness as he delivered his talk.

It is worth remembering that, just as valued information can come from students, parents, workers, and other laymen we interview as well as from faculty, psychiatrists, supervisors, and other experts, so good ideas can come from little-known authors as well as from prominent ones. For example, a view expressed by a layman in a letter to the editor of a newspaper may offer some valid comments.

Guidelines for Selecting Reading Materials

1. Determine whether the author is qualified to make a valid comment. Does he have experience and knowledge about his subject?

2. Study the author to see whether you can determine that he is relatively free from prejudice.

3. Carefully analyze the supporting evidence and reasoning used.

4. Examine his written statements closely to determine whether there are any inconsistencies or fallacies.

5. Attempt to ascertain the solution an author offers to the problem.

Using the Library and Other Sources

Although libraries can be extensive in their arrangements and vary in their systems of classification, they have enough common characteristics to call attention to. Obviously, the sooner we familiarize ourselves with the resources available in our local library, the less time we will spend in merely looking around.

Locating Books

The *card catalog* is without question the most important source of information about books available in a library. In the catalog, books are listed under the author's name, the book's title, and the subject listing. In some instances the book we want may be assigned to a reference reading room or to a divisional library instead of the regular stacks.

It is essential, of course, that we locate relevant source materials for our investigation. For example, if our topic involves early settlements in the Midwest, we can study the writings of the period—diaries, memoirs, and the like. These *primary sources*, although they are subjective in nature, will yield much worthwhile information. Works published in later years that cite these original sources are known as *secondary sources;* their value lies in the disclosure of additional conclusions and broader perspectives.

Recent publications will furnish materials on contemporary issues — such as the increase in crime, changes in modern theology, jobs for the poor, urban renewal, and cleaning up the country's rivers and lakes. Since such current publications are often found in a reserved-reading shelf, looking here first could be the most fruitful course in our search for books related to a timely topic.

Suppose you are interested in biographical information. First, check the card catalog to determine the whereabouts of full-length biographies and other books written by or about the person concerned. If you need additional sources, most libraries have on reference shelves *Biography Index*, which is concerned with leaders in various walks of life; *Who's Who in America, Dictionary of American Biography, American Authors,* and other American biographies; *Who's Who* and *Dictionary of National Biography,* which contain information about persons in England and other countries.

Searching for Materials in Magazines

Periodicals must not be overlooked as valuable sources of materials. If we browse, we may find recent issues in racks or shelves in the main reading rooms. Bound editions of older copies are usually found in nearby stacks.

To locate materials on specific topics, we must, of course, refer to indexes. *Readers' Guide to Periodical Literature* will prove invaluable. Prominently displayed on a table in almost every library, this index, printed annually with semimonthly supplements, dates back to the turn of the century. Poole's *Index to Periodical Literature* may be consulted for articles from 1802 to 1906. Among other indexes are the *International Index to Periodicals,* which is particularly helpful for materials in the fields of science and humanities, *Agricultural Index, Public Affairs Information Service, Art Index, Education Index, Congressional Record indexes,* and *Song Index.* For one of the most complete sources covering a wide range of topics, there is *Ulrich's Periodical Directory.*

Collecting Materials from Newspapers

The newspaper is one of the chief sources of information concerning daily occurrences in international, national, state, and local affairs. News items include finance, education, entertainment, politics, war and peace, and a variety of other subjects. So far as indexes are concerned, the *New York Times Index* and the *London Times* are without doubt our best sources for news events on most conceivable topics. Unfortunately, most newspapers are not indexed; and if we are searching for material in them, we will have to look through many issues of the period.

Bound and unbound newspapers are ordinarily found in basement rooms of libraries, while current issues are normally displayed on racks in reading rooms. We must not overlook the possibility that our library may have microfilm collections of some leading newspapers as well as magazines and unpublished graduate theses.

Using Documents

Documents are original, written or printed items conveying information or evidence. Often to be found in personal or public files, they include historical papers, maps, newspaper clippings, certificates, letters, and countless other records and reports; and they constitute information that could be valuable for our speaking.

Special materials concerning a region or state can be found in local or state historical museums. Other materials may sometimes be obtained from private collections, as in, for example, the various departments of an educational institution.

Specialized leaflets on many topics are issued by the government and are available in libraries. These government documents are not entered in the card catalog, but rather are located in a separate index entitled *Monthly Catalog: United States Government Publications.* In using this publication, we should (1) look for specific topics (avoid looking for names of authors), (2) use cross references, (3) try to determine the approximate date of publication, and (4) ask the librarian for assistance if we can't locate the correct publication.

Special Collections

There are many publications of a different nature that will yield valuable categorial information, and many of them will be found in the reference shelves of our library. For material concerning population figures, athletic records, geographical statistics, and other such data, we will refer to the *World Almanac and Book of Facts, Information Please Almanac, Statesman's Yearbook, Statistical Abstract of the United States,* or *United States Census Reports.* For brief summaries of historical developments, physical phenomena, or fields of thought, we will turn to *Encyclopaedia Britannica, The Encyclopedia Americana, Columbia Encyclopedia,* or other standard encyclopedias. For a broad view or for pros and cons on many topics, we will refer to the *Reference Shelf* series, the *Debate Handbook* series, or the *Annals of the American Academy of Political and Social Science.* For materials on business topics, we may wish to examine a number of scholarly journals, popular magazines, and trade and professional journals; the obvious ones are *The Wall Street Journal, The New York Times,* and *Dun's Review.*

A wide variety of materials may be obtained by writing to private organizations such as insurance companies and radio and television stations for copies of proceedings, reports, bulletins, discussions, and speeches. We shall note in the chapter on audio-visual materials (Chapter 13) many other forms of materials that can be used to dramatize or illustrate ideas.

Recording Materials for Use

Whenever we find a noteworthy piece of evidence in the newspapers or magazines we read regularly, let us cultivate the habit of clipping it out, making sure we have written on the document the source, the date, and the page. For other findings, we can write this single item on a 3 × 5 or 4 × 6 card, using only one side of the card so that its wording can be seen and found easily when it is filed in a packet or filing box.

Obviously we should exercise extreme care when we record materials to avoid omission or addition of words or even taking material out of context. To be certain about the precise recording of factual statements or views, we should check the original material with our own copy.

Exact statements should be set within quotation marks. If any statement is too lengthy, it can be pared down by inserting three spaced periods to indicate the omitted portion; if the omission, which presumably will not destroy the original intent, occurs at the end of a sentence, four spaced periods are used. Should we wish to paraphrase (put the author's views in our own words), we should make every effort to avoid any distortion. We can put our own interpolations in brackets and indicate italicized words by underlining them.

At least four major items should ordinarily be recorded on a card: the *subject*, the *material*, the *author's name*, and the *publication data* (title, place, publisher, date of publication, and page numbers). Take a look at the sample cards.

Sample Quotation from a Book

How Details Are Interpreted

"One's perception, then, is obviously influenced by which aspects he abstracts from a given situation. There is, however, another factor which contributes to the phenomenon of differing perceptions. How one interprets what he abstracts is equally important."

William V. Haney, Communication Patterns and Incidents (Homewood, Illinois: Richard D. Irwin, Inc., 1960), p. 244.

Sample Quotation from a Magazine

Executive Interviewing

"More often than not, he deserts his desk entirely, and pilots you to a nook on the opposite side of the room. As you loll back on a couch, he draws up a chair and begins to talk to you from across a coffee table, and not necessarily, for the moment, about business at hand."

Robert Sheehan, "Business Manners," <u>Fortune</u>, Vol. 54., No. 1 (January 1957), p. 106.

In addition to preparing cards correctly for easy reference and filing, we should plan also to prepare a bibliography in which the materials are classified as books, magazines, documents, and newspapers. Books are recorded or set down in this way:

McBurney, James H., and Kenneth G. Hance, *Discussion in Human Affairs* (New York: Harper & Row, Inc., 1950).

A journal article is arranged like this:

Wiksell, Wesley, and Milton J. Wiksell, "Improving Clarity in Interpersonal Communication," *Adult Leadership*, Vol. 19, No. 8 (February 1971), pp. 252–254.

A newspaper article is set down in this way:

"Want to Keep Your Friends? Try Double Talk on Them," *The Milwaukee Journal*, February 16, 1970, The Green Sheet, p. 4.

A pamphlet is recorded in this manner:

Highway to Successful Committee Meeting, Chamber of Commerce of the United States (Washington, D. C., 1964).

To sum up: Useful materials can be collected from close observation and real experiences, careful interviewing procedures, correspondence and questionnaires, telephone procedures, and research in libraries and other places. The search, however, involves much more than the casual reception of ideas; rather, it demands the ability to weigh the relative value of available materials.

Suggested Assignments

1.   Conduct a brief survey of opinions among both students and faculty regarding some academic question such as the value of the lecture method of teaching. Compare the findings from these two groups.

2.   Write a brief report on the kinds of materials you collected for your most recent speech. Indicate where you found the materials and justify your selection of them.

3.   Ask a local speaker about the methods he uses in collecting materials for speeches.

4.   State ten sources of material for which you can claim at least a fair amount of reliability so far as a specific problem is concerned. Explain why the sources may be considered reliable.

5.   For your next talk collect various kinds of materials from libraries and other places mentioned in this chapter. Note the reactions among your listeners to these different materials.

6.   Listen to some speaker or conversationalist. Evaluate the kind of materials used to support ideas he or she asserted.

7.   Select listening and observing teams to witness some event. Discuss before the class in an unrehearsed panel what was heard and seen. Observe the different reactions stated by each member.

8.   Join with your class in a guided tour of the campus library. Following this tour exchange selected topics. For the topic you receive, indicate where you would look for materials. Then seek the combined thinking of the class to supplement your views.

9.   Investigate the kinds of materials used by some outstanding speaker by reading his speeches. Make note of these materials and make brief reports of them to your class.

Suggested References

Adler, Mortimer J., *How to Read a Book* (New York: Simon & Schuster, 1940).

Babcock, C. Merton (ed.), *Ideas in Process* (New York: Harper & Row, 1958). Part 5, "Seeing What Stares Us in the Face" by Wendell Johnson.

Barker, Larry L., and Gordon Wiseman, "A Model of Interpersonal Communication," *Journal of Communication*, Vol. 6 (September 1966), p. 173.

Freeley, Austin J., *Argumentation and Debate: Rational Decision Making*, 3rd ed. (Belmont, Calif.: Wadsworth Publishing Co., 1971). Chapter 5, "Exploring the Problem."

Haselerud, G. M., *Transfer, Memory, and Creativity* (Minneapolis: University of Minnesota Press, 1972). Chapter 4, "Retrieval."

Logan, L., V. G. Logan, and Leona Paterson, *Creative Communication* (New York: McGraw-Hill Book Co., 1972). Chapter 3, "Perceptive Listening."

McLaughlin, Ted J., Lawrence Blum, and David M. Robinson, *Communication* (Columbus, Ohio: Charles E. Merrill, 1964). Chapter 14, "Gathering Information for Management Reports."

Miller, Melvin, "When Found, Make a Note of," *Today's Speech,* Vol. 10 (September 1962), pp. 10–11.

Moyers, Bill, *Listening to America* (New York: Dell Publishing Co., 1971).

Stevens, John O., *Awareness: Exploring, Experimenting, Experiencing* (Moab, Utah: Real People Press, 1971). Chapter 1, "Awareness."

Tandberg, Gerilyn, *Research Guide in Speech* (Morristown, N. J.: General Learning Press, 1974). Part 2, "Annotated Listing of Basic References."

Wiksell, Wesley A., and Milton J. Wiksell, "Evaluating Programs," *The Speech Teacher,* Vol. 18 (January 1969), pp. 68–71.

10
Outlining for Speaking

"The major and minor points in bold relief"

Some students take to outlining enthusiastically for the succinctness, clarity, and orderliness that it entails. Others—from their first introduction in elementary school—exhibit a vagueness about the process that raises a number of questions particularly important in composing talks and speeches. What is an outline? What is its relationship to the complete composition? What are the purposes of outlines? What kinds of outlines are there? What distinguishes a good outline from a poor one?

Let us consider these questions in turn.

The Nature of the Outline

The outline presents a series of ideas or topics in abbreviated form, a form usually characterized by symbols, indentations, and schematic relationships. It represents ideas that the speaker will later expand into a complete presentation or ideas that have already appeared in complete form. In short: *An outline's major value lies in its format, which distinguishes major and minor points by structural methods.*

The following are typical structural divisions of an outline:

```
        I.                  I.
        II.        or       A.
        III.                   1.
                                  a.
```

(The distinctive qualities of an outline are not determined by the differences between sentences and words or phrases. Outlines may consist of words or phrases or sentences. In most instances, too, the outline's structure is not related to the variable of words, phrases, or sentences.)

The outline structurally organizes the ideas contained in the complete composition. In its briefest form, it may set forth merely the major topics or headings; in its most complete form, it may include virtually the entire composition, but not in paragraph form. Furthermore, as previously stated, it may foreshadow the complete composition, or it may be derived from a composition. The amount of detail in an outline depends upon its purpose — contrary to what is sometimes believed, the omission of illustrations, examples, quotations, and the like is not a requisite to outlining. *An outline's identifying characteristic is its structure, not its content.*

Purposes of Outlines

When viewed in its proper perspective, the outline becomes a graphic presentation of the content of a composition (such as a speech or an essay or a chapter). It presents material in such form that the major points are readily discerned, while minor points are clearly set forth in their proper relations to the major points as well as to each other.

To answer the question — Why construct an outline? — we must consider the connections between outlining and speech composition, on the one hand, and outlining and speech delivery, on the other.

Outlines and Speech Composition

The outline is an invaluable instrument in analyzing a subject. By means of it, we can set down the main points in parallel order, and then develop or expand each of them in similar order. In this way we can see our major and minor points at a glance, and ascertain whether our analysis and developments are orderly and "make sense." Here are two examples, one pertaining to *informative speaking* and one to *speaking on a controversial subject.*

Let us assume that we are developing a subject such as "My College" or "My University" and constructing an outline as we go along. Let us also assume that we shall proceed from main point to main point and then return to develop each main point. Perhaps we think of such points as the *location,* the *history,* the *purposes,* the *physical plant,* the *personnel,* and the *traditions* of the institution. We might, then, construct an outline like this:

I.	*Location*
II.	*History*
III.	*Purposes*
IV.	*Physical plant*
V.	*Personnel*
VI.	*Traditions*

Now let us look back at what we have done and see whether we have made a good analysis. Are these six points *coordinate* in terms of content? If so, the outline is satisfactory thus far. If not—if, for example, one of these points is actually subordinate to, or a part of, another—our outline is defective; and by the same token, our analysis is defective. At this point, the outline's value becomes apparent: Its structure combines sequence and subordination.

On the assumption that our analysis and outline are satisfactory thus far, let us proceed to develop the first two points.

> I. *Location*
>   A. *Within the nation*
>   B. *Within the state*
>   C. *Within the city*
> II. *History*
>   A. *From the date of founding to 1930*
>   B. *From 1930 to 1955*
>   C. *From 1955 to the present*

Now let us see what we have done. Are the subordinate points actually coordinate in content, or have we incorrectly related certain points? For example, do they overlap? Again, our outline enables us not only to extend the analysis but also to keep a constant check upon its validity. (Before leaving the whole-part, or explanatory, outline, we should realize that we have still to observe another major consideration: *Do the several main points add up to the whole?* For instance, does the sum of points I to VI represent all of the *major* points that may be included in the subject "My College"? Let us not impose this test here since it appears later in connection with the requirements or tests of outlines.)

Let us briefly develop a portion of an outline that is concerned with a matter of judgment or controversy, stated in the form of the speaker's position: "Television News Programs Should Hire More Women."

> I. *News comment based on women's experience enriches news coverage.*
> II. *Informed women news commentators serve as models for women viewers.*
> III. *Capable women are available for open competition.*

As we look at our outline, we should ask two questions: (1) Are points I to III related to the main subject as reasons for the "truth" of this subject? (2) Are these three points actually coordinate in *meaning* as well as in *structure*? If the answer is *Yes* in each case (and this appears to be the correct answer in our example), our outline is satisfactory thus far, and our analysis of the subject is also satisfactory thus far.

Let us now develop two of these points:

I. *News comment based on women's experience enriches news coverage.*
  A. *The feminine viewpoint adds a new dimension to straight reporting formerly reserved for men.*
  B. *Interests of women reporters will affect news selection.*
II. *Informed women news commentators serve as models for women viewers.*
  A. *Competent female reporters prove that women can deliver essential news without girlish apology.*
  B. *They show the housewife that matters of national importance are within her domain.*

Are the subordinate points actually subordinate—do they pertain to the main points? Are the subpoints reasons for the truth of these main points? Are the subpoints related to one another? If the answers are *Yes* (and it appears that such answers are valid here), the outline is satisfactory thus far, and our analysis is also satisfactory.

Thus the outline has aided us in the development of our subject and has provided us with means of testing our analysis. This is the primary value of an outline in speech making.

Outlines and Speech Delivery

The outline is also a useful instrument in preparing for delivery and in delivering the speech. On the assumption that the speaker chooses not to compose his message word-for-word or chooses not to speak from a manuscript he has already composed, some form of assistance is probably needed in preparing for delivery—and perhaps in the actual delivery. Here is where the outline comes in.

Because the outline sets forth the major and minor points in bold relief, it keeps the structure of the message clear. Also, it enables the speaker to see at a glance the points of the speech as he progresses through the subject. (Consider how much more easily we can spot separate points in an outline than we can in ordinary manuscript form.)

Many speakers, even though they may not be speaking impromptu, are capable of speaking without an outline—that is, without a written outline; however, more often than not, the speaker will have an outline in mind. The more competent he is in making an outline, the more satisfactory will be this unwritten, but none the less real, outline.

Types of Outlines

Outlines may be classified according to subject-matter relationships and according to form. Let us consider these in order.

Subject-Matter Relationships

In this category there are two types of outlines: (1) whole-part (for informative speaking) and (2) reasons or proofs (for argumentative speaking).

Whole-Part Outlines   When the speaker's purpose is to provide information or to increase understanding about a topic, the subject-matter relationships are *whole-part*, in that the development of the subject consists of analyzing the subject or of breaking it into its several parts.

The Department of Speech

I. *History*
    A. *The years as a "service department" only (1940–1950)*
    B. *The years of development into a department with a major (1950–1960)*
    C. *The years of expansion into graduate work (1960–   )*

II. *Purposes*
    A. *Teaching*
        1. *Undergraduate*
        2. *Graduate*
    B. *Research*
        1. *Departmental*
        2. *Private*
    C. *Service*
        1. *On-campus*
        2. *Off-Campus*

III. *Areas of activity*
    A. *Oral Interpretation*
    B. *Radio and television*
    C. *Rhetoric, public address, communication*
    D. *Speech education*
    E. *Audiology and speech sciences*
    F. *Theatre*
        (etc.)

Here, then, is a breakdown of the *whole* subject (The Department of Speech) into at least some of its parts — together with a similar breakdown of some of the first-degree parts into additional parts. If this outline were to be expanded, it could, of course, be made to include more parts of the whole subject or more subdivisions of the existing parts.

The outline can reflect as many parts as the subject itself warrants or as the speaker wishes to include in his analysis. In every case, however, there is the whole-part relationship, with subpoints consisting of parts of the points to which they are immediately subordinate; and, not surprisingly, if a point is divided, *it must be divided into at least two parts.*

Reasons or Proofs Outlines   When the speaker tries to prove to others the truth of some idea in which he believes, the subject-matter relationships are of the nature of support or proof. Here the development of the subject consists of setting out arguments in support of the subject or proposition.

You Would Find Speech Teaching a Satisfying Career

I.   *It has an ancient and honorable tradition and past.*
   A.   *In ancient Greece and Rome it was at the heart of education.*
   B.   *In the Middle Ages it also occupied a central position in education.*
   C.   *In the United States, with a few exceptions, it has been prominent in education since the Colonial Period.*

II.   *It has one of the highest possible objectives — the development and nurture of the human mind, character, and personality.*

III.   *It is the epitome of individualized instruction.*

IV.   *It offers opportunities and satisfactions for nearly every interest.*
   A.   *It has opportunities for those with aesthetic interests.*
   B.   *It has opportunities for those with rhetorical interests.*
   C.   *It has opportunities for those with scientific interests.*

V.   *It is a dynamic, expanding, and demanding field.*

Here, then, is a series of *reasons or proofs* for the alleged truth of the subject, thesis, or proposition. Each of the major points is related to the subject as a reason for its truth, not as a part of the whole subject as in the whole-part outline. Each subpoint stands as a reason for the alleged truth of the main point above it. If this outline were to be expanded, there would merely be more statements of proof at various points — more major points (VI, VII, etc.) or more points of the next degree (A, B, etc.) or points of the next degree (1, 2, etc.), and so on. ·

Outline Forms

The three forms of the outline are: (1) a list of *words,* (2) a list of *phrases,* and (3) an array of *complete sentences.* Let us consider each kind.

List of Words This is the simplest type of outline—an organized list of words representing the divisions and subdivisions of a topic. Even though bare and necessarily brief, its very compactness and terseness make it a most useful type of outline.

For one example of the list-of-words outline, let us recall the one that we constructed on "My College" (see page 160). Or let us outline the subject "Methods of Delivering a Speech":

> I. *Impromptu*
> II. *Extempore*
> III. *Manuscript*
> IV. *Memoriter*

Another example might be "The Colleges in Our University":

> I. *Arts and Letters*
>   A. *Art*
>   B. *English*
>   C. *History*
>   *(etc.)*
> II. *Natural Sciences*
>   A. *Astronomy*
>   B. *Botany and Plant Pathology*
>   C. *Chemistry*
>   *(etc.)*
> III. *Social Sciences*
>   A. *Geography*
>   B. *Political Science*
>   C. *Psychology*
>   *(etc.)*
> IV. *Communication Arts*
>   A. *Advertising*
>   B. *Audiology and Speech Sciences*
>   C. *Communication*
>   D. *Journalism*
>   E. *Speech and Theatre*
>   F. *Television-Radio*

This type of outline, simple as it may appear, is *more than a random list.* Rather, it observes all features of good outlining as to subject-matter relationships and form.

List of Phrases   This type is essentially the same as the first, the only important difference being in the use of groups of words (phrases) instead of single words. It serves the same basic purposes, and the subject-matter relationships are essentially the same. For an example, let us show the development of Chapter 6 ("Materials of Development") in an outline of this type.

I. *Materials common to all speaking*
    A. *Materials found and used by the speaker*
        1. *Examples*
        2. *Narratives*
        3. *Statistics*
        4. *Quotations*
    B. *Materials created by the speaker*
        1. *Repetition*
        2. *Restatement*
        3. *Comparison*
        4. *Contrast*

II. *Materials and procedures of reasoning and the argumentative process*
    A. *The nature, sources, and uses of evidence*
    B. *The nature of reasoning*
    C. *Types and tests of reasoning*
        1. *Reasoning from example*
        2. *Reasoning by analogy*
        3. *Reasoning from cause*
        4. *Reasoning from sign*
    D. *The structure of reasoning*
        1. *The traditional model or pattern*
            a. *Induction*
            b. *Deduction*
                (1) *The categorical syllogism*
                (2) *The hypothetical syllogism*
                (3) *The disjunctive syllogism*
        2. *The Toulmin model or pattern*
            a. *Data*
            b. *Warrant*
            c. *Claim*
            d. *Backing*
            e. *Qualifier*
            f. *Rebuttal*

III. *Common uses of the materials of development in speaking*
    A. *In an explanatory message*
    B. *In a message of advocacy*

Here, as in the list-of-words outline, we have more than a random set of phrases. Whether it is a simple outline, consisting of only one or two points and no subdivisions, or a long one with considerable development, it must observe all features of good outlining (such as proper analysis and parallelism in form).

Complete Sentence As its name indicates, this outline consists of complete sentences at every point—major points and all minor points or subdivisions. It *may* be used in *whole-part* outlining, where it differs from the briefer forms in the extent to which it states the nature of each point (a sentence instead of a word or a phrase). It is the only type that may be used to indicate *reasons or proofs* relationships of a speech of advocacy or argument, inasmuch as it is only by means of complete sentences that judgments, opinions, or propositions can be clearly expressed. (It is impossible to state a judgment, for instance, via a word or a phrase—a complete sentence is required.)

The complete-sentence outline is used to express *whole-part* relationships in the following example for the subject "Milestones in the Teaching of Speech-Making in the United States":

I.   *The first period (1635–1730) may be called the Period of Ornamentation and Embellishment.*

II. *The second period (1730–1785) may be called the Period of Classicism.*

III. *The third period (1785–1850) may be called the Period of Classicism with Elements of Elocution.*

 (etc.)

To express *reasons or proofs* relationships, the complete-sentence outline can be applied, for example, to the statement "A Course in Group Discussion Should Be Added to Our Program":

I.   *The present program is inadequate.*

 A. *It fails to include instruction in reflective thinking.*

 B. *It places undue emphasis upon advocacy.*

II. *The addition of a course in group discussion would solve this problem.*

 A. *It would provide for instruction in reflective thinking.*

 B. *It would place discussion and advocacy in proper balance.*

(It would also be helpful to review two outlines previously developed, "Television News Programs" and "Satisfactions in Teaching.")

In each of these outlines we have a complete sentence at every point, whether it is major or minor. Because a complete thought (not a label or a term) is presented, a reader will be better able to discern each unit without the necessity of relying upon another person's interpretation of a word or phrase.

As we look back upon these three types of outlines (word, phrase, sentence), we may well ask: What are their relative values and limitations? What are their respective uses?

First, a complete-sentence outline is the only type that is applicable to reasons or proofs (in advocative speaking). This is true because reasons cannot be expressed in single words or in phrases; only words connected into complete statements can express propositions, judgments, convictions, or opinions. (While it *is* true that a speaker may use a list of words or phrases as an aid to delivery, this list merely represents the *propositions* of the message, with the words or phrases serving as "reminders."

Second, in whole-part situations (informative speaking), all three types of outlines have values and uses, depending upon the wishes of the speaker and the uses to which the outline will be put. Specifically, the list-of-words outline is valuable in the preliminary stages of analysis in setting forth briefly and pointedly the major and minor divisions. In addition, it can serve a speaker well by providing him with a brief set of headings (we might call them notes) to which he can refer easily. Of course, this outline has its limitations. Since it is but a set of labels rather than statements, it depends upon the mind of its maker for interpretation. The list-of-words outline has values in both analysis and delivery, provided we do not ask it to do more than it can legitimately do by its very nature.

As for the list-of-phrases outline, it, too, can facilitate analysis and delivery, in that we can set down in comparatively brief form the essentials of the subject being developed.

The complete-sentence outline spells out the intended meaning of each point, providing us with a complete statement at every stage, a full revelation of the whole-part or reasons relationships. Perhaps it is less helpful during delivery, although even here it provides a complete guide for the speaker; and it makes on-the-spot interpretation and development unnecessary. Its principal limitation may rest in its very completeness, its lack of the eye-catching, bold-relief aspect of the single-word or the phrase outline. Undoubtedly, its value lies in its requiring full attention to analyzing the subject prior to delivery.

We have considered each type of outline as a separate entity. However, some speakers and teachers, at times, combine these types in whole-part discourses. For instance, they may develop the main headings with sentences and the subordinate points with words or phrases. Also, it is true that in series-of-reasons speeches, references to evidence merely name the source of the supporting material. While there is no harm in combining types of outlines, we should remember that *each has a specific purpose* and *each has good reasons for its use.*

The Requirements of a Good Outline

Features of a *good outline*—in addition to systematic indentation and subject-matter relationships—include *form* and *subject matter.*

Form

The rules for outlining fall quite naturally into three categories: (1) indentation, (2) symbols, and (3) phrasing.

Indentation Every good outline exhibits systematic indentation, or steps from left to right. For example, an outline representing the typical, or *deductive* (see Chapter 11), pattern or plan should look as follows:

    I.
      A.
        1.
          a.
            (etc.)

However, this principle of indentation applies only to succeeding degrees and subdivisions. In other words, we move toward the right *only* as we move "down the stairs" in terms of points and subpoints. If there are two or more coordinate points, they fall on the same vertical plane, as:

    I.
      A.
      B.
        1.
        2.
      C.
        1.
        2.
        3.
          a.
          b.
            (etc.)

If the material of one point extends to a second line, the second line begins at a point directly under the beginning of the first line, as:

    I.
      A. ....
         ....
        1. ....
           ....
            (etc.)

By this principle, *the following form is incorrect:*

I.
  A. ....
....
    1. ....
....

As noted above, the examples we have just reviewed pertain to the deductive plan of organization, in which we proceed from major points or statements to particulars. While this plan is more typical and commonplace than the inductive, the latter (as noted in Chapter 11) is, indeed, a valid and useful plan of development sometimes employed by writers and speakers.

Almost by definition of the *inductive* pattern, the outline form is an inversion of the more typical form. Consequently, the proper form for the outline of a message of this type would be:

    a.
   1.
  A.
 I.
(etc.)

(Of course, each step may be expanded as the *subject* and the *speaker's wishes* dictate. For example, there may be a., b., and c., as well as 1., 2., and 3, etc.)

What is the rationale behind these principles of indentation? First, the very essence of outlining requires a form that clearly sets out major and minor points; and indentation is *the* means of making this "profile" possible. Second, equal or coordinate points should be arrayed equally; hence, the same indentation for these points. Third, the "stair-step" form (or indentation) should be complete and readily discernible; hence, nothing should be placed to the left of a given point's beginning location.

Symbols   Ordinarily, and ideally, the points of an outline are designated and preceded by symbols (numbers or letters). Two readily apparent reasons are (1) to provide distinguishing marks for the sections in the outline and (2) to set forth clearly the degrees of subordination. These symbols should be systematically used to represent both coordination and subordination.

Ordinarily, the major points are designated by *Roman numerals,* the second-degree points by *capital letters,* the third-degree points by *Arabic numerals,* the fourth-degree points by *lower-case letters,* the fifth-degree points by *Arabic numerals in parentheses,* and subsequent points, if any, by other types of symbols. In all cases there must be consistency, lest the symbols lose all value.

The following outline form (in the deductive pattern) represents the proper use of symbols through six steps or degrees:

I.
  A.
  B.
    1.
      a.
      b.
    2.
      a.
      b.
        (1)
        (2)
          (a)
          (b)

Phrasing For the *whole-part* outline, any one of the three modes of phrasing is satisfactory: (1) list of words, (2) list of phrases, (3) complete sentence. The choice rests entirely with the maker of the outline[1] and is made according to the values and limitations that we have previously considered.

For the *reasons or proofs* outline, on the other hand, *only the complete-sentence outline is acceptable* because only sentences express thoughts, judgments, opinions, or propositions. The points in this type of outline are not topics or representations of topics but are *judgments* and *opinions*, or *propositions and subpropositions*.

Subject Matter

Again, we shall refer to two kinds of subject-matter relationships: (1) whole-part (the speech of information), and (2) reasons or proofs (the speech of advocacy).

Whole-Part Here the properly constructed outline represents a breaking down of a subject. The movement (in the deductive pattern) is from the whole subject to its principal parts, to the parts of each principal part, and so on.

Hence, the basic test is: Is each part of the outline properly related to each other part regarding the sense of the subject matter? For example, are the parts designated by Roman numerals actually coordinate parts of the whole subject, and so on? Also, is a part designated by a capital letter actually a part of the subdivision above it—the one represented by a Roman numeral?

---

[1] In the instructional setting, the student may be required to prepare speech plans using complete-sentence outlines for all types of discourses. In this way, the instructor can check more carefully the nature of the student's preparation.

Inasmuch as there must, of necessity, be *at least two parts* to every *whole,* this type of outline should ordinarily have at least two points at every stage of subordination. Note the following (in the deductive pattern):

I.
  A.
  B.
    1.
    2.
      a.
      b.
II.
  (etc.)

Exceptions to this principle may be permitted only if the speaker deliberately *chooses to develop only certain aspects of the subject.* For instance, in I.B. above, he may choose to discuss only point 1. In such an instance, however, the speaker should make clear that this analysis is deliberately incomplete, lest he create the impression that he has violated the basic principles of good sense and good outlining.

Reasons or Proofs   Here the properly constructed outline represents the arraying or listing of reasons, proofs, or statements that support propositions or statements to which the former are subordinate. In other words, as we go "down the stairs" (deductive), we go from statement to support, statement to support, and so on. This relationship is such that, in subject-matter relationships, the best test of this type of outline is indicated by the question: Is each subpoint related to its immediately superior point by "for" or "because" or "since"? An affirmative answer indicates a good outline. (We should, of course, note a corollary relationship and test. As we go "up the stairs" (inductive), the relationship represented by "therefore" is evident in a properly constructed outline.) This can be seen in a previously studied outline supporting "Television News Programs Should Hire More Women":

(for – because – since)
  I.   *News comment based on women's experience enriches news coverage.*
    (for – because – since)
    A.   *The feminine viewpoint . . . .*
    B.   *Interests of women reporters . . . .*
  II.   *Informed women news commentators serve as models for women viewers.*
    (for – because – since)
    A.   *Competent female reporters prove . . . .*
    B.   *They show the housewife . . . .*

(Note that the for-because-since relationship exists only between statements of two different degrees or on two different "stair steps." It does not exist between statements of the same degree.)

The Place of Evidence in the Outline

One question about outlining remains to be considered: How do we handle evidence (examples, illustrations, narratives, testimony, and the like) that we use to illustrate or prove the points or statements in the outline? Actually, there is no one answer, except to say that there must be a place for such material, inasmuch as it is closely related to the points or lines of thought contained in the outline.

There are three common methods of handling this material: (1) treat it as an integral part of the outline by inserting it, with appropriate symbols, at the relevant points; (2) include it at relevant points but separate it from the outline by brackets and do not identify it with symbols; (3) array it in a column at the side of the outline, virtually as a separate document although spatially adjacent.

This material and these methods pertain to all types of speeches and subject matter, although we shall use examples only of the *reasons or proofs* relationship.

Included in the Outline—With Symbols

I. *News comment based on women's experience enriches news coverage.*

   A. *The feminine viewpoint adds a new dimension to straight reporting formerly reserved for men.*

      1. *"The presence of women on our 'broadcasting team' broadens the base of our programming and introduces several features not inherently present when the staff consists solely of men." Statement made by Charles E. Smith, Manager of WABC-TV, Broadcasting Notes, Vol. 10, No. 2, p. 85.**

      2. *A survey of 25 programs which include both men and women reporters and 25 programs which include men only shows substantially greater breadth of features in the former than in the latter. Broadcasting Notes, Vol. 11, No. 1, p. 10.**

---

* Hypothetical sources.

Even though this evidence is material discovered by the speaker, rather than his own statements, it is regarded here as an integral part of the structure. Hence, it is included in the outline.

This method has two possible disadvantages, which may outweigh its advantages. First, it does not readily distinguish between the speaker's own ideas and the materials he has found to develop them (evidence). Second, it may create problems of division and subdivision. If, for instance, he wished to develop point A with subpoints, and if he were to list them as 1, 2, etc., there would be confusion between the two types of material bearing these symbols—quite clearly, this material would not be of the a-b-c order. (Some persons might attempt to avoid this confusion by using other symbols —parentheses or other distinguishing marks. Even then, some confusion almost certainly would exist.)[2]

Included in the Outline—With Brackets

I.   *News comment based on women's experience enriches news coverage.*
   A.   *The feminine viewpoint adds a new dimension to straight reporting formerly reserved for men.*
      ["The presence of women . . ."   *p. 85]*
      [A survey of 25 programs . . .   *p. 10]*

This is an effective method, inasmuch as it arrays the evidence at the most relevant points, at the same time avoiding the two elements of possible confusion noted in the first method.

Separated from the Outline

I.   *News comment based on women's experience enriches news coverage.*

   A.   *The feminine viewpoint adds a new dimension to straight reporting formerly reserved for men.*

      "The presence of women . . ."   *p. 85*
      A survey of 25 programs . . ."   *p. 10*

This is also a workable method, inasmuch as it arrays the evidence at relevant points, at the same time avoiding the two elements of confusion noted in the first method. Perhaps it is slightly less effective than the second method in that it separates the evidence quite noticeably from the point to which it refers.

However, the second and the third methods are perhaps equally effective in meeting the demands of *clearness* and *relevant position* and in avoiding possible confusion between the speaker's own statements and the evidence presented to develop, illustrate, or support these statements.

---

[2] Note that the student speaker whose speech plans are included in Chapter 11 chose to use this method of handling evidence.

Suggested Assignments

1.   Assume that you are to speak upon "The History of My College" and that you will present the material in time sequence. Compose a list-of-words outline that meets the appropriate tests considered in this chapter.

2.   With respect to the same situation as in assignment 1, compose a list-of-phrases outline.

3.   Assume that you are to speak for or against the proposition that "A Course in Public Speaking Should Be Required of All College Students." Also, assume that you are to use the *deductive* speaking plan (see Chapter 11 for further discussion). Compose an appropriate complete-sentence outline with a maximum of three major points, a maximum of six points of the next degree, and a maximum of twelve points of the succeeding degree. Include only your own assertions, not any evidence to "underpin" these assertions.

4.   Assume that you are to speak on a proposition of your choice, and that you are to use the *inductive* speaking plan (see Chapter 11 for further discussion). Perform the operations as in assignment 3.

5.   Expand the outline in assignment 3 or in assignment 4 by adding evidence (facts, testimony) at certain points.

6.   Prepare a practical, usable set of speaker's notes upon the longer outline prepared in assignment 5.

Suggested References

Baird, A. Craig, *Argumentation, Discussion, and Debate* (New York: McGraw-Hill Book Co., 1950). Chapter 7, "Organization: The Outline and the Brief."

Freeley, Austin J., *Argumentation and Debate: Rational Decision Making*, 3rd ed. (Belmont, Calif.: Wadsworth Publishing Co., 1971). Chapter 13, "Building the Brief."

Joffe, Irwin L., *Developing Outline Skills* (Belmont, Calif.: Wadsworth Publishing Co., 1972).

McBurney, James H., and Kenneth G. Hance, *Discussion in Human Affairs* (New York: Harper & Row, 1950). Pp. 170–184 ("The Discussion Outline").

McBurney, James H., and Glen E. Mills, *Argumentation and Debate: Techniques of a Free Society*, 2nd ed. (New York: The Macmillan Co., 1964). Chapter 13, "Briefing and Outlining."

Winans, James A., *Speech-Making* (New York: Appleton-Century-Crofts, 1938). Pp. 116–130 ("The Outline").

11
Organizing for Speaking

"Without structure there is no content"

A public meeting took place at which plans for increased students' rights and greater student involvement in the affairs of the local university were to be discussed. The speaker began by stating the problem: (1) College students are better educated, more sophisticated, and wiser about national and world affairs today than a generation ago; (2) because of this growth and because their greater knowledge makes students want to play a more active role in their society, increased student participation in governmental affairs of all kinds is needed; and (3) the university, as a major institution in society and as a training ground for future leaders, must face up to its responsibilities and make student participation in its operation and government possible.

The speaker then proceeded to discuss various means by which the university administrative officials could work with student leaders in solving their mutual problems. He next reiterated his views of the educational attainment of entering freshmen and concluded the major portion of his message with a strong appeal for college students to seek out areas of the university where their leadership was most needed.

After a brief pause, the speaker concluded by reminding his listeners that his message had consisted of three major points: the need for student involvement in university affairs, the university's obligation to initiate cooperative measures, and the increased educational standing of today's college student. He then sat down, and the floor was open for questions and comments.

Immediately, one of those embarrassing silences descended upon the audience of over a hundred. No comments were forthcoming for more than a minute; and when the audience participation finally did commence, it varied from actively hostile to vague and unrelated responses to the message. Yet, invitations to the meeting had been sent to one hundred people known to be friendly toward the point of view expounded in the message!

Now, what was wrong with the message? It certainly showed evidence of some interesting ideas. But what was most conspicuously wrong was its insane organization; there appeared to be three different orders of presentation of the material—the one the speaker forecast, the one he actually followed, and the one he offered as a summary (not to mention his arranging the wrong subheads under the stated main heads—a "detail" which our brief account did not reveal).

Lest this example seem to be bizarre and atypical, consider some of the lectures you have been exposed to in college. Unless yours is an unusual school, some of your notes will reflect lectures and other presentations no better organized than this formal speech on student rights—and without reasonable organization, oral messages simply do not come across.

Once we understand the elements of organization—organizing and developing the speech plan (including the purpose sentence, body, conclusion, introduction, transitions, and internal summaries), there *should be* no valid reason—no excuse—for poor organization. While this chapter is concerned mainly with organizing the formal speech, the principles of organization are the same for all speaking. In ordinary conversation, we make our decisions about the basic structure of our remarks in the split second we may have between another's message and our own rejoinder.

The Elements of Organization

As we begin our discussion of the elements of organization, it is necessary that we clearly distinguish between the concepts of *outlining* and *organization*. Certainly they are related, closely related, and perhaps one does not often exist without the other; but an understanding of organization depends upon an understanding of the function of outlining. Outlining is a tool, a vehicle, an instrument by which organization is attained; it consists of a set of schematic relationships explained by symbols and indentations. Or it may, in the same fashion, represent ideas that have already appeared in complete form. In short, an outline's major value lies in its format, which distinguishes major and minor points by structural methods.

Organization, on the other hand, is the pattern of development or arrangement of a communication—in this instance, an oral message. It is the manipulation of the various thought structures of the message into the form that the speaker believes will best accomplish his or her goal, which is to affect the listener's behavior. This structure or organization is achieved by means of the tool of outlining, at least in the early stages of the development of the message.

Essentially, we organize messages because (1) we want to make sense and (2) we recognize our listeners' psychological need for unity. What we have to say—particularly in speaking at any length—arouses no meaning, or at least not our intended meaning, within the listener unless we organize the message to form a pattern for the listener that both reasonably satisfies him and reflects the source's meaning. The importance of order or structure in this sense has long been recognized by rhetorical theorists.

Some theorists look upon the message and its structure as two separate entities; others, as a unit. But in almost all cases, considered separately or together, their inherent relationship has been perceived; and today,

> It is enough simply to point out that the most impressive and truthful matter conceivable can lose lustre and attractiveness through faulty organization, and conversely that perfect organization can never transform drivel into shining truth. Form is not a sterile concept. It makes a difference whether material combines into a unified whole or remains an incoherent mass of disjointed particulars; under no circumstances, however, should we regard form as an independent virtue. . . . Disposition, as the rhetorical counterpart of form in its broader sense, must be viewed as a *means;* through it the potency of subject matter asserts itself and makes its purposes evident to the perceiving mind. But it remains a means—not a terminal value.[1]

Simply stated, organization is a means, not an end; it is a way of patterning the materials of speaking. As such, it is important not in itself but in what it can do to the materials of speaking as an aid to listener understanding.

Basic to all organization are three concepts: (1) purpose, (2) development, and (3) relationship.

Purpose, in this context, relates to what the message is all about, or, looked at in another way, what behavioral changes are expected in the receiver as a result of the message preparation. The concept of purpose is best expressed by the purpose sentence (also called topic sentence, subject sentence, lead sentence, "gut" sentence), which is briefly discussed in Chapter 2 and considered in more detail in Chapter 8 and in the section "The Purpose Sentence" later in this chapter. The purpose sentence, in its various states of development, ranges from the most general statement of the speaker's intent to the most specific, but *the entire concept of organization hinges upon this statement of intent.*

The concept of *development* in organization of the message includes the sum total of all the materials of speaking—materials of development, personal proof, and materials of experience—addressed to the listeners involved, arranged so as to make particular, to make concrete, to reinforce, to enliven, to support, or otherwise to fill out the meaning and significance of the purpose sentence.

The development is the heart of organization, the explanation or justification of the purpose sentence. In developing the ideas expressed in the purpose sentence, we call upon our experience in the subject matter, our powers of observation and investigation, our understanding of the listeners' probable attitudes, and our abilities as oral communicators. In the development stage of organization, the real integration of idea and form takes place; the raw materials are molded into the package that is our completed message.

---

[1] Lester Thonssen and A. Craig Baird, *Speech Criticism* (New York: Ronald Press Co., 1948), p. 404.

With these two concepts—purpose and development—in mind, let us now consider the third concept of organization, the *relationship* between the two. This relationship is easy to grasp in theory but sometimes difficult to put into practice: The development is always subordinate to the purpose, as stated in the purpose sentence. Regardless of where it may appear in the speech plan or in the speech, the purpose sentence must dictate the development—the development must develop the purpose sentence. If the organizing process does not spring from the statement of purpose, the purpose sentence will not express the real intent of the finished speech, and the speech may end up having no purpose at all or one far removed from what the speaker meant to say.

Organizing the Speech Plan

The speech plan is the blueprint of the speech, worked out by the speaker as thoroughly and as carefully as time will allow before presentation. By the time we settle down to block out our blueprint, we will already have given some thought to our purpose as a preliminary step in selecting the subject (see Chapter 8) and collecting the materials (see Chapter 9). Our task now is to assemble our materials into effective form for presentation of the speech.

A beginning speaker may well ask, "How many parts are there in a speech plan? And what are they?" Rhetoricians have not always agreed in their answers; indeed, speaking is such a personal art that agreement is neither possible nor desirable. Aristotle stated that the "indispensable constituents are simply the Statement and the ensuing Argument" (in our terms, the purpose sentence and the body of the speech) and further that "at most, the parts cannot exceed four—Proem, Statement, Argument, and Epilogue"[2] (introduction, purpose sentence, body, and conclusion). Other rhetoricians have conceived of as many as seven parts to the speech or speech plan: introduction or exordium, narration or explanation, proposition, division, proofs or argumentation, pathetic (or emotional) excitement, and conclusion or peroration.[3]

In our day, however, most writers in the field of communication tend to agree with Aristotle in limiting the parts of the speech to those necessary to all speaking, while conceding that particular kinds of speaking may demand particular forms of speech plans and particular parts of the plan. For our purposes, a division into four basic parts is practicable, listing them in the order in which they are prepared: (1) the purpose sentence, (2) the body, (3) the conclusion, and (4) the introduction.[4]

---

[2] Aristotle, *The Rhetoric*, trans. Lane Cooper (New York: Appleton-Century-Crofts, 1932), Book III, p. 220.

[3] Charles Coppens, *The Art of Oratorical Composition* (New York, 1885), p. 107, as quoted in Thonssen and Baird, p. 400.

[4] For an explanation of this statement, see p. 190.

The Purpose Sentence

In practice, the purpose sentence (see Chapters 2 and 8) becomes a declarative sentence formulating an idea, a feeling, a judgment, or a matter of inquiry, which we want our listeners to accept or understand or consider. It is declarative because at this stage of preparation we no longer have a question in our mind about the topic. We have decided, and we declare in our purpose sentence what our communication will be about. This is not to suggest that, either here or at any other stage of message preparation, we must harden our mind as to the purpose of the message to the degree that it cannot be modified. Our organization must reflect our decision as to the purpose; should that purpose be modified, we simply amend the purpose sentence.

The Body of the Speech

The development of the purpose sentence is called the body of the speech; it is the structured organization of the message. It incorporates the materials of speaking (see Chapters 5, 6, and 7) we have chosen for the particular speech, with intent to adapt to the occasion and to our listeners' wants and desires, biases and prejudices, potential attention or lack of it, and degree of knowledge about us and our subject.

Ordinarily, the development, or the body of the speech, will be constructed most effectively from an outline that uses complete sentences. In Chapter 10 we learned that ideas and thoughts require complete sentences in order to be adequately stated. The outline form is essential in structuring the body of the speech because it allows us to weigh the relationships among the materials we have chosen, to check the arrangement and logicality of our

---

Suggestions for Planning the Body

1. Place your purpose sentence in a prominent spot on your desk or table, and refer to it constantly as you structure the body. Make sure the development supports and explains the purpose sentence (unless you conclude that the purpose sentence itself must be altered).

2. Select and phrase the major ideas you wish to develop. Normally, they will be few in number—two to four. Occasionally, a one-point speech is desirable, and a speech of considerable length or complexity may have five or more main points.

3. Decide upon the basic organizational pattern dictated by the subject, the occasion, the audience, and your own goals, abilities, and limitations.

4. Select and arrange your subpoints and other supporting material, taking into account the purpose of the speech, the basic structure chosen, the need for logical support, the desire for listener adaptation, and any time limitations.

5. Consider the need for transitions and internal summaries, depending primarily upon the complexity of your material and your own limitations as a speaker.

points in support of our arguments, and to preserve the whole-part division of our materials.

The outline, in itself, does not help us get from point to point; it does not assure us that our listeners will be able to keep earlier parts of the speech in mind as they listen to later portions. The beginning speaker—or any other speaker faced with a complicated development of a subject—should build into his outline at least clues to transitions from point to point and internal summaries that will keep him and his listeners aware of what has been said and of the relationships between what has been said, what is being said, and what will be said.

Basic Plans of Organization   The structure of the body of the speech may vary from the strictly logical to the primarily psychological, according to our topic and our estimate of the particular situation and the nature of our audience. Speaking plans are usually personal, subjective, each experienced speaker having his own ways of organizing a talk for delivery. However, as beginning speakers we need some orientation and assistance in organizing the development of our purpose sentence. There are two basic types of organization—*deductive* and *inductive*—and several means of developing or implementing them.

The Deductive Speaking Plan   Probably the simplest and most often used kind of organization in speaking is the *deductive,*[5] which proceeds from statement of purpose to particulars. It consists of the purpose sentence; then one or more major statements in support of or in explanation of our purpose sentence; and evidence, further reasoning, and additional explanation supporting our major points. Furthermore, we introduce illustrations or other experience and sensory materials to help make our message interesting and persuasive. We then compose a conclusion and an introduction, and our speaking plan is ready for use.

The straightforward deductive speaking plan is simple and easy for the listener to follow. It is useful when the nature of the talk is primarily logical and when the listener group is objective or neutral. It usually does not turn people on when they are not already interested in the subject, and it often fails to produce an address of beauty or power. At its worst it is downright dull. Furthermore, it is not likely to reach listeners who are opposed to the speaker's ideas. The straightforward presentation often antagonizes rather than conciliates and persuades a hostile group. It may also provoke mild disapproval among listeners who feel that they already understand and agree with the speaker's position; such people want less reasoning and more stimulation.

For an example of a deductive talk, let us consider the professor of

---

[5] The terms "deductive" and "inductive" are used here to refer to the basic plans of organization, not to types of reasoning.

sociology who has been asked to speak to a politically mixed group on the trend of the administration toward socialism. He states his belief: Socialism is not intended to replace free enterprise in the United States, only to supplement it. He then says that the American citizen has certain fundamental rights: worthwhile employment for every citizen who is able and willing to work; high standards of teaching for his children in public schools, with adequate classroom space and high enough salaries to attract able persons into the teaching profession; medical care at public expense for all who need it. To whatever extent free enterprise cannot or will not provide these essentials, government must do so by "socialistic" measures, says the professor.

So far his talk is strictly deductive and straightforward. It probably appeals to the neutral, thinking members of his audience, who have not yet made up their minds and are interested in his point of view. However, it probably antagonizes his more conservative listeners, bores the liberals with solutions they have long ago accepted, and disgusts the smattering of convinced socialist listeners, who consider the professor's socialism much too mild. The professor is aware of this resistance and suddenly thrusts a series of questions at his audience: "Shouldn't we get rid of our public school system and turn education over to private enterprise? It is a socialistic institution; it exists not for profit but for public use. And what about tariffs? Why shouldn't our industry compete with foreign industry on a free enterprise basis? Why shouldn't our national magazines compete with other entertainment on a free enterprise basis? Why subsidize them through postage rates that are far from meeting the cost of handling them?" Even the hardrock conservative hostility to the professor's views may yield a little to interest in his argument.

What rhetorical device did this speaker use in his attempt to persuade? Anticipating opposition to his ideas, he turned to *reductio ad absurdum* — reducing the opposing argument to the absurd by carrying it out to its logical extreme. This is one of the techniques that we can develop to make the basic deductive speech plan more interesting or more persuasive to listeners with varying reactions to the subject.

The Inductive Speaking Plan   The other basic plan, known as *inductive*, proceeds from particulars to statement of purpose; it is the inverse of the deductive sequence. In speaking, we present a series of particulars or incidents in a connected order leading to the general conclusion, which states our purpose. For example, if we are to argue the proposition that "Business should give financial aid to deserving college students of the lower income groups," we may describe a series of cases of deserving students who were able to get a college education only through industrial scholarships; or cases of high-ranking high school students who did not go to college because no aid was available; or cases of medical students who ruined their health by working their way through medical school. Or we may use all three kinds of cases, leading our hearers through a series of specifics to the desired general conclusion.

© 1966 United Feature Syndicate, Inc.

The inductive method of organization is especially useful when the audience is not particularly interested in the subject or when, for other reasons, gaining its attention may be difficult. It can be used to arouse curiosity. Also, when we have to face an audience hostile to our ideas, by using the inductive method we can approach our subject more indirectly, with less shock effect; and sometimes we can guide our listeners to the conclusion before we speak it. When this happens, some of them may come to the very desirable belief that the idea is their own.

A disadvantage of the inductive method is that it usually takes longer to develop skillfully than the deductive method. Specific instances cannot ordinarily be stated as economically as can an opening statement of purpose and its developing particulars. Furthermore, unless we are very careful in the construction of transitions from point to point, our listeners may get lost among the particulars and never arrive at the conclusion at all.

Combinations and variations of the two basic patterns are commonly employed in constructing messages. We may, for example, announce our proposition in the deductive fashion and then proceed inductively toward a concluding restatement of the proposition. Or we may present a connected series of specific instances leading to a statement of the proposition or purpose, and then follow the statement with developing materials. Or we may use one or the other of the two basic plans but substitute for the usual summary conclusion an emotional appeal, urging approval and support of our position.

Means of Developing or Implementing the Basic Speech Plans   The two basic plans of organization may be developed in a number of ways. Good speech plans are personal, and they must be worked out by each of us as we take into account our subject, our listeners, the occasion, and our own abilities. We will be more impressive speakers if we think through our message carefully and develop the plan that best fits our particular problem. The following discussions present a variety of ways the beginning speaker can organize material in order to present it effectively. Without help, a beginner may tend to stick with a plan that happened to work the first time, no matter how haphazardly, and use it over and over again, to the detriment of ideas that need different management and to the boredom of listeners who have heard it all before.

Time   Sequential development is used for materials whose relationships can best be described according to the time of their occurrence or whose time sequence is inherent in the subject matter, as with a historical account, a process, or a narrative of personal experiences. For example, in telling about the Chautauqua movement in our country, we would logically begin with its founding and proceed as follows:

  I.   *The early Chautauquas from 1900 to 1910*

  II. *The circuit Chautauquas from 1910 to 1920*

  III. *The decline of the Chautauquas after 1920*

Space   Sometimes an arrangement of speech material according to areas or spatial topics works best. For instance, materials may be organized in respect to spatial relationships, such as from north to south or from east to west or from top to bottom or from center to outside. The following example about "Working Conditions in a Coal Mine" works from bottom to top:

  I.   *Hazards deep in the mine*

  II. *Conditions a worker faces as he transports ore to the surface*

  III. *Working conditions on the ground level*

Causal   While this sequence is more often associated with speeches of advocacy, it is used effectively also in talks that inform. For example, we may tell of the causes of certain effects or, in reverse, the effects resulting from causes and resultant further effects, as in this illustration delineating "Effects of Recent Changes in Operation of X Company Chain Stores":

  I.   *Growing slump in initially huge profits*

  II. *Hiring of comparison shoppers*

  III. *Discovery through them that, while X Company charged comparatively low prices in general, it charged higher on some items than did small grocer*

  IV. *Reduced prices of items involved*

  V.   *Mounting profits*

Implicative   The implicative technique consists of presenting a problem and then considering, one after another, the possible solutions. For each solution we show, through reasoning and evidence and perhaps through materials of experience, that the solution is false or inadequate, until we have eliminated all solutions except the one we believe to be right. If we have done our job well, our hearers should arrive at the sole remaining solution as soon as we do, or sooner. In a closely reasoned talk, we then proceed to offer our solution as the only one that will solve the problem.

However, if we are dealing with an audience that comes to the meeting opposed to our solution, we will probably merely hint at it—or else not state it at all but consider and reject the other possible solutions and then ask our hearers to make up their own minds. The implicative technique is best used in dealing with a hostile group of listeners. For an audience already on the side of the speaker it is a somewhat awkward method, and it may arouse resentment in listeners who want all of the available facts in order to choose their own solutions objectively.

Problem-Solution This development technique is related to the implicative plan but is more commonly used. It consists of stating the problem, proposing a solution, and then presenting evidence and reasoning to support it. Although the plan usually makes major use of materials of development, it may be adapted to a hostile audience by the use of more indirect means than bluntly stating the problem and the solution. Like the implicative technique, it may avoid a specific statement as to the solution, if the speaker prefers to steer clear of it.

A problem-solution sequence in an *informative* address falls naturally into two major parts: (1) a description of a problem and associated problems followed by (2) a description of a solution or solutions that are being proposed. Here is an illustration of a problem-solution sequence for an informative speech on "Meeting Chicago's Traffic Problem":

   I.   *The relation of Chicago's area to its population (including suburbs)*
  II.   *Resultant traffic congestion*
 III.   *Proposal to double the number of one-way streets*
 IV.   *Proposal to create free parking lots in fringe of city for commuters*

Topical In this sequence we divide our material into major parts without paying any attention to chronological, causal, spatial, or problem-solution sequences. The most frequently used sequence, the topical can fit almost any kind of talk. It can be used to describe races of people, kinds of political parties, types of educational programs, kinds of leadership. The following is an example of topical arrangement—its subject, "The Executive Training Program":

   I.   *The objectives of executive training*
  II.   *The training courses best suited for executives*
 III.   *Qualifications of instructors*
 IV.   *Recreational facilities for trainees*

Narrative   The name "narrative" explains the nature of this plan, which consists of presenting the major points of the speech as a connected story, often historical in nature. Instead of arguing that Lincoln was our greatest president by offering three or four or more reasons, we can demonstrate our claim by telling the story of the wartime years in Washington, the frustrations in trying to find adequate military leadership, the opposition of the Copperheads, the demands of the extreme abolitionists, and the homely, honest Abraham Lincoln moving firmly through the chaos. This is one way we can demonstrate our claim that Lincoln was our greatest President. The method is not strictly logical, nor is it necessarily nonlogical. We may or may not explain our entire reasoning process, but our facts should be correct and our conclusions based on careful research. To the extent that we introduce descriptive words and word pictures into the narrative, we add some elements of interest by using experience and sensory materials; and if we display a good knowledge of Lincoln and his time, we strengthen our personal proof.

Because the narrative method relies so much on description and exposition, it may not, in the Lincoln illustration, satisfy listeners who want strict reasoning; but it may please listeners who admire Lincoln and it may entertain apathetic listeners who have heard all the rah-rah "Lincoln stuff" before. Even hostile audiences may be intrigued by a story with word pictures and may be persuaded to abandon some of their hostility.

Comparative   This plan compares a proposed solution to a similar solution of a similar problem, which is understood and accepted by the listeners. If the Wagoner University campus has a serious parking problem and we believe that barring freshmen from parking privileges is the sensible and suitable solution, we may point out that the University of Graustark, an institution highly respected among our listeners, solved its parking problem this way.

We may use a less direct comparison than the above. Supposing the city in which Wagoner University is located has solved its parking problem by eliminating downtown parking altogether, and its citizens approve of the measure, we may note this fact and propose that the university apply the same principle, but in a limited sense—bar freshmen, and only freshmen, from the university parking places.

The comparative technique is logical in nature; but, like the implicative and problem-solution methods, it uses materials of experience to meet a particular situation and audience. The comparative method helps our hearers visualize our proposal, even if the situation with which we compare it is imaginary.

Suggestion   Basically this plan is akin to the comparative; it may even have a narrative quality. The difference is that the suggestion technique makes no direct reference to the real problem. We use it when we realize that direct reference to the problem we want to discuss will meet with immediate disapproval. Instead, we talk about a similar problem whose similar solution will meet with little opposition. We imply, but do not state, that our hearers ought to apply the acceptable solution to the problem we are really concerned with.

If the poor of our city receive inadequate help, and our hearers are not disposed to increase taxes to meet the situation, we might talk about the splendid care the city gives to stray animals. We could go on about the animal shelter in its smart, new building, about the promptness with which animals are picked up, the care they receive, the trouble taken to place them in suitable homes, the money the city spends on this service, and the interest various organizations take in it. We would probably conclude by congratulating our fellow citizens upon their thoughtful and generous care of animals, and then, as subtly and cleverly as possible, suggest that perhaps human beings in distressful situations should be given more consideration than they presently receive.

The Conclusion

The specific purpose of the conclusion of a speech depends upon the nature of the speech itself, the nature of the occasion, the goals of the communicator, and the audience. However, we should design all conclusions so that they lead the listener in the direction we want him to go. The conclusion is our last chance to accomplish what our purpose sentence states that we set out to do — to explain a process, to make clear a concept, to request a vote, to suggest a course of action, to satirize a public figure, to poke fun at a convention of society. It is estimated that the average listener cannot be expected to remember more than one fifth of what the speaker says — and that is probably a liberal estimate. This makes clear the need for a strong, intensive conclusion that will help the listener recall the most important parts of our talk.

Nearly all conclusions to talks should perform another function: to signal "the end." Nothing about a speech is more psychologically unsatisfactory to the listener than a conclusion that trails off, backs and fills, never quite succeeds in concluding. A speech is an artistic unit, with a beginning, a middle, and an end; no matter what specific purpose the conclusion is intended to perform, it ought to wrap up the speech. It ought to say to the listener, "There! I have done it! It is finished!" Lew Sarett, one of the greatest of all teachers of speech, used to tell his classes in persuasion, "When you quit, quit all over."

Keeping in mind the basic goals of the conclusion — to urge the listener in the direction we want him to go, and to satisfy his desire for a completed message — we must consider three specific aspects — (1) the relationship of the conclusion to the purpose of the speech; (2) the relationship of the conclusion to the listener; and (3) the relationship of the conclusion to the occasion of the speech — before we can get down to the business of constructing our conclusion. (See inset, page 188.)

Methods of Concluding   There are many varieties of conclusions, and they are not mutually exclusive. A given method of concluding may contain elements from other methods; or we may combine elements from various methods into an original conclusion. Let us consider four basic methods of concluding a message:

Purpose-Sentence Conclusion   If we use strictly inductive organization, we usually conclude our talk with the full statement of our purpose in speaking. While this kind of speaking does not seem to be widely used, it succeeds very well when the purpose sentence is carefully constructed to serve both as the proposition and the conclusion. If we have chosen to present the materials of our talk indirectly, we will most often want to be indirect in our conclusion as well. The purpose sentence of the speech plan may then be stated less specifically, perhaps even watered down or deliberately obscured, so that we only hint at the real purpose of the speech. Of course, we would not choose this method of concluding unless the occasion or the attitude of the listeners warranted it. We must remember, too, that while the sense of

---

**Considerations in Composing
the Conclusion**

1.   *What is the real purpose of your speech? What does your purpose sentence tell you? What hidden goals do you have in mind? Is your purpose expressed directly or indirectly in the body of the speech plan? Are you clearly advocating a change of policy or subtly suggesting a flaw in some cherished social institution? Are you attempting primarily to explain the administrative structure of a governmental body? Is your goal general or specific? Are you interested mainly in promoting understanding in your listeners or do you really want them to agree with your criticisms? Is your humor intended to relax and please or are you using it to take the edge off a bitter and controversial criticism?*

2.   *What is the relationship of the listener to your speech? Is he knowledgable about the subject, or is he ignorant? Is he likely to be opposed to your ideas, enthusiastic, apathetic? Surely in your conclusion you will want to sustain and*

even heighten his interest; perhaps you will want to motivate him to action. At any rate, the way he is likely to feel about your subject, as you approach the conclusion, will heavily influence your choice of concluding statements.

3.   *Finally, you will want to consider the relationship between your speech and the occasion of its presentation. Are you the featured speaker, a guest of the organization? Will you violate any of the norms of the host group? Should you express appreciation for the opportunity to speak? Is there an audience beyond the visible one—will your words be carried in newspapers, on radio or television? Will you be expected to link your message with the one before or after yours? If your speech is truly "occasional," in that it relates to its specific setting, consider this connection before you decide upon your conclusion.*

the message may be stated indirectly, the *form* of the conclusion must satisfy the second goal of all conclusions—to leave the listeners satisfied that the speech has ended.

Summary Conclusion   The summary is possibly the most common form of conclusion. In it we repeat our purpose sentence and main points, sometimes by repeating the phrases we used in the body of the talk, but more often by reducing their content to a number of very short sentences.

Avoiding such phrases as "To summarize," "Now, in conclusion," and "Let me conclude by saying" is sensible not only because they are trite but even more because they clearly signal the approaching end. The audience may respond by immediately turning off their attention and reaching for hats and coats. It is better to ease into a conclusion unobtrusively and then hit our listeners hard with the ending.

Appeal Conclusion   In this form of conclusion we directly ask our hearers to agree with us or to take certain action, or to entertain the possibility of a "brighter future" if they think and act as we suggest. The appeal ending is a useful way of concluding a persuasive talk.

When he was England's Prime Minister, Winston Churchill employed a classic type of appeal conclusion in an address delivered a few months before the United States entered World War II:

> We shall not fail or falter; we shall not weaken or tire. Neither the sudden shock of battle, nor the long-drawn trials of vigilance and exertion will wear us down. Give us the tools, and we will finish the job.[6]

Roger M. Blough, Chairman of the Board of the United States Steel Corporation, concluded a talk with an appeal ending:

> The future is for men who dare to have great expectations, and who—with the guidance and encouragement of all the people for whom they strive— will also have the courage, the persistence, the wisdom, and the patience to transform those expectations into realities![7]

Illustration-Quotation Conclusion   Some speakers like to conclude with either an illustration or a quotation. For instance, a speaker advocating creation of a monorail system to provide rapid transit between his city and its suburbs illustrates the point in his conclusion by describing the efficiency of operation of the original monorail system in Germany.

Illustrations will help to focus and hold the listener's attention upon

---

[6] "Put Your Confidence in Us," an address broadcast February 9, 1941, printed in *Blood, Sweat, and Tears* (New York: G. P. Putnam's Sons, 1941), p. 462.

[7] From "Great Expectations," an address to the Economic Club of Chicago, March 13, 1957. Printed in pamphlet form and distributed by the Public Relations Department, U. S. Steel.

some specific matter which he can remember. The quotation may strike a familiar chord in the listener's memory; it may bring the added authority of some well-known and well-respected person into the speech; and it may serve to bring together the main points of the speech into a succinct, easily remembered statement.

Recently, a student speaker, campaigning against his best friend and supporting another student for a campus office, concluded his talk with these words from Shakespeare's *Julius Caesar*, "If, then, that friend demand why Brutus rose against Caesar, this is my answer, — Not that I loved Caesar less, but that I loved Rome more."

It is a common failing among speakers to spend too small a proportion of their preparation time on the conclusion of the talk. Some make the mistake of working on the introduction before they prepare the conclusion. These speakers either fail to understand the importance of the conclusion, run out of preparation time by spending it all on the body of the talk, or, lulled by their wide knowledge of the subject, think mistakenly that they "can handle the conclusion."

The conclusion is structurally the most important part of the formal talk (although it is true that with a poor introduction we can lose the interest of the listener and never regain it). In the conclusion we have our last and most important chance to "make our pitch."

All these methods of concluding assume that we are presenting a solo performance, that we occupy a climactic position in the speaking occasion, that we want to leave our listeners with specific ideas to remember or to accept, or that we ask them to alter their behavior in a relatively specific way. Sometimes, however (and this view violates certain basic principles), we prefer not to be so specific. We may wish to leave questions in the receivers' minds to provoke further, immediate communication on the topic, or additional thought and study, perhaps leading to delayed change of attitude or behavior. We may wish to invite our listeners to contribute their knowledge or experience to the subject, or we may want them to ask questions to clarify unexplained points. Our message may be not a formal one-shot affair, but informal and part of a continuing dialogue. In these cases, we may choose to modify drastically the norms of good speech conclusions — or even deliberately omit a conclusion altogether.

The Introduction

The introduction of the speech plan is placed, of course, at the beginning of the plan, since the introduction of the speech is at the beginning of the speech. However, the introduction is planned *last*, not first as so many inexperienced speakers believe. Common sense tells us why. If the introduction is to introduce something, then it follows that we must know what we are introducing before we can plan the introduction.

Purpose of the Introduction   All introductions have three basic purposes: (1) to arouse the listener's attention, (2) to enhance the speaker's personal proof, and (3) to lead the listener to a consideration of the message or content of the speech. As with conclusions, introductions are intensely personal matters; even though they depend in large measure upon the purpose of the speech, the listener, and the occasion, the individual characteristics of the speaker influence their makeup a good deal. (See inset, page 192.)

Methods of Introducing   Since we may have to prepare an introduction before we have mastered these fairly complicated relationships, let us first look into the basic approaches to introducing a talk, some of which are described below. These somewhat contrived techniques will serve as substitutes for the personal introduction that we will eventually learn to prepare for every formal speech.

The Illustration-Quotation Introduction   In this kind of introduction, we begin by trying to catch our hearers' attention with a story, a description of some event or situation, or a striking quotation. It differs from the unrelated introduction (described below) in that it has a connection with the occasion or purpose of the talk. Many clergymen begin their sermons by quoting from the morning scripture reading. A speaker who wanted his hearers to support missile research began his talk with an eyewitness description of the launching of a Saturn rocket.

A quotation may serve as an interesting introduction if we are good at reading or quoting the words of others. If we have had little experience in reading aloud, we should practice carefully before trying this kind of introduction, or get the help of someone who has had training or experience in oral reading.

The Direct Introduction   In this brief, forthright, and often refreshing introduction, we announce to our listeners exactly what we intend to talk about. Such an introduction is: "It is my purpose, ladies and gentlemen, to ask you to vote for me for the House of Representatives. I believe that I am the best qualified candidate for the job." Although it is less frequently used than some other introductions, it works well with listeners who are friendly or neutral toward the topic or speaker.

This form has several variations, not all of which are as brief and direct as the example above. Sometimes we combine two kinds of introduction, first acknowledging our hosts or referring to the occasion, and then telling our listeners what our major points will be. Sometimes we tell only part of what we really want to say.

The Acknowledgment Introduction   In this approach we devote the entire introduction to greeting the assembled dignitaries and other guests, in acknowledging the chairman's speech of introduction, and in paying compliments to the audience. Such matters should be included in many, if not most, introductions, but an introduction that covers only these suffers because it fails to prepare the audience for the message to come.

The Occasion Introduction   Here we build our introduction out of aspects of the occasion. We may review its historical significance; we may praise individuals and organizations connected with it; and if the purpose of the talk permits, we will also include a "preview" of the purpose. This kind of in-

Considerations in Composing the Introduction

1.   *Consider the relationship of the introduction to the purpose of the speech. The questions about the composition of the conclusion also apply to the introduction. If your purpose is to be expressed clearly, deductively, in the body of your speech, you may wish to put the purpose sentence at the end of the introduction, and expect most of the introduction to lead to this statement. If your purpose is to be expressed indirectly, or your organization is inductive (with the purpose to be revealed later in the speech), you would instead keep your introductory remarks general, as far as the purpose is concerned; indeed, the audience might not be able to determine much about your purpose from your introduction.*

2.   *No matter how directly related or unrelated to the purpose of your speech, the introduction must be designed to attract and hold the listener's attention. It must reach out to your listeners' interests; it must strive to increase your personal proof or at least maintain that which you have, and finally, it must relate as a whole to the body of the speech. An introduction perceived by the listener as completely hanging in space will most often mean that less attention is paid to the content of your speech and may damage your personal proof in the long run.*

3.   *Evaluate the relationship between your introduction and your listener. Ask yourself essentially the same questions as you asked about your listener and your conclusion: how much does he know*
about your subject? What is his attitude toward what you intend to say? What does he know and feel about you?

4.   *What is the relationship between your introduction and the occasion of your speech? Will you be expected to acknowledge the occasion, to express appreciation at being asked to participate in it? Are there important officials or visitors to be acknowledged? Should you begin by relating your subject to the occasion? These decisions will affect not only the attention of your listeners but your personal proof as well. The way in which you relate yourself and your subject to the occasion of the speech may easily spell the difference between the success and failure of this particular message.*

5.   *Finally, consider yourself, as a person and as a speaker, in relation to your introduction. What can you give to the introduction? Suppose the occasion calls for a humorous anecdote, but you simply cannot tell a funny story well. Suppose, on the other hand, you thrive on jokes in your introductions—you love to tell them, and you tell them very well —but the occasion is a serious one. Suppose you have a tendency to be quite nervous at the beginning of a talk, but you know certain tricks that will reduce this nervousness, certain words you can say, certain visual aids you can use, certain movement patterns that tend to relax you. Can you adapt them to the peculiarities of this particular speech, set of listeners, and occasion?*

troduction is extremely useful when the occasion is important and the message ties in with it directly. On occasions of lesser importance, this sort of material should be abbreviated and combined with material of another category.

The Unrelated Introduction In this introduction we tell jokes or stories or make other frivolous comments that we think will gain attention. We make little attempt to relate the introduction to the subject or the occasion or the audience. Although this type of introduction is easy to prepare, it has a serious disadvantage in that it fails to start the listeners toward an understanding of the purpose of the talk. The most suitable place for the unrelated introduction is the extremely informal situation in which the audience is friendly and the subject not particularly controversial. However, breaking a longer introduction with an interesting, only slightly related remark here and there will not harm the speech and may help relax the audience.

Developing the Speech Plan

Now that we have assembled all the parts, let us proceed to the task of building a specific speech plan, beginning with the purpose sentence, continuing with the body, then the conclusion, and, finally, the introduction. Our topic will be "Let's Revise Our Primary System."[8] (The complete speech plan, essentially deductive, is reproduced on pages 197–199.)

Developing the Purpose Sentence

In this case, the speaker apparently had a specific objective in mind: to advocate a change from the present haphazard primary system of selecting a presidential candidate to a regional system, supervised by the federal government. His purpose sentence, therefore, was a straightforward declarative statement; it advocated a change; and it stated the desired change. (Note that the purpose sentence, as with all other parts of the plan, is a *complete sentence*.)

The critic, however, might make two observations, one in the nature of a commendation, the other negative: (1) The traditional "we should" of the advocative speaker was replaced with "we need to . . ." Quite possibly the speaker made this change because he intended to deliver the purpose sentence as part of his speech and believed his listeners would respond more favorably to an appeal to fulfilling their joint need than they would

---

[8] The authors are indebted to Roger E. Williams, graduate student in Communication at Michigan State University, now temporarily in public service, for permission to use a speech plan developed by him. The plan was selected, not as an example of a perfect model but as an example of a real plan by a real speaker for use in a real speech. If in studying this plan we find errors in concept or construction and can suggest methods of improving it, then we are making use of the example as a learning device.

to a flat pronouncement of the speaker's own personal objectives. (2) An examination of the body of the speech plan clearly indicates that the speaker felt a compulsion to discuss and reject an alternative plan, that of a national presidential primary.

This critic is unable to determine why the speaker wanted to introduce and discard the alternative. The point is, however, that the purpose sentence does not include or forecast any of the material in the second major part of the body; thus it does not accurately state what the speech was to accomplish. The solution, in this case (assuming a genuine desire of the speaker to consider the national presidential primary), would be to include the national primary in the purpose sentence as prepared for the speech plan:

> Since neither the present haphazard primary system nor the proposed national presidential primary is likely to be effective, we need to institute a system of regional presidential primaries under the supervision of the federal government.

The speaker might still opt to deliver the purpose sentence as he originally designed it, but the corrected one would be of much greater help to him as the major guideline for preparing his entire speech plan.

Developing the Body

As we can observe, the body of the speech plan consists of three major points (only two of which are reflected in the purpose sentence): Point I lays out the faults in the present system, thereby developing the "need for a change" implied in the purpose sentence. Point II introduces and then discards the alternative proposal of a national presidential primary. Point. III sets out the speaker's solution and argues for it.

The speaker's first main contention, that the present primary system needs revision, is well developed, and it makes good use of the materials of speaking (see Chapters 5, 6, and 7). The speaker's personal proof should be enhanced when he demonstrates his knowledge of the problem and offers his listeners specific factual information (twenty-three state primaries, for example). He uses reasoning and evidence, and cites sources of his evidence, examples of the materials of development. Phrases such as "helter-skelter" and "winner-take-all" should help to hold the listeners' attention as well as suggest that the speaker is one of them, not some remote expert from far off Washington (materials of experience). His major subpoint under his first main contention (the proliferation of primaries argument) is developed in greater detail than the other major subpoints; this concentration tends to reflect the speaker's interest as shown in his introduction.

The second major contention is something of a puzzle, not alone because it is not mentioned in the purpose sentence, but because its statement is not in "contention" form but is an objective, expository statement, supported by four points of argument. The critic can only guess that the speaker did not think through this part of his proposed speech as carefully as he did the others—or conclude that our principle about the purpose sentence contributing to the development of the speech plan is vindicated.

The final major contention contains the "plan" or solution to the problem described in the introduction and point I. It is well developed, in general, and is strengthened by the inclusion of a specific proposal by a member of Congress, which must pass the legislation required to implement the plan supported by the speaker.

Developing the Conclusion

Our speaker developed his conclusion by combining three recognizable types (points A, B, C). He began by summarizing the need for a change from the present disorganized, multiprimary system—he appealed to authority by citing Senator Thomas Eagleton as support for his (the speaker's) position. He then combined an appeal with a quotation by closing his speech with a statement by Senator Robert Packwood—appropriate for its reflection of the speaker's views and for its "onward and upward together" spirit, with which speakers advocating a policy change like to conclude and which American listeners have come to expect of such speeches. (Note, however, that the speaker ignored his own major point II in his conclusion.)

Developing the Introduction

The speaker apparently was concerned, throughout the preparation of his speech plan, that his listeners might not be very interested in his subject and that they might not know much about it. He chose a variation of the illustration-quotation introduction in an attempt to overcome these obstacles. He began with a figurative analogy or comparison—in narrative form—probably calculated to arrest his listeners' attention. Then he made his comparison or relationship with his topic very clear, in case some of his audience did not get the point.

Description is another technique of this introduction, along with historical allusions and an attempt to take the edge off his criticism by citing Senator Eagleton's contention that the original primary system was developed in good faith to remedy an evil of an earlier period.

A good argument can be made for the claim that the speaker's introduction, especially points C and D, serves the double purpose of introducing the audience to the subject and also inductively (in the sense we are using that term) leading toward a statement of the purpose sentence. Thus this speech plan, as is the case of many if not most of the "real" speech plans we see, is not a pure form of the deductive, but actually is inductive-deductive in structure (see page 183).

Note that in this plan the introduction is much longer and more detailed than the conclusion, supporting the critic's belief that the speaker had some concern with initial listener interest in his topic. Note, also, that the major divisions of the introduction (and this applies to the conclusion, as well) are *not* indicated by Roman numerals, which represent major arguments or divisions of the purpose sentence, but by capital letters, representing, in this instance, major divisions of the introduction.

Developing Transitions and Internal Summaries

The speaker apparently felt that the relationship between his first major contention and the second (in the body of the speech plan) might not be clear to his listeners; and he inserted, in parentheses, a transition between these two parts of his plan: "(As we think about revising the primary system . . .)." The same technique was used between major points II and III:

> (As we consider revising the primary system, the national primary idea seems to pose more problems than it solves.)

We know that the speech plan is an outline of what the speaker intends to say, not a manuscript, and he frequently has to supply transitional statements to remind himself of his intended meaning and his obligation to be clear to his listeners.

The same point can be made for internal summaries. The speech outline does not contain connective devices that would help the speaker and the listener keep in mind what has been said previously as they move together to another section. In this case, the speaker inserted in his plan, as the last main subpoint of the body just prior to his conclusion, a statement that may be considered, in part at least, an internal summary:

> While the regional primary concept is not a perfect solution, it would preserve much of the direct contact that is integral to primaries; it would retain the ultimate party conventions; it would eliminate wasteful travel and unnecessary fatigue; and it would provide enough time, over a 5-month period, to scrutinize the candidates.

In this way, the speaker presumably hoped to aid his receivers in relating the body of the speech to the upcoming conclusion.

Now that we have "looked over the speaker's shoulder" as he prepared his speech plan, we can study it in its entirety (see the inset of the deductive plan) and annotate it carefully in the margins of this book. Let us look especially for (1) examples of how the principles set down in this book are brought together to produce the plan of the speech and (2) examples of the misuse of these principles. In these ways, we should be able to improve our own speech plans and thus our own speaking.

Similarly, study the inductive speech plan on "New Energy for Energy" on pages 200–202.

A Specimen Speech Plan: Deductive

Let's Revise Our Primary System

Introduction

A. *According to venerable British tradition, the steeplechase began as a wild race among the landed gentry of 18th century England. Horsemen sighted a distant steeple, aimed their steeds, and took off—over walls, water, chicken coops and picket fences. James Kilpatrick, "The Mad Primary Steeplechase Has Got to End,"* <u>Washington Star</u>*, April 23, 1972, p. C4.**

    1. *They terrified livestock and left village natives perplexed.*

    2. *They left a trail of bruised bodies and broken bones, and the weary winner limped home on a winded horse.*

B. *According to recent American tradition, we have inaugurated a new steeplechase of our own. Every four years, zealous politicians enter a wild race that could be labeled the "Grand National Presidential Primaries Steeplechase" as they set their sights on being named a presidential nominee.*

    1. *Candidates dash from state to state promising great things, spending great sums, with election results often leaving the natives (and nation) perplexed.*

    2. *Behind them lies a trail of typewriters and telephones, dollars and debts, and the weary winners limp to the conventions with their vigor and resources drained.*

C. *The primary system was the product of good intentions. Senator Thomas Eagleton,* <u>Congressional Record</u>*, Vol. 118, No. 67 (April 27, 1972), p. S6847.*

    1. *The Progressive reformers around the turn of the century wanted to take the selection process out of the so-called "smoke-filled rooms."*

    2. *They also wanted to expose the candidates to public scrutiny prior to election day.*

D. *However, the present system of 23 different state primaries—each run by its own set of rules and each producing varying results—has become unmanageable. Former White House counselor, Robert Finch, describes the present system as being "to the point where it is insanity compounded— demeaning to the participants, and exhausting the candidates as well as resources." "Finch Suggests Primaries Be Made Uniform, Simpler,"* <u>Washington Star</u>*, April 5, 1972, p. A2.*

Purpose Sentence
E. *We need to institute a system of regional presidential primaries under the supervision of the federal government.*

Body

I. *The present presidential primary system needs revision.*

A. *The state-by-state primary system functioned well when there were roughly ten scattered states using this means of delegate selection. Kenneth Crawford, "An Orderly Pattern of Regional Elections,"* <u>Washington Post</u>*, April 18, 1972, p. A18.*

---

* *For a discussion of the place of evidence in the outline of the plan, see Chapter 10, pages 173–174.*

B. Now there are 23 state primaries, with more states considering this option. Senator Packwood described this situation by stating "the noble dream of democratization has become a nightmare. The innovative reform . . . has been tarnished in practice." Senator Robert Packwood, _Congressional Record_, Vol. 118, No. 54 (April 7, 1972), p. S5598.

C. The proliferation of primaries, and their lack of uniformity, has produced numerous problems.

    1. The number of primaries makes campaign financing difficult. "Do Primaries Have a Future," _National Civic Review_, Vol. 61, No. 5 (May 1972), p. 224.

    2. The "helter-skelter" scheme is needlessly exhausting physically. James Kilpatrick, "That Costly Trail to Miami," _Washington Star_, July 9, 1972, p. D1.

    3. In many states, the primary election results have no binding effect on delegate votes. "Daley's Regional Primaries," _Chicago Tribune_, July 12, 1972, p. 20.

    4. State primaries often involve obscure local issues which have little consequence in national perspective. "And Now a Word for Primaries," _Chicago Tribune_, April 2, 1972, p. S–1A.

    5. Some states follow a winner-take-all-delegates law that distorts election results. "The Primary Extravaganza: Time for Reform," _Washington Star_, April 23, 1972, p. C1.

    6. Primary laws allowing crossover voting defeat the objective of producing a nominee that is the first choice of his own party. James Kilpatrick, "That Costly Trail to Miami," _Washington Star_, July 9, 1972, p. D1.

Transition: (As we think about revising the primary system . . .)

II. A national presidential primary is one alternative.

A. This idea has been proposed by Senator Mike Mansfield and Senator George Aiken in the form of a constitutional amendment. Senator Mike Mansfield, _Congressional Record_, Vol. 118, No. 38 (March 14, 1972), p. S3886.

B. While this would bring needed uniformity, most observers feel that a national primary would be going from bad to worse. "Are Primaries Necessary?" _Time_, Vol. 99, No. 15 (April 10, 1972), p. 13.

C. It would compound problems extant under our present primary system. "And Now a Word for Primaries," _Chicago Tribune_, April 2, 1972, p. S-6A.

    1. Primary campaign spending would be aggravated to the extreme.

    2. It would lengthen the primary campaign considerably, especially in the vote-rich states of the North.

D. It would also produce new problems.

    1. A national primary would favor those candidates with access to the national news media center in Washington, D. C. Senator Robert Packwood, _Congressional Record_, Vol. 118, No. 54 (April 7, 1972), p. S5598.

    2. Direct contact with the voters would be lost. "Are Primaries Necessary?" _Time_, Vol. 99, No. 15, p. 13.

    3. Relatively unknown candidates would be put at a distinct disadvantage. "Are Primaries Necessary?" _Time_, Vol. 99, No. 15, p. 13.

4. It would favor those candidates with easy access to enormous sums of money. Senator Robert Packwood, *Congressional Record*, Vol. 118, No. 54 (April 7, 1972), p. S5598.

5. If a run-off election were necessary, it would mean three national elections in four months.

Transition: (As we consider revising the primary system, the national primary idea seems to pose more problems than it solves.)

III. A regional primary system is the most sensible plan.

A. An orderly pattern of regional elections would provide the best formula for maximizing the benefits and minimizing the faults of primaries.

B. Under a plan introduced by Senator Robert Packwood now pending in Congress, the following would occur. Kenneth Crawford, "An Orderly Pattern of Regional Elections?" *Washington Post*, April 18, 1972, p. A18.

1. The country would be divided into five regions (Audio-visual aid: Use coded map).

2. Each of these regions would conduct a primary according to a staggered timetable. The first election would be held in March, and the other regional primaries would be held at one-month intervals thereafter.

3. The order of regional elections would be determined by lot, 70 days prior to each election, thus discouraging lengthy campaigns.

4. The same slate of candidates, picked by a 5-man commission as all "nationally recognized" candidates, would run in each primary. Provisions are also made to include relatively unknown candidates.

5. Convention delegates would be appointed by the candidates on a proportional basis according to the percentage of votes received.

6. The regional primary system would be supervised by a Federal Primary Elections Commission of five members appointed by the President and approved by the Senate.

C. While the regional primary concept is not a perfect solution, it would preserve much of the direct contact that is integral to primaries; it would retain the ultimate party conventions; it would eliminate wasteful travel and unnecessary fatigue; and it would provide enough time, over a 5-month period, to scrutinize the candidates. James Kilpatrick, "That Costly Trail to Miami," *Washington Star*, July 9, 1972, p. D1.

Conclusion

A. A serious appraisal of the present primary system reveals a number of severe problems that contribute to a "steeplechase madness."

1. Senator Eagleton, in supporting revision of primaries, stated that the "present system has terrible disadvantages with few, if any, advantages." Senator Thomas Eagleton, *Congressional Record*, Vol. 118, No. 67 (April 27, 1972), p. S6848.

B. Integrity and credibility must be restored to our presidential selection process in keeping with the dignity and responsibility of the presidency.

C. As Senator Packwood has stated, "If we are to return 'government to the people' and restore their confidence in that government, we have an infinitely better opportunity through the regional primary concept." Senator Robert Packwood, *Congressional Record*, Vol. 118, No. 54 (April 7, 1972), p. S5599.

A Specimen Speech Plan: Inductive*

[Audience Analysis: This speech is to be given to a student audience. Receivers are personally experiencing some consumer effects of the energy shortage, but they do not have an overall perspective as to the extent or the urgency of the problem. The speaker's intent is to convert their unfocused concern into energetic support for the speech's purpose. The inductive approach† is used due to the fact that, by suggestion, the receivers will realize that to support a massive energy research and development program will cost staggering sums of money—taken from tax revenues and industry profits. Thus, in the long run, the individual (as a consumer and taxpayer) will end up supporting this essential endeavor.]

New Energy for Energy

Introduction

A. *In California, last week, fifty truckers found their visit to a San Jose truck stop indefinitely extended. They were out of diesel fuel . . . and so was the service station.* "Cold Comfort for a Long, Hard Winter," *Time, Vol. 102, No. 24 (December 10, 1973), p. 33.*

B. *In Pennsylvania, 3000 employees of an electronics firm were laid off for a week while their plant closed to conserve fuel.* "The Fuel Crisis Begins to Hurt," *Time, Vol. 102, No. 25 (December 17, 1973), p. 33.*

C. *Along the Gulf of Mexico, fishing boats sat idle. The fish were there, but the fuel wasn't.* "Cold Comfort for a Long, Hard Winter," *Time, Vol. 102, No. 24 (December 10, 1973), p. 33.*

D. *In New Hampshire, the fuel shortage left some 25 towns without police and fire protection, garbage pickups, road repair, or school transportation.* "Cold Comfort for a Long, Hard Winter," *Time, Vol. 102, No. 24 (December 10, 1973), p. 33.*

E. *These reports do not depict isolated and unusual events. Instead, they are representative of a growing pattern of problems facing America as the oil shortage becomes a reality.*

Body

1. *America's present shortage is around 1.4 million barrels of oil a day, or about 10% of total demand.* "The Fuel Crisis—Nixon Acts," *Newsweek, Vol. 82, No. 23 (December 3, 1973), p. 25.*

2. *Residual oil supplies, used by utilities, are now at "minimum operable inventories" in New England. Never before in peacetime have these oil supplies been this scarce.* "The Fuel Crisis—Nixon Acts," *Newsweek, Vol. 82, No. 23 (December 3, 1973), p. 25.*

   a. *Further residual oil shortages will result in power blackouts.*

   b. *According to an OMB report, these shortages—and subsequent power cuts—will continue to spread. After New England, they will move down the East Coast and into the Midwest.*

---

* The authors are grateful to Roger E. Williams for permission to reproduce this example of an inductive speech plan (see also footnote on page 193).

† Note that the speech plan is not perfectly inductive in structure; you may wish to check your knowledge of the two forms by identifying the internal deductive structure in Part III of the Body.

3. *New Englanders are currently receiving about 25% less heating oil than normal. "The Meanest Winter of the Century," Time, Vol. 102, No. 25 (December 17, 1973), p. 35.*

A. *Our present oil situation is critical.*

   1. *Lawrence Goldstein, senior economist for the Petroleum Industry Research Foundation, predicts our shortage during the first three months of 1974 will increase to 2.8 million barrels of oil a day. "Hill Moves Daylight Saving, Mileage Goal," Washington Post, December 11, 1973, p. A16, Col. 4.*

   2. *Other economists predict the shortage during this period at anywhere from 2.6 up to 6 million barrels of oil a day — depending on the effectiveness of conservation measures and the Mideast situation. "Next, the Oil Recession," Newsweek, Vol. 82, No. 23 (December 3, 1973), p. 86.*

   3. *Further demand upon our already short supply of oil will be made by our military forces. They will need an additional 300,000 barrels a day to replace supplies cut off by the Arab oil embargo. "Hill Moves Daylight Saving, Mileage Goal," Washington Post, December 11, 1973, p. A16, Col. 4.*

B. *The future oil situation looks even more critical.*

I. *America's oil shortage is increasing.*

Transition: As our oil supplies decrease, what is happening to our energy demand?

A. *Energy consumption in the U. S. over the last two decades had been increasing about 7% a year. "What Went Wrong," Time, Vol. 102, No. 24 (December 10, 1973), p. 50.*

B. *President Nixon underscored our increased demand for energy when he told Congress, "Some forecasts say that we will double our usage of energy in the next ten years . . . In fact, it is predicted that the United States will use more energy and more critical resources in the remaining years of this century than in all of our history up until now." "Executive Reorganization: The President's Message to the Congress." March 25, 1971. Weekly Compilation of Presidential Documents, Vol. 13, March 29, 1971, pp. 54 –560.*

C. *In discussing the demand for oil, John Love, former Director of the President's Energy Policy Office, stated, "We're doing everything we can, but we're not going to produce petroleum supplies that will meet the demand curve." "The Man in the Middle of the Energy Crunch," Nation's Business, Vol. 61, No. 10 (October 1973), p. 78.*

II. *America's energy needs are also increasing.*

Summary: Our nation's oil shortage is increasing as our demand for energy keeps increasing. What alternatives do we have?

A. *John Love, former Director of the President's Energy Policy Office, lists two necessary steps in solving the energy problem. "The Man in the*

Middle of the Energy Crunch," <u>Nation's Business</u>, Vol. 61, No. 10 (October 1973), p. 78.

    1.   First is the problem of "dampening the demand."

    2.   Second is the problem of developing alternate sources of energy.

B. To "dampen" energy demand, our nation is now participating in a series of conservation programs. "Energy Shortage Strikes Home," <u>U. S. News & World Report</u>, Vol. 75, No. 24 (December 10, 1973), pp. 18–19.

    1.   These include reduced highway speed limits, lowered thermostats in homes and offices, restricted hours for service stations, etc.

    2.   While these actions are important in dampening the short-range demand, they will not help our long-range energy shortage.

C. To achieve a long-range solution to the oil shortage, we must speed the development of other conventional and nonconventional energy sources, states J. K. Jamieson, Chairman of Exxon Corporation. <u>Newsweek</u>, Vol. 82, No. 23 (December 3, 1973), p. 64.

D. Our natural resources and technical expertise provide us with a number of energy options. "Alternatives to Oil," <u>Time</u>, Vol. 102, No. 24 (December 10, 1973), p. 43.

    1.   The U. S. has perhaps one-third of the world's coal supply.

        a. We must develop ways to de-sulfurize coal for direct use.

        b. We must develop the capacity to convert coal into synthetic oil and gas.

    2.   We must greatly increase our energy output from nuclear power plants.

        a. We should encourage the development of breeder reactors, and also the inexpensively fueled, low radioactive fusion reactors.

    3.   Solar energy should be harnessed to supplement and even replace other energy sources.

    4.   Geothermal energy could provide low-cost, pollution-free electric power in certain parts of the country.

    5.   Other alternatives include tidal power, wind power, fuel cells, and the use of waste products for power generation.

III. There are energy alternatives to oil.

Conclusion

A. As oil supplies become less available and our national demand for energy keeps growing, it becomes increasingly important that we explore alternative sources of energy.

B. President Nixon emphasized the need for energy research and development when he stated that "it is clear that the answer to our long-term needs lies in developing new forms of energy." Statement by the President Announcing a Series of Additional Actions to Deal with the Nation's Energy Problem. June 29, 1973. <u>Weekly Compilation of Presidential Documents</u>, Vol. 9, July 2, 1973, pp. 867–874.

Purpose Sentence   C. We need to encourage and actively support research efforts to develop new sources of energy.

Using the Speech Plan for Effective Speaking

There is a type of student who "prepares" his speech, and *then* writes an "outline" to satisfy his instructor's requirements. He scoffs at the speech plan as busy work—and complains that he gets low marks on his speeches. This student gets nothing worthwhile from our discussion of organization; the prepare-first-outline-later method is the Royal Road to bad speaking.

If, however, you want to pull together the principles of speaking you have been studying and use them constructively in the presentation of your message, you can make the speech plan work for you. Here is a suggested plan of action for developing and using your speech plan:

1. Analyze and adapt to your listeners throughout your preparation. Keep in mind at all times the people with whom you are talking.

2. Limit and adapt your topic until you have phrased it into the best purpose sentence of which you are capable.

3. Force yourself to make your entire plan support and develop your purpose sentence. (If your purpose sentence is faulty, modify it.)

4. Choose a basic plan (deductive or inductive) for your speech and develop the unique approach that best suits your purpose, your material, your listeners, and yourself as speaker.

5. Develop your speech plan carefully, selecting from among the materials of speaking you have gathered those that best appear to accomplish your purpose. As you outline, use complete sentences whenever possible. Choose your outline symbols for consistency and workability. Check for logical consistency. Remember to use materials of development, personal proof, and materials of experience in accordance with the principles and methods you have read in this text.

6. Speak your thoughts aloud as you prepare. Try out ideas, relationships of ideas, and wordings of ideas. Do *not* attempt to memorize, but experiment with different ways of expressing your ideas.

If you follow these procedures, you will find that, by the time the speech plan is completed, you are nearly ready to deliver your extemporaneous speech. There will be no need to memorize. After you have prepared one or two small note cards with indications of the main headings and major subheadings of your speech plan printed in large block letters; and after you have prepared any quotations you wish to read verbatim; and after you have attended to the matters of style and the principles of delivery, which are discussed in the following chapters—then you will be ready to begin practicing your speech for delivery. Now that you know your subject, your materials, and your organization, your fear of speaking extemporaneously should be greatly reduced. And thus, the attention you have paid to organizing your speech will pay off in its presentation.

Suggested Assignments

1. Prepare and deliver a speech offering direct support for a single point on a current events topic. Be sure that your topic is a single point worthy of consideration, capable of expansion and clarification. The point should be developed with materials that you have recently read and reacted to. For example, how did you react to the latest unidentified flying object or military crisis? Why did you react in this way? After thinking about the general subject area, you should synthesize your idea to a single declarative sentence (purpose sentence). State it simply (for example, "The large American cities are going broke"). After determining the purpose sentence, you should set about explaining why you reached this conclusion, calling upon any materials you feel are pertinent. Prepare a speech plan for this speech, carefully following the instructions in this and other relevant chapters. Consult the sample speech plans in this chapter. Include a bibliography of the sources you used.

2. Carefully choose and limit a topic, according to the principles and instructions in Chapter 8. Collect your materials, and record them according to the instructions in Chapter 9. Then, following the deductive speaking plan described in Chapter 11, outline and organize your speech for presentation. Prepare your speech plan according to the principles of outlining explained in Chapter 10. At the top of your plan, immediately below the title, indicate what modification, if any, of the deductive plan you are using. Identify the types of evidence you have used, according to the information provided in Chapter 6. These identifications should be made in the speech plan at the point where the evidence occurs. Identify the types of reasoning you used, according to the information provided in Chapter 6. These identifications should be made in the speech plan at the point where the reasoning occurs. Include the sources of your evidence within the speech plan, following the example of the sample plans in this chapter. Add a bibliography of any general sources you used.

3. Repeat assignment 2, using the inductive speaking plan or modification of it.

4. Choose a subject in which you strongly believe. While taking into account your listeners' attitudes toward that belief, see how many attention-arresting devices you can work into your speech (do not lose sight of the message). Employ appeals, along with reasoning and evidence, in an effort to convince your audience. Prepare your speech plan, following the instructions in the assignments above. Include the sources of your evidence according to the sample speech plans in this chapter, and a bibliography of the general sources you used. Indicate, in the righthand margin, each appeal you plan to use and each attention-arresting device growing out of the composition of your speech.

5. Prepare a speech in which you report a process—how something is made, how something operates, how something is marketed, how a product is used, how an idea has developed, or the like. You are to take a fairly elaborate idea and reduce it to a short speech that can be understood by an audience not knowledgable about the topic. So far as is possible, you are to reduce the process to a series of steps, employing one of the speech plans discussed in Chapter 11. Each of the main points is to be amplified with specific, concrete materials. The report must be interesting as well as informative. To assist in accomplishing these goals, you must make use of

visual or auditory aids (see Chapter 13). Prepare your speech plan according to the instructions in the assignments above. Include your sources of evidence, a bibliography, and a list of the visual or auditory aids you plan to use.

6. Prepare a speech of advocacy in support of or against a current policy or significant custom of our society. Analyze your subject, your audience, the occasion, and your own prejudices in order to determine your exact use of the materials of speaking and your pattern of organization. Review the entire textbook up to this point, selecting and adapting those ideas which you believe will best aid you in your task. Materials of development, personal proof, and materials of experience will all form a necessary part of your speech. You should have a specific audience reaction in mind. You may be more or less direct in your efforts to secure this reaction, depending upon your analysis of the situation. Prepare your speech plan according to the instructions in the assignments above. Include sources of evidence, a bibliography, and notations of the materials of speaking in the righthand margin. If your speech is in any way indirect, include a statement of the rationale upon which you are operating in the preparation and presentation of your speech. The rationale should include basic assumptions about your listeners' knowledge of and attitudes toward your subject, as well as a statement of your ultimate purpose in speaking, if the purpose sentence does not reflect it. (If yours is a speech-communication class in which subjects of current interest are continually discussed, discard the "choose a topic" approach in these exercises and substitute a "respond to the exigence" approach (see Chapter 8 for details).

Suggested References

Aristotle, *The Rhetoric*, trans. Lane Cooper (New York: Appleton-Century-Crofts, 1932). Book III, pp. 220–241.

Bettinghaus, Erwin P., *The Nature of Proof*, 2nd ed. (Indianapolis: Bobbs-Merrill Co., 1972). Chapter 7, "Strategy and Tactics in Message Preparation."

Cohen, Arthur R., *Attitude Change and Social Influence* (New York: Basic Books, 1964). Chapter 1, "The Communication."

Ehninger, Douglas, *Influence, Belief, and Argument* (Glenview, Ill.: Scott, Foresman and Co., 1974).

Freeley, Austin J., *Argumentation and Debate: Rational Decision Making*, 3rd ed. (Belmont, Calif.: Wadsworth Publishing Co., 1971). Chapter 13, "Building the Brief."

Mills, Glen E., *Message Preparation: Analysis and Structure* (Indianapolis: Bobbs-Merrill Co., 1966). Chapter 5, "Outlining and Patterns of Arrangement"; Chapter 6, "Introductions, Conclusions, and Transitions."

Thonssen, Lester, and A. Craig Baird, *Speech Criticism* (New York: Ronald Press Co., 1948). Chapter 14, "The Structure of Oral Discourse."

12
Phrasing Materials: Language and Style

"Words! Words! Words!"

"Words! Words! Words!" This expression is probably more frustrating than it is revealing, for any speaker knows that his study of the principles and the methods of speaking must lead, ultimately, to the oral presentation of a message. This chapter is not concerned with the actual delivery of the message, but it focuses upon the essential vehicle of the message — words and combinations of words. *Style* is the term that describes the uniqueness of a communicator's combining of words.[1] *Style* is the term we often use in distinguishing between speakers whose words we like and those whose words we don't like: "His style of speaking is poor"; "I don't like his style"; "He has a good style"; "He speaks with a compelling style." Well, what is this "good" style that effective communicators presumably have and ineffective communicators lack?

For centuries, speakers and writers have tried to define, describe, or in other ways identify the word *style*. Lord Chesterfield held that style is "the dress of thoughts." Others claim that a man's style is the man himself. *Webster's Dictionary* defines *style* as "mode of expressing thought in language . . ." This last definition is perhaps the broadest and most useful starting point for our attempt to discover what style is. From this definition, we know that the vehicle of style is language, and language is a system of symbols called words. It is through words that communication is carried on, and those of us who study oral communication are called upon to study words in many ways.

Words interest us as sounds, begun by the voice-producing apparatus, amplified by the resonators, and formed into words by the articulators. We are also concerned with words and sounds as they are perceived by the hearing mechanism and the nerve tissue associated with hearing.

---

[1] It is important to distinguish here between style in the rhetorical sense, which has to do with language; and style, as the layman sometimes uses the word, which refers to all elements associated with speaking.

When we consider style in speaking, we are concerned with words as they are spoken and words as they are heard. We are concerned with words as sounds, and with four attributes of sound: loudness, pitch, quality, and time (see Chapter 14). We are concerned with the relationship of the sound of a word to the thing it names or describes.

We are especially concerned with words and meanings. Words are but symbols for meanings that are within us; and meanings are not transmitted or sent from the message source to the receiver—they are aroused within the being of the receiver. Words (and other symbols), however, are the instruments that arouse these meanings. And while we must avoid confusing the symbol with the meaning—and we must refrain from a simple "meaning-transfer" analysis of communication—we must recognize that it is primarily through our language that meaning arousal is achieved in the receiver. Furthermore, we must recognize that we can never be sure that our receiver will make the distinction between words and meaning, and we can be almost certain that he will confuse our words and our meaning, and that the meaning we arouse with our words will not necessarily be what we intended. Thus, oral style refers not merely to beauty or form or acceptability, but to a basic message sense. Style can literally spell the difference between meaning arousal in the receiver that approximates the meaning within us, the source, and meaning arousal that does not.

Moreover, style is more than a matter of choosing the right words to arouse meanings. We must consider not only the words themselves but the way we put them together in phrases, sentences, and paragraphs. It is the process of choosing single words, constructing phrases and sentences of these words, and building paragraphs of these sentences that makes the style of one person different from, or better than, that of another. Take, for example, the following illustrations: one from Ecclesiastes and the other a rehashing of that passage. In content, the two are somewhat similar; yet their success in arousing meaning differs sharply:

To everything there is a season, and a time to every purpose under the heaven: A time to be born, and a time to die; a time to weep, and a time to laugh; a time to mourn, and a time to dance; a time to keep silent, and a time to speak.	In the course of human life, we observe that the events of life have definite cyclical characteristics, awareness of which will lend to the observer a certain appropriateness in his actions.

One clue as to what makes the style of one interesting and delightful to read, and the other drab and boring, is that the verse from Ecclesiastes uses simple, concrete words. Another clue might be that the original verse is easier to read than its prosaic counterpart because of the structural simplicity of the original; it is made up of a series of short, parallel phrases that enter the reader's understanding with ease. The new version, on the other hand, requires some mental gymnastics before it can be grasped. Still, there is something else — some magic — that makes the original style better, and it is this ingredient that has for centuries escaped definition and made necessary countless attempts to find out what we mean when we use the word *style*.

Bear in mind that both of the examples above are of written style. When we consider that our problem is to use words orally, the question of effective style becomes much harder to pinpoint.

Oral Style and Written Style

Most speaking is impromptu or extemporaneous in mode. Consequently, we have little opportunity to "build in" the characteristics of good style, as we can in writing an essay or term paper. This means that we must study these characteristics even more carefully — learn them so well, in fact, that we can develop the ability to create good style on our feet, at the moment of delivery. This is hard to accomplish, very hard, but *it can be done* — by learning the principles of good style, adapting them to our purpose as a speaker in a given communicative situation, and delivering the message. We do this over and over again, as often as we have the opportunity. This is the "magic formula."

"A speech is not an essay on its hind legs," remarked one teacher of communication. She was pointing out simply that there are differences between the style of spoken language and the style of written language. Because of these, the conventions of written English do not always apply to spoken English, simply because words and phrases are perceived in one instance by the eye of the reader and in the other instance by the ear of the listener. Therefore, our mode of expression must be adapted with this principle in mind.

Furthermore, the kind of English that is often regarded as proper for writing may not be proper for speaking, because of the varied speaking situations we meet from day to day. The more informal the situation, the more informal must be our words, phrases, and sentence structure. Consequently, we may often find that an effective speaking style will appear to have been used in almost total ignorance of the rules of good formal writing. A manuscript sermon delivered from the pulpit of a large, dignified, urban church may be set in print for wider distribution and may stand as a well-written essay; but the remarks of a shop foreman explaining the gears of a new fork-lift truck to the employees, clear and efficient as his speaking may be, might appear in print to be almost infantile because of the short sentences and oversimple, repetitive language.

If, in working from our speech plan, we choose words, phrases, illustrations, sentences, and whole paragraphs according to the standards of good essay writing, we will most likely deliver a speech that sounds strained, overdone, and ultraformal. It is important, then, to examine some of the basic distinctions between the styles of written and oral communication.

Instant Intelligibility

The most important difference between oral and written styles is that the oral message must be composed so that it can be understood immediately. An oral message is presented only once, usually, and the receiver is expected to grasp the message as it is delivered. Written materials, on the other hand, may be read and reread; they may be compared with other writings; unfamiliar words may be looked up in the dictionary. The fact that the printed word is so accessible, that the reader can spend as much time and effort with it as he wishes, gives the writer the privilege of indulging in obscure language, if obscure language suits his purpose; of expressing his thoughts delicately, if delicacy suits his purpose; of being subtle, if subtlety is what he needs. He is, in short, free to write what he wants to write in the language of his choice.

In speaking, we have no such privilege. Oral style does not demand kindergarten language, but we are nonetheless restricted to words and combinations of words that our audience can understand on first hearing. Even when we fulfill this requirement, we must frequently use more repetition and restatement than the formal writer would find necessary. If we are grappling with a difficult concept, we must explain it again and again, sometimes using exactly the same language, sometimes approaching the subject from a variety of angles. And all the while we are repeating and restating, we must take care not to let our message drag or sound repetitious.

Where a simple, clear-cut explanation will suffice for the writer, as speakers we may find it necessary to illustrate our explanation, to compare our point with a similar point, or to ask rhetorical questions or otherwise enliven and enrich our message. We may also find it necessary to use vivid language, language more vivid than the writer would find necessary (or could get away with), because it helps our listeners form images of the ideas and feelings we are trying to get across to them. (See the section in this chapter on "Vividness.")

Sometimes a word of four syllables or more is exactly the right word to express an idea in print; but, knowing that the listening vocabulary of our audience is far smaller than its reading vocabulary, we may have to substitute a series of short, plain words — words that might sound awkward in print but convey the idea clearly in speaking.

In short, the requirement of instant intelligibility means that the speaker must use shorter words, phrases, and sentences; more oral punctuation, more imagery, more illustration than would the writer with the same message.

Personal Address

Because of the direct, face-to-face, and immediate contact of the speaker with his listeners, we are permitted, and, indeed, often required, to use a more personal form of address than the writer customarily uses. We may use the impersonal, third-person approach if we wish; but, to test its wisdom, compare the following two passages as if you were hearing them orally:

> The student of oral communication must be aware of the importance of proper language in his messages.
>
> You must learn how to choose the right words when you talk.

The sentence on the left is remote, dignified, and impersonal; the one on the right is directed right at the immediate audience. Chances are that the first sentence might need a second reading for its message to be clear. In an oral message, a sentence that abstruse would be lost.

Effective as "you" may be, there are many occasions in which greater informality and warmth are desired and the speaker must demonstrate oneness with his hearers. This can be achieved through the use of the first person plural, *we*—not the editorial *we*, but the one that means "you and I." President Franklin D. Roosevelt knew the value of this feeling of unity with his audiences, and his phrase "you and I know" has become almost a cliché.

Sentence Structure

Although in one sense the speaker lacks the writer's freedom in his use of language (because of the instant intelligibility requirement), in another sense he enjoys more freedom: The comparative informality of most speaking situations permits and encourages greater liberty in the construction of sentences than traditional writing patterns allow. Splitting an infinitive, for example, scarcely causes a raised eyebrow among listeners, but in formal writing it is still regarded with some distaste. Contractions (*don't, won't, you'll,* for example) are commonly accepted in speaking, as are incomplete sentences—fragments. In fact, much of our oral communication is done in fragments today, especially in informal situations. A student speech that was received with almost unanimous approval by the audience contained the following passage:

> You wouldn't want a child of yours to grow up never seeing a tree or a bird, would you? Would you? Of course you wouldn't! Yet you show no signs of alarm when somebody wants to cut a school playground in half. No, you don't. You just turned a deaf ear. Said nothing. Let 'em get away with it. Went right on about your business of eating and sleeping and making a living. Wake up! Open your eyes! Look around you. When did you see a cow last? Hear a bird sing? Remember?

This piece has several contractions. It is full of fragments. The tense shifts. There are colloquialisms, like "let 'em" and "wake up!" We may find the style a bit strange, a bit lacking in dignity; but those who heard the speech found no strangeness, no lack of dignity; and none of the listeners criticized it for bad style.

There are, of course, many more differences between written and oral styles. We cannot run through them all here; some we will pick up with experience if we read and listen for the distinctions. The passage above is from a speech that was exciting to hear. Written style can also be exciting through the use of methods peculiar to writing. The important thing is that the two styles are not the same; each has its own devices and its own audience, and skill in the use of one does not automatically bring skill in the use of the other.

Without negating what has been said about the differences between oral and written style, it must be recognized that the two are not always sharply differentiated — our analysis, for example, has tended to contrast formal writing with relatively informal speaking. Written style also seems to be changing from rigid correctness to greater informality; the conventions of written English are not so strict as they have been traditionally. In fact, it would appear that much of modern writing is taking on more and more of the characteristics of good informal speaking style.[2] Also, modern speaking appears to be a great deal more informal than ancient speaking — as far as we can learn from the transcripts of old speeches, which have probably been edited somewhat as they have been passed on to us (which means, possibly, that we read the words of a skillful writer rather than a speaker).

Whatever may be said of style in speaking and its differences from style in writing, one thing is certain: to be effective, speaking style must be geared to the immediate understanding of our listener.

The Characteristics of Good Oral Style

With the underlying requirements for oral style of instant intelligibility, personal address, and informal sentence structure, we may consider now the *characteristics* of oral style — the qualities that are present in a good oral message and lacking in a poor one. Style, as has been often observed, is an intensely personal canon of rhetoric, and laying down strict rules for all occasions and all circumstances is impossible. It is probably safe to assert that there are as many systems of style standards as there are writers and

---

[2] D. Gordon Rohman, Professor of English and Dean of the Justin Morrill College of Michigan State University, writes that "Modern taste prefers the sense of spontaneity in prose, the sense of talk rather than 'writing,' the sense of 'thinking out loud' rather than premeditation." *The Good Writer*, Vol. 5 (April 1967), p. 1.

speakers. Although the ancient classification — unity, coherence, and emphasis — is comprehensive and acceptable, language changes, and so does our information about language. Therefore, for our purposes today, the standards of an adequate speaking style can best be described with these four qualities: clarity, forcefulness, vividness, and adaptability.

Clarity

Above all, style should be clear (precise, accurate); whatever the speaker says should be easily understood by his audience. To illustrate, these lines from Lewis Carroll's "Jabberwocky" have bemused readers and critics for years:

> 'Twas brillig, and the slithy toves
>   Did gyre and gimble in the wabe;
> All mimsy were the borogroves,
>   And the mome raths outgrabe.

"Jabberwocky" may have meant something specific to the author, and very likely does mean something to scholars of Lewis Carroll, but it means little to most listeners — unless it is used to illustrate some specific point, such as the need for clarity.

Clarity is essential to style, no matter who the source is, no matter who the receiver or what the occasion. All the speaker's subtleties, rhythms, images, power, and authority count for nothing when the audience cannot understand what he is talking about. This is true for persuasive speaking as well as explanatory; to be convinced, the audience must first understand. Of course, there are occasions — as when the receiver is hostile to an idea — when the communicator will want to approach his subject indirectly and merely hint at the central idea; but, although he may be using subtleties of meaning, he must say something to the audience and say it clearly, for an audience will not listen to double talk.

The lack of clarity in speaking can often be blamed on the speaker's failure to recognize that listeners tend to equate words and meanings, words and things. So does the speaker. The problem is that *dog* to the speaker may "mean" a large, fierce German shepherd pursuing the mailman down the street, while to the listener the word *dog* "means" a small, docile French poodle lying on a silk pillow in a basket. No wonder listener and speaker cannot understand one another.

The problem can never be completely solved, for communication by its nature is imperfect, but improved clarity may be achieved in numerous ways. For most speakers in most speaking situations, simple words will be grasped more easily than complex words. Why use *domicile* when *home* will do the job? Perhaps unfortunately, about forty words account for half of all American speech, and these include the articles *a* and *the* and the pronouns *I, that, you,* and *it.*

Concrete words are more easily grasped than abstract words. We can easily note the differences in the two passages below, which Herbert Spencer used to illustrate how vague abstractions can be turned into concrete realities:

In proportion as the manners, customs, and amusements of a nation are cruel and barbarous, the regulations of their penal code will be severe.	In proportion as men delight in battles, bull-fights, and combats of gladiators, will they punish by hanging, burning, and the rack.[3]

Or, suppose a member of the city council were to make one of the following statements. Which would be more satisfying to the public?

We are going to improve public transportation in this city.	By the end of this year we will have an extra bus on the Broadway, the Third Avenue, and the Cedar Street lines. By the end of next year we will have twenty new buses and we will operate on fifty routes as compared with the present thirty-five.

Not only the words themselves but also the structure of sentences and paragraphs should be simple and concrete. Speakers and writers who lack skill in expression often find themselves bogged down in a succession of dependent clauses and parenthetical phrases. Their product is cluttered with *ands, buts, whichs,* and *whiles,* which may be understandable in an essay but unworthy of strict attention in speaking, when the listener hears each sentence only once.

Again, oral style does not demand kindergarten simplicity. It is possible for us to achieve simplicity of style without being infantile or dull. Edward FitzGerald, in his translation of Omar Khayyam's *Rubaiyat,* might have said (although it is unlikely): "My arrival could have been compared to a state

---

[3] Herbert Spencer, *The Philosophy of Style,* ed. by Fred N. Scott (Boston: Allyn and Bacon, 1892), p. 8.

of liquidity, and my departure, to air in motion." FitzGerald preferred simplicity: "I came like Water, and like Wind I go." Similarly, in conceding the election of 1952, Adlai Stevenson could have concluded his remarks with some stiff, formal comment. Instead he chose to let people know how he felt by alluding, in simple words, to what Lincoln had said after losing an election: "He said that he felt like a little boy who had stubbed his toe in the dark. He said that he was too old to cry, but it hurt too much to laugh."

Forcefulness

No sailor during World War II ever heard the public-address system squawk across the decks of the attack transport ship the words "Please let down your boats into the water." Yet countless hundreds of times, when the moment for making the landing came, sailors, soldiers, and marines leaped to action when they heard the call "Away all boats!" This curiously archaic phrase may have puzzled the landlubbers; but to the men who had to go over the side, the behavior demanded was quite clear—and the order compelled their attention because it was forceful.

Forcefulness is another standard of good style in speaking; the term implies drive, excitement, urgency—qualities that are necessary in many speeches. Forcefulness does not, however, imply loudness; we can be forceful with a whisper as well as with a shout. Perhaps compelling is the best way to describe forceful speaking, for the style should at all times compel the audience to listen, to try to understand, to welcome persuasion and information. One of the most forceful speakers of modern times was Winston Churchill, yet it was not loudness that conveyed this forcefulness but the choice and combination and arrangement of words and sentences. Churchill's style almost defied the listener not to listen.

One element of forceful style is directness. Compare these methods of issuing orders: "It should be brought to your attention that the term papers are expected by Thursday"; "Term papers are due Thursday"; and "You must turn in your term papers on Thursday." Which of these statements would stimulate the student to begin his work tonight? Clarity, too, besides ranking as a basic quality of style is a concomitant of forcefulness, for no audience can be compelled by something it does not understand. In short, for a forceful style, we should choose words, phrases, and sentences that say, "Look, this is important; listen to me."

Vividness

Vivid language appeals to the senses through words that call up sensory impressions, emotions, and experiences. It helps the listener see, hear, feel, even taste and smell, the images the speaker produces in his attempt to make ideas real to his audience. Of utmost importance in persuasion, vivid language can also direct and hold the listener's attention to an idea intended primarily to inform.

Vivid language is a primary means of appealing to basic motives (see Chapter 7). It lifts the potential receiver from his routine of half-listening; it dashes other thoughts from his mind and helps him to feel what we are trying to put across.

Shakespeare knew well the value of vividness. His plays are full of imagery, of references to places, people, and happenings that were at once familiar to his audiences and yet expressed with sufficient distinctiveness that, despite their knowledge, the listeners (or at least many of them) paid full attention. His description of the witches in *Macbeth*, for example, is short, yet full; although this description is merely a bit of exposition that forms no part of the narrative of the play, we are unaware that it is a technique and we find that Shakespeare leaves us receptive to the images of these creatures:

> What are these,
> So wither'd and so wild in their attire,
> That look not like th' inhabitants o' th' earth,
> And yet are on't? . . .
> You should be women,
> And yet your beards forbid me to interpret
> That you are so.

How can we make our speaking styles vivid? For one thing, we can choose words that sound like what they stand for. The simple word *slippery*, for example, well describes the feel of a fish freshly caught. *Spatter* tells us what large raindrops do when they hit the sidewalk. We need not use bizarre or foreign words, or dig deep into our vocabulary for odd and esoteric words — these may smack of artificiality; we need only select, carefully, some relatively common words and phrases that arouse meanings through their sounds as well as through what they describe.

Another device we can use is to combine words and phrases in new, original ways. We can avoid, whenever possible, the stereotyped phrases that have been overused, like the chairman's beginning his introduction of the final speaker of the evening with the words, "Last, but not least, we have . . ."

Words and combinations of words have definite rhythms — in speaking and in prose as well as in poetry. A succession of short, clipped, one-beat words will sound monotonous; so will a steady onslaught of the polysyllabic, hypermetrical articulations of a superintellect. We can vary the length and rhythm of our words to help avoid monotony.

Vivid language, because it adds color to speaking, helps our receiver listen easily, concentrate with some intensity, and thus receive our message and give it meaning that is somewhat akin to the meaning we intended. Let us think about the vivid language in these examples of speaking:

There is poor teaching, very poor teaching, going on at the University right now! I've experienced it. I think as students we have all experienced it. How many of you have had the instructor who mumbles or talks so fast that you can't take notes or pauses so much between words that you get lost? How about the instructor who is never there during his office hours? Or makes the students feel like peasantry, while he is the aristocrat? Or assigns a ten-page paper on Monday and makes it due on Wednesday? Or says we're having a little quiz on Friday and it turns out to be your midterm? Or the instructor who writes the most important point on the board and you can't read his writing? *Believe me,* this is my fourth year here and I've had every one of these happen to me.[4]

Finally, I continue to urge the need to explicate to our students the values of the political, social, economic, ethical, and moral system under which we live. As I study student protest, I get the feeling that students often do not understand just what it is they are rejecting. If they do not understand, whose responsibility is it to see that they do understand?

All of us would agree that we should not insist upon unquestioning acceptance by students of current stands of society, not by any means. Too many of us are engaged in the struggle to right wrongs and eradicate intolerance to adopt that posture.

But young people need to be reminded that our society was not built on shifting sands, or it would not have stood firm so long. They need to be reminded that with all of its faults and ills, this is still a nation motivated by lofty ideals. They need to be reminded that where their elders have fallen short of perfection, it has not been for lack of effort or honest intent. They need to be warned that to discard all values out-of-hand, just because they have been inherited from the past, would be to open the door for a return to barbarism and anarchy.

I invite your attention to these unanswered questions:

Do universities have some responsibility to help students work out a viable set of standards by rational process?

We say that universities are established to preserve and impart the best of the accumulated *knowledge* of the past. Do they not have the duty to preserve and impart the best of mankind's accumulated *wisdom* as well?

The Rector of St. Andrew's University, in his address to the faculties many years ago, said this: "Mighty are the universities of Scotland, and they will prevail. But even in your highest exultations never forget that they are not four, but five. The greatest of them is the poor, proud homes you come out of, which said so long ago: 'There shall be education in this land.'"

Michigan State University, too, exists because the people in poor, proud homes of another century decreed that there should be education in Michigan. To what end? Not that great libraries and laboratories might be erected to grace the scene, not that trustees and presidents and professors might have interesting occupations, not that bright young people might enjoy an interesting interlude between adolescence and maturity. No, they estab-

---

[4] Introduction to a student speech in a beginning speech class.

lished this university because they saw in higher education the brightest hope for those who came after them to achieve the quality of life to which only the members of a free society dare to aspire.

Next Sunday, on Founder's Day, we should pause to remember with humility and gratitude those whose wisdom and courage and sacrifice made possible all that Michigan State University is today. We should hope that they would be proud of what has been built on the foundations they laid down—a *strong, vital, dynamic* university with *bright prospects* of achieving true greatness in the years just ahead.

Let us agree that if Michigan State University continues constant in its sensitivity and responsiveness to the needs of people, adapts its programs and procedures wisely to the imperatives of the times, and cherishes true excellence as the only goal in all it undertakes, there is no limit to what we can achieve. Such is the state of our university in 1967.[5]

Adaptability

Good style must be adaptable to various occasions and listeners. Although language that is clear, forceful, and vivid will possibly fit into any speaking situation, different occasions and audiences require different stylistic approaches. In the latter part of the eighteenth century, Edmund Burke, the English statesman, was probably one of the great speakers (or writers of speeches) in the English language. Let us look at a passage chosen at random from his speech on conciliation with the American colonies:

> In forming a plan for this purpose, I endeavoured to put myself in that frame of mind, which was the most natural, and the most reasonable; and which was certainly the most probable means of securing me from all error. I set out with a perfect distrust of my own abilities; a total renunciation of every speculation of my own; and with a profound reverence for the wisdom of our ancestors, who have left us the inheritance of so happy a Constitution, and so flourishing an empire, and what is a thousand times more valuable, the treasury of the maxims and principles which formed the one, and obtained the other.

No doubt in Burke's time, and for his particular audience, this language was excellent; but how would it suit a contemporary communicator—speaking, for example, to a public speaking class? Certainly not very well, for the times are different, the occasion is different, the audience is different, and the speaker is different. We might even reduce the paragraph to a statement as simple and succinct as this:

> To be fair to you, I have tried hard to avoid my own prejudices and to take advantage of the great thinking of the past.

---

[5] Excerpt from a speech, "There Shall Be Education . . . ," delivered at a faculty convocation at Michigan State University, East Lansing, Michigan, on February 8, 1967, by the university's president, John A. Hannah. Reprinted by permission.

No business executive would give instructions to his six-year-old son in the same language that he uses to give instructions to his secretary. Most college professors modify their language from the graduate seminar to the freshman class in the lecture hall. We talked earlier about the necessity for adapting our message and our manner of speaking according to the total situation (Chapters 3 and 4). One of the methods of adapting is to vary the style to fit the situation. We can select words, phrases, and sentences that are suitable to the age of our listeners. There are undoubtedly a large number of words that would be well received and understood by an audience of senior citizens but would be neither received well nor understood by an audience of college freshmen (and vice versa!). We can choose words also according to the part of the country our listeners come from: An audience in Louisiana prefers to hear the word *bayou* for creek; Californians would have no trouble understanding *arroyo*. Our listeners will not only understand our message more easily if we speak their language; they will also accept our ideas more quickly, because they will like us better than they would a "stranger." We can also choose our words and examples according to the occupations of our listeners, their social background, and their education.

In short, all the principles of understanding and adapting to the audience and the occasion should be considered when we choose the words and phrases that will make up the message our listeners hear. In making this adaptation of language, however, we must be very sure not to patronize our listeners or misuse any words or terms. These mistakes could be fatal to our personal proof and, therefore, to our purpose in speaking.

There is not space in a single chapter to cover all of the elements, characteristics, and standards of good style in oral communication. One way we can learn about style in speaking is to study good speeches; take a speech of Churchill's, for example, and read every word and phrase in it with an eye to discovering what effect that word or that phrase might have on the listener. Would a synonym have done as well? We can also study good writing with the same critical eye, remembering that good writing style is not always good speaking style, and vice versa. Still, any good writing—prose and poetry—will teach us a great deal about how to use words.

Style and the Other Principles of Speaking

Although we have been mainly concerned with style itself, scattered through our discussion have been references to the occasion and the audience. Style, like the other parts of the speaking process, does not exist in a vacuum; rather, it is one of the vital parts of the entire process of communicating. (And good style, too, is one of the consequences of attention to the communication process.)

In adapting our speaking to particular audiences and individuals, our choice of language can easily determine whether our listeners will accept or reject our persuasion. Suppose you should, by some wild stretch of the imagination, go to your political science instructor, and ask him: "Wudja mind if I turned my paper in late? I ain't got it ready on account my Mom got sick and I hadda go home." You might get permission to present your paper late, but your instructor would probably have mentally recorded an "F," because he could not believe that an "A" paper could come from the same brain that produced those sentences.

A fine minister, an excellent preacher in many respects, was let go by his church because the congregation simply could not take any more of his poor and inappropriate word choices in the pulpit and in the community. Style in speaking can lose a sale, can influence a co-worker's thinking about you, and can stamp you as an undesirable neighbor. Personal proof and style, then, are inseparably related.

What about exposition or information? Have you ever asked directions of a person whose manner of speaking was so unskilled as to choice of words and sentence structure that his language *got in the way* of your understanding? This fault is understandable in the very young, and parents and teachers strain their patience to the utmost to try to understand. However, with other adults, we ignore them or half understand them or, if possible, dismiss them from our world.

Even the logical sense of a speech may be altered by poor style. One speaker used danglers in his sentences to such an extent that, in addition to his meanings' being almost always obscure, his reputation as an unintentional humorist was widespread. "Having closed our windows, the rain soon came" was one of his dandies. And, similarly, "His wife was successfully operated upon for appendicitis at the Good Samaritan Hospital which suddenly attacked her Monday at her home on Mozart Avenue." Poor style in speaking, besides sometimes sounding funny, frequently destroys the listener's understanding.

"We are what we say" is not necessarily true, of course, but most people react as though they believe it. We would probably all agree that poor style in speaking is one of the greatest deterrents to finding oneself accepted as a person.

Improving Your Style

How can you improve your style? This is not an easy question to answer, for there are no formulas to be memorized. Moreover, developing good speaking style is a long-term project, which should start as soon as possible and literally never end. However, many speakers have been able to improve their speaking style by developing a keen ear for language and by continual self-appraisal—and so can you (see inset, page 220).

Suggestions for Improving Speaking Style

1. Constantly strive to increase your vocabulary — especially your speaking vocabulary. As an adult, your speaking vocabulary will probably not grow much unless you make conscious efforts. The easiest way to build a good vocabulary is to read widely, remember words, and look up "meanings"; for instance, choose ten new words from each day's reading to remember, discover the "meanings" of, and use in conversation. Listen to the words others use, too; look up their "meanings" and try to fit them into your speaking. Be careful lest you become "word happy," saying words for their own sake or using words that are inappropriate for the subject, the occasion, or the audience (or, if this is a necessary stage in your development as a speaker, try to pass through it as quickly as possible!).

2. Study the various combinations of words that you read and hear. Although words by themselves are helpful in building effective style, it is the combinations that make the real difference.

3. Constantly work to adapt your oral language to the people you talk to, to the situation that exists as you talk, and to the subject under discussion. Never make the mistake of assuming that any old word or phrase or sentence will do, any old time.

4. Make a study of language as an instrument of communication; look at its relationships to things. Learn to appreciate its capabilities and its limitations, too.

5. Practice speaking in public as often as you have the opportunity, as often as you have something worthwhile to say.

It is fashionable today to regard the subject of style in speaking with a suspicious eye, to relegate it to a position below reasoning and evidence, organization, and adaptation. However, let us remember that words, alone and in combination, form the major vehicle through which reasoning, evidence, and all of the other constituents of persuasion and exposition reach our listeners.

Suggested Assignments

1.   Instead of participating, listen in on the next informal conversation at lunch or coffee break, or between classes. Focus on the words, the combinations of words, the sentence structure. Make mental notes concerning the degree of instant intelligibility of the messages exchanged, the amount of personal address used, the sentence structure itself. Transcribe your notes as soon as you are alone, and make an evaluation of the style of the communication you overheard.

2.   Apply the criteria for good oral style (clarity, forcefulness, vividness, and adaptability) to an informal exchange between your instructor and a student in one of your classes. Rate both participants in the communication situation. Who "won"? How did style affect meaning arousal between the speakers? How did style affect your own understanding of the messages exchanged?

3.   During the next round of speeches in your class, select one of them for a careful analysis. Make no notes during the speech—just listen as hard as you can. Would you label the speech as "instantly intelligible"? Whether your answer is Yes or No, try to decide what part the language of the speech played in your decision.

4.   Select a current speech from *Vital Speeches*. Study its language. Then analyze the style of the speech, using the principles of clarity, forcefulness, vividness, and adaptability as your bench marks. Make judgments about the speech by using these principles as criteria.

5.   Ask your instructor to record your next speech and have at least portions of it transcribed. Study the manuscript of your speech. Does it *read* well? If it does, do you feel that this is a sign of good oral style? Now, listen to the tape. Which do you like better, the essay or the speech? Justify your answer.

6.   Attend a lecture or other public speech or, if this is impossible, listen to a speech on television or the radio. As you listen, try to focus your attention on the language— the words, the phrases, the sentences, the larger units. Using this chapter as your guide, write a short essay on the style of the speech.

7.   Listen to a recording of one of your earlier classroom speeches. Analyze it according to the principles of style in this chapter. How well did you do? What seemed to be your strong points? Your weak points? If you had the opportunity to deliver the speech again, what changes in style would you make?

8.   Select an essay from your freshman English textbook. Read it aloud. How does it sound? Try it on your roommate. Now, keeping your classroom audience in mind, rewrite the essay in good, informal oral language. Perhaps your instructor will permit you to read portions of the original and the revision to the class. Take a vote. Which version do your fellow students like best *as a speech?* What conclusions can you draw from their responses?

9.   Choose a technical subject for a speech, one with which you are very familiar but which is unfamiliar to most of your audience. Plan and organize a speech in which you explain some aspect of this subject. Modify your technical language—find words that express simply and clearly the technical nomenclature and concepts. Give your listeners a simple quiz in which you attempt to discover whether they really understood what you were talking about.

10.   Deliberately choose as the topic for your next bull session a big, broad subject like Democracy, Communism, Education, Freedom, or Peace. Try to make your remarks as meaningful and specific as you can through your choice of language. (Note: This is a learning assignment only, to help force you to study your language carefully. You would not choose such a topic for formal speaking.)

11.   Prepare a speech that is composed entirely of description or narration; that is, describe something you have seen or experienced, such as an automobile accident, the sun setting behind a low cloud bank, or a thrilling circus performance. Or, tell a story about some entertaining, compelling, or frightening event. You will find that following the principles of good style will greatly assist you in putting across this kind of speech.

12.   Write out a short speech on any subject that interests you and might interest your audience. Choose every word in the speech with special care—get it just the way you want it. Then memorize the speech and deliver it to your classroom audience. In this way you will have the experience of delivering a speech using the lan-

guage you wish to use. (Note: This is another learning assignment. Most of your *formal* speaking should be extemporaneous and most of your informal speaking will be impromptu, but an occasional experience with memorized speaking may help to sharpen your ears so that they hear good and bad style.)

13.   Your instructor will ask each of you to choose a topic for an impromptu speech. He will collect the topics and ask you to draw one. You will have ten seconds to prepare a two-minute speech, which will be recorded. Besides concentrating on your message, try to choose language that is clear, forceful, vivid, and adapted to your listeners. You will be given an opportunity to hear and study the playback of your speech; then you will have one week to prepare a five-minute extemporaneous speech on the same topic. As a result of your impromptu experience, the opportunity to study it, and the week's preparation time, your prepared speech should be rated considerably better in style. Your instructor will compare your two speeches and offer suggestions concerning your style.

14.   Prepare the speech plan for your next classroom speech. Practice your speech and present it to the class. Now, assume that you have been asked to give the same speech to a different audience (your instructor will define and describe your new audience) without your having time to modify your plan. Study your speech plan again, and practice your speech once, keeping your new audience in mind. Remember to adapt your style and language to your new listeners. Present your speech, and note the contrasting language between the two speeches. If both speeches have been recorded, your comparison will be more meaningful.

Suggested References

Alexander, Hubert G., *Meaning in Language* (Glenview, Ill.: Scott, Foresman and Co., 1969).

Aristotle, *The Rhetoric*, trans. Lane Cooper (New York: Appleton-Century-Crofts, 1932). Book III, Chapters 1–12.

Benjamin, Robert L., *Semantics and Language Analysis* (Indianapolis: Bobbs-Merrill Co., 1970).

Berlo, David K., *The Process of Communication* (New York: Holt, Rinehart and Winston, 1960). Chapter 7, "Meaning and Communication"; Chapter 8, "Dimensions of Meaning"; Chapter 9, "Observations and Judgments: The Structuring of Perception."

Black, John W., and Wilbur E. Moore, *Speech: Code, Meaning, and Communication* (New York: McGraw-Hill Book Co., 1955). Chapter 5, "The Vocabulary of Speech"; Chapter 10, "Style in Speech."

Blankenship, Jane, *A Sense of Style* (Encino, Calif.: Dickenson Publishing Co., 1968).

Flesch, Rudolf, *The Art of Plain Talk* (New York: Harper & Row, 1946).

Langer, Susanne K., *Philosophy in a New Key*, 3rd ed. (Cambridge, Mass.: Harvard University Press, 1957). Chapter 5, "Language."

Lee, Irving J., *Language Habits in Human Affairs* (New York: Harper & Row, 1941).

Samovar, Larry A., and Jack Mills, *Oral Communication*, 2nd ed. (Dubuque, Iowa: Wm. C. Brown Co., 1972). Chapter 8, "Language: Verbal and Nonverbal—The Medium of Communication."

13
Using Audio-Visual Materials

"Objects, instruments, or devices—either audible or visible—
help to clarify ideas"

Throughout history man has used, in a meaningful, artistic, and creative way, some form of audio-visual aids to make his ideas more clearly known. In earliest times he is known to have used simple diagrams as a basic means of communication. With the awareness that language is abstract and subject to misunderstanding, man increasingly turns to some form of audio-visual material in order to reinforce the spoken word and to improve his communication.

Researchers indicate that increased learning is directly related to multi-sensory appeals—especially the audio and the visual in combination.[1] Tests by the Armed Forces reveal that learning by such audio-visual aids is retained about 55 percent longer than facts learned in the usual way.[2] Complex objects and ideas become even more apparent to us through the combined stimuli of sight, sound, touch, taste, and smell.

It is obvious that audio-visual materials are widely used by speakers, teachers, and other leaders in educational, religious, and medical institutions—to name but a few. Information for today's generation is increasingly depicted through television and other media in that category. Television itself uses various kinds of audio-visual materials described in this chapter. Some media people predict that cable television will practically revolutionize our homes into widespread educational centers. No doubt, audio-visual materials will be used and observed more extensively in the future than ever before.

---

[1] According to a study by Thomas Dahle, the combined use of oral and written comments is more effective than the single use of oral, written, pictorial, or grapevine methods. See Thomas L. Dahle, "Transmitting Information to Employees: A Study of Five Methods," *Personnel*, Vol. 34 (1955), pp. 243–246.

[2] R. M. Goetz, *Visual Aids for the Public Service* (Washington, D. C.: Public Administration Service, 1954), p. 3.

The Nature and Uses of Audio-Visual Materials

Stated simply, audio-visual materials are objects, instruments, or devices—either audible or visible—that are designed to help clarify ideas. They are extremely advantageous for situations in which relationships must be readily grasped. Pictures, charts, recordings, chalkboards, motion pictures, and any object or living thing, such as a ship model or a plant or animal, can be classified as audio-visual aids. To illustrate how such materials can bolster the communication process in your own speeches, suppose you are to explain how to take better pictures for slide projection. To describe the process by means of words alone would prove to be an involved and laborious process, which your audience might find difficult to follow. However, the same situation with a camera and several friends available for placement in unposed groupings would clarify your ideas for taking better pictures for slide projections. Thus, it becomes apparent that audio-visual materials can assist both speaker and listeners in sending and receiving messages. They can help in these ways:

1. *Aid understanding* by adding a new impression.

2. *Spark attention* in bored, apathetic, or sleepy audiences. Some speakers use a visual aid in the opening of their speeches to arouse listeners.

3. *Improve the memory of the speaker.* For example, if your material is a skeleton outline of the talk, it will help you remember the points you are going to develop.

4. *Reduce tension and stiffness in the speaker* by making you move about as you handle the aids. You can also focus your listeners' attention on the material as you point to it.

5. *Increase audience concern about the topic.* In a speech on highway fatalities, pictures of demolished cars would have this effect.

6. *Simplify complex materials* involving statistics by using charts.

7. *Produce more accurate sensory images in your listeners.* Words often wear smooth and lose their force.

8. *Aid in retention of information and images.* Your listeners can learn more and remember your message better.

Planning the Use of Audio-Visual Materials

While some aids, such as chalkboards and diagrams, are easy to plan and use, others may require much time and energy to procure (and it may be costly). For this reason we must be doubly certain that the results are worth the effort—that the inclusion of some audio-visual material will make our message more understandable. For instance, let us suppose that a speaker is considering using a motion picture in a talk. It is evident that he will need to select an appropriate film, preview it, and evaluate its effectiveness; procure the equipment, and possibly an assistant, and return the equipment after using it. While startling improvements have occurred in audio-visual programming and equipment—such as the invention of videocassettes, slide-tape programs, machine-made transparencies, instant-load and jam-proof projectors—a speaker probably could profit by simply using whatever equipment is available for his short talk.

Still other factors in planning the use of audio-visual materials are these: (1) Will the aid furnish additional information to what we can provide in our speech? (2) Is the aid available or possible to produce fairly easily? (3) Does the aid provide interesting information in a clear and concise way? (4) Is the aid relatively easy to manipulate? Is it durable and neat? (5) Will the aid present a true example of actual conditions? (6) Will the time we spend on the aid get in the way of necessary explanation and class discussion? (7) Will the aid be too costly for a limited budget?

There are several principles that govern the usage of audio-visual materials. Foremost is the need for recognizing their function as a means to an end—an instrument of communication. Of secondary importance is the need for skill in their selection and presentation; the speaker must know which aid is best suited for the clarification of his ideas and how to use it. Sometimes an audience learns more easily when we use more than one kind of aid. Perhaps the best test in choosing audio-visual materials is this question: Will the specific aid actually illuminate or develop the idea? If not, it might be better for us to consider another type of aid or to abandon plans for audio-visual help altogether. Of course, before we can make decisions about audio-visual material, we must be thoroughly familiar with all of the aids at our disposal.

Audio-Visual Media

The Chalkboard   In view of the numerous aids that are available for use, students often overlook an inexpensive and versatile one—the chalkboard. The chalkboard, or blackboard—usually green in modern buildings, and sometimes hidden behind curtains—is one of the most popular visual aids.

When leading a meeting or presenting a message, keep in mind that there is something about writing the subject on the chalkboard that attracts immediate attention and keeps the listeners oriented to its consideration. No doubt you can recall how some instructor actually filled the chalkboard with written comments during his presentation. You saw him move about as he used the chalkboard; and you were intrigued by his skill in making this subject clear. Students were impressed by William James, the first American experimental psychologist, who constantly used the blackboard to illustrate his points.

Chalkboards are advantageous in other ways: (1) They are immediately available and can be repeatedly erased. (2) Their size allows for a considerable amount of visual material. (3) Major points in the discussion can be highlighted. (4) Spur-of-the-moment comments can be put into writing. (5) The audience can be exposed to special terms, concepts, and illustrations; technical, foreign, and key words; explanations of issues and policies; outlines of summaries, diagrams, maps, and other graphics. (6) Mounted pictures and charts can be hung from the chalkboard. (Some of these possibilities may not be planned ahead of time, but if you are using the chalkboard as your principal visual aid, you may wish to keep handy for possible use such materials as colored chalk, a pointer stick, masking tape, and cover sheets.)

When we work on a chalkboard, it is important that we draw distinctly, write legibly, allow an adequate amount of spacing between words, and use large enough letters and drawings for the audience to see without straining. For example, letters should be at least three inches high for a room thirty feet deep. Although printing requires more time than writing, it is preferable because of its greater legibility. For an extensive amount of drawing, we should arrive early in order to complete the work before the group arrives.

We should keep in mind that the chalkboard is not effective (1) when the material we write is not large enough for distant viewing, (2) when the lettering is poor or carelessly inscribed, and (3) when intricate drawings require more time than is practical.

Precautions in Using the Chalkboard

1.   *See that the chalkboard is clean and free from distracting materials.*

2.   *Use colored chalk to provide interesting contrast.*

3.   *Letter or write clearly, legibly, and large enough for the people in the back row to see.*

4.   *Make sketches simple, bold, and large enough.*

5.   *Use a yardstick in drawing lines.*

6.   *Draw or write quickly to hold interest.*

Actual Objects   Three-dimensional forms with height, width, and depth provide a reality that cannot be duplicated by any other form of audio-visual aid. Ideas relating to material objects can be more readily comprehended when the listener can handle or manipulate the object itself. Thus, if we could see and touch a rock from the moon, we would undoubtedly have more insight into its character than if we merely had it described to us in words. The student who, in a speech about homing pigeons, brought one to class to illustrate how to attach a message on its leg, and then released it out the window to carry the message back home thirty miles away, provided her listeners with a demonstration they probably will never forget. In this case the movement of the pigeon made the live object stand out prominently.

We can also use contrast to make an object noticeable; for example, objects that are large in relation to others attract attention. A speaker can be a visual aid by exhibiting colorful costumes from other countries. The use of a small puppet in costume could provide an interesting contrast.

We can use an object to exemplify a certain category. Rocks, butterflies, or arrowheads, for example, can be shown as specimens of their category.

Here are some questions concerning the use of objects:

1. Does the object aid in communicating your purpose?

2. Will it be easy to use?

3. Is it large enough for distant viewing?

4. If there are workable portions, will you be able to take them apart and place them back easily and quickly?

5. Is the object safe for demonstration purposes?

Models Models are three-dimensional representations of actual objects that would be impractical or impossible to display because of their unusual size or weight. Their advantage lies in the possibility of reducing large or heavy objects or of enlarging small objects so that they may be assembled, displayed, and dismantled conveniently. In many instances, models are also more serviceable than the actual object and more readily available.

A model has the same scaled dimensions as the actual object and shows exactly how it would appear. In explaining the human eye, for example, we can arrange to show a cut-away model to help the viewer perceive the eye as if he were looking through it. Models of public buildings or bridges can sometimes be held up, tilted, or turned for careful scrutiny. Even more eye-catching effects are possible when we apply movement to the model, as in the case of a glider, a parachute, or a motor. These three-dimensional materials can often be obtained from libraries, public agencies, or private sources. In addition, almost any manufacturer would probably provide samples of his products or models of his equipment. Food, clothing, oil products, rubber products, miniature cars, skeletons, and tools are a few of the materials that may be obtained from such sources.

Precautions in Using Objects, Models, and Pictures

1. *Use aids that are large enough to see.*

2. *Hold objects and pictures up high, facing them toward different parts of the room and holding them there long enough for good comprehension.*

3. *Use only a small number of pictures, carefully paced with your talk so as not to confuse the viewer.*

4. *Place smaller objects, certain specimens, drawings, and pictures in the opaque projector.*

5. *Use models only if they work effectively.*

6. *Invite your group to examine and perhaps operate some of these aids after the talk.*

Photographs   Pictures play a prominent role in the communication of many events. We encounter almost anywhere pictures in magazines, newspapers, comics, posters, billboards, and the like. Excellent pictures catch the eye of people, increase meaning arousal, and stimulate imagination. They also reduce "overcommunication," or the overuse of the verbal load. Photographs can, in essence, verify the words of a speaker and say to listeners, "These conditions are real, I'm not exaggerating, and you can see that they really exist."

For use in the speaking situation, enlargements of still photographs are most appropriate. While motion, as such, is not depicted, spatial relationships are indicated. Their widespread use in newspapers, magazines, and books shows that rather large photographs are effective in presenting a message. The small-sized photographs can be enlarged for a group by means of an opaque projector. Photographs, in general, are (1) convenient to handle and use, (2) reasonably easy to obtain, and (3) easily examined.

The best picture to accompany a speech is one that reveals actual conditions. For example, for a speech on water pollution we might include a colored picture of a polluted stream showing waste from a nearby plant. Pictures can also create a mood or an emotion. A large-sized photograph of a starving child in front of a dilapidated house would provoke increased feelings of concern. Realistic color in pictures (just as in the case of color television) adds a considerable amount of reality to our topic. In selecting pictures for speeches, we should choose those that (1) highlight the intended purpose, (2) represent a typical situation, not an isolated instance, (3) represent dramatic qualities to enhance interest, (4) contain contrasting shades or color combinations, and (5) provide sharpness or clarity of detail.[3]

Our best procedure is to use only a few pertinent pictures and to give the viewers ample time to study each one as we display it. We should keep in mind that pictures are subject to misinterpretations—what people see is bound to be interpreted in accordance with their own experience. Facial expressions are a good example. Is a person smiling or smirking? Is a wide-eyed child looking at something in horror or wonder? Therefore, it is necessary to allow for the first impressions and then proceed to present a factual account of what the picture truly presents.

Maps   As we are becoming increasingly global-minded in the consideration of common problems such as war, pollution, trade, and air transportation, the use of maps can offer better understanding of their various implications.

Representations of the earth's surface through the use of color, symbols, lines, and words often make useful visual aids. Maps can denote a variety of detailed information, and are economical with regard to space, time, money,

---

[3] See W. A. Wittich and Charles F. Schuller, *Audio-Visual Materials: Their Nature and Use,* 3rd ed. (New York: Harper & Row, 1962), pp. 81–92.

and simplicity. Also, they pinpoint essential facts about the areas they represent. Their popularity is evident in their frequent use as a supplementary mass communicative aid in the current television news programs in both news and weather reporting.

The map usually features (1) political boundary lines between states and countries, (2) surface features such as water and land areas, rivers, valleys, deserts, and mountains, (3) locations and dimensions of extensive uninhabited areas, (4) social and cultural information such as language and population data, (5) information about economics, agriculture, and international trade routes, and (6) climate, in respect to rainfall, latitude, and altitude. A pointer stick can bring some specific area into immediate focus.

Finding appropriate maps can be tricky. Recently printed ones of the size needed for good viewing for those seated in the last rows of our room may not be available. Due to changing political conditions of the modern era, maps quickly become outdated. For example, between 1959 and 1968, thirty-nine new countries came into existence, thirty-four altered their names, and thirty-two changed their boundaries; also, 2,500 towns and communities changed their names. The forces of nature also contribute to changes in maps — volcanoes make new islands, and lakes shrink.

In searching for maps, we should not overlook color as an attractive feature in depicting areas like mountains and flat lands. We can contact travel bureaus, government agencies, companies, airlines, bus and rail information centers, foreign diplomatic offices, state tourist offices, foreign-language and history departments on the campus, as well as newspapers and magazines.

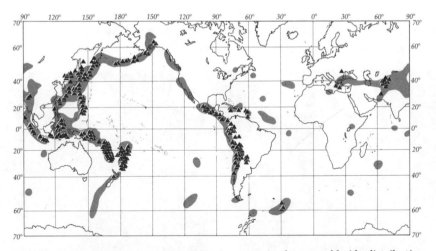

Fig. 13.1   A map coded for a specific purpose—to show worldwide distribution of deep earthquakes (triangles) and shallow earthquakes (gray areas). (From Oceanology: An Introduction by Dale E. Ingmanson and William J. Wallace. © 1973 by Wadsworth Publishing Company, Inc. Reprinted by permission of the publisher.)

It may be desirable for us to prepare our own maps, tailoring them to the focus of our talk. When making them, we should circle important areas, ideas, or relationships with colored pencils and crayons. If the drawings are made on large sheets of paper, they can be attached to a chalkboard with tape. Or we can draw our large area map on the chalkboard before the class begins. Should we wish to use a road map, or some other small map, an opaque projector or transparencies for the overhead projector (to be described later in this chapter) will create the enlargement.

The Flannel Board   The flannel board is a piece of gray or black flannel stretched over a sturdy veneer or masonite board. Pieces of paper — symbolic caricatures, major headings, or pictures from magazines and newspapers — when glued with rubber cement to the backs of strips of sandpaper or to flannel will cling to the flannel. These "slap-ons" can be carefully prepared in advance and can be moved about freely during the presentation of a message.

By means of the flannel board, we use cleverly constructed slap-ons to capture and hold attention and to point up our major ideas. Slap-ons can, for example, be used to visualize a step-by-step process. They are much faster to apply than writing on the chalkboard, although careful rehearsing is needed to achieve good timing and coordination in manipulating them. Becoming confused or hesitating in the selection of the appropriate slap-on tends to nullify the desired effect. Other advantages of flannel board usage are (1) slap-ons can be used again and again, (2) the items can be used in various combinations, and (3) the presentation can be adapted to the listeners.

Its possible limitations include (1) the work required in obtaining or making it, (2) the difficulty in finding a sturdy easel high enough for good viewing, (3) the work and time involved in creating slap-ons (they are ex-

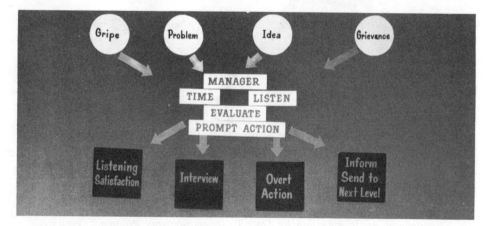

Fig. 13.2   A flannel board used in discussing communication (Courtesy: The University of Wisconsin – Extension)

pensive if made by an artist), and (4) the possibility of listeners' becoming more interested in an elaborate display than in our ideas.

If you don't have access to a flannel board, a local audio-visual aid center will often provide one. For slap-ons, the drawings for original designs need not be artistically perfect as long as they are neat, understandable, and clearly visible.

Closely resembling flannel boards are hook-and-loop boards, which permit three-dimensional objects, diagrams, and pictures to be hooked to any one of numerous nylon hooks attached to the board.

Graphs Using a *bar graph* is a simple procedure in the picturization of data in a speech. The bar graph is relatively easy to construct and read, its key feature being the grouping of comparative data into either vertical or horizontal bars. These bars, usually dark in color, are drawn on stiff cardboard, or slides or other projector materials.

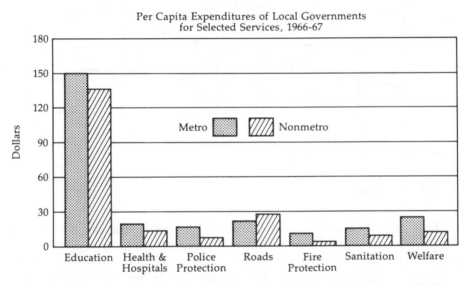

Fig. 13.3 Bar graph showing local government expenditures (Source: U. S. Department of Agriculture)

If, for example, we are planning to compare college enrollment figures over several decades, we can use a bar graph to good advantage. In this case, the length of each bar would represent the total number of enrollees, while each individual bar would represent a certain year. Using a small number of bars (six to eight) makes the best results. Larger numbers of bars together with small-sized captions tend to destroy its chief purpose — simplicity in the use of statistics.

Similar to the bar graph, and used quite effectively for indicating percentage materials, is the *line graph*, which portrays a series of facts with two variables — time and quantity.[4] On such a graph, we can plot a fact in respect to time intervals on a series of vertical and horizontal lines equidistantly spaced. When there is more than one line, we distinguish one from another by using different colors or different types of lines (a series of dots, dashes, or a continuous line). Such devices (and a legend explaining what the particular line indicates) serve to keep the listeners from getting lost in the statistics.

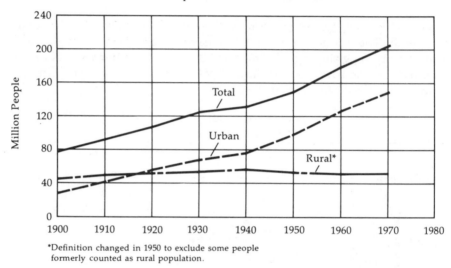

Population of the United States

*Definition changed in 1950 to exclude some people formerly counted as rural population.

Fig. 13.4   Line graph depicting population growth and distribution (Source: U. S. Department of Agriculture)

Line graphs can inform the listener about current trends — in education, the stock market, social problems, labor, international trade, military might, and the like — and delineate increases or decreases in these trends. By checking current magazines, newspapers, and pamphlets, we will find line graphs indicating various late developments and trends in many of our contemporary problems.

Another way to focus attention on condensed statistics is the *pictorial graph*. A variation of the bar graph, this graph employs various numbers that are represented by symbolic figures, such as a soldier or an aircraft carrier. Yet, if actual numbers are not given along with percentages, understanding may be somewhat difficult. To be effective, these symbols should (1) be ample in size for easy viewing and be easily identified by the listeners (for

[4] According to Hugh Culbertson and R. D. Powers, "Study of Graph Comprehension Difficulties," *Audio Visual Communication Review*, Vol. 7 (Spring 1959), p. 109, bar graphs proved better than line graphs for comparing statistical information.

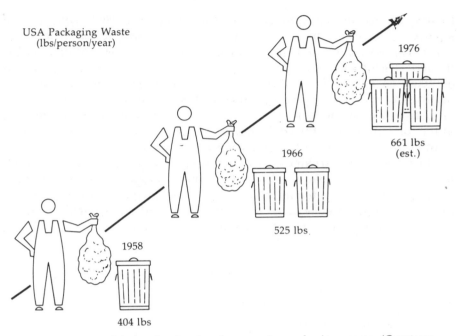

USA Packaging Waste
(lbs/person/year)

1976

661 lbs
(est.)

1966

525 lbs

1958

404 lbs

Fig. 13.5 *Pictorial graph showing increase in packaging waste (Courtesy: David P. Cook of The University of Wisconsin – Extension)*

example, the comparative number of college graduates in different countries or the comparative number of men in uniform in various nations), and (2) be consistent in size to eliminate misunderstanding. Because these picture materials are easily understood, these graphs have sometimes been called an international statistical language.

Pictorial graphs are not as accurate as line graphs; the use of symbolic figures is intended to reveal approximate numbers, rather than specific ones. The addition of these simplified graphs, however, may increase interest as well as understanding.

Choosing a simple graph is essential; if it is too complex, it loses its value. The best graph highlights only one or two ideas. If the copy of the graph is too small to be viewed clearly, as in the case of one that is published in a magazine, it can still be used if an opaque projector is available.

For use in the slide machine, on the chart, and on the chalkboard, we must, of course, draw our own graphs. Our main concern, in this case, will be clarity of the relationships depicted, through the use of a minimum number of fairly large-sized bars or lines. We should make graphs simple, large, and bold enough for everyone to see. A large-sized colored picture may be pasted in bare portions of the bar graph to suggest the subject matter. Sometimes an entire blown-up photograph from a magazine can be used as the background for the line graph. A pictorial graph can be made quite easily with careful drawing or with forms cut out of construction paper.

Charts In the *pie chart*, which is another commonly used visual aid, differences in quantity are indicated by the relative size of the portions of a circle. The whole amount, represented by the circle, may be divided into numerical proportions or percentages. While such percentages cannot be depicted as accurately as they can with line graphs, such divisions are particularly helpful in indicating a breakdown of expenses, sources of supply, or distribution of goods. If we stress the relationship of the various portions to the total amount of the circle, our pie chart will be a valuable instrument in the communication of the idea we want to convey.

In a talk on the current expenses of the national government, for example, the pie chart could clearly indicate the relative amount of money allotted to education, defense, veterans' affairs, and other such departments, through the use of appropriately sized segments portrayed in different colors. Pie charts are easy to draw and can be quickly understood.

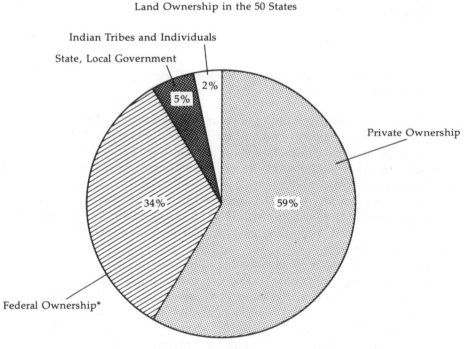

Land Ownership in the 50 States

Total Area, 2.3 Billion Acres

*94% is in the 11 western-most states and Alaska.
About 50% is in Alaska.

Fig. 13.6   Pie chart of land ownership (Source: U. S. Department of Agriculture)

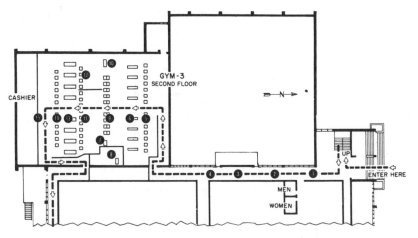

Fig. 13.7   Flow chart of a part of a registration sequence

The *flow chart* is an excellent way to explain the steps in a process and how various elements relate to one another. Through the use of arrows and lines, a flow chart drawn on a chalkboard, chart, or slide can show, for instance, either the basic sequence by which a bill becomes a law or the step-by-step process involved in the manufacturing of some product.

Composed of assembled and carefully prepared data, flow charts are sometimes known as work simplification charts.[5] Among the advantages of the flow chart are (1) it can explain a complicated process which would take an enormous amount of words alone; (2) it can disclose a series of operations; (3) it permits the listener to visualize rather difficult, confusing, and intricate processes; (4) it can indicate the flow of material or the travel route of a public conveyance. For example, we may wish to present in detail a proposed new bus route on our campus or the course of some commodity from its raw condition to its manufactured state at the time of purchase by the consumer. A similar chart is known as the *tree chart*, which depicts the relationship between products and their source, such as a family tree, or the results of some important invention. In the same classification, we find the *stream chart*, which presents the sources that create a product, such as small streams uniting to produce a large river.

The *organization chart* indicates each division of an organization and its breakdown into various departments. It naturally begins with the top officials and goes down, each step being indicated by rectangles, circles, or other graphic representations.

By displaying such a chart, we can explain specifically and easily (1) who is responsible to whom, (2) the nature of the work in each unit, (3) the functional or area grouping of units, and (4) the levels of administrative

---

[5] See H. S. Hall, "Putting Work Simplification to Work," *Business Management Service Bulletin*, No. 605 (Urbana, Ill.: University of Illinois, 1956).

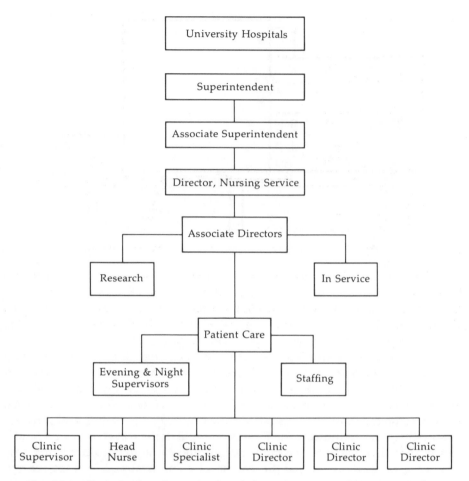

Fig. 13.8   Organization chart of a hospital nursing service (Courtesy: Audio-Visual Instruction, University of Wisconsin)

officers with their successive ranks of supervisors and subordinates. We can make clear the flow of authority and the role each employee plays in the organization.

Organization charts of this nature are often published in magazines and newspapers. Other sources include schools of business, administrative offices, and libraries, as well as local industrial firms and state or federal agencies. An opaque projector may be used to enlarge small charts for easy viewing on the screen. Original drawings can be made on stiff cardboards, transparencies, slides, the chalkboard, or slap-ons for the flannel board.

To make a chart, we should purchase a cardboard about 28 inches by 20 inches. We can work out the major lines by penciling them in lightly and, once we are satisfied, making them darker by the use of lettering pens. It is important to leave ample space between the lines — this can be checked by studying our tentative plans at the approximate distance at which viewers will see the chart. Explanatory lettering should be at least two inches high.

Diagrams   These are bare outlines or simple sketches, which are perhaps among the oldest methods of depicting objects and living things. Recent discoveries on the rock walls of a Mexican cave show line drawings of animals believed to be the work of artists around 800 B.C. In our times this method of sketching or drawing is used to a considerable extent in presenting descriptions of such things as houses, fashions, recreation areas, and machines. (See Fig. 13.9, pages 238–239.)

Generally, a diagram's effectiveness is increased if it is not too detailed or involved. We should be aware that diagrams are, like most other aids, abstract and symbolic. Even more important is that they are the most condensed of all aids and, therefore, need more interpretation. In this event, supplementary aids such as photographs or models can be used in conjunction with more careful or detailed explanations.

As an illustration of combining the diagram with other aids, a student talked about a proposed state park, skillfully using the diagram together with colorful slides. She had procured a large sheet of paper, which she attached to the top of the chalkboard. On it was a simply drawn diagram of the park in bold lines, with several colors depicting the proposed areas for a number of recreational activities. In addition, she used slide projections showing scenes of newly developed recreational areas in a nearby state to illustrate her recommendations.

Diagrams may be procured from a variety of publications and sometimes from audio-visual aid departments. We may even draw our own sketch — of a new building, say, or a new kind of vehicle — on a slide, a cardboard, or a chalkboard, or use it in an opaque projector. Copies of diagrams may be passed out to listeners, before, during, or after the presentation, depending upon the situation. In preparing such diagrams, we should make lines clean and avoid too many details. Usually, it is a good idea to rough in a simple diagram on a sheet of paper and then reproduce it in bold and attractive form on the chalkboard or cardboard, using colored chalk or lettering pens. The diagram and its captions should be sufficiently large so that all viewers can study them without strain.

Posters   These are representations of ideas or facts on cardboards ideally measuring 22 inches by 28 inches, for use in small rooms, and 28 inches by 44 inches, for display in large rooms. Simple, bold in design, and vivid in color, posters cover a single theme for instant contemplation.

A good poster is like a miniature billboard — it is designed for a momentary glance and must tell the intended story quickly. Thus, posters may contain graphs, charts, maps, or cartoons, as well as pictures, to promote such causes as health, conservation of resources, fire prevention, athletics, the armed services, or safe driving. As a rule, the messages that posters dramatize should be capable of expression in three or four well-chosen words. They may be used to highlight items of information or personal viewpoint. As with diagrams, it is often best to reinforce posters with other visual aids such as slides, maps, charts, and pictures that provide additional information.

Ordinarily, it is easier to obtain posters from outside sources than it is to draw them. Attractive posters can be obtained from travel bureaus, railroad companies, government agencies, foreign news and information offices, steamship lines, airlines, the armed services, lecture-concert offices, and conservation or health departments. Many of these are distributed free of charge.

On the other hand, let us say that we want to make a poster, because we're good at it or because finding one might be difficult. Various types of material such as construction paper, wrapping paper, and even the back of a used poster can be used, or we may purchase a colored cardboard about 22 inches by 28 inches in size. We may also attach objects to the poster to produce a three-dimensional effect. It is a good idea first to work out a miniature sketch of our plans for this cardboard. If, for example, we have chosen "Conserving Wildlife" as our topic, it would be desirable for easy viewing to use a large-sized colored photograph of the head of one animal, not a number of animals; also to avoid using a glossy print since it may reflect a glare. Following our roughly made plans, we will paste our picture in the appropriate area and print carefully a two- or three-word phrase beside the picture. We might also paint our picture with two or three trees, or a distant mountain, to suggest a natural background. We want to make our poster as dramatic in color and design as possible.

Fig. 13.9   Diagram showing smog and smoke pollution in a city (Reprinted with permission from the UWM Magazine)

Here are a few suggestions:

1. Use catchy wording.
2. Make the poster large enough to convey the message—no larger.
3. Use lower-case letters since they are easy to read.
4. Capitalize the letters in important words for emphasis.
5. Make letters at least 2 inches in height for a distance of 25 feet.

Flash Cards and Sequence Charts   *Flash cards* are compact cards—about 9 inches by 12 inches or larger in size—usually displayed high enough on an easel so that each person in the audience can easily observe them. They are used to assist the listener to concentrate on the subject to be discussed. We print the subject at the top of the first card; on the other cards, we print the major headings (obviously brief and to the point), which are "flashed." In some cases, we may wish to include all major headings on one cardboard. In a flash card series, the word or phrase should be at least 2 or 3 inches high—so that it can be read from a distance of 20 feet. Words may be emphasized by (1) underlining, (2) color, (3) larger lettering, or (4) a combination of these three elements.

Both lettering and illustrations can appear on flash cards, although lettering by itself is more commonly used. No fewer than two or three and no more than five cards are recommended. Flash cards offer several opportunities for stressing major points: (1) We can present a major point orally and then emphasize it for a brief period with a flash card. (2) We can have all cards displayed at once to indicate the outline of our talk. (3) We can inform our listeners in a time-saving and relaxed way. (4) For summary purposes, we can use the cards to review the key ideas.

Two types of *sequence chart* design can be used in presenting information in sequence: the strip chart and the flip chart. The *strip chart* is made as a

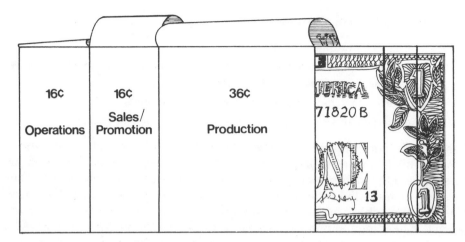

Fig. 13.10   *Strip chart used in presenting industry costs*

single chart on which important words are covered with strips of paper, often fastened by scotch tape. Important points may be stressed by tearing off or turning over a paper strip at the appropriate moment.

In the *flip chart*, headings and supporting material are shown in condensed form on several sheets, each of which is flipped over the top of the easel the moment exposure is desired. These charts are particularly useful when specific procedures are to be outlined in a sequential arrangement.

In both types of charts, we set down the main points of our talk in letters large enough for those in the last rows to see. Sometimes the presentation is "sparked" by one or two drawings or ample-sized photographs pasted next to the point they are to develop. The flip chart is especially useful because the extra sheets can serve as a welcome substitute for the chalkboard. Brief

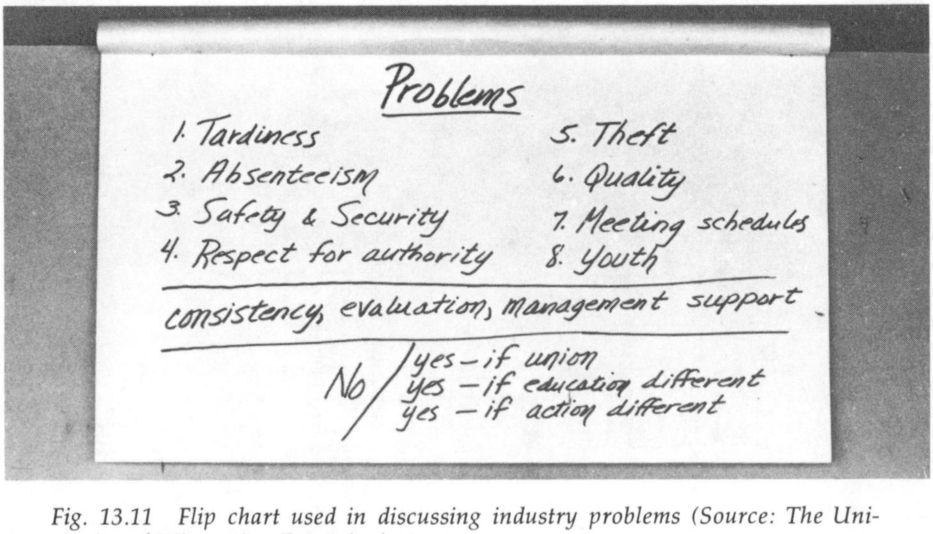

Fig. 13.11   *Flip chart used in discussing industry problems (Source: The University of Wisconsin – Extension)*

comments can be written or lettered on the sheets as we talk. Many of us find that paper charts are preferable to the chalkboard for the outlining of major points, ideas, or relationships between ideas. These charts, with their dark lettering, placed on an easel close to the audience, permit us to reveal the specific point at the right moment and, therefore, tend to make our key ideas stand out. In addition to serving as a visual outline, they can foster continuity in our talks and can be referred to again and again in review.

Flash cards and sequence cards are generally easy to make. The most important factor concerns lettering and spacing. To insure adequate results, we should make a rough draft on thin paper of the same size as the final cardboard. Then, on this cardboard, we draw and accurately center key words or phrases about two inches high in straight lines. To achieve maximum clarity, we should avoid crowding or using too many words and major points.

Flash cards are usually 9 inches by 12 inches in size and contain but one major point, while the strip chart can be three or four times that size in order to contain the entire schematic and drastically reduced outline of the talk. For the strip chart, we use scotch tape to secure thin masking sheets over the lettering temporarily. For flip charts, the printed headings are lettered on the pages in much the same manner as is done on flash cards. In all types of graphs and charts, attention should be directed to the most effective color contrasts for easy reading. These combinations are recommended:

Black on yellow	Black on white
Dark green, red, or blue on white	Yellow on black
White on dark blue	White on dark red, dark green, or black

Printed, Typewritten, and Written Materials The thoughtful speaker recognizes the urge audiences have to collect printed information related to the speech. He or she often distributes this information to create an awareness of a need for further knowledge of the subject. These materials may include copies of the complete speech, statistical portions of it, outlines of it, or supplementary articles related to it. Such handout materials have several values: (1) they free the listener from note taking during the talk; (2) they permit him to concentrate more fully on the talk; (3) they allow him the opportunity to refer to the handout at a later date; and (4) they give the speaker an opportunity to discuss a rather complex problem in a relatively short time. Needless to say, several of the aids already discussed in this chapter can also be handed out. Pictures or objects that we hold up and discuss during the speech may be distributed among the audience before, during, or after the speech. Outlines and agendas may be handed out before the speech. However, longer or more detailed materials, unless they are needed for study as the speech progresses, should not be handed out until afterward because they may distract the listeners. Handouts used after a presentation permit the listeners to check their own thoughts regarding what was said.

Articles, messages, instructions, or statistical information may be reproduced by any of various methods, including carbon copies, photocopies, or printing. The choice depends on the cost, the number of copies desired, and the availability of machines. Photographs, printed materials, and objects are usually distributed and then recalled by the speaker.

Precautions in Using Flannel Boards, Graphs, Charts, and Printed Materials

1.   *Obtain a sturdy easel to hold placards, or display them on the sill of the chalkboard so that they will be visible from the extreme ends of the front row.*

2.   *Be thoroughly familiar with what the visuals mean.*

3.   *Introduce each one in a different, not a trite, way.*

4.   *Explain each one carefully — don't assume that everyone understands even the simplest ones.*

5.   *Keep the visual covered until you are ready to use it.*

6.   *Practice using the more intricate visuals, such as the slap-ons.*

7.   *Maintain eye contact with the listeners, not the visuals.*

8.   *Keep the presentation moving ahead, avoiding unintentional hesitations.*

9.   *Announce each point on the visual briefly, then develop it with a sufficient amount of material.*

10.   *Have printed materials displayed on the table at the end of the talk.*

Slides and Filmstrips   *Slides* are mounted transparent images or pictures that can be projected individually with a slide projector. They can be used singly to provide enlarged images of almost anything — charts, drawings, diagrams, tables, cartoons, and other such materials; or they can provide continuity of thought when the individual slides, in color or black-and-white, are shown in a logical sequence.

For the inexperienced speaker or for one who has difficulty in expressing himself, much of the content of a speech can stem from these visual images. In addition, the attention of the listeners can be focused on the screen rather than on a shy speaker.[6] When using slides, we should make sure that we include only those of special significance, that they are in the correct order, that the proper side is up, and that we are adequately prepared to give a satisfactory explanation of each one. It is advisable for us to number and thumb-tab slides so that we or the projectionist will have no difficulty in finding the correct one.

A *filmstrip* consists of a small number of transparent images or still pictures (in color or in black-and-white, either silent or sound) on a strip of

---

[6] For a further analysis, see Richard E. Barnes, "Establishing a Climate Conducive to Reducing Communication Apprehension," Kansas University Extension Center Bulletin, 1972.

film that can be shown in a partially darkened room. Although the roll of filmstrip does not permit rearrangement or omission of certain pictures, as is the case with slides, this sequential order of pictures provides a carefully planned step-by-step process. For example, we may project scenes of a national forest without the fear of our slides being out of sequence, while we ask our listeners to think about means of conserving such areas in various states. For such a talk we can operate the frames manually (slowly) in order to develop important points at our own pace and to build a cumulative effect. We can use the audible element in the filmstrip, or we can adapt to the occasion by giving our own comments instead—whichever seems better. As in the selection of good motion pictures, it is well to preview filmstrips before committing ourselves to their use.

Making slides requires two-inch squares of cellophane, binding tape, and pieces of cardboard. A typed message or figure can be lettered or drawn on cellophane material, which is then mounted on a cardboard frame. Filmstrips can be made by anyone who has access to a 35mm camera.

Precautions in Using Slide Projectors

1. *Find out in advance what kind of projector is available—manual or automatic.*

2. *Practice with the machine before your presentation.*

3. *Check to determine that the slides are right side up and in order.*

4. *Ask someone familiar with the projector to aid you in setting up the instrument for showing.*

Silent Motion Pictures   Well-chosen *silent films* can depict animation, motion, and continuity that play a leading role in dramatizing significant ideas, people, objects, and events. These motion pictures can portray better than any other medium such phenomena as (1) living organisms too small for the eye to perceive, (2) rapidly moving events in slow motion, (3) extremely slow processes portrayed more speedily through timed-interval photography, and (4) abstract or complex procedures produced in simplified form. Silent films give us the opportunity in speaking to relate our own personal impressions, and they permit adaptation to a particular group or occasion. However, they may not necessarily be preferred substitutes for demonstrations of actual objects—the size of the audience, the complexity of the demonstration, and the skill of the demonstrator being important variables.

Besides the possibility of using our own silent films, a number of first-rate films are available for a mailing fee or a small rental charge. Audiovisual aid centers or religious, social, and political groups offer catalogs of films and instructions for use. Commercial firms, public libraries, museums, and governmental agencies are other possible sources. Many films having to do with mental health, safety, prevention of fires, precautions against burglaries in the home and in industry, and the prevention of disease can be obtained free from the organization producing them.[7]

In addition to acquiring a film we will need to find a projectionist. For a classroom speech, often a student assistant trained in projection techniques can be contacted in the audio-visual center. Perhaps a student in the speech class knows operating techniques and can be called upon for assistance.

Sound Motion Pictures   With realistic background sounds, a motion picture has the capacity to present an almost firsthand impression. Several advantages of sound films to the speaker are apparent—they are natural and lifelike, they make a presentation vivid, and they may provide expert commentary. From another viewpoint, they are moving pictures, plus words, plus personality—all creating "believability." While it is not to be expected that a student would often use sound motion pictures, since rental fees are expensive and most films are too lengthy for a short speech assignment, nevertheless, it is important to keep this realistic form of communication in mind for other speaking occasions. Of the short, thought-provoking films produced by various film distributors, some are surrealistic and provide challenging ideas. Most educational films, which are ordinarily ten to thirty minutes in length, might fit well, for example, into convention programming and workshops which we might be planning or in which we might be a workshop leader. To stimulate such groups to think about the film content, we might ask our listeners questions involving key ideas to be depicted.

Recordings   Recordings comprise original sounds that have been registered by mechanical or electrical mechanisms using tape, wire, or discs. A speaker can use such sound mechanisms to amplify a point of his speech effectively. Recording devices can capture a wide range of unusual sounds. Although music most often constitutes the subject matter of recordings, many other presentations are available. We can, for example, make use of recordings to supplement discussions of historical or current events, dramatic presentations, nature studies, scientific phenomena, and outstanding personalities.

Recorders and recordings are recommended for special occasions when the sound element is highlighted. For instance, following a talk about the songs of certain birds, we could shut off the lights and in the darkness listen to the various "calls" by waterfowl. Or with a portable tape recorder, we could record various students expressing their views on some group project or contemporary problem. By listening to the playback of such a discussion, listeners can evaluate their own ideas.

Recording equipment is usually available in communication or speech

---

[7] For added information regarding free films, see *Educators Guide to Free Films,* Educators Progress Service, Randolph, Wisconsin.

departments and campus audio-visual aid centers. Also, a number of re-cordings are sometimes made available by these departments and, in some instances, by libraries and other institutions of higher learning.[8] Disc and tape recordings may be purchased through local record shops, and some-times they may be borrowed from agencies and people with private collec-tions.

Precautions in Using Motion Pictures and Recordings

1. Preview or pre-hear the materials to determine whether or not they will enhance your ideas.

2. Carefully practice using the equip-ment to insure a good performance.

3. Set up the equipment in advance of the talk and recheck it so that delay will not occur.

4. Check the volume of the sound sources to determine the best level.

5. Keep the room well ventilated to help insure attention.

6. Point up the key ideas so that the listeners will know the reasons for the projection.

7. Use a pointer stick to spot critical areas in the projected image or picture.

8. Limit the amount of listening or viewing to just enough to illustrate your main points.

9. Pause at intervals to dwell on some significant point that needs special emphasis.

10. Review any portion of the presen-tation by returning to the specific place in the audio or visual aid. If needed, show the whole film or sequence again.

Audio-Visual Apparatus

Opaque and Overhead Projectors These projectors dramatically repro-duce facts, figures, and other images directly to the screen. Both the opaque and the overhead projectors were designed to assist the speaker to present his ideas with increased impact.

The *opaque projector* works best in a darkened room. It allows us to project on a screen images of a variety of different materials—fabrics, coins, drawings, old books, and other such objects—in addition to photographs and graphics. (Ordinarily a projector will accommodate not only mounted pictures or sheets of paper but also pages in books, pamphlets, albums, and the like.) The opaque projector is easy to operate and projects materials that could not conveniently be made into slides or filmstrips. Moreover, an entire group can study the enlarged image of a small or large object for any rea-sonable length of time.

---

[8] For a list of available tapes, write *Audio-Visual Aids,* San Jose State University, San Jose, California.

The *overhead projector* is a great boon to us as speakers because we can face our audience as we insert prepared plastic (such as that used to cover windows in winter), carbon, or cellophane transparencies that reflect images on the screen; we can write, trace or draw on the transparencies with felt pens or pencils while talking to the audience; we can build up pictures with overlays; and we can leave some lights on. Upon these transparencies we can (1) project the major headings of our speech, (2) plan sketches, numerical data, and graphs — or draw some of them in during the speech to emphasize some added point, and (3) make the major conclusions easy to remember.

Slide Projectors   These are machines that rely on the aid of an efficient lens system and a sufficiently powerful lamp in order to project transparencies onto a screen in a partially or completely darkened room. Modern slide projectors are compact and relatively light in weight. They can be equipped with a push-button control wired to the projector, which affords the speaker the opportunity to change the slides in the slide carriage as he speaks in the vicinity of the screen.

A variety of other features are characteristic of the latest slide projectors. With some models we can repeat a slide if needed by dialing the number of the desired slide and pushing a button. Others feature (1) a jam-proof mechanism and (2) slide images that seem to move. Through the use of two carousel slide projectors, a form of animation or an illusion of motion results.

Filmstrip Projectors   A filmstrip projector is a relatively simple mechanism that includes a lamp, a reflector, lenses, and a smoothly operating channel through which the filmstrip passes. By means of a simple knob, the filmstrip (usually about 20 to 50 frames in length) is conveniently moved from one projection to another. These machines, which in some instances can operate as slide projectors, are usually light and easy to operate. This makes it possible for us to set up the projector and test it just a few minutes before we present our speech.

Newer models are fully automatic so that planned sound effects or descriptive materials emanate from a record player, providing a realistic effect. We can operate these with considerable confidence because easy slot threading, positive framing, and no sticking are assured. The film moves quickly and smoothly. A "spin-back" control provides an easy summary or review of some important point.

Motion Picture Projectors   Motion picture machines are designed to project rapidly a series of still photographs, thus providing animation and in many instances sound. Since they are rather heavy and the preparation for their use is somewhat involved, it is imperative that we set them up and test them before a speech or meeting begins. Although motion picture projectors differ in design, they are basically the same in their operation. In each instance the operator must be familiar with the entire process of threading the film, focusing the picture, and adjusting the sound. While significant changes have occurred in projectors and screens recently, the presentation still depends on the efficiency of both.

New models feature snap-out reel arms and rapid automatic threading and rewinding apparatus. Modern wall model screens are desirable since they are easy to use and suffer little damage from use. Of much interest to any speaker interested in showing movies is the fact that we can now show a film in a lighted room instead of one with black shades. In addition, a film can be stopped on a single frame to emphasize an essential point, and portions of the film can be rerun if desired.

Disc Recorders and Playbacks   These mechanisms, which are the oldest types of recorders in use, can record and play back sounds on discs. While the recording feature is a requisite in preparing audio effects, it is the playback feature of this and other recording machines that we use at the time of our speech. As playback materials, both homemade and commercially produced records are useful aids while speaking. Obviously, we should give particular attention to suitable volume when playback occurs.

Tape Recorders   These highly flexible mechanisms, now available in stereo, permit magnetic signals to reproduce sound imprints on rolls of metallic-coated tape. Tape recorders offer such advantages as easy mending of tapes and editing, and easy marking of especially important passages that the speaker may wish to repeat.

The recent models are much lighter than any formerly available—a factor of much importance when we consider transporting them to and from the place where we are to speak. Also, these new machines possess a fidelity output that rivals recorders weighing thirty to forty pounds more and costing up to three times as much. Besides their ample power output and improved quality, the newer models contain a built-in recording level meter and a standard phone jack for external speakers or head-set listening.

We should not overlook the intriguing possibilities of cassette tape recorders and the even more dramatic potential of video tape recordings. With them, we can record the testimony of "outside" experts in support of our topics, or we can record pertinent views expressed in our own group. With the use of simple cartridges we can replay a variety of materials for analysis in classroom discussions. There is no need to fumble with the threading processes of cumbersome tape recorders or film projectors; all we have to do is insert the cartridge into the cassette recorder or video equipment and it is ready for recording or viewing purposes. We simply flip a switch or press the necessary button, and in a matter of seconds recordings or playbacks will occur. A rapid rewind system allows us to remove the cartridge quickly or to replay key ideas for increased understanding.

When we have plans to utilize special equipment during our talk, we should arrive on the scene early. Keeping in mind that we can ordinarily be seen most easily when we're in the center of the platform, we should, whenever possible, place the visual aid in this area. Moreover, *we should stand at the side of the material and concentrate our attention upon the group and on getting the message across, rather than on the audio-visual aid.*

In this chapter we have considered the various audio-visual materials and procedures in common use in speaking situations. This list of audio-visual materials and principles might be extended, but a fundamental knowledge of the basic types is all that is necessary. The choice of audio-visual aids will depend upon the subject of the speech, the physical situation, the availability, the cost, and the efficiency of operation. In addition, the time for preparation of the visual material is sometimes sharply limited by circumstances over which the speaker has no control. Whatever the case, as long as the aid makes a distinct contribution toward interest, understanding, and conviction, the speaker can be certain of its worth.

Suggested Assignments

1.   Show photographs featuring people in some dramatic incident. Ask several persons how they interpret the scenes. Note the variations in feedback.

2.   In a talk explain or compare certain economic, military, or housing conditions in various countries. In clarifying these problems, use either a bar graph, a pie chart, a pictorial graph, or a line graph. Consider using a unit such as the last decade or the amount of money allocated for a given cause.

3.   Select a talk in which you explain or describe a product or a process. Give the talk without visual aids. Then use visuals to note their advantages.

4.   Plan a talk about the customs of people in a given country. Use one of the following technical devices with suitable recordings, or pictured effects: a tape recorder, a slide machine, a filmstrip machine, or a motion picture machine.

5.   For a forthcoming speech of advocacy, include flash cards, posters, or a flannel board to bolster interest and desired action.

6.   In a speech designed to explain a procedure, use either a diagram, a flow chart, or an organization chart.

7.   Make a note of the talks yet to be delivered in your course. Consider the ideal types of audio-visual aids and/or combinations of them one might use. Consider handouts, the chalkboard, the opaque projector, and recording machines. State how each could be used.

8.   Observe the audio-visual aids used in some television program or lecture. Analyze their use on the basis of the principles learned in this chapter.

9. Make preliminary plans for an hour-long workshop or conference presentation on some specific phase of your major field. List what audio-visual aids you would need for this presentation.

10. Visit your audio-visual aid department and ask to examine the latest equipment available for classroom use. Be prepared to discuss this equipment in class.

Suggested References

Braden, Waldo (ed.), *Speech Methods and Resources*, 2nd ed. (New York: Harper & Row, 1972). Chapter 22, "Making Effective Use of Audio-Visual Aids in Teaching Speech" by Wesley Wiksell.

Dale, Edgar, *Audio-Visual Methods in Teaching*, 3rd ed. (New York: Dryden Press, 1969). Part 2, "Materials for Audio-Visual Instruction."

Fensch, Thomas, *Films on the Campus* (New York: A. S. Barnes & Co., 1970). Chapter 9, "The Ohio State University."

Gold, Leon S., "Using Film in Management Development," *Training in Business and Industry*, Vol. 8 (August 1971), pp. 19–25.

Howell, William S., and Ernest G. Bormann, *Presentational Speaking for Business and the Professions* (New York: Harper & Row, 1971). Chapter 11, "Multimedia Aids to the Presentation."

Maynard, R. A., *The Celluloid Curriculum* (New York: Hayden Book Co., 1971). Chapter 17, "Teaching with Films."

Pluss, Ruth, "Sharpen Up Your Bulletin Board!" *The Clearing House*, Vol. 38 (March 1964), pp. 437–438.

Power, Gertrude Levore, *Making Posters, Flashcards, and Charts* (Washington, D. C.: U. S. Government Printing Office, 1956). Pp. 3–18.

Starr, Cecile, *Discovering the Movies* (New York: Van Nostrand Reinhold Co., 1972). Pp. 131–135.

Williams, Catherine M., *Learning from Pictures* (Washington, D. C.: National Education Association, 1963). Chapter 1, "Choosing Pictures."

Wittich, W. A., and Charles F. Schuller, *Instructional Technology: Its Nature and Use*, 5th ed. (New York: Harper & Row, 1973). Chapter 3, "Teaching with Pictures and Graphics."

Wright, Andrew, *Designing for Visual Aids* (New York: Van Rostrand Reinhold Co., 1970). Part 2, "Visual Materials."

14
Delivery in Speaking

"Delivery is essentially the presentation of the message to the listener via the visible and audible codes"

We have probably all heard people speak in a manner that sounded almost flawless: every syllable was very clearly enunciated, the sound of the words was almost music, even the rhymes and rhythms rang in our ear with freshness and variety; yet, when it was all over, we had the feeling that nothing had happened. Why? In most situations like this, the speaker has usually lost touch with what he had to say—with the ideas, the content, of the message. He concentrated so heavily on making a "good delivery," instead of on communication, that delivery became the chief end of his speaking effort. We all deplore this overemphasis on delivery for its own sake—as an end rather than as a means.

On the other hand, we have probably all heard people who deliver their oral messages with a droning voice, insipid body action, and careless pronunciation. Their speech comes through to us as a big nothing; and we all deplore their lack of attention to the importance of telling us what they're thinking in a way that turns us on.

The nature of delivery and its relationship to the substance of the message are frequently misunderstood. Delivery is essentially the presentation of the message to the listener via the visible and audible codes. The ideas and feelings that we want to express to our audience are determined as much by nonverbal behavior and by vocal signals as they are by the words we use. Through various tones of voice and facial expressions, we can change the receivers' attitudes toward almost anything we wish to utter. Therefore, delivery becomes a tool or means, not an end—but a most important means.

Effective speakers keep the communication process in balance by thinking of delivery as a tool to help them get their ideas across. Successful delivery of content and feelings requires extraordinary skills. Like any other proficiency, it is learned through hard work. Ted Williams, former batting star of the Boston Red Sox and baseball manager, differs with baseball followers who think that a good hitter has superior eyesight, reflexes, and timing. "Not so," Williams has said repeatedly, in effect, "my eyes and reflexes aren't any better than a lot of those in other people." In other words, in Williams's view practice, hard work, and willingness to stay with it are more important than natural ability.

We are not all equally gifted in the art of delivery. Some people can stand up and speak to us and hold our attention with the most trivial of subjects; others can mutter something of considerable significance and fail to get any kind of message across. While the latter may be remiss in their handling of the message itself, they also lack skill in delivery; and they need to devote much attention to learning how to present a talk.

The speaker delivers his message to the listener by way of two distinct paths—the visible and the audible, or he is the speaker the receiver *sees* and the speaker he *hears*. If either of these "speakers" is deficient, only one of the two channels of delivery is working well. Thus, while the two aspects of delivery naturally operate together in the speaking situation, it will be interesting to examine them separately.

The Speaker We See

In every face-to-face communication situation, both the verbal and the nonverbal channels are in operation. While one may be dominant in some instances, each is potentially as strong as the other. With respect to the nonverbal, we can imagine some of the cues of personal proof that a person waiting to speak reveals by yawning and daydreaming during another's speech. He could go a long way toward creating a good image (good personal proof) by good posture and conduct, by confident and alert walking to and from the platform or rostrum, and by a respectful and understanding attitude while other persons are speaking. Everything adjacent to us creates "images" in the eye of the beholder. The general appearance of a room, an office, or an outdoor setting all communicate a message. This is something we must remember as we plan the background for our talk. Is the blackboard clean? Is the whole area from which we speak cleared of distracting objects or pictures?

According to Harrison, nonverbal communication is not only extensive but often functions at such a low level of awareness that we may not realize that we are part of it. Yet these nonverbal cues may be some of the key dimensions of source credibility, which, in turn, is regarded as a vital element of persuasiveness.[1]

Ray L. Birdwhistell, anthropologist at Temple University, believes that we do most of our "talking" with our body movements. He coined the term *kinesics*, the study of all body movement in interpersonal communica-

---

[1] Randall Harrison, "Nonverbal Communication: Explorations into Time, Space, Action and Object," in James H. Campbell and Hal W. Hepler, *Dimensions in Communication*, 2nd ed. (Belmont, Calif.: Wadsworth Publishing Co., 1965), pp. 257–259.

tion. Birdwhistell believes that we pour out information with our shrugs, our hand and body movements, our eyes, our facial expressions, and even our silences. These signals are often *more* reliable messages than are the words we utter.[2]

Thus, whether conscious or unconscious, overt or covert, the nonverbal cues emanating from "the speaker we see" demand consideration and careful examination. Such cues are revealed by (1) attitude, general appearance, and posture, (2) movement and gesture, (3) facial expression, and (4) eye contact.

Attitude, General Appearance, and Posture

Among the more observable elements making up "the speaker we see" are those commonly called *attitude, general appearance,* and *posture.* As a general rule, a person's attitude is the key to his personality. Personal attractiveness depends on a genial disposition, confidence, alertness, pleasing appearance, good posture, knowledge, and interest in others. Although they may not know it, listeners are continuously sizing up—assessing and interpreting the impact of—these behavior practices.

Generally in our society we prefer neatness and propriety in dress, a friendly and courteous manner and attitude, an alert, appropriate, standing position for formal speaking situations, and an equally alert and suitable manner of sitting in an informal speaking situation.

The bearing of the body and the position of the head—the speaker's posture in any position, sitting or standing—suggest to the listener the *dominant* or *submissive* roles people play. The dominant speaker usually looks relaxed while the submissive speaker is often given away by the rigidity of his body, suggesting fear and "inferior" feelings (which may indicate that the person is afraid to use his emotional resources).[3] The confident and relaxed speaker carries with him an air of assurance and conviction about his message. However, relaxation can be carried to the extreme of seeming indifference, and confidence can look like conceit. Because these impressions can destroy the very effect we want to create, we should be careful not to overdo. Let us keep these procedures in mind:

> 1.   As you *stand,* try to keep your shoulders back and your head up. Good posture makes you look alert and helps you really be alert. Try to stand naturally and comfortably. Do not give the impression that you need to lean against the stand for support. Give your body solid support by having your feet far enough apart. Shift your weight when you stand or sit to alleviate that "frozen" look. (Remember that the speaker's posture gives clues about his attitude.)

---

[2] For additional information, see Ray L. Birdwhistell, *Introduction to Kinesics: An Annotation System for Analysis of Body Motion and Gesture,* (Washington, D. C.: Foreign Service Institute, Department of State, 1952).

[3] See Bonaro W. Overstreet, *Understanding Fear* (New York: Harper & Row, 1971), p. 99.

2. When you *sit*, don't slump down in the chair with your shoulders hunched over and your chin on your chest. Don't put your feet on the table, or cross and uncross your legs conspicuously. Sit up straight, shoulders back; look alert. Let your bones support your body, and you can sit straight and be relaxed at the same time.

While we need to be aware of the norms and conventions of a given speech situation—in this case, a formal one—we must remember that listener expectations regarding the speaker and the goal of the interaction tend to have a modifying effect.

Let us take a professor in the classroom. Normally, he would stand, wear a coat and tie, manifest a dignified manner, and have a friendly tone of voice. But this man sits on the desk, does not wear a coat, has the tie at one side, and is at times quite loud in volume. Is he wrong? No, not necessarily! While he departs from the norm and while this is not generally praiseworthy conduct, it is possible that for this particular person and his subject, occasion, and audience, he may be right (whether he be teacher or student).

The important thing is that we each know the norms, the nature of the variations, and why and how we vary from the norms. The norms should always be our point of reference!

Movement and Gesture

While we are speaking, purposeful movement helps to point up certain ideas and to impart our interest in our topic. Such movement can be used, for example, when we want to introduce a new idea; we can take a step or two away from our original position and move back once the idea has been sufficiently developed. We can walk to the chalkboard to write down some important figures. We may need to cross the room to make use of a visual aid. Whatever the direction, our movement should have a purpose, and we should move in moderation.

Some speakers have difficulty holding attention because they remain motionless; they stand up, recite their words like an automaton, and sit down when they are done, without ever having come into contact with any of the ideas in their message. Other speakers go to the opposite extreme and pace restlessly back and forth, revealing their own uneasiness and disturbing the listeners' concentration. Their movement is without purpose; it is caused, in most cases, by excessive self-consciousness—stage fright.

We may frequently have to adjust the kind and amount of movement in relation to the occasion and audience. An abundance of overt, vigorous action may be appropriate in some situations wherein people engage in active pursuits, while before sedentary listeners, more restrained—even quite dignified—bodily responses may be required even of a normally animated person. We might think of the difference, in this respect at least, between a pep rally and a church worship service.

In addition to general body movement, the hands, arms, and face have a definite function in communication through gesture. Like other body movements, gestures help to point up ideas, enhance the listeners' interest, and relieve the speaker's tension. Apart from functioning in the conveyance of logical ideas, gestures help portray such emotional feelings as fear, friendliness, anxiety, warning, satisfaction—all of which can aid social interaction. Gestures change in harmony with facial expressions, the voice, and other behaviors in a "cluster" to "characterize any subtle nuance of feeling."[4]

Beginning speakers frequently discover for the first time that they have, at the end of each arm, seemingly useless appendages: their hands. Because they don't know what to do with these "ridiculous" objects, many speakers put them in their pockets; some put them behind their backs; those who are fortunate enough to have a speaker's stand put them on the stand, or hold notes with them. No matter what the speaker has done with his hands, even if he is not conscious of them, his body will have enough energy to expend to start them moving. One hand will go up to scratch his head or chin; soon the other will rub his nose or adjust his glasses or retract the point on a ballpoint pen. This purposeless movement calls attention to itself and hinders the communication process. Such uneasiness, in what some call "nonverbally handicapped" people, stems from their not knowing how others feel toward them and perhaps from having a negative attitude toward themselves.

On the other hand, the speaker can take advantage of this nervous energy. By controlling the movements that his hands are going to make anyway, he can help get his ideas across clearly and forcefully. He can write on the blackboard or show pictures, objects, and other kinds of visual aids. He can point to maps. He can indicate dimensions (". . . about so high"). He can enumerate specific points by holding up an appropriate number of fingers as he develops those points. He can emphasize significant ideas by pointing, indicating sizes and areas, and so on.

In general, experienced speakers use gestures to stress ideas and to express emotional feeling. Sometimes they use them as a substitute for words. However, we should avoid talking too much with our hands, lest our actions draw attention away from the message itself. Nor is it wise to use only one or two gestures repeatedly, lest they become meaningless.

Facial Expressions

Facial expressions, like other physical movements, can help or hinder communication. Smiles and frowns, even though unintentional, stimulate their appropriate responses from the listener. A common misconception is that interest and/or enthusiasm can be faked. Sincere enthusiasm is the

---

[4]See Albert Mehrabian, *Silent Messages* (Belmont, Calif.: Wadsworth Publishing Co., 1971), pp. 61, 113.

expression of authentic feelings within us. In this regard, psychologist Carl E. Seashore believes that the smile is a sign of well being, approval, satisfaction, attraction, and affirmation, and, conversely, that the frown expresses ill-being, dissatisfaction, negation, disapproval, and repulsion. When spontaneous, the smile and the frown tell the truth.[5] The best thing we can do about facial expressions when speaking is to permit them to reflect our genuine interest in, and responsiveness to, the ideas in our message and to reveal our genuine desire to communicate with our listeners.

Whereas facial expressions vary from culture to culture, there is rather general agreement that they reveal pleasant and unpleasant attitudes and are among the most commonly understood behavior traits. A crucial factor in "sending" messages by facial expression, or by any other means for that matter, is the extent to which we express what is thought or felt within. Are we believed to be honest and forthright or are we not ringing true? In addition, do we express through our face what we wish to communicate? If, for example, we are distressed about a problem, does our face show it?

Strangely enough, if our facial expressions reveal our intended meaning and feeling, our audience will not be observing them—rather they will be subsumed as part of the total communication process. For the same reason, listeners will, however, become more aware of any physical activity that is not in harmony with the message.

Eye Contact

The eyes are perhaps the most effective nonverbal means of communication that we have as speakers. If we look directly at our listeners most of the time we are speaking, we will probably help to awaken their personal interest in the information or advice we are giving. We will also have the opportunity to observe their reactions and adjust accordingly. Through their feedback, we can tell whether they are "still there" and awake (or appear to be attending); also, we can gain some indication of their attitude toward us and our message.

A common fault among speakers is failure to direct our remarks to our listeners. We will gaze at the wall or out the window or down at our shoes. Also, some of us have mastered something of the technique of eye contact but nothing of its real nature. We display "pseudo eye contact"—the outward form; we look, but we do not see. Nobody in the audience is certain about where our remarks are directed; and because the listeners do not feel personally involved with our message, they will probably pay less attention to it.

To avoid these faults and achieve direct contact with the listeners, we should plan to look at one listener or, in the case of a larger group, one area

---

[5] Carl E. Seashore, "Your Smile and Your Frown," *Household Magazine* (January 1943), p. 1.

at a time—then at another, then another. We should continue this eye contact all the while we are speaking.

Eye contact with the speaker should serve as a stimulus to each of the persons in the audience and help greatly in maintaining their attention.

The Speaker We Hear

What speakers do, of course, is speak. Speaking is a means of conveying messages, orally, from one mind to another by means of a system of symbols called language. Most of us think of language as words that are put together into recognizable and meaningful patterns. True enough, but spoken language is more than words and sentences; it has elements that communicate ideas and feelings every bit as important to the message as the words that make it up. Thus, a speaker's voice reveals his physical condition and his emotional state as well as his ideas. Fear, surprise, unhappiness, sickness, and other feelings can be detected in the tremor of the voice, its loudness, its rate, and its pitch. Studies at Kent State University suggest that neurotic and other negative tendencies are revealed in the voice, while better adjusted people generally have pleasant voices.[6] Thus, we might find that while garbled speech may indicate nervousness—or angry tones, inferiority and resentment—clear and melodious speech may indicate the very opposite.

Why does one speaker have a pleasing voice and not another? Why does one talk with vigor and conviction, while the other speaks monotonously and timidly, and seems to be lethargic and indifferent about what he is saying? The first speaker, of course, enjoys greater success in communication; the second, even though his efforts are sincere and his convictions deep, is almost totally ineffectual. The deficiencies that cause his failure are often complex, far from easy to analyze and correct; yet he can improve a good many of them by concentrating on the vocal elements of delivery.

Articulation and Pronunciation

Articulation is the production of clear and distinct sounds in words, which sounds are produced by modifying, interrupting, or filtering the exhaled breath stream through the larynx, throat, mouth, and nasal cavity. Actively engaged in this process of forming graduated obstructions of the emitted breath stream are the appropriate movements of the tongue, lips, and velum as they make proper contact with the teeth, hard palate, and posterior pharyngeal wall.

It is generally recognized that the vowels contribute largely to the in-

---

[6] *The State Journal* (Lansing, Mich.), June 26, 1960.

tensity or carrying power in the voice, while the consonants relate to intelligibility of words. Consonants, therefore, are of prime importance for the hearer's understanding of a word or a sentence. Much of his ability to distinguish one word from another depends upon the speaker's attention to the consonants.

Errors in articulation obviously occur when we carelessly form the vowel or consonant sounds. Do we run our syllables together? — muffle the sounds so that they are indistinct? — try to hide behind an indistinct shield in order to cover up inadequacies in our reasoning? — add extra sounds so that our speech calls attention to itself? Let us watch particularly to determine whether the vowels are given proper voicing in such words as *cruel, mayor, ruin, really, dairy, poem, violet, fool,* and *room.* As far as consonants are concerned, the *ct* in *correct, exact,* and *expect* must have a firm *kt* sound, and special attention must be paid to other consonant combinations such as *st, lp, vd, nd, ng, ld,* and *pt* in words like *cast, help, arrived, around, fling, field,* and *wept.*

Pronunciation is the customary or acceptable method of sounding the parts of words by selecting the proper vowel and consonant sounds and by stressing the proper syllables. Common examples of misplaced accents are the words *preferable, comparable,* and *abdomen,* in which the accent belongs on the first syllable; yet many people consistently stress the second.

Typical errors may be classified in four categories: (1) omitting sounds, or passing over them lightly, such as dropping the final *t* in asked, the *g* in recognize, the *h* in *human* and *humble,* and the first *r* in *February;* (2) substituting sounds, such as *b* for *p* in *Baptist* and *w* for *hw* in *why;* (3) reversing sounds and accents, such as saying *prespiration* for *perspiration* and *ROmance* for *roMANCE, HOtel* for *hoTEL, POlice* for *poLICE,* and *GUItar* for *guiTAR;* (4) adding sounds, as in the case of *r* added to *idea* so that it becomes *idear* and *y* to *column* so that it becomes *colyumn.*

One of the best ways to overcome these errors is to listen to a recording of your own voice; you will probably be surprised at the number of words you mispronounce, or slur over, or articulate badly. Speech deficiencies, when not caused by physical disorder, are often the result of habits developed in childhood; and it is probably true that environmental conditioning is, in most cases, responsible for poor articulation and pronunciation. Whatever the speaker's background, the problem is related to careless use of the speech modifiers: the lips, tongue, teeth, jaws, and hard and soft palates. The careful speaker will make sure these mouth structures are doing their job in modifying the sound produced when the vocal cords are vibrated by a stream of air from the lungs.

As we begin the task of correcting errors brought to our attention by the recording of our own voices and by the comments and criticisms of teachers and friends, we should jot those errors down on a piece of paper so we will know what to work on. Then we should make a real effort, each time we speak, to expend the energy necessary to form correct and distinct sounds. Practicing these words over and over again will help us form a new habit. If, however, we have difficulty in correcting our errors or if there are too many of them to correct alone, a course in phonetics will acquaint us with the exact vocal procedures involved in the formation of sounds. If we believe our speech defects to be serious, it would be wise to visit a speech clinic.

Many mispronunciations occur as a result of indifference, imitation, carelessness, affectation, or lack of knowledge. However, the pronunciation of some words naturally varies from one region of this country to another; what is correct in Biloxi may sound peculiar in Poughkeepsie, and vice versa. If we mix these pronunciations of different regions indiscriminately, we can expect negative reactions from our listeners. For instance, when middlewesterners use pronunciations common to the New England area, they are sometimes suspected of being snobbish or of "talking down to people." The same offensive mingling of regional pronunciations in words like *either, ask,* and *dance* among social leaders, certain academicians, actors, and others often appears to be an attempt to gain prestige.

Raven L. McDavid, an authority on social as well as regional dialects, recently observed that mispronunciations can betray the speaker as uncultured and of low social status. He contends that ever since Professor Higgins made a "fair lady" out of Eliza Doolittle, people have realized that a person's speech can determine her social status.[7]

To improve our pronunciation, we can refer constantly to a good dictionary, noting therein the diacritical and accent markings. But also we can observe that there is no standard pronunciation for many words in American English. Whereas *brush, seeing,* and *desk* are pronounced essentially the same everywhere in the United States, a large number of words are not pronounced alike. We can hear the *r* sound at the ends of words in the Middle West and West, but not in the South or in New England. *Either* and *neither* are pronounced differently in these areas. These cause no serious problems in communication; quite the opposite, they remind us that speech is a social commodity.

So that we may remain consistent and natural in communication, authorities have accepted three major American dialects: the *Eastern,* which is spoken in the New England area; the *Southern,* which is evident in the

---

[7] *Chicago Sun-Times,* March 7, 1969.

states of the "old South"; and the *General American,* which exists in the remaining Midwest and West. Since no exact line separates any of these areas, there may be some natural mixing of dialects along the borders. In any case, the most acceptable pronunciation is probably found among the educated people in our native region, although academic eminence does not always insure good pronunciation.

Some linguists, such as A. S. Hayes, approach the subject of pronunciation through a person's first and second languages—the latter, in the case of minority language groups, to be used in jobs and in contacts with the majority of American people.[8] Thus, we need not reject the use of the first language for anyone among the foreign population or other minorities, for every person deserves the privilege of relating intimately with his own group. On the other hand, as we look back into history, the cultured groups looked severely at Abraham Lincoln for his baggy clothes, unshined shoes, melancholy tone of voice and mispronunciations like "sich" for "such," "thar" for "there," and "Mr. Cheerman" for "Mr. Chairman." Yet he related extraordinarily well to his Illinois listeners in his debates with Stephen Douglas.

Loudness

For the listener, loudness refers to intensity, or the strength of the sensation he receives; for the speaker, it is the amount of breath that he forces through his vocal cords and amplifies in the air-filled cavities in and around his mouth. To be good speakers we will control the amount of air and its amplification to fit the situation; in a large room, or in any place where there are conflicting sounds, we will increase our loudness; in a small room, we will adjust the loudness to the size of the room and the number of listeners. In all cases, we will vary our loudness—to provide emphasis and variety, as our message dictates.

In any speaking situation sufficient loudness indicates that we have no fear of speaking up—which means that we will use energy, animation, spontaneity, and enthusiasm. With conviction, sincerity, and genuine interest, we should have little trouble attaining the proper loudness for the situation. However, because large rooms often present acoustical problems, it is a good idea, before we deliver a prepared speech in such a room, to ascertain whether we can be heard in the back row. Professor Ralph Nichols, a listening researcher, feels that one of the leading factors in increasing listening comprehension is audibility—can you be heard easily, distinctly, and clearly?[9]

---

[8] *Wall Street Journal,* January 19, 1966.

[9] Ralph G. Nichols, "Factors in Listening Comprehension," *Speech Monographs,* Vol. 15 (1948), pp. 154–163.

For the ideal general degree of loudness, there are two conflicting opinions, each believed sincerely by its proponents and each totally unreasonable if taken as a general rule. One opinion is that we can maintain attentiveness by speaking in a rather quiet voice; but this does not acknowledge that such low volume can soon become dull monotony—not to mention that many of the listeners may experience difficulty hearing the speaker at all. The other school of thought holds that loudness, or explosiveness, is stirring. The weakness in this belief lies in the speaker's inability to emphasize anything when everything he utters is loud.

Actually, the best level to maintain in most speaking situations and throughout most of the speech is somewhere between the two extremes—a middle ground from which we can depart when we want either to emphasize a major point by speaking loudly or dramatize other material by lowering our volume. By maintaining a moderate loudness, we can save the extremes for those moments when we must stress important words, pertinent quotations, and major ideas; or when we want to subordinate words and ideas of minor importance.

Pitch

Simply defined, pitch is highness or lowness of voice. Pitch itself can reveal, among other things, a speaker's emotional and physical condition: to some people, a high pitch suggests anger, excitability, and uncertainty; conversely, a low pitch suggests assurance, relaxation, confidence, and trust. It is a good idea to learn to avoid either extreme. However, if one's voice is naturally high, trying to lower it for a sustained period of time will only strain the vocal cords; if it is naturally low, raising it for a lengthy period of time will do the same.

Variations in pitch are commonly called melody. Without this quality, our voices would sound dull and monotonous, and they would soon put our listeners to sleep.

The beginning speaker often uses little if any inflection (pitch changes) to make his message become interesting and meaningful. Evidently, he does not realize that effective communication requires mastering a range of inflections, which are actually glides from one key to another on a hypothetical musical scale. These pitch changes may be *rising inflections, downward inflections,* or combinations called *circumflex inflections;* and in all cases we associate "shades of meaning" with their use. Usually, we think of rising inflection at the end of a sentence as expressing doubt or reluctance to be aggressive and emphatic. We are likely to feel that downward inflection indicates something important and definite. Circumflex inflection, wherein the pitch rises and falls, we are apt to think of as expressing doubt, surprise, or sarcasm. As with loudness, we should vary our inflectional range in accordance with our intended meaning, the size of the room, and the size of the audience.

Most of our speaking should be confined to our natural pitch with variations up and down the scale to indicate different degrees of enthusiasm,
doubt, and conviction, or statements and questions. Reading the following
question aloud is a good example of the way pitch varies to indicate meaning. "Where did you leave my class notes?" Notice how our voice seemed
to rise in pitch as we approached the end of the question. Now let us say,
"That's great!" with a circumflex inflection indicating a sarcastic tone. In
all probability we will be communicating two messages—one indicated by
the words and the other by the conflicting tone of voice—resulting, therefore, in an inconsistent message or *double bind*. We can lose friends, jobs,
prestige, and money by inadvertently communicating in such a manner. In
any event, in considering the tones and the words, we must be certain that
inflections reinforce, rather than contradict, the intended meaning of our
message.

Quality

Vocal quality can be described as harsh, resonant, nasal, breathy, melodious,
hoarse, dull, husky, or flat. The physicist might say that this quality is determined by the complexity of the sound wave.

Quality of voice may depend upon the physical structure of the mouth,
jaws, teeth, and lips. Differences in size and shape of mouth structure make
the sound of one voice distinctly different from another. Vocal quality may
also vary with the emotional state. It can reveal timidity, enthusiasm, boredom, and other feelings. In this regard, a person's "good morning" can be
about as unpleasant or as pleasing an experience as you can recall; a whisper
can irritate or charm. Bossy and overanxious people or relaxed and congenial
people likewise reflect these feelings through their voices. Vocal quality also
tells something of the physiological condition of the body or the vocal mechanism. Fatigue, sickness, or damage of some kind in the vocal apparatus
can often be detected in the voice quality.

If our vocal mechanism is by nature incapable of producing pleasing
tones, or if we have some chronic physical condition, we may need to compensate by working diligently to excel in the other elements of speaking:
choice of materials of speaking and use of audio-visual materials, for example. Speakers with various vocal or visual handicaps have used *compensation* with positive results.

With respect to emotions and bodily fatigue, the wisest course is a preventive one: that—to do our best to maintain emotional and physical well
being—we should provide our bodies with plenty of rest, exercise, and relaxation.

Naturally, a resonant, pleasing voice quality that reveals inner feelings
of health, enthusiasm, well being, and friendliness promotes effective communication. Warmth does much to assist us in reaching people. Moreover,
the way we handle a problem vocally influences our listeners' responses.

When a person in the open forum period raises a highly controversial issue, other things being equal, we will secure a more favorable reaction from our listeners if our voice quality remains free of any sign of irritation, defensiveness, or hostility. We will be more effective if we talk in a voice that registers feelings of assurance, enthusiasm, helpfulness, and calmness, together with concern for the purpose of our message.

Time

Time is the speed or pace of utterance. We think of it in two ways—the overall *rate* of speaking and the *amount of time* devoted to a pause, a syllable, a word, a phrase, or a sentence. (We are not referring here to timing. See Chapter 17.)

Common faults in the overall rate of speaking include (1) a monorate, or sameness of rate, (2) rushing too rapidly at different speeds through the message, or (3) plodding or laboring along too slowly, perhaps jerkily. In each of these situations we stand a good chance of losing our audience.

The rate of utterance, or basic speed, is of primary importance in aiding understanding. For most speaking, the optimum rate for achieving understanding is from 125 to 175 words per minute. Consequently, if we are inclined to fall short of this number to a considerable extent, or to go beyond 200 words per minute, some adjustments in rate may be necessary.[10]

Of paramount importance, however, are the other variables that determine the proper rate: (1) the amount of material to be covered in the allotted time, (2) the complexity of the material—if it is highly complicated, we should slow down, (3) the nature of the audience—let us bear in mind that people take in ideas at different rates, (4) the mental and physical nature of the speaker, as well as his fluency and his personality, (5) the occasion, the physical structure of the room, and the equipment available, such as microphones, and (6) the listeners and their familiarity or unfamiliarity with names, words, and statements. Let us hear the testimony of a person who speaks a great deal:

> Since in my work I have to talk a lot, I have fallen into the habit of talking rapidly. Lately I decided to alternate rapid speech with periods of slowing down, weighing each word, and letting its implication have full play. And this, I find, keeps the auditor's attention on edge, and makes me phrase more clearly the ideas I want to convey. But it does more—it affords me a new sense of confidence.
>
> Haven't you, on the other hand, known dreary, hesitant people who ought to try talking fast for a change? While they fumble vaguely with facts,

---

[10] Recent research indicates that comprehension is not greatly affected if compressed speech through tape recordings is increased to around 200 words per minute. See Charles M. Rossiter, Jr., "Some Implications of Compressed Speech for Broadcasters," *Journal of Broadcasting*, Vol. 15 (Summer 1971).

ideas and phrases, you'd like to jolt them into thinking a sentence swiftly through before they began it, so that words would follow one another with logical sequence and zip. Deliberate speeding up would not only add tremendously to their conversational effectiveness, but would also transform them by giving them a new and more sparkling personality.[11]

With respect to the second factor—the amount of time devoted to pauses, syllables, words, phrases, or sentences—the speaker can vary the duration in the interest of attention, emphasis, and intelligibility. Although these ends may be achieved by variations in force and *pitch*, they are also a product of variations in *time*. A pause may serve both emphasis and clarity, and so on. Lyndon Johnson, for instance, sometimes made effective use of the pause when he simply stopped his speech and gazed at his listeners in order to emphasize some point.

Generally speaking, how do we know when to slow down, when to speed up, when to pause? As we speak, let us consider (1) the listeners' familiarity or unfamiliarity with names, words, phrases, and statements; (2) the relative importance of these elements; and (3) the denotative or connotative meanings involved. And let us remember that decisions about time are subject to modifications, depending upon the materials, the group, and the specific occasion.

Modes of Delivering Talks

Delivering a message may be accomplished by four different methods: (1) impromptu, (2) extemporaneous, (3) manuscript, and (4) memorized. Each has its values, limitations, and unique features, including reasons, or circumstances, that determine when and when not to use each of them in a given situation. In fact, two or more of these types can be combined in one speech.

While we may think that conversational quality (see Chapter 2) is more easily adapted to the impromptu and extempore modes of speaking, there is nothing inherent in either the manuscript or memorized modes to prevent its use. Indeed, in any mode of speaking, the speaker should introduce as much conversational quality as the subject, the occasion, and the nature of the audience will permit.

Impromptu Speaking

Impromptu speaking is speaking that has not been planned in advance for a given situation. We can expect it any time—whenever a real situation calls

---

[11] Hilton Gregory, "Change Your Pace," *Reader's Digest* (March 1942), p. 10. Reprinted by permission.

for spontaneous communication. For instance, in a conversation after a concert we may find ourselves ready to defend our ideas about classical music. We may wish on the spur of the moment to make an announcement at a club meeting or to pay special tribute to one of the members. Impromptu speaking also occurs in consultations, discussions, open forums, and in the give and take of everyday living.

No one questions the value of being able to improvise. For example, in a staff meeting of the campus newspaper, when some controversy is brewing, it is to our advantage if we can "think and speak" to the problem. By skillful improvising we can often contribute more than by remaining silent or relying exclusively on material that has been prepared in advance. Impromptu speaking also gives us the opportunity to talk directly to the point and offer pertinent facts as the need for them arises.

Five rules to consider when called to speak on the spur of the moment are: (1) Be brief. (2) Don't apologize for having had no time to prepare. (3) If you have no new ideas, try supporting or rejecting some idea already stated. (4) Talk about a relevant thought, not about generalities. (5) If you have no worthwhile comment to offer, admit it.

There are serious limitations in the use of impromptu speaking, primarily related to the embarrassment or ignominy of being unprepared. Organization, specific materials of speaking, and language may suffer. Worse than that, some remark we make may be misunderstood or we may regret an impetuous statement or opinion. For these several reasons, we should carefully plan our remarks when we know in advance that we will be called on.

Because impromptu speaking requires the ability to formulate ideas quickly and the capacity to organize them, we should train ourselves by participating in everyday conversations, bull sessions, class discussions, and open forums so that we will gain confidence and experience. We can also achieve some degree of skill by listening, observing, and reading extensively, as was discussed in the chapter "Collecting Materials."

Extemporaneous Speaking

When speaking extemporaneously, a person will first select and limit his topic (if he has a free choice), do research, organize his thoughts in outline form into a speech plan (see Chapter 11), and rehearse this material. Keeping his speech plan in mind, he will talk through the ideas to become familiar with the main headings. At the time of the speech he will follow his pattern of thought and select the wording of the ideas at the moment of delivery.

Extemporaneous speaking may be used for any type of speech at almost any time—audio-visual demonstrations, lectures, instructions, entertaining speeches, political addresses, debates, and special forms of address (such as those to be discussed in Chapter 18). The method has several advantages:

(1) we can adapt our message and style to a particular group; (2) it allows flexibility in the use of content; (3) we can note feedback from the group and make suitable adjustments; and (4) it makes for naturalness in delivery. All of these advantages are conducive to interest, understanding, learning, and retention. In extemporaneous speaking, we more or less deliberately sacrifice some quality of language and exactness of organization in order to increase flexibility and adaptability of thought.

This method has limitations as well. A number of talks have failed for lack of practice with cards or notes, fairly essential to extemporaneous speech; too much reference to them can create poor communication.

Manuscript Speaking

In manuscript speaking, we not only plan our message for a particular audience but also write it out word for word for the purpose of reading the prepared manuscript at the time of delivery.

This method is preferred in every circumstance where exact language is of paramount importance. It is the one used most frequently for radio and television speaking, resolutions involving tributes, announcements regarding important policies, and papers before academic societies.

Manuscript speaking has distinct advantages. Rigid time limitations imposed upon the speaker by radio and television producers or by a program chairman make this mode of delivery necessary. Furthermore, since the speech is in complete form (as far as the verbal message is concerned), it allows the speaker more security with exact words and ideas. (Often, when we are speaking extemporaneously, accuracy or personal proof may be increased if we read *specific materials* from the printed page — an evidence card, a slip of paper, a motion, or the like.)

On the other hand, it is very easy to read a manuscript in such a dull fashion that the speech is virtually a failure. The specific disadvantages involve (1) the loss of some eye contact, (2) a general restriction in movement and spontaneity, and (3) the loss of opportunity to adjust to feedback (when we stick to the manuscript). Manuscript reading, additionally, may possibly involve (1) an unnatural vocal quality, (2) the restriction of meaning and feeling, and (3) an unrehearsed delivery of the script.

You may wish to follow these suggestions in planning the manuscript speech: (1) Use a variety of sentences of short and medium length. (2) Bring out your key ideas by using vivid words. (3) Steer clear of words with difficult sound combinations that could cause you to stumble. (4) For easy reading, type the manuscript double- or triple-spaced, with wide side margins to make room for last-minute revisions.

Before rehearsing the speech, you should read it over silently to determine whether you've said what you intended to say and to check the pronunciation of unfamiliar words. In striving for a conversational style, you will want either to subordinate or to emphasize certain words and ideas, depending on their weight in the message. Underlining the important words or thoughts will remind you to give them special emphasis. Pauses need to be marked, too, by whatever system seems most reliable. Here are a few suggestions for rehearsing the manuscript talk: (1) Read the talk over to become familiar with the message you want to convey to your listeners. (2) Learn to take in sufficient material at a glance. (3) Read the written material as if you were speaking it. (4) Use the principles of movement, attitude, gesture, and the elements of voice to help get your message across.

Memorized Speaking

Memorized speaking means speaking a prepared text word for word from memory. This method also has certain advantages. For example, we can arrive at a speech occasion knowing that we will (1) be letter perfect in what we are to say, (2) suffer no last-minute pangs over precise wording, (3) be free from the encumbrance of a manuscript, and (4) have an opportunity for direct eye contact with our listeners. Offsetting these advantages, however, are certain disadvantages or problems: (1) Memorized speaking requires extra time beyond all other steps. (2) It offers little if any flexibility in content. (3) It establishes the possibility of forgetting. (4) It presents a danger of speaking indirectly with an unnatural or "canned" effect.

To prepare for a memorized address, we must (1) understand the ideas we are memorizing and keep the central theme before us at all times; (2) memorize passages, concepts, or phrases as a whole—not thinking in terms of words; (3) rehearse the talk again and again to avoid the possibility of forgetting; and (4) think in terms of *ideas* so as to preserve elements of the conversational manner.

There may be occasions for which we will want to memorize only portions of a message, such as poetry, prose passages, the scriptures, famous quotations, and excerpts from great speeches that must be stated verbatim.

Combination of Modes of Delivery

Many speakers combine one or more of these "pure" modes, sometimes intentionally, sometimes unintentionally. When we interpolate remarks within the manuscript of our speech we are using a manuscript-impromptu combination. As we look over our manuscript the night before we speak, we may wish to add notes to the manuscript, thereby using the manuscript-extempore combination. It is easy to see how memorized-impromptu and memorized-extempore combinations of modes can be used, and combinations even of memorized-manuscript-extempore-impromptu modes are not uncommon.

A very common combination is extempore-memorized or even impromptu-memorized. In these combinations we may prepare our speech plan and expect to speak extemporaneously; but we may deliver material that we have presented many times before, drawing even the exact words from memory without being aware that we are doing so. And speaking without specific preparation on a subject that we have thought about for some time, we may repeat words from memory — words from long-forgotten speeches or other materials — without knowing that we are, in part, using the memorized mode.

Furthermore, when we deliver a message without preparing it in advance, we may be drawing so much of the talk from material we have studied previously that it is impossible for our listeners to determine whether our speech is extemporaneous or impromptu. No matter what label this presentation wears, in order to be a proficient speaker in the great variety of circumstances in which present-day man must talk, we should gain experience in all of the basic modes of delivery. Only in this way will we be able to use the modes and combinations of modes that best fit the circumstances in which we are speaking.

It should be apparent that how you deliver a message plays a significant role in communication. While it is essential that you keep your message and your audience uppermost in mind, both the *way* you deliver a message and the *mode* of delivery are extremely important factors in communicating with people.

Suggested Assignments

1.   Tape-record your voice. With the aid of your instructor and the class, note all the words slurred and mispronounced. Also, determine whether proper variations in time, pitch, loudness, and quality were used to enhance proper meaning and feeling.

2.   Prepare a brief talk for television playback. Note the "silent messages" you sent in addition to the thoughts expressed.

3.   Listen to the speech of those about you for a period of one week. Record on a paper the mispronunciations you have noted.

4.   Prepare a list of topics of current interest on your campus and in your locality. Submit this list to your instructor for his use in conducting a round of impromptu speeches in class. Discuss this mode of speaking.

5.   Memorize a quoted excerpt for class presentation. Discuss the advantages and disadvantages of this technique.

6.   Write an announcement to be delivered word for word. Read it to the class, observing the procedures discussed in this chapter. Evaluate the effectiveness of this form of speaking.

7.   Study the nonverbal behavior of people you contact in the period of one week. Be prepared to discuss the impact they had on your feelings.

8.   Appraise the voice of some student or teacher. Note in what way this person's voice aids or hinders the communication process.

9. Determine the correct pronunciation for the following words. Add to this list an equal number of words that people in your part of the country (or in your cultural group) commonly pronounce differently from people elsewhere (or in other cultural groups). In each instance note the region or group wherein a different pronunciation is more frequently heard.

room	Missouri	apparatus	defect	Cincinnati
creek	guarantee	Baptist	already	data
juvenile	research	New Orleans	chasm	America
mayor	February	column	comparable	preferable
gather	relevant	Chicago	Baltimore	chicanery
Cuba	regular	champion	idea	culinary
recognize	athlete	physician	abdomen	library
sects	luxury	picture	experiment	statistics
tomato	aunt	government	chef	advertisement
literature	which	fish	irreparable	mischievous

10. Watch your *final* consonants:

right	kept	wept	slept	respect	district	conflict		retrospect
exact	exactly	direct	correct	correctly	strict	strictly		defects
selects	facts	thinks	thanks	desks	risks	next	first	rests
lost	tastes	hosts	resists	wrists	costs	forest	artists	guests
last	test	posts	results	west	went	president	and	hand
understand	thousand	round	found	sounds	seconds	almonds
tends	called	old	holds	bold	child	field	tomorrow

11. Watch your *middle* consonants:

understand	laboratory	library	arctic	particular	gentlemen	all
right	always	advantage	government	exception	didn't	couldn't
soldier	adjective	interpretation	recognize	yesterday	twenty
going to	got to	want to	don't want to	let me	give me	let us
of them	with the	to them	see them	have them	for them	couple of
lot of	out of	let them

12. Watch for consonants *added, inserted,* or *transposed:*

drown	drowned	gown	attacked	only	twice	once	across
height	nowhere	somewhere	pretty	hundred	children	brethren
introduce	prescription	pronunciation	irony	tragedian	larynx
pharynx	Des Moines	Illinois	luxury

13. Watch for *incorrect consonants:*

accept	length	strength	depth	with	other	gesture	escape
chimney	handkerchief	February	something	seven	eleven	diphtheria
diphthong	dilapidated	taciturn	gibberish	dishevel	content
fifth	orgy	why	when	which	while	whether	wheel	wharf
wanting	having	doing	seeing	coming	going	being	morn-ing	singing

14. Watch for *incorrect vowels:*

get	can	gather	just	again	sense	catch	wrestling	such
since	six	milk	men	any	because	fish	wish	dish	piano
Italian	pronunciation	suite	column	heroine	syrup	prowess
wander	cupola	abroad	daughter	taught	caught	sought
thought	water	wash	watch	lost	cloth	rinse	poor	deaf
been	pretty	coupon	measure	Roosevelt	our

Suggested References

Barbara, Dominic A., "Nonverbal Communication," *Journal of Communication,* Vol. 13 (September 1963), pp. 166–173.

Bronstein, Arthur J., and Beatrice F. Jacoby, *Your Speech and Voice* (New York: Random House, 1967). Part 5, "The Voice."

Campbell, J. H., and Hal W. Hepler (eds.), *Dimensions in Communication,* 2nd ed. (Belmont, Calif.: Wadsworth Publishing Co., 1970). Section 3, "Nonverbal Communication: Explorations into Time, Space, Action, and Object" by Randall Harrison.

Eisenberg, A. M., and Ralph Smith, Jr., *Nonverbal Communication* (New York: Bobbs-Merrill Co., 1971). Chapter 3, "Nonverbal Meaning: A Behavioral Approach."

Eisenson, Jon, *The Improvement of Voice and Diction* (New York: The Macmillan Co., 1965). Chapter 7, "Pitch and Voice Improvement."

Gibb, Jack R., "Defensive Communication," *Journal of Communication,* Vol. 11 (September 1961), pp. 141–148.

Gray, Giles W., and Claude M. Wise, *The Bases of Speech,* 3rd ed. (New York: Harper & Row, 1959). Chapter 5, "The Phonetic Basis of Speech."

Jensen, J. Vernon, *Perspectives on Oral Communication* (Boston: Holbrook Press, 1970). Chapter 2, "Perspective on Delivery."

Hall, Edward T., *The Silent Language* (New York: Fawcett World Library, 1959). Chapter 10, "Space Speaks."

Harris, Thomas A., *I'm O.K. – You're O.K.* (New York: Harper & Row, 1969). Chapter 5, "Analyzing the Transaction."

Harrison, Randall P., *Beyond Words: An Introduction to Nonverbal Communication* (Englewood Cliffs, N. J.: Prentice-Hall, 1974).

Mehrabian, Albert, *Silent Messages* (Belmont, Calif.: Wadsworth Publishing Co., 1971). Chapter 1, "Immediacy: Liking and Approach."

Oliver, Robert T., *Making Your Meaning Effective* (Boston: Holbrook Press, 1971). Chapter 6, "Presenting Your Speech."

St. Onge, Keith R., *Creative Speech* (Belmont, Calif.: Wadsworth Publishing Co., 1964). Chapter 4, "Delivery."

Part Four
Forms of Speaking

Part Four provides specific advice for the speaker focusing on particular types of speaking—advocacy or persuasion (Chapter 15), informative or expository speaking (Chapter 16), entertaining or humorous speaking (Chapter 17), and "special occasion" speaking (Chapter 18).

15
Speaking to Advocate

"The basic purpose of all advocacy is to change or deepen attitude or behavior"

Tradition has often divided speaking into advocacy (persuasion, argumentation), information, and entertainment. Although all speaking potentially affects the human organism, messages directed at people differ considerably because of the *intent* of the speaker. And even though the principles of speaking apply to all original oral communication situations, the specific purposes of the speaker require special applications.

Advocacy does not stand alone, unmixed with elements from the other two kinds of speaking. Information almost always goes along with it in the same message; the communicator informs or reminds his listeners of certain facts and then tries to persuade them to action based on those facts, or he tries to instill an opinion that may later produce the desired action. If the facts on which the persuasion is to be based are sometimes not explicitly stated, they are implied.

Some types of advocacy can be entertaining—take, for example, court-room drama. From the *Merchant of Venice* to *Perry Mason*, court advocacy has achieved a special following in literature and the theater and, more recently, in radio and television. Many people regularly visit real courtrooms, especially criminal courts, to witness the dramas enacted there, just as they would go to a movie or a play. Drama, entertaining or not, is more often an expression of advocacy than it is of informative speaking. It ranges from the President's plea to the American people to adapt to a continuing energy crisis, down to the citizen's appeal to the municipal judge to let him go because he has never violated a law before.

The Nature of Advocacy

Speaking to advocate, or persuade, covers a wide range. A formal speech, such as a prosecuting attorney's closing address to the jury, in which he may depend upon evidence and reasoning for persuasive power, is only one kind

272

of advocacy. A mother's appeal to her son to drive safely for a happier, longer life is another. Let us define advocacy here as an attempt to change the attitude and behavior of an individual or a group or to strengthen an attitude or behavior already present.

Advocacy is found just about wherever speakers speak. Political leaders talk on television and radio to persuade citizens to support their actions; and political aspirants address masses of listeners through the same media, or talk informally to little groups in somebody's living room. Legislators in fifty state capitals and in the national capital debate issues before one another and before the public, and meet in committees to argue the public business. Attorneys in hundreds of courts, high and low, argue to persuade judge or jury to accept their interpretations of the cases under consideration.

Women in the marketplace, men on the construction job, and youngsters at play all engage in some kind of persuasive effort every day. A mother tries to persuade her neighbor to push for stop signs at the school intersection; a father tells his associate they should build the new hamburger stand in such-and-such suburb, and why; a boy tells his friend down the street, "Tell your Dad to cool it. The grass can be cut any old day."

Clergymen from the pulpit urge their parishioners to a better life. Teachers and professors, while they deal in information daily, at the same time try to persuade students to accept and retain it. Salesmen, with foot in door, by radio-television or telephone, or over the counter, make their pitches.

Although the basic purpose of all advocacy is to change or deepen attitude or behavior, the method or technique of the speaking varies according to the subject under discussion, the occasion, and the person or group on the other end. The technique may be simple: "Buy this lawnmower." Or it may involve a chain of action: "Clean up your city; stop throwing candy wrappers and cigarette butts on the sidewalk; put your trash in the garbage can; wash your windows; curb your dog." Or the speaker may try to persuade us to support a national policy: "Our country should stay out of foreign wars." Or he wants us to accept an idea: "Libraries have a special importance in a democracy; they encourage good citizenship." Or the advocacy has an intellectual level: "The success of Western civilization rests upon a proper understanding of the relative worth of material possessions and spiritual values."

Obviously, a single technique would not be used for all these varieties of persuasion. The persuasive speaker varies his use of the materials of development, personal proof, and experience and sensory materials according to his analysis of the audience, the situation in which he is to speak, and the subject itself. Not only do the amounts of these resources vary, but also the ways in which they are used.

To distinguish between these different kinds of speeches of advocacy, with their respective treatments, writers in the field of speech communication have classified speeches of advocacy by various subtypes—among them the "logical" persuasive talk, the "nonlogical" persuasive talk, the debate, the argument, the mixed informative-persuasive talk, the goodwill talk.

These subtypes are not mutually exclusive—a given one may contain elements from others. Their descriptive labels indicate some of the ways speakers may adapt the materials of persuasion to the many subjects, occasions, and audiences that confront them.

Two selections are offered (see insets) to illustrate the range of speaking for advocacy. The first is a transcription of a speech delivered and recorded in the persuasion course at Michigan State University; the second is a speech plan, submitted originally by a student in the basic communication course

A Specimen Speech of Advocacy

Once upon a time there lived a king named Babylon. He was the king of a vast land rich in resources which was named Rhetorica.

One day in the village the people became aroused. There were rumors that the savage Ignoramuses were invading their country, destroying their homes, robbing them of their possessions, and worst of all—eating the citizens!

"What shall we do?" cried the people. "The Ignoramuses are coming and we are not nearly as strong as they. They will surely eat us!"

King Babylon began to speak. Everyone became silent and listened. "Have no fear, my subjects," he said, "I will lead you away from the Ignoramuses. We will flee to a new land where we will be able to build even better homes and be much happier than we are now."

"Praise our king! He will save us from the terrible fate of the Ignoramuses!" cried the people.

Early the next morning the Rhetoricians all met in front of the palace. They had packed all of their valuable possessions and stood waiting for their leader. Soon the king's trumpeters appeared and blew their horns to announce the coming of Babylon. Then came a page bearing the king's flag. Next came the king's council of knights and nobles. Within a few minutes the king had appeared and everyone began to assemble into position to begin the long journey.

When they became assembled, one subject spoke up and asked the king, "Which way are we going?"

"Never fear," answered Babylon, "I will get you there. Let's see—we can't use the path to the East—it is not wide enough. The path to the North is infested with vicious, snarling beasts. The path to the West is a dead end. I guess we can try the path to the South then."

So, they were off. They traveled for three days and still didn't recognize where they were. By this time the people began to wonder about the king. They would ask the nobles, "Do you think the king will ever lead us to this new land?

and adapted for use as a sample plan and included in the Communication 102 syllabus.

It is evident that each of these speeches requires special handling of the principles of speaking and that each one is very different from the other. Yet each speech made use of the same basic principles of communication. Let us turn our attention, therefore, to the organization of speeches of advocacy and observe some of the modifications of these principles.

Organizing the Speech of Advocacy

The Topic

Except in the public speaking classroom, the speaker does not ordinarily "choose a topic" for a speech to advocate. Advocacy arises out of the everyday issues with which we are confronted. Perhaps we rise to oppose a plan

---

We have been traveling for three days and still don't know where we are."

One of the nobles spoke up. "I know things are looking bad now, but we will just have to wait—the king will get us to that new land somehow."

Two weeks passed. The king kept leading the people. To <u>where</u>, they were not sure, but he kept leading them. One day they came to a fork in the road. "Which way shall we go?" cried the people.

"We cannot take the road to the right," answered the king; "it is infested with poison ivy. Therefore, I suppose we should take the road to the left."

So they went left. Four weeks later they were still on their journey. The subjects were deeply distressed by this time, as they were afraid the Ignoramuses were catching up with them. And they were tired of traveling aimlessly.

One subject spoke to the king. "Where are we going, King Babylon?"

King Babylon looked the subject in the eye. "I hope to lead you to a land

full of promises. Now I am beginning to wonder, though. We had come this way because we had to go South when we started, in order to avoid misfortune from the East, the West, and the North. Two weeks ago we had to go left to avoid the poison ivy. Never fear—I will get you somewhere, though."

About three days later it happened. The king and his subjects reached their stopping point. The only problem is that when they got there, they recognized it as the land they had originally left. Not only that, but the dreaded Ignoramuses were hiding behind the bushes and ambushed them and <u>ate them all up</u>! And they were worse off than when they started their journey.

*There is some good news, however. King Babylon managed miraculously to escape the terrible Ignoramuses, and the last I heard he found some new kingdom to lead.**

---

* Reproduced here through the courtesy of Diane Sadewasser.

A Specimen Plan for a Speech of Advocacy (Deductive Form)

Compulsory Arbitration

Introduction

A. *During the 1959 steel strike, President Eisenhower made the following statement: "America will not — indeed, it cannot — tolerate for long the crippling of the entire economy as the result of labor-management disputes. The choice for free employers and employees is clear. Voluntarily, in the spirit of free collective bargaining, they will act responsibly; or else, in due course, their countrymen will see to it that they do act responsibly." Theodore H. Kheel, <u>The Pros and Cons of Compulsory Arbitration</u> (New York: New York Chamber of Commerce, March 1961).*

Purpose
Sentence

B. *The federal government should adopt a program of compulsory arbitration in labor-management disputes in the basic industries.*

Body

I. *Strikes in the basic industries are detrimental.*

A. *Many persons are harmed by major strikes.*

1. *Both labor and management suffer losses.*

Factual
Evidence

a. *There is a loss of wages. "After a Three Month Shutdown What Striking Printers Got," <u>U. S. News & World Report</u>, Vol. 54, No. 11 (March 18, 1963), p. 98.*

Factual
Evidence

b. *Often there is a loss of markets. "Effect of the Mere Threat of a Strike in Steel," <u>U. S. News & World Report</u>, Vol. 58, No. 12 (March 22, 1965), p. 91.*

Reasoning
from
Example

Factual
Evidence

c. *Sometimes workers even lose their jobs. "Effect of the Mere Threat of a Strike in Steel," <u>U. S. News & World Report</u>, Vol. 58, No. 12 (March 22, 1965), p. 91.*

2. *The consumer suffers.*

a. *There is a loss of product or service.*

b. *Higher prices result from the fact that the supply of products is down.*

Factual
Evidence

3. *The economy as a whole is adversely affected. "Can the U. S. Still Afford Big Strikes?" <u>U. S. News & World Report</u>, Vol. 58, No. 18 (May 3, 1965), p. 87.*

B. *The number and scope of strikes are increasing.*

   1. *More strikes are occurring within the basic industries.*

      a. *Shipping between Maine and Texas has been tied up by two 39-day strikes in recent years by East Coast Longshoremen.*

Factual Evidence

      b. *Major airlines have been shut down twice in recent years. "Can the U. S. Still Afford Big Strikes?"* U. S. News & World Report, *Vol. 58, No. 18 (May 3, 1965), p. 87.*

Reasoning from Example

      c. *Experts believe that a steel strike is probable in the near future.*

         (1) *The contract is about to expire.*

         (2) *Steel companies are stockpiling.*

         (3) *Steel imports are up significantly.*

Reasoning from Sign

   2. *There is a concentrated loss due to strikes.*

      a. *Strikes are longer today than in the past.*

      b. *The record shows that there are more man-days idle per striker today than in the past.*

II. *The present system of settling labor-management disputes is ineffective.*

  A. *Collective bargaining is ineffective.*

Opinion Evidence

   1. *Secretary of Labor W. Willard Wirtz has said: "Collective bargaining as we have known it is obsolete." W. Willard Wirtz, "Union Friends Dominate Federal Labor Panels,"* Nation's Business, *Vol. 51, No. 2 (February 1963), p. 56.*

Opinion Evidence

   2. *Walter Lippmann, writing in the* Washington Post, *said: "The country has outgrown the existing machinery for dealing with big labor disputes." Walter Lippmann, "Today and Tomorrow,"* Washington Post *(August 20, 1963), p. A-13.*

  B. *Voluntary arbitration is an ineffective preventive to strikes. Kurt Braun,* Labor Disputes and Their Settlement *(Baltimore: Johns Hopkins Press, 1955), p. 159.*

III. *The adoption of compulsory arbitration by the federal government is a feasible alternative.*

   A. *It has been adopted in other countries.*

   B. *Polls indicate that the public favors compulsory arbitration in labor-management disputes in the basic industries. Benjamin Wyle, "Compulsory Arbitration and the National Welfare," The Arbitration Journal, Vol. 19, No. 2 (1964), pp. 98–102.*

Reasoning from Analogy

   C. *Management has things to gain from such a program. "New Calls for Arbitration," U. S. News & World Report, Vol. 54, No. 6 (February 11, 1963), p. 90.*

Reasoning from Cause

   D. *Unions would gain from submitting to compulsory arbitration. W. Willard Wirtz, "Union Friends Dominate Federal Labor Panels," Nation's Business, Vol. 51, No. 2 (February 1963), p. 56.*

Conclusion

   A. *Today a serious problem exists concerning the settlement of labor-management disputes.*

      1. *Strikes are detrimental.*

      2. *The number and scope of strikes are increasing.*

   B. *The present system is ineffective.*

   C. *Compulsory arbitration should be adopted.*

   D. *Dr. Orme W. Phelps, Senior Professor of Economics at Claremont Men's College, sums up the situation this way: "Our whole system of jurisprudence relies on the idea that anyone with a grievance is able to compel an antagonist to meet him peaceably at a public hearing where, after argument, a binding third-party settlement is handed down. No one apologizes for this: more often than not the courts are referred to as protectors of our liberties, defenders of our freedom. The unanimity with which it has been held that labor disputes must be exempted from this process is remarkable in itself." Orme W. Phelps, "Compulsory Arbitration: Some Perspectives," Industrial and Labor Relations Review, Vol. 18, No. 1 (October 1964), pp. 81–91.*

presented by someone in our group; perhaps a community problem inspires us to prepare an answer. Speakers do not, then, prepare "speeches of advocacy." They speak on issues, and critics label their efforts "speeches of advocacy." Even as an exercise in the speech classroom laboratory, when we present a talk advocating something, that "something" should always be real to us; we should regard our speech not only as an exercise but as an opportunity to speak out on subjects we have opinions on.

The Purpose Sentence

For speeches of advocacy, we normally phrase the purpose sentence so as to suggest a behavioral change expected in our listeners (sometimes, as in patriotic speeches, we want to help our listeners maintain an attitude already held). The exact wording of the purpose sentence varies according to the nature of the subject and the kind and amount of behavioral change desired. If we wish to advocate a policy change, the purpose sentence contains the word *should*. "The United States should increase its support of major space programs." When taking a stand against a policy, we avoid the use of the negative in the purpose sentence, whenever possible, because a negative connotation there will tend to confuse us as we prepare our message; and, if the purpose sentence is actually spoken, it may also confuse the listener. Thus, we avoid "The Congress should not change the present electoral system of choosing the President;" but do use "The United States should retain the present electoral system of choosing the President."

However, not *all* purpose sentences for speeches to advocate need to contain the word "should." We may wish to argue that "The community college is a better place to send your freshman daughter than the large state university," or "Erecting Christmas decorations before Thanksgiving violates the true spirit of Christmas," or "Smoking marijuana is more injurious to mental health than drinking." Generally speaking, the purpose sentence for a speech advocating a policy includes the word "should"; that for a speech of advocacy concerning a matter of fact or value may be phrased in a variety of ways.

In every case, however, the purpose sentence should be clear, as concise as possible, and as complete as necessary, and it should state specifically what the listener is asked to think or believe or do.

A special problem arises when we are forced to be indirect. It is one thing to argue that air pollution is bad and should be reduced. Even if the listener is opposed to our specific solution, he is not likely to deny the existence of the problem. Other controversial issues may find the listener willing to consider our arguments with some detachment. But, suppose we wish to argue that hippies form a vital part of our society or that the automobile should be banned from the highway in favor of public transportation. We know that we may not be able to present our reasons directly because some listeners are strongly set against us. What, then, do we do about the purpose sentence? First we remind ourselves that the primary purpose of the purpose sentence is to aid us in clarifying our goal in composing the message. *There is no requirement that the purpose sentence be stated in the message exactly the same way we phrased it for our speech plan.* Therefore, we compose our purpose sentence precisely as we would if listener bias were not a worry. Now, we know what our goals are, what our intent is. As we construct our speech plan, we can work in the message of the purpose sentence so that it helps assure us of a fair hearing by our listeners. With a very controversial subject, we may decide not to make a statement of purpose to our audience at all; but whenever possible, we will announce our purpose but modify the purpose sentence so that our listeners will not immediately reject us and our subject.

The Speech Plan

In Chapter 11, we considered two basic plans for the organization of a message — deductive and inductive — and discussed a number of modifications for them. Let us now look at these modifications as they apply specifically to speaking to advocate.

The *causal sequence* is perhaps the most logical modification. Ordinarily, it is used in its deductive form, where we announce our proposition and proceed to support it causally, but it may be developed with an inductive speech plan as well. The causal sequence is commonly used when we perceive the listeners as relatively neutral in their attitudes toward our subject, although this pattern is not limited to a neutral audience.

The *topical sequence* is a catch-all in that it is principally used when we have a variety of points to be discussed in a given message. By means of the topical sequence, we are able to develop each point within the sequence according to its own fashion. If our subject is "foreign aid," we first explain the overall aid program; argue against military aid, using a causal pattern; and then support economic aid in various parts of the world, employing a *space sequence.*

As attractive as the topical sequence may seem for advocative speaking, it often suffers from a lack of internal relationship between the topics. By planning our transitions and internal summaries carefully, we can offset this problem. Another difficulty is that this pattern is sometimes used to justify discussion of a number of points that should really be presented in separate speeches.

The *time sequence* is useful to the speaker who believes that the strength of his argument lies in its time relationships. A speech attempting to show the causes of World War II, for example, might be organized in this way. We might choose to begin with the Treaty of Versailles in 1919, proceed to the assumption of power in Italy by Mussolini in 1922, to the rise of Hitler in the early 1930s, to the swallowing up of the Rhineland in 1936 and of Austria and the Sudetenland in 1938, and on to the invasion of Poland in 1939.

The *narrative sequence,* which is related, of course, to time, is usually a good attention-arrester, because listeners usually enjoy a good story, well told. While its use is not determined exclusively by the listeners' attitudes, the narrative sequence is perhaps most advantageous in speaking situations where we suspect that our listeners will be apathetic or would be hostile to a more direct approach.

The narrative sequence may tell a story very directly, thus making its point directly; or it may be used subtly, as an analogy. The narrative about King Babylon, which appears earlier in this chapter, was actually intended as an attack on irresponsible political leaders. Only the speeches that preceded it on the program gave listeners the necessary hint.

The *problem-solution approach*, like the causal sequence, usually comes into play when the speaker wants to rely on reasoning and evidence; and, like the causal sequence, it may be developed either from the purpose sentence or to the purpose sentence. While it is most often attempted before audiences that are presumed to be relatively neutral, we can also reduce doubt, apathy, and even hostility by this method, in which we carefully develop the problem before we propose our solution.

The *implicative approach*, an adaptation of the problem-solution approach, is usually reserved for the hostile listener. By developing the problem fully and then considering and rejecting each possible solution in turn, we lead our listeners to our conclusion before we arrive there or even without our having to state it at all. The principle behind the implicative approach is that listeners will be more likely to accept what they believe is their own solution than they will the solution of the speaker, especially if he does not possess high credibility with them.

The *comparative approach*, which has many advantages for the advocate, is one of the most appropriate to use when the listener's knowledge about our subject is low. A direct comparison between that which the listener understands well and that which he is in doubt about often helps him to accept our argument. The comparative approach can also be used indirectly, however, even analogically, when a controversial subject is being discussed.

The *suggestion approach*, a combination of several others, introduces the subject of the speech indirectly and suggests rather than proclaims our intent. Since it is reserved for hostile listeners, its advantages are obvious; its disadvantage is that it may become too obscure, so that not even a hint of our real message gets through.

Except for the most indirect ones, all these plan modifications are available for the speaker who faces a friendly audience. For such listeners we increase the amount of materials of experience and decrease the amount of materials of development, or we reduce the materials of development with which our listeners are familiar and present new information to them.

Listener Adaptation

When we are advocating, it is very important that we know as much as possible about our listeners' probable reactions to our message. Then we can make "educated guesses" about the kinds and amounts of materials of speaking to use. For the neutral listener we will use a heavy concentration of materials of development; for the friendly, materials of experience and fresh or new materials of development; for the apathetic, materials of experience, until the listener loses his apathy and develops a positive or a negative attitude toward the subject; for the hostile listener, personal proof is urgently needed, although all listeners have to feel assurance of it.

Conclusions

We know that the purpose of all conclusions is to assist in leading our listener in the direction we want him to go (see Chapter 11). In advocative speaking, the purpose of the speech may range from our desire for overt behavioral change by the listener through a subtle alteration of attitude to the maintenance of the status quo. The conclusion, in each case, should reflect the purpose of the speech and advance it.

The means of achieving the given purpose, however, varies with the speaker's analysis of his listener's knowledge of the subject, and, more importantly, with his analysis of the listener's attitude toward the subject and toward the speaker. Often the occasion plays a powerful role in determining the method of concluding.

For straightforward advocacy, when we have announced our purpose sentence and gone about convincing our receivers, the most common method of concluding is with an open appeal for acceptance of the idea or for a more overt behavioral change—to vote, to give money, or to participate in an activity. This method is equally useful when our purpose, though still obvious, is to gain acceptance of a belief or concept. Sometimes in the conclusion we will appeal to the listener to think about what has been said, to give the idea a fair hearing, and then to vote his own conviction. Lew Sarett referred to this as the "absolute candor plus appeal to good sportmanship" conclusion.

When the advocacy has a slightly elevated quality, as to either its goal or its language, the illustration or quotation method of concluding may be efficacious in swaying the listener, while maintaining the dignity of the address. Such an ending may add to the credibility of the speaker, as when the speaker, urging the adoption of a program of students' rights by the faculty of a university, concluded with "The only thing we have to fear is fear itself. . . ." When the talk advocating a change has been developed inductively, the speech may conclude with the statement of the purpose sentence. This technique may provide a dramatic note; it may be used to spring a surprise on the listeners; or it may simply arrive as the culmination of a careful, slow, steady building of the listeners' interest and attitude to an acceptance of an idea that they might have received with hostility had it been presented earlier.

The summary conclusion is probably less useful in speaking to advocate than it is in informative speaking, but, combined with either an implied or a direct use of the appeal, it can achieve a double purpose—to remind the listener of the major points in support of the purpose sentence and to urge his acceptance of our goal. Some summarizing of the main points is almost always required when the speech is relatively long or complicated, or when we have chosen to digress from our theme. After all, it will do little good to appeal for the listener's support when he cannot quite remember what he is being asked to do or why he is supposed to do it!

Introductions

The introduction serves to arouse the listener's attention, establish or maintain the source's personal proof, and direct the listener's thoughts (overtly or covertly) toward the subject matter of the message. As with the body and the conclusion, the introduction to the message must be designed with the purpose of the speech, the listener's knowledge and attitudes, and the occasion in mind.

In speaking to advocate, we can use the unrelated introduction to disarm our listener when we want to put off jumping too quickly into our subject. We have to be careful, however, that the listener does not interpret this maneuver as an attempt to trick him or camouflage the issue.

Some acknowledgments are frequently necessary, especially in more formal speaking situations, and acknowledging guests or other important persons may help our credibility, especially when our subject is highly controversial. This is also true of the occasion approach to the introduction, but we are usually more successful when we combine either of these styles with an illustration or quotation, preferably one that ties the acknowledgments or occasional remarks to some aspect of our subject.

Probably most often used and most successful is the illustration or quotation form of introduction. It has the advantage of being potentially attention-arresting; it can lead easily into the subject; and it can go with either deductive or inductive speech patterns. Student speakers often find that this introduction is personally satisfying, as well; if they encounter a reasonably favorable response, their own nervousness tends to decrease.

For the direct approach to advocacy, of course, the direct approach to the introduction may best serve our purpose. We may begin with the purpose sentence or we may precede it with a brief acknowledgment of the listeners and a reference to the occasion. Conversely, when we wish to conceal part of our purpose for a while, we may jump directly into the portion of our purpose that we believe will find a favorable audience, and reserve the statement of the remainder of our purpose for later in the speech.

Delivering the Speech to Advocate

Contrary to what some persons say, there is no one best method of delivery to use for advocating. Like all other principles of effective communication,

presenting the talk depends upon our old friends—the purpose of the message, the listener, the occasion, and our own abilities as speakers.

With a friendly audience, we can usually speak more emphatically than when our listeners are hostile. Apathetic listeners can sometimes be waked up with a vigorous presentation. The more directly we approach our advocacy, the more forcefully we can present our arguments. But table-pounding does not always work with the favorably disposed listener; and loudness and logic do not always march hand in hand (though many high school debaters appear to think they do). Undoubtedly, the smartest thing is to play it loose, adapting our delivery, audible and visible, to our analysis of the speaking situation—always ready to change and change again, if we do not obtain the results we expect.

Refutation in Advocacy

Refutation—or replying to an argument—might be called advocacy in reverse. Rebuttal in debate is only one form of refutation. A salesman's effort to overcome a customer's expressed reasons for refusing to buy his product represents another form. In the give-and-take of an informal meeting, if we take issue with what a speaker has just said, we are practicing refutation just as much as if we had been called upon to respond formally.

Many speakers, masters at presenting a prepared advocative talk, fold up and fail to defend their arguments effectively when confronted with objection or counterargument. Refuting an opponent's argument is not easy; but if we think enough of our belief to present it in public, we should think enough of it to defend it against attack. Of the possible ways to defend our beliefs when they are under attack, let us discuss five typical ones. Once we become familiar with them we will be in a better position to refute an argument.

Rejection

You may reject an opponent's argument as being irrelevant, or you may reject his analysis as naive. A speaker may argue that, since X country has seven battleships while we have only four, "the X navy is stronger than ours." You point out that the evidence submitted is irrelevant; that "atomic weapons and air power have made the battleship obsolete." You then challenge the speaker to compare our strength in aircraft carriers and atomic submarines with that of X country.

Matching

You may match your opponent's evidence with an equal or superior quantity or quality of your own. Some speakers feel that greater quantity defeats less quantity; that twenty-four pieces of evidence automatically beat twenty-three. But it is obviously better to match your opponent in quality by offering evidence that is more recent, more complete, or more specific.

Testing

You may refute your opponent's evidence by applying tests of evidence (see Chapter 6); that is, by questioning the reliability of the evidence. If your opponent quotes Senator A to the effect that replacing overage mail delivery trucks will seriously damage the country's economy, you may point out that three years ago Senator A predicted the collapse of the national economy when the housing bill was passed, but the economy seems to be in pretty good shape. Last year Senator A demanded a reduction in government salaries, threatening the nation with economic downfall if his bill was not passed. "How much are Senator A's predictions worth?" you ask.

Utilizing

Utilization is "turning the tables" on your opponent. You are opposed to a proposed local tax on haircuts. Your opponent refers to your shaggy look and asks, "How can this man, who obviously hasn't seen the inside of a barber shop in weeks, be an authority on haircuts and taxes on them?" You turn the tables very simply: "Ladies and gentlemen: I can't afford a haircut very often as things are. How can I ever get one if you raise the price by putting a tax on it?"

The speaker must be careful in resorting to this form of refutation, for it can easily lead to a damaging and embarrassing counter-turning-of-the-tables by his opponent. But when wisely used it is often an effective way to deal with an opponent's argument or evidence.

Admitting

The speaker may decide it is expedient to admit his opposition's point and then find other ways of advancing his argument. Suppose your opponent says, "Paving this road will cost more than a hundred thousand dollars, and that's a lot of money." You may reply: "One hundred thousand dollars *is* a lot of money, but even so a hundred thousand dollars is only one tenth of the amount we have appropriated for road paving in this county, and the county commissioners say this stretch of road should have first priority. . . ."

Since advocacy is one of the three basic purposes of speaking — and is more often used than the other two, information and entertainment — we will likely be persuaders all our lives. This pleads for more effort than just "speaking our minds." We need to learn the principles of persuasion; comprehend the full range of argument and counterargument; study all sides of issues we plan to debate; become familiar with the techniques of advocacy; and carefully choose the best material from the storehouse of our minds and the accumulation of the ages so as to present effectively our worthwhile ideas to those who may benefit from them.

Suggested Assignments

In the following assignments make full use of materials of development, personal proof, and experience.

1.   Choose a topic for a persuasive talk. Prepare two complete speaking plans (including introduction and conclusion), selecting them from those we have described. Keep in mind your audience, the subject, the occasion, and your own abilities. Select the better plan (in your judgment) and present your talk to the class. Submit both plans to your instructor, together with a statement explaining why you chose the one you did.

2.   For your next speaking assignment prepare at least three different introductions. Select the best one (in your opinion) for delivery to your class, but hand all of them to your instructor. Explain briefly to your listeners why you chose the one you did. Be prepared to defend your choice.

3.   Carry out the same assignment, this time preparing three conclusions instead of introductions.

4.   As an exercise in preparing speaking plans for use in advocacy, your instructor will gather together all of the plans submitted to him for a persuasive speaking assignment, mix them up, and distribute them at random to all the students in the class. You will study the plan you have received, recall the talk (you are wise if you have taken notes on all the talks in this round), and rewrite the speaking plan as though you were to deliver a talk on this particular subject.

5.   Choose a topic for a persuasive talk toward which your listeners will, you believe, give an attentive and objective ear. Research your talk carefully. Prepare a purpose sentence and a complete speaking plan (including introduction and conclusion) of the deductive type. Submit these, plus your evidence cards and speaker's notes (if you are allowed to use them) on the day you deliver your talk. Your talk should be evaluated and graded on the basis of your entire preparation, not merely on the presentation.

6.   Choose a topic for a talk toward which you believe your listeners would show a lack of interest. (Be sure the topic interests *you*, however, and that it is worthwhile.) Prepare for the talk in the same manner described in assignment 5, but this time use an inductive speaking plan.

7.   For the next series of speeches, your class will form two groups. Group A will prepare and present straight advocative speeches, using the deductive speech plan (or a variation), announcing the purpose sentence in the introduction, and employing a heavy concentration of the materials of development, especially evidence and reasoning. Group B will reply to these talks at the next class meeting. Speakers in Group B will be expected to use refutation (rejection, matching, testing, utilizing, admitting). Your instructor may wish to assign certain types of refutation to each of you; he may require that a minimum of three types be used in each refutative effort.

8.   Carry out the same assignment, described just above; but this time your speeches of refutation will be presented impromptu, each one following one of the prepared advocative talks.

Suggested References

Andersen, Kenneth E., *Persuasion: Theory and Practice* (Boston: Allyn and Bacon, 1971).

Anderson, Jerry M., and Paul J. Dovre, *Readings in Argumentation* (Boston: Allyn and Bacon, 1968).

Bettinghaus, Erwin P., *Persuasive Communication,* 2nd ed. (New York: Holt, Rinehart and Winston, 1973).

Freeley, Austin J., *Argumentation and Debate: Rational Decision Making,* 3rd ed. (Belmont, Calif.: Wadsworth Publishing Co., 1971).

Johannesen, Richard L., *Ethics and Persuasion* (New York: Random House, 1967).

Larson, Charles U., *Persuasion: Reception and Responsibility* (Belmont, Calif.: Wadsworth Publishing Co., 1973).

Miller, Gerald R., and Michael Burgoon, *New Techniques of Persuasion* (New York: Harper & Row, 1973).

Miller, Gerald R., and Thomas R. Nilsen (eds.), *Perspectives on Argumentation* (Glenview, Ill.: Scott, Foresman and Co., 1966).

Minnick, Wayne C., *The Art of Persuasion,* 2nd ed. (Boston: Houghton Mifflin Co., 1968).

16
Speaking to Inform

"Let us know what is going on"

Sharing information is a matter of concern to everyone. Whenever two or more people actively involve themselves in some task, project, or problem, they depend upon the sharing of information in order to achieve understanding in their particular endeavor. In this regard, one of the most important discoveries in communication research is the extent of *undercommunication*, or the failure of one of us to let others know what is going on. Equally disturbing is our deficiency in communicating effectively the knowledge we have. All too often, information is received through the *grapevine*, which, as many of us have observed through experience with the *rumor clinic game*, is very prone to distortion of the original message as it is repeated "down the line." Although correct information is frequently transmitted, more often than not additions, omissions, and loss of detail permeate our messages. It comes as no surprise then that Peter Drucker observes an increasing demand for informed persons to impart knowledge concerning people's needs.[1] Of particular note is Eleanor Roosevelt, who continued for sixteen years after her husband's death to absorb and dispense information, both informally and as an adviser to the United Nations. Her days were crowded with speaking engagements and interviews with people seeking her ideas on the status of women, the minorities, and countless other problems.

In preparing his information for presentations, the sender of a message must decide how to present ideas so that a particular listener or a specific type of audience can easily understand and profit from it.[2] Many of us no doubt have had the experience of knowing what information we want to present, yet after our speech we found that the information had not been accurately perceived by our listeners. Perhaps we did not attempt to determine in advance whether the receiver was receptive to our idea. Perhaps we failed to present our information in an organized and interesting way. Perhaps we failed to put our facts in a sequence that would make the process, product, or concept we were describing understandable.

---

[1] Peter Drucker, *The Age of Discontinuity* (New York: Harper & Row, 1968), pp. 266–267.

[2] The problem is not a single one inasmuch as the preferred method of receiving information varies from individual to individual.

So as to view informative speaking from a variety of angles, let us consider such questions as: What are some of the occasions that call for informative speaking? What are the underlying purposes of an informative speech? What are some of the principles the speaker must heed in order to bring about learning and retention by the listener? What are some special kinds of informative speaking?

Occasions for Informative Speaking

The occasions for informing people are increasingly numerous in this modern era. We use the informative process in formal speeches, reports, personal interviews, radio, television, and telephone conversations, to name but a few. We use it not only in person-to-person relationships but also with larger groups who must know about policies, welfare programs, processes, achievements, investigations, contributions, future plans, progress, or the prospects for the expansion of some worthy institution or cause. (However, we must not claim that "effective communication" is the sole factor in the solution to problems.)

In informing a person or a group about such matters as these, we find that information is best understood if it is received at a time convenient to the listeners and at the place involved, such as at a specific hospital, river, workbench, art gallery, laboratory, or home.[3] However, because assembling in this way is obviously not always practical, we must rely on sharing information in the office, the classroom, the conference room, the radio or television studio, the lecture hall, or through letters, memos, and bulletin boards.

Informative Speaking as a Purpose in Communication

The words "speaking to inform" in a broad sense suggest the clear and impartial treatment of ideas in order to achieve, as closely as possible, maximum understanding of some process, product, procedure, or instruction. Three factors in the communication of information are evident: (1) to transmit information (*downward communication*); (2) to obtain suggestions, opinions, reactions, and feelings from peer groups (*horizontal communication*); (3) to ask for information from those in subordinate roles or positions

---

[3] According to a recent survey by the Carnegie Corporation, children learn most of their information outside the school, not in it. *The Milwaukee Sentinel*, July 5, 1967, p. 15.

(*upward communication*—sometimes the hardest to get, the most needed). Whatever the kind of informational speaking—report on conditions or explaining a process or a product—we strive to answer the listeners' prospective questions as well as those that occur to us. To these ends, we answer such questions as: What does this information mean? What will it do for me? How does it work? How do I use it? How did it come to be? What is its importance? How well does it meet its intended function? What are its advantages and disadvantages? How has it affected others?

As we look over these questions, we can readily see that a planned interchange of ideas or facts is called for, to be offered in a clear and interesting manner. As the speaker, we have an obligation to give as much information as time permits and to be credible, bearing in mind that people respond positively to direct, factual presentations.

From polls we find that people want above all a leader whose words they can believe, whose intentions they can trust. For if we engage in partiality as we give information, we may provoke the listener into rejecting our message itself as well as stirring up other undesirable responses. There is no substitute for truth, logic, and factual accuracy. Inevitably, a listener is going to detect unwarranted half truths or lack of accuracy. For example, if a chairman of a committee seeking a site for the organization's clubhouse inadvertently leans heavily toward the purchase of one plot over another, he might be indulging in *unintentional communication*—that is, giving his listeners the opportunity to sense that personal gain may be his real objective. More important, however, is the realization that the primary intent of the message—to maintain a fair and accurate account of facts—was not fulfilled. (On the other hand, a combined informative-persuasive message is acceptable, in which the source offers certain interpretations and even recommendations if they are requested. He exonerates himself from unintentional communication by qualifying his persuasive remarks with "in my experience," "I have found that," or "the committee recommends.")

Lincoln Steffens, famous journalist and editor of *McClure's Magazine* in the early 1900s, recognized the effect of impartiality. As a student he heard various visiting scholars, who no doubt had well-established convictions, but who, in their speeches to inform, managed to maintain impartiality. Those experiences, said Steffens, allowed him freedom to think for himself.[4] Even in interpersonal relationships, people are apt to resent advice unless they ask for it. The salesman who says, "You ought to buy a new car," never stands as good a chance as the one who says, "There are both advantages and disadvantages in buying a new car—let's talk about them." Human beings have a tendency to "turn off" those who offer hasty declarations and opinion couched in instruction.

Keeping free from partiality is, of course, extremely difficult as the speaker explains, describes, or relates happenings. It has often been said that

---

[4] Lincoln Steffens, "I Become a Student," *Modern Minds*, compiled by H. M. Jones, R. M. Ludwig, and Marvin Perry, Jr. (Boston: D.C. Heath & Co., 1949), pp. 20–21.

© 1958 United Feature Syndicate, Inc.

no one can report anything exactly as it occurred and that no two people agree completely on anything. To David Brinkley on NBC, fairness is the key to responsibility, but to go through life subjected to various environments and still claim total objectivity is sheer insanity.[5]

Perhaps the words of S. I. Hayakawa, the general semanticist, are relevant here:

> How, then, can we ever give an impartial report? The answer is, of course, that we cannot attain complete impartiality while we use the language of everyday life. Even with the very impersonal language of science, the task is sometimes difficult. Nevertheless, we can, by being aware of the favorable and unfavorable feelings that certain words and facts can arouse, attain enough impartiality for practical purposes. Such awareness enables us to *balance the implied favorable and unfavorable judgments against each other.*[6]

The Informative Process

The informative process is complex, and it is up to the speaker to see that his information is understood by his listeners. Listeners, in turn, have the responsibility of listening actively in order to interpret the ideas of the speaker. In this two-way process, the chief burden lies with the speaker. He has the time to make a thorough investigation of his topic and to plan his presentation of the material with care. Therefore, he should make allowance for the listener's having to do his thinking after he receives the information.

Unfortunately, we often become so engrossed in our material that we forget that a person may hear our message and yet not understand it, and that the informative process is not complete until the information is fully understood. To get through to people, we must, therefore, put ourselves in the listeners' place and try to recall how little we knew before we studied our topic. We can test this principle by listening to the information some person is attempting to give us about a policy or a project; then in our own words relate to this speaker what he has said, and continue the process until the

[5] Barbara Delantiner, "Cool but Not Cold," *The Milwaukee Journal,* December 1, 1968, p. 2.

[6] S. I. Hayakawa, *Language in Thought and Action* (New York: Harcourt, Brace & World, 1941), p. 48.

speaker is satisfied that we have the information correctly in mind.[7] During this process, we will probably find omissions, additions, or substitutions entering into the content, particularly in our first attempt, and continuing until we have been thoroughly corrected.

To reduce these chances for errors, we can learn to adjust our remarks in accordance with the type of listener we face. Since no one method of presenting information to an individual supersedes all others, we have to study our particular listener carefully and select the method he or she seems to prefer. Some persons cannot absorb information quickly; for them, repetition of the main points is essential. For listeners who need to see the object in order to remember it, a visual aid or a demonstration is helpful. For those who need specific details, many data may be necessary.

The matter of adjustment becomes increasingly difficult when the group listening is large and heterogeneous. Here we confront wide differences in experience, attitude, education, and receptivity. For this situation, we will probably make use of several materials of development and audio-visual aids rather than one alone. In all cases, we will briefly summarize each of the major points as we go along and briefly repeat them in our concluding remarks. At this part of the message — the conclusion — we will take care not to stop abruptly or indulge in an anticlimax dealing with irrelevant material.

In this learning environment (the face-to-face situation), we have an opportunity to ascertain whether our information is being understood. We can observe the listener carefully for signs that indicate lack of understanding. We can invite comments and thereby seek to clarify our subject. According to Schramm,[8] there is opportunity for a considerable amount of feedback[9] in this process.

Learning and Retention

Every speaker would profit considerably in time and effort saved if he could be given a set of principles for creating an ideal learning process for the listener. Unfortunately, so many variables exist in this area that a common solution is impossible. However, it is generally recognized that learning is change, conditioning, and adjustment; that adults as well as young people can learn; that we learn through imitation and through experiences (unhappy as well as happy ones); that we learn through trial and error; that we

---

[7] William V. Haney, *Communication and Organizational Behavior*, Rev. ed. (Homewood, Ill.: Richard D. Irwin, 1967), pp. 89–90.

[8] Wilbur Schramm, "Communication Research in the United States," in Wilbur Schramm (ed.), *The Science of Human Communication* (New York: Basic Books, 1963), p. 13.

[9] It is recognized that feedback is not always of value and sometimes even harmful to the speaker. See David S. Brown, "Some Feedback on Feedback," *Adult Leadership*, Vol. 15 (January 1967), pp. 228–251.

Principles of Learning

1. *Learning should be adapted to the experiences, felt needs, and future plans of the listener.*

2. *Learning is more likely to occur when the listener understands the goals or reasons involved in the topic itself.*

3. *Learning should be planned with specific attention to the uses the learner can make of the materials explained.*

4. *Learning occurs more easily when relationships are stressed—comparisons of ideas, techniques, objects.*

5. *Learning depends upon clarity in organization and preciseness of words. Where there is vagueness, learning suffers.*

6. *Learning is a sporadic process, not a steady and gradual one. Rest periods, or the introduction of a change in procedure, are needed.*

7. *Learning is enhanced through various kinds of demonstrations—live scenes, audio-visual aids, and the like.*

8. *Learning happens when the learner perceives some form of meaningful reward—praise, recognition, promotion, or financial gain.*

9. *Learning occurs when there is an intention to learn.*

10. *Learning profits by repetition.*

11. *Learning responds to proper timing. We learn best during periods of good mental and physical health, and least in times of fatigue and ill health.*

12. *Learning occurs to the extent that listeners are actively participating, actively listening, or actively engaged in discussing the problem.*

13. *Learning depends upon seeing relationships between the unknown and the known.*

14. *Learning depends upon the emphasis given to major points.*

15. *Retention depends upon applying the principles learned.*

retain what we want to retain; and that we see what is of advantage to us. It is apparent, too, that learning of a theoretical nature occurs through the use of planned methods in more formal circumstances, such as in the classroom, the conference room, and the lecture hall.

When we plan our message, our hope, of course, is that learning will occur and that our listeners will see some need for making an effort to remember and retain the ideas we offer them (see the list of principles in the inset). At the same time, any knowledge that we have about learning and retention will do much to shape our informative speaking. The following procedures make use of theories of learning and retention that can be applied to speaking.

Choose Topics of Interest to Your Listeners

It is evident that a subject that interests the listener is easier for him to absorb and comprehend than one that is not. A topic that cannot be attended to cannot be understood. If a person is interested in what he is seeing, hearing, or doing, he is inclined to learn more without conscious effort. According to psychologists, people work more diligently when they observe others being interested or concerned in them. For example, Babe Ruth, with the concern and helpful communicative assistance of someone (in his case, a Catholic priest) worked like a demon to excel in hitting home runs for the New York Yankees. If someone is vitally interested in a skill or an idea, his struggle to get the message might succeed despite poor instruction, or even unfavorable conditions. According to Nichols, there is much evidence to indicate that real interest in a topic, no matter how it is attained, will promote comprehension.[10]

Choosing a topic that interests people is not easy. People have vastly different interests, likes, and dislikes. For example, teachers generally rate themselves high on social interests and low on mechanical interests, while airplane pilots rate themselves highest on scientific interest. Yet in all of us there are common interests — how to stay well, saving money, crime prevention, mental health, safety on the highways, and sex. Even though our subject interests our listeners, we may be certain that initial curiosity and attention will fall off rapidly unless they are sustained throughout the speech by interesting materials.[11]

Give Listeners New and Valuable Information

As long as people are satisfied with their status, content with the knowledge they possess, or comfortable with common practices, they will tend toward apathy, which has always been a barrier to progress. A speaker, therefore, should provide his listeners, not with a rehash of old ideas, but with late developments that are profitable to them. Such timely subjects as new time- and labor-saving devices, maintenance of clean restaurants, prevention of crime, recycling of metals, hydroponic gardening, and means of saving our cities, will unquestionably stimulate interest and thought. Some revealing or "confidential" statements can provide the introduction to such new ideas. The late Governor Alfred E. Smith of New York used to say to his listeners, "Now, I'm going to let you in on something." Similarly, a speaker could begin with "Have you thought about ways to bring the beer can out of the woods?," "I'm going to explain to you some new methods of staying well," or "Let me tell you some recent experiences I have had in interviewing for a job."

Learning implies the introduction of new information. It may, to be sure, be something we know about but about which we are presently unconcerned or oblivious. Perhaps we are unaware of the value of the topic and must be

---

[10] Ralph G. Nichols, "Factors in Listening Comprehension," *Speech Monographs*, Vol. 15 (1948 Research Annual), pp. 161–162.

[11] Carl I. Hovland, Irving L. Janis, and Harold H. Kelley, *Communication and Persuasion* (New Haven: Yale University Press, 1965), p. 115.

apprised of its importance. To illustrate: A talk on the newest way to curb disrespect for law enforcement officers would no doubt create renewed interest and concern; a report on current methods of controlling the use of harmful drugs should grab your group. On the other hand, we cannot limit ourselves to sure-fire subjects, nor do we want to. There is so much that people *should* and *need* to know, even though they don't always care to know.

As we plan our talk, let us ask ourselves questions about our subject and our listeners: What is new and valuable to my listeners in this talk? Can they use this information right away? Why is it desirable for them to have it now?

Be Clear and Use Precise Words

One of the basic objectives in presenting information is the arousal of meaning in the listener through the use of words. In the treatment of complex materials particularly, this procedure is often so difficult that misunderstanding occurs. According to Weaver, even when people talk directly to one another, misunderstanding is the rule, whereas understanding is a happy accident.[12] We know that high-flown language, gobbledygook, or pedagese is chiefly used to impress listeners rather than to give them an idea they can easily grasp. A beautiful example is the cumbersome style of this excerpt from Richard D. Gay's translation of the Gettysburg Address in pedagese:

> Eight and seventh-tenths decades ago the pioneer workers in this continental area implemented a new group based on an idealogy of free boundaries and initial conditions of equality.
>
> We are now actively engaged in an overall evaluation of conflicting factors in order to determine whether or not the life expectancy of this group or any group operating under the stated conditions is significant. We are met in an area of maximum activity among the conflicting factors. The purpose of the meeting is to assign permanent positions to the units which have been annihilated in the process of attaining a steady state. This procedure represents standard practice at the administrative level.[13]

In addition to this kind of jargon, we can also avoid long and overly repetitious messages so full of unrelenting details that few people can absorb them. Critical feedback such as "keep it short" and "boil it down" indicates a demand for brevity. This means the weeding out of meaningless statistics, long lists of records and dates, lengthy explanations, and other paraphernalia of *overcommunication*. Dr. Samuel Johnson once said that a man who uses a great many words to express his meaning is similar to a poor

---

[12] Andrew Weaver, *Speech: Forms and Principles*, 2nd ed. (New York: David McKay Co., 1951), p. 152.

[13] Reprinted with permission from the *Harvard Alumni Bulletin* of February 24, 1951. Copyright 1951 by Harvard Bulletin, Inc.

marksman who, rather than aiming a single rock at an object, gathers a handful of stones and throws them in hopes of hitting his mark.

Essentially then, familiar words, relatively short sentences, clear transitions, and brevity[14] are recommended in order to get the message across rapidly, to make an impact on the listeners, to save time, to increase interest, and to afford the opportunity of meaningful thought. Moreover, short words and shortened forms of titles are often easier to digest and easier to pronounce, such as UN for United Nations and PERT for Program Evaluation Review Techniques. However, unexplained abbreviations create a barrier to communication almost like a foreign language. John O'Hayre makes a strong case for making use of only a few commonly known words when he says that the average American understands perhaps only one word in ten of those found in a desk dictionary.[15] It is said that even language experts understand no more than 10 percent of the entries in an unabridged dictionary. The alternative, then, is to concentrate on words that most people understand. For meaning can exist only through what we have in common in our lives, minds, and language.[16]

With modern technology and research everywhere about us, we are likely to discover strange new words as we prepare our message for speaking. One way to handle this problem is to consult the latest edition of a dictionary that contains current interpretations of these words. If any *bypassing* is likely to occur—in which case the speaker has one meaning in mind and the listener has another—we can help resolve this *miscommunication* by (1) being person-minded, not word-minded—ask, "What does the word mean to you?"; (2) questioning and paraphrasing—ask the speaker (after you have received his message) if what you are thinking or restating is correct; (3) being sensitive to contexts—ask yourself if you are really thinking about the accompanying words, not the word itself.[17]

Sometimes our listeners will find it difficult to comprehend complicated explanations and instructions. When this occurs, our knowledge that *meanings are in the receiver* will keep us from "blaming the listeners" and resorting to such defensive comebacks as "You do not understand . . . "It is unfortunate that you do not see . . ." "You are wrong in thinking that . . ." "But I told you . . ." "You failed to listen to me when . . ." "You misinterpreted my . . ."; they only compound the error in interpretation, arouse defensiveness, and embarrass the listener.

---

[14] See Rudolf Flesch, *The Art of Plain Talk* (New York: P. F. Collier, 1946), pp. 21, 56, 58, and 145.

[15] John O'Hayre, *Gobbledygook Has Gotta Go* (Washington, D. C.: U. S. Government Printing Office, 1966), p. 26.

[16] See John R. Pierce, "Communication," *Scientific American* (September 1972), pp. 31–36.

[17] See William Haney, *Communication and Organizational Behavior* (Homewood, Ill.: Richard D. Irwin, 1967), pp. 230–236.

Instead, pleased that a listener is interested enough in what we are saying to seek further clarification, we can respond to him with such phrases as "That is a good question . . ." "I'm afraid I did not develop that point far enough . . ." "I'm sure I overstated that idea . . ." "Please do not feel that I intended that remark as meaning . . ." "Perhaps I did not make myself clear on that point . . ." "Let's look at it this way . . ." These will tend to assuage the listener's fear that he is incapable of grasping our explanation and, far from hurting our credibility, may actually enhance it.

Get the Audience to Think with You

In order to capture and hold thought processes in our listeners, we can utilize a considerable number of principles that play an important part in getting people to think with us.

The first step is for us to think with them — our audience — instead of thinking solely of ourselves and what we want to say. We must try to discover their concerns and build our speech to inform around them. We must attempt to present a sequential arousal of ideas that in some way stimulates their past experiences or combinations of them. Once aroused, one thought will lead to another, and with this continuous thought pattern in operation, listeners should be thinking with us. Putting it another way, before we can get people to think, we must perceive thinking as a process or function that demands continuous stimulation of meaningful ideas within the minds of listeners. In his speech on inflation, a student used incidents in everyday life with which his listeners could identify. He showed, through the use of an organized plan and a pictorial graph, what could be bought with a dollar ten years ago as compared with what it will buy today. He moved from one point to another with clear transitions and included examples of purchases normally made by the group.

The buzz session provides an excellent method of stimulating thought through the involvement process. Immediately following our presentation (talk, film, role-playing, or panel discussion), we ask the audience to form into smaller groups of five or six, with each group selecting its own chairman (who keeps the discussion relevant) and recorder (who writes down the contributions). After the members of the group have had about five or ten minutes to respond freely, their recorded questions and comments are reported back to the larger group. In such small buzz groups, people seem to feel freer to ask questions and contribute ideas from their own experiences, thereby giving the speaker an opportunity to clarify a number of confusing details.

In classrooms, workshops, staff meetings, and other group meetings, the use of questions and answers increases the thought process. At a recent International Communication Association convention, a participant complained that her chief frustration was the lack of time for give-and-take between speakers and their listeners. She liked sessions wherein members of the audience could ask many questions, talk back, and sometimes even criticize the presentations. Sometimes, such questioning may be encouraged during a more formal communication situation, such as a lecture. At the Bell Laboratories, Alex Bavelas, professor of psychology at Massachusetts Institute of Technology, found that permitting questions during a talk increased the amount of thinking and improved its quality.[18]

However, too many such interruptions during a presentation can badly damage an organized body of knowledge. For the beginning speaker it may be wise to limit questions to an open-forum period and even to request in the beginning of a talk that people hold their questions until afterward for the sake of continuity and the possibility that the answer may be forthcoming in the talk. Here are suggestions for the handling of answers during such question periods:

1.   Restate the question, loudly enough for all to hear, to determine whether you and the rest of the group have heard it correctly.

2.   Take your time in answering. By so doing you will probably come up with a better answer.

3.   Compliment the person who asked a pertinent question. Maintain a friendly attitude in other answers as well.

4.   Draw the questioner out if you don't understand the point he is raising.

5.   Admit ignorance when it is advisable to do so. Offer help in finding the answer or ask if any other person can provide an answer.

Rhetorical questions, which require no oral answers, are thought-provoking, especially if there is a sustained pause after each question. Another method is to invite some further involvement of the listeners, like asking them to respond with a show of hands, or calling on them to take part in a demonstration before the group or to engage in *role playing*—which is essentially "acting out" ideas, feelings, and understandings regarding some policy, procedure, or method of handling a situation. For such a procedure, we should choose people who are neither shy nor apt to be embarrassed. Following the "scenes," the group can discuss (1) omission of facts, (2) mistaken ideas, (3) strong or weak solutions, and (4) suggestions for other methods of handling information. In addition, we might ask listeners to participate in a brief written or oral quiz on the highlights of our message or to interpolate certain comments after "Now what have I said?" or to contribute pertinent feedback. Many communicators fail to realize that this two-way communication or feedback is a splendid way to get people to think with us.

---

[18] Alex Bavelas, "Pause for Pleasure," *Chemical Week* (June 26, 1954), p. 26.

Special Types of Informative Speaking

The way we impart information depends a good deal on what the subject of the information is—a process, a product, an organization, a concept, or an oral report.

A Process

The listener will more likely understand the explanation of a process if the speaker presents it carefully step by step. This kind of procedure calls for an explanation of what specific step comes first, why it comes first, and how it is to be done. Why must the succeeding steps be taken?—and so forth. Illustrations, enumerative symbols, and well-chosen transitions help to clarify the step-by-step process. In discussing the correct order of business in parliamentary procedure, we could use these transitions: "We come now to the first step in the order of business . . ."—"The second step is roll call (if necessary)," and so on.

In explaining processes—such as how to plant a new lawn, how to operate a voting machine, how a bill becomes a law, or how to make cuff links out of beautiful stones found along the shore—we generally use the *time sequence*. For example, in an explanation of the *incident method*—a variation of the case method in problem solving developed by Paul and Faith Pigors[19]—we would explain (1) how a brief incident is presented to a group, (2) how the group obtains facts through asking the leader questions, (3) how the group decides what decisions need to be made, (4) how each member of the group is expected to write a solution, and (5) how the group discusses the incident and how it reaches a final decision.

In the explanation of a process we should note necessary equipment, procedures, and a statement of the consequences of mistakes. We should remember to illustrate or clarify the process with audio-visual materials whenever possible. Moreover, we should briefly repeat the important points we have covered and demonstrated; and if the process is to be learned, they should be repeated and practiced by the listener.

A Product

This type of speaking refers to end products (a canoe, a purebred animal, a synthetic fabric, a monorail car) created by man or nature. If, for example, a railroad is to keep pace with the needs and tastes of the public, it must be on the lookout for new and improved methods of operation. Year in and year out, the development of new products and the changes made in existing

[19] See Paul and Faith Pigors, *The Incident Process: Cases in Management Development* (Washington, D. C.: Bureau of National Affairs), 1955.

products make it necessary for the railroad to inform the general public about such new features. This information process can be achieved by talks that focus public attention upon improvements over previous products in regard to specifications, simplification, stability, durability, and economy of operation.

For talks of this kind we usually use the *topical sequence* in order to achieve an orderly discussion. For example, if we want to talk to a group about a new kind of ski or recent developments in air conditioning units, we will explain how these products satisfy needs by discussing their operation, their functions, their ease of handling, and their economy of operation. We will also supplement these explanations and descriptions with appropriate models, actual objects, pictures, brochures, and other forms of visual aids.

An Organization

Suppose you are called upon to explain the line of responsibility in some organization such as the city government of Atlanta, Michigan State University, the Ford Motor Company, or the World Council of Churches. Since a common complaint of poorly informed members of some groups is made known through the phrase "We don't know exactly where we stand in our responsibilities and roles," for good understanding to occur, look up the aims, purposes, creeds, or philosophies involved. Explain major changes, areas of responsibility, where authority is delegated and where there are relationships within the organization.[20] Use a topical sequence, an organization chart, and whatever illustrations and comparisons are needed to aid understanding.

A Concept

In conversations we are likely to hear such questions as: "Just what do you mean by *democracy?*" "What is *socialism?*" "What is a *Republican?*" "How does he differ from a *Democrat?* Aren't they the same?" As our listeners become better educated, as our civilizations become more complex, we, as speakers—formal and informal—are confronted more and more with the necessity of discussing and explaining abstract ideas—concepts.

Examples of concepts, or intangible topics, are justice, goodwill, integration, faith, crime, brotherhood, and the presidency. Mass, velocity, inertia, and time are concepts basic to physics; in psychology, we have personality, motivation, identification, emotional behavior. Successfully or even provocatively explaining such abstractions requires more than ordinary skill in speaking, for they are intangibles that are seldom easy to understand.

An explanation of socialism, for instance, would require not only

---

[20] Silence on these matters can be worrisome. Does it mean that a leader doesn't trust you, that he doesn't care about you, or that he is willing to permit rumors to spread information?

defining the word but comparing it with other forms of economic systems, explaining its functions, describing its effects, giving concrete examples of how it works in countries that practice it. Audio-visual aids—in the form of photographs, slides, or motion pictures—may be very helpful in illustrating functions and effects.

Reports

In a report every speaker aims to give information based on facts and findings, which his listeners can weigh in a rational way. A report, therefore, draws its chief value from accuracy. It may be an account of progress on a bridge, a statement on the uses of a new type of medicine, or a message updating a group on what occurred at a recent convention; it may be an article, book, or other publication that is reviewed before a group.

Generally speaking, the oral report reflects the highlights of a detailed written report, which may be a handout to be given to each member in the group. Usually we present these highlights extemporaneously, quoting only those portions that demand accuracy in the choice of words.

We are often at a loss to know where to begin our report of a study we have made and what order the details should follow. We will cover the basic assignment if we follow these steps:

1. Give the reasons for your report.
2. Tell the general conclusion reached.
3. State the method of reaching this conclusion.
4. Reveal several possibilities if a solution to the problem is to be considered.
5. Invite audience questions and comments.

To sum up the principles for imparting information: We should offer information that is (1) carefully organized, (2) adapted to the listeners' capacities, and (3) easily learned and retained. It is most important to keep in mind that the mere "handing out" of information is not enough. Informative speaking, quite as much as any other kind, requires consideration of the listeners' interests, an attempt to satisfy individual needs, and a fair and impartial discussion of the information.

Suggested Assignments

1. Plan an "informative session" in which you impart information for a period of two minutes. Then invite questions from the class. Note the interest and concern in their queries.

2. In a brief period of time, give your class instructions regarding some skill as, for example, threading a projector. Then call on certain members to thread the film, explaining why certain procedures are followed.

3. Investigate a local problem. Follow the principles of reporting this presentation.

4. Involve the members of the class with buzz sessions or role-playing in order to demonstrate some point in your speech.

5. Plan a six-minute talk in which you explain the delegation of authority in some organization. Use an organization chart to help get the information across.

6. Give a two-minute talk in which you define a concept. Ask your classmates to write the information you gave them on a piece of paper. From these papers determine how effective you were in explaining the concept.

7. Plan a brief explanation of some new product, policy, or procedure. Use the various methods outlined in this chapter to get the message across.

8. Investigate for a report to your class the "Communicative Climate" of some industry or organization.

9. Plan a Community Communication Service Project in which you spend some of your spare time in attempting to develop better communication with some foreign student, parent, brother or sister, senior citizen, parent without partner, or physically handicapped or culturally disadvantaged person. Develop the results into a brief report before your class. Invite questions and comments.

Suggested References

Alexander, H. G., *Meaning in Language* (Glenview, Ill.: Scott, Foresman and Co., 1969). Chapter 5, "The World of Meaning."

Barnlund, Dean C., "Toward a Meaning-Centered Philosophy of Communication," *Journal of Communication*, Vol. 12 (December 1962), pp. 197–211.

Davis, Keith, *Human Relations at Work*, 3rd ed. (New York: McGraw-Hill Book Co., 1967). Chapter 19, "Communicating with Employees."

De Vito, J. A. (ed.), *Communication: Concepts and Processes* (Englewood Cliffs, N. J.: Prentice-Hall, 1971). Part 3, "Clear Only if Known" by Edgar Dale.

Hill, W. F., *Learning: A Survey of Psychological Interpretation* (San Francisco: Chandler Publishing Co., 1971). Chapter 9, "Learning Theory, Present and Future."

Jain, Nemi C., and William R. Stroud, "A Conceptual Framework for Studying Intercultural Communication," a paper delivered at the International Communication Convention at Phoenix, Arizona, April 23, 1971.

Lee, Irving J., *How to Talk with People* (New York: Harper & Row, 1952). Chapter 2, "They Talk Past Each Other."

Linkugel, Wil A., R. R. Allen, and Richard L. Johannesen, *Contemporary American Speeches*, 3rd ed. (Belmont, Calif.: Wadsworth Publishing Co., 1972). Chapter 3, "Speeches That Impart Knowledge."

Pace, R. Wayne, and R. R. Boren, *The Human Transaction* (Glenview, Ill.: Scott, Foresman and Co., 1973). Chapter 5, "Clarification."

Siegel, Lawrence (ed.), *Instruction: Some Contemporary Viewpoints* (San Francisco: Chandler Publishing Co., 1967). Part 2, "The Facilitation of Significant Learning" by Carl Rogers.

Wiksell, Wesley A., *Do They Understand You?* (New York: The Macmillan Co., 1960). Part 4, "Patterns for Communicating."

17
Speaking to Entertain

"The entertaining remark can ease tensions and help clear the air"

Spoken entertainment has a much wider range than is generally realized. It extends from the rawest kind of bachelor-dinner humor through the talk full of brilliant wit to the essentially serious speech whose purpose is achieved through entertainment.

The prevalence of entertaining speaking in the United States is plain to see. At almost any time of the waking day, television audiences are settled back in their armchairs waiting for the comedian to come into view and entertain them. Tens of thousands listen to radio entertainment every day, often over the car radio as they drive along the highway. Thousands more crowd the movies and theaters to be amused, in part by entertaining speech. And, of course, there are the late evening TV talk shows. . . .

Not only is the outright entertainment speech prevalent; so also is communicating that contains entertainment. Clergymen liven up a sermon with stories or remarks that are intended to amuse while not straying too far from edification. College teachers weave into their lectures not only bits of classical wit but also the latest sophomore jokes. Political speakers poke fun at their opponents. Lecturers amuse as well as inform and persuade crowds at Farmers' Day exercises, union meetings, sales conventions, banquets, and the like. Professional people relax their dignity and exchange the newest witticisms. Conversations, interpersonal communication, and informal messages of all kinds contain attempts at humor.

Entertainment comprises far more than humorous speaking. Any communication that has for its purpose, or one of its purposes, helping the listener to relax, enjoy himself, and forget his cares for a short time is an entertainment talk. Travelogues, descriptions of happy scenes or experiences, and light subjects of all kinds may be used to entertain an audience.

Sometimes a communicator resorts to entertainment for presenting a controversial topic because he doesn't dare state it openly. He may thereby win the attention and even the partial or entire approval of an audience that would greet his idea with open hostility if it were seriously presented. One student speaker gave an entertaining talk entitled "Teachers I'd Rather

Forget." The student listeners hugely enjoyed laughing at professional foibles. But they also listened intently, without quite being aware of what they were absorbing, to a portrayal of senseless student behavior. This latter result was just what the speaker wanted.

One of the greatest exponents of humor in communicating was Abraham Lincoln. While his best-known addresses were exclusively serious—the Gettysburg Address and his inaugural addresses, for instance—in more informal situations he often employed humor to put across a serious idea that was unwelcome. When challenged to a duel—and he was challenged more than once in those turbulent times—he is said to have replied that, since he was the challenged and had the choice of weapons and distance, he chose cornstalks at twenty paces. He could have said that he disapproved of duels and the stupid idea of fighting to "save one's honor." However, his humorous reply got his message across far more effectively.

Entertainment depends upon the same basic principles and techniques of communication as advocacy and information. Moreover, speeches of entertainment are very often—one is tempted to say most often—intended to influence or inform listeners, as the examples above clearly indicate.

Preparing an Entertaining Talk

Choosing the Topic

To choose a topic wisely for an entertaining talk, the speaker needs to take into account the nature of his audience, the occasion, the possible treatments he can give the topic, and his own talents and limitations as a communicator.

Good topics are always hard to come by, but students of speaking seem to have the most difficulty in finding a humorous topic. It is hard to think of something clever or funny, especially if you sit down to "think up" a humorous talk. The truth to keep in mind, when you are looking for a humorous topic, is twofold: (1) there are relatively few topics in the world that are funny, and (2) any topic may be treated entertainingly. If you struggle to think of something amusing, you are likely to get nowhere; but if you let your mind wander over almost any subject that interests you, you will probably begin to remember lighthearted, entertaining, even downright funny incidents connected with it.

In Chapter 7 we read a short description of a very bad storm at sea. Now, what could be funny about such a terrifying experience? Plenty. The speaker who somehow survived that storm also recalls the tray filled with cups of hot coffee that sailed through the air and struck him on the chest. He was not hurt, and the entire crew burst out laughing at the sight of him, dripping with coffee from head to foot. A book he had not been able to find for six months jumped out from its hiding place and banged him on the nose. The strange object on the ship's deck proved to be a porthole—the ship was rolling so badly that he mistook the wall for the floor. He has been able to elicit laughter from many audiences by recounting these tales.

The speaker who plans to give an entertaining talk will profit from re-reading the chapter on responding to and selecting the subject, and then letting his imagination roam for a while, even run riot. If we look at a subject as it might appear to someone else, for example, we will have considerably less trouble finding a good subject for spoken entertainment.

It is essential to take into account the nature of the audience when we choose a topic. A humorous talk about the titles of Ph.D. dissertations might be amusing to the graduate faculty of a university but probably would not entertain an audience unfamiliar with college life. Activities at sea would bore a soldier whose only shipboard experience consisted of the trip to the battle area and back in a crowded hold, but it could be quite amusing to an audience of former sailors attending a reunion dinner. A humorous treatment of "My First Day in a Teller's Cage" would leave most of us cold, although it would probably crack up a convention of bankers.

Formulating the Purpose Sentence

The basic principles of formulating the purpose sentence (Chapter 8 and Chapter 11) apply to speaking to entertain in two specific ways: (1) Since "a speech of entertainment" may be intended either just to entertain or to serve as a vehicle for presenting information or for advocating a point of view, it is important that the purpose sentence accurately reflect the real purpose of the talk. (2) The purpose sentence, in this type of speaking, may serve primarily as a guide to the speaker in preparing his message and differ significantly from the purpose sentence as spoken to the listeners, especially when the entertainment elements provide the means of informing or persuading.

For example, "Earth monsters will meet space monsters before we are much older" may be the purpose sentence we wish to present to our listeners, whereas "Earth monsters will meet space monsters unless we develop our social knowledge to the level of our scientific knowledge" may be the purpose sentence that appears in our speech plan.

Selecting the Type of Speaking Plan

The second step in preparing an entertaining talk is the selection of a speaking plan, or the approach. In choosing our speaking plan, which may be developed concurrently with, or even before, the selection of the topic, we must keep in mind the nature of our audience, the occasion, and our own speaking talent and limitations. (Chapter 11 will refresh our understanding of the basic speech plans.) There are endless ways to shape an entertainment talk, among them the long narrative, the short narrative, satire, and exaggera-

tion and understatement. There is no need for us to imitate these four slav-
ishly, but we can use them as a starting point from which to devise our own
particular approaches.

Single Long Narrative   Organizing a talk as a story is almost sure to make
it attractive. Curiosity makes people pay attention to a narrative even when
it is poorly told. While almost any story, reasonably well told, will attract
and hold attention, telling it so that its message will also impress the audience is a difficult art.

Using *one long narrative* requires that we know our story perfectly — not
by words or phrases but by the proper sequence of events. If we find ourselves forced to say, "Oh, I forgot to tell you that before the boys went into
the cemetery the moon disappeared under a cloud bank — that's how the
night happened to be dark, you see," the flow of the narrative has been
interrupted and the audience diverted from its spell and the sequence of
events. Other instances of this kind of storytelling are "Did I remember
to tell you that . . . ?" "I think you would get the point if I went back and
. . ." If we do not have the sequence clearly and firmly in mind, we will
frustrate our listeners and lose their interest.

A long narrative demands an excellent vocabulary and the ability to
vary the style. A story is rarely told without some description, and description may often form a major part of the narrative talk. If you were telling
the story of your first bout with registration at a large university, you would
be lost without descriptive language because the actual event probably
consisted merely of your standing in various lines. But the descriptions of
the thousands of students jammed into the auditorium, the perspiring
registration personnel, the endless arrow signs pointing this way and that,
the insistent signs directing you to pay your money first or see your adviser
first or get your course cards first, the faintly disguised contempt of the man
behind the desk as he explains that when a course is marked closed not even
your senator-uncle can open it for you, the feeling of being lost and un-
wanted — these descriptions make your story exceedingly interesting to
those who have had the experience and can even make it real to those who
have not.

Some of the principles of writing a good narrative apply to the telling of
one. To make a story seem more alive, we can assign definite names and
personalities to our characters, whenever possible. We can give our story a
locale, a definite place, and a definite time. Instead of the vague and boresome
"She told him that . . ." or "The old man informed his grandchildren that
. . . ," we can use dialogue between characters. Stephen Leacock achieved
a seriocomic effect in his essay "The Approach of the Comet" with this
dialogue:

> I heard a little boy last Sunday, on his way into church, say to his
> mother, "Mother, is it true that a comet is going to hit the world?" And she
> said, "Yes, dear, the newspapers say so." "And where shall we be after it

hits us?" "I suppose, darling," she answered, with a touch of reverence, I admit, in her voice, "that we shall be dissolved into a nebular nucleus with an enveloping corona of incandescent hydrogen." After that they passed into the church, and I heard no more.[1]

Let us remember that a good narrative has a plot; it tells a story. In most cases it should work up to a climax; there should be suspense, so that the audience constantly wonders what will happen next.

Short Narrative with Theme   This type, consisting of a series of stories related to the overall theme, is probably the most common kind of entertaining talk. The stories or jokes or descriptions must be relevant to the theme, which, in most cases, should be clearly stated, and the speaker should remind his listeners of it from time to time, possibly before or after each story. Because this type of talk is so common, and because many speakers are so fond of their stories that they tell them whether they pertain to the main theme or not, many speakers shy away from it.

Used by a master, however, the short narrative technique can be highly entertaining. Even a speaker who is something less than a master, by following the simple rules discussed here, may rise from the status of a mere storyteller to that of a communicator of ideas.

Satire   Satire may be defined as holding folly up to ridicule. Carefully selected, carefully handled, and delivered with a friendly smile, it is a very appealing form of entertainment. There are various degrees of severity in the use of satire; we may poke fun lightly or deride; we may expose in a friendly fashion or with deadly seriousness. Experienced speakers may succeed with bitter or vicious satire, but it is best for the beginner to keep it light, humorous, and friendly. Also, it will be wise to study the principles of satire before trying it for the first time.

Satire, or "poking fun at," may be applied in a number of different ways. The safest and one of the most entertaining is to make fun of yourself. It is a safe form, because no one's feelings can be hurt except perhaps your mother's. You may even be a bit vicious toward yourself. Your listeners will probably enjoy chuckling at you if you signal them by a friendly manner that all is in fun, with no hard feelings.

A former major-league first baseman has entertained many groups of young baseball enthusiasts with talks flavored with details of his ineptness as a player. Such as this:

> I remember attempting a tough double play one afternoon against the White Sox when I grabbed an infield chopper and threw to the left fielder who pegged the runner out at second; but I couldn't get back to first base

---

[1] Stephen Leacock, *Over the Footlights* (New York: Dodd, Mead & Co., 1923), pp. 269–270. Reprinted by permission.

> in time to complete the double play. They always played me at first base because it was easier for the bat boy to carry me out there from the dugout. I almost never missed a ball that was hit — slowly — in the air — straight at me — into my glove — waist high — on the side where my good eye was.

Incidentally, this man was a first-rate first baseman, and his listeners all knew it.

Making fun of *other* people is a somewhat dangerous business, unless we are sure that our audience wants to laugh at the expense of someone else — Democratic convention delegates listening to a satirical attack on a Republican candidate, for instance, or vice versa. We sometimes poke fun at persons for whom we have a great deal of respect, doing so with no malice. This kind of satire, however, often backfires, as in the circumstance that prompted Queen Victoria's most quotable quote. She is said to have caught one of her grooms-in-waiting — the Honorable Alexander Grantham Yorke — doing an imitation of her, presumably for the entertainment of everyone at court. When the Queen saw this mimicry, she commented: "We are not amused."

Making fun of others, however, can be an effective form of entertaining speaking, provided that the occasion, the audience, and the subject or subjects of the satire are carefully studied and taken into account. It is better, as the great humorist Will Rogers knew, to satirize important people, people in good health, people whom the satire cannot harm, rather than the old or ill or helpless or otherwise unfortunate. An audience's sympathy tends to go out to the latter groups, and the communicator who ignores that fact may find himself looked upon as a hostile figure. The same principle applies to satire directed at institutions or ideas. Listeners would probably be amused at a talk making fun of college students living in a dormitory or apartment house, but they would probably not enjoy a satiric picture of old folks in a home for the aged — unless the satire was very gentle.

It is also quite possible to satirize situations. Jack Benny, the comedian, brought down the house (Carnegie Hall in New York City) when he was scheduled to play his violin and appeared on the stage having "forgotten" his bow. A university play successfully satirized life on the production line of an automobile manufacturing company. This kind of satire is perhaps the easiest for the beginning speaker; it allows him to create humor and lightness in a situation he himself has observed.

Exaggeration and Understatement   As to *exaggeration,* most of us have heard about the Texas mosquito that carried off the grand piano — one of the several variations of the mosquito story. The fables of Paul Bunyan, the tall stories of the mountain people, and the weird exaggerations of children are all examples of this kind of humor. Most amateur attempts at using exaggeration come off fairly well, if the speaker remembers to limit their total space in the talk. The most successful exaggerations — with some exceptions — seem to bear some resemblance, however slight, to the truth.

Understatement is harder for the beginning speaker to handle. It seems to demand more skill in composition and more finesse in delivery. It is found most frequently as just one element in a humorous setting. "Jolly good show," said the movie Englishman when three blocks of buildings were reduced to rubble by a German bomb. "He was a little het up," drawled the cowboy after the dude managed to escape from the corral where he was charged by an enraged bull. While we may not be able to think of a subject that will allow us to use understatement throughout an entertaining talk, we will probably be able to use it as one ingredient.

Other types of entertainment speaking develop from these basic forms. By listening carefully to after-dinner speakers, studying the entertainment talks that are found in books on public speaking, noticing the methods of television and movie comics and humorists, and paying close attention to the most popular conversationalist in your crowd, you will begin to discover ways of communicating that will make the best use of your talents and will entertain your hearers.

Presenting the Entertaining Talk

"Delivery in Speaking" is discussed in some detail in Chapter 14, but certain peculiarities of the entertaining talk make its delivery rather special. At least three aspects should be considered: (1) the communicator's mental set, or attitude; (2) the preparation of the audience for the talk; and (3) the talk's timing. If the speaker tries to understand these factors, he will find his task easier; he may begin to enjoy the prospect of being entertaining; and if he does, he probably *will* be entertaining.

Speakers seem to complain more about the job of preparing an entertainment talk than any other kind. The same lament is heard about delivery; "I just can't be funny when I'm up before a group," they say.

Being funny is certainly not easy, especially for the speaker who has had little experience with the role. However, you do not have to be funny in order to entertain. Furthermore, even within the context of being funny there exists a wide range of desired reactions, from guffaws to smiles. No communicator should consider himself a failure if his listeners indicate enjoyment of what he says, whether they break out into uproarious laughter or not.

The Communicator's Mental Set

A speaker must want to speak, and he must want to speak on a subject that he chooses or adapts. Nowhere is this principle more true than in an entertaining talk. If you tell yourself you can't be funny, then you can't. It's as

© 1960 United Feature Syndicate, Inc.

simple as that. But to the extent that you convince yourself that your message is worthwhile, that your audience will enjoy hearing it, and that you will enjoy delivering it—to that extent you will be preparing the way for a successful entertaining message. To sum up: Tell yourself that you will have fun with the audience, and the chances are that you will.

As in all types of communicating, you will find it easier to make yourself believe that you will enjoy the experience if you take care in selecting and adapting your subject, search for the right kind of speaking plan or approach, organize and construct your message in the best possible way, and rehearse or practice it—not overlooking a careful consideration of the nature of your audience and of the occasion. When you have done your best by way of preparation, mount the platform (if you are to speak from a platform), relax as much as you can, and enjoy yourself. Try it. Aim at real interaction with your listeners, and be prepared for a pleasant surprise!

Preparing the Audience

Listeners at many an entertainment event fail to relax and enjoy it because they are not sure they ought to. It is up to you (as speaker) to change this attitude. Do not depend on the occasion or the chairman, for these may fail you. Your manner, your smile should convey to your listeners that the talk is to be enjoyed; if necessary, tell them more or less directly. If you appear nervous or strained, your audience will undoubtedly feel insecure. If you relax and enjoy yourself, the audience will be encouraged to do likewise.

Among those who fail to react favorably to spoken entertainment are some of the people who see a Shakespearean play for the first time. They grimly refuse to laugh at Shakespeare's bits of comedy because their conditioning is that Shakespeare is a tragic writer whose "works" are to be "appreciated." They don't happen to know him as one of the world's greatest comic writers, and so they fail to notice anything to laugh at. Nobody invited them to laugh.

Timing the Talk

Good speakers, like good actors, time their lines precisely. Good actors and good speakers, incidentally, usually can't explain how they do this. Those of us who have acted in plays have probably developed our timing—line by line. Let us try to carry this experience over into speaking.

To use an example from a fictitious play: Suppose that the line you are to read is "I must have that money," and the associated action that is indicated is to strike a kitchen match on the fireplace mantel. Try the line and accompanying movement. You will find that if you strike the match at the word *must* or the word *money*, the line will give an impression of force or determination. But if you strike it just before or just after you deliver the line, the line will be a bit humorous.

The timing in that little scene is important. The same is true in an entertainment talk. If we deliver the punch line too soon or too late, we will fail to produce the desired reaction in the audience. There are many theories about timing, and one prime principle to heed is to try to anticipate the listeners' reaction and hit them with the punch line just before they see it coming or as they are halfway to sensing it.

We can ride our laughs, too. Many a good message has been ruined because the speaker didn't know how to handle audience reaction and kept on talking through the laughter. We should wait until the laughter has reached its peak and begins to decline before starting our next point. We should give our listeners a chance to appreciate the subtleties of what we say. Nor should we be in too much of a hurry. After all, our listeners are hearing our message for the first time.

Timing is such an important matter that it deserves very serious attention. We can learn a good deal by studying clever conversationalists, good speakers, and comic monologuists whenever we have an opportunity to hear them. We can train ourselves to listen to the way they time their remarks. While we can't imitate them successfully, and we don't want to, we can learn techniques and adapt them to our personality and talents.

Although entertaining speaking may not be the most significant method of communication in our society, it does have an undoubted importance. The entertaining narrative, humorous phrase, or witty insight in a persuasive speech, for example, often helps to ease tensions when serious matters are under discussion. Adlai Stevenson, presidential candidate in 1952 and 1956, was liked and respected by many intellectuals, although the professional politicos feared that this image might harm his prestige with the common man. Aware of this danger, Stevenson thought that by poking fun at himself he could make himself more appealing to the majority of voters, and endear himself further to his intellectual supporters. On one occasion, he gave the call to arms: "Eggheads of the world, unite! You have nothing to lose but your yolks!"

The same kind of entertaining witticism can help clear the air in a tense business conference or in a highly competitive debate or in an interpersonal exchange. Entertainment has a place in almost every communication situation, because it serves an important purpose—to relax tensions and open closed minds.

Suggested Assignments

1.   Listen to your favorite television or radio comedian as he delivers one of his monologues. Instead of merely enjoying him, study his language, the organization of his talk, and the relation of his humor or gags to the theme of the monologue. Pay particular attention to his timing. Write a brief analysis and note possible application of his technique to your own speaking on light, entertaining subjects.

2.   Read "How to Live a Hundred Years Happily" by John A. Schindler, in W. Hayes Yeager's *Effective Speaking for Every Occasion,* 2nd ed. (Englewood, Cliffs, N. J.: Prentice-Hall, 1951), pp. 236–250, or a similar talk assigned by your instructor. How do you classify the talk: persuasive? informative? entertaining? Justify your answer. What are the elements in this talk that give it a lighthearted quality?

3.   Attend a travel lecture or listen to a sermon by your favorite clergyman or pay especially close attention to a lecture by your favorite professor. These talks are not necessarily entertaining in character, but look for the light touches. Try to interview the speaker and ask him why he inserted these remarks. What conclusions do you draw? Then read one of Shakespeare's serious plays. Note especially the light or comic scenes. Why, in your opinion, are they there?

4.   Reread Chapter 8. Most of the topics listed on pages 134–139 of that chapter are not especially intended for entertainment talks. Choose one topic and look at it from every possible angle to discover its humorous or lighthearted elements. Then select an approach from those suggested in this chapter. Organize your speech and present it in class.

5.   Choose a topic for an entertainment talk. Outline at least three speech plans for the talk, using three of the approaches discussed in this chapter. Select the best approach (in your opinion) for a talk to be delivered in class. Submit all three plans to your instructor for his analysis.

6.   Select a scene from a play, round up the necessary number of fellow students, and present the scene. Pay especial attention to the timing of the lines and movements. Try various methods of handling the timing. Perhaps the drama instructor in your college or university will help you perform this exercise.

7.   Choose a topic that is essentially serious, though not momentous or world-shaking. Outline your talk in a straightforward, deductive pattern. Then go back through the plan and insert lighter material such as narration, description, satire, exaggeration, or understatement. Present your talk. Finally, by means of a short questionnaire, ask your listeners whether your lighter material helped them to enjoy the talk more, to listen more carefully. Also ask them whether the added material detracted from their understanding of your message.

8.   Obtain a recording by one of the current crop of humorists. Play one of the humorous bits over and over until you think you know everything the comedian is doing. Now, write a paper in which you analyze the humor—the topic chosen, the speaking plan or approach used, the speaker's mental set, his adaptation to his audience, and, especially, his timing of his lines. In your final paragraph, summarize what you have learned—*what you can adapt to your own speaking.*

9.   Select what you regard as the most serious flaw in your character or personality. Develop a humorous speech in which you satirize this flaw in yourself. Try to give your speech a wider application by *subtly* relating your character fault to your listeners.

10.   Adapt a fable or fairy tale so that it comments upon one of the significant social problems of our day. ("The Sleeping Beauty," for example, can be adapted to show the need for our society to wake up to the necessity of solving problems of war, poverty, race relations, waste of natural resources.) Tell your story humorously, using satire and exaggeration as part of your narration.

11.   Describe a serious event, such as an automobile accident, and draw a moral from your description. Now, assume that you have been asked to give an after-dinner talk. See if you can adapt your serious description so that it amuses your listeners but still makes the original point.

12.   Try some impromptu humor in a conversational or interpersonal situation and see whether your presentation has changed as a result of studying this chapter. Try it first on a good friend, someone whose friendship you are very sure of (and who, preferably, is smaller than you are). Don't memorize a joke or a "funny." Just talk, relax, and let it come naturally. (*Note:* The authors are not responsible for the results.)

Suggested References

Gilman, Wilbur E., Bower Aly, and Hollis L. White, *The Fundamentals of Speaking*, 2nd ed. (New York: The Macmillan Co., 1964). Chapter 9, "Social Speaking: Entertaining."

Ketchum, Richard M., *Will Rogers: His Life and Times* (New York: American Heritage Publishing Co., 1973).

Monroe, Alan H., and Douglas Ehninger, *Principles and Types of Speech Communication*, 7th ed. (Glenview, Ill.: Scott, Foresman and Co., 1974). Chapter 18, "The Speech to Entertain."

Rogge, Edward, and James C. Ching, *Advanced Public Speaking* (New York: Holt, Rinehart and Winston, 1966). Chapter 11, "The Speech of Entertainment."

Samovar, Larry A., and Jack Mills, *Oral Communication*, 2nd ed. (Dubuque, Iowa: Wm. C. Brown Co., 1972). Chapter 11, "Special Occasions — The Unique Communication Situation."

Yeager, W. Hayes, *Effective Speaking for Every Occasion*, 2nd ed. (Englewood Cliffs, N. J.: Prentice-Hall, 1951). Chapter 10, "How to Make Entertaining Speeches."

18
Special Types of Speaking

"As a speaker, he could rise to any occasion"

Some persons show considerable skill in summing up in a few words the ideas and aspirations of people. One of these was the great dissenter Justice Oliver Wendell Holmes, a master of word selection in his legal decisions as well. Today, Eric Sevareid of CBS can in but a brief space of time on the air beautifully wrap up some highly critical problem of the day.

Some kinds of speaking are uniquely related to special circumstances, ranging from a specific occasion to the use of the broadcast media. They are apt to be brief, highly pertinent remarks, and since they can be important to the listeners, they require the same care in preparation as other oral message forms. They all belong in one or another of the categories of advocacy, informative speaking, and entertainment. However, their peculiar problems in subject matter, structure, and delivery require our special attention.

Introducing a Speaker

A very common type of talk is introducing a speaker to a group. It is particularly applicable when the speaker is a visitor, more or less a stranger. The introduction is usually made by the president of the group or the chairman of the program committee, or by somebody who knows the speaker well. Its purpose is to create in the audience a friendly, receptive attitude toward the speaker, to present him as one who is qualified to talk on the subject, and to stimulate a desire in the audience to listen to him.

If the speaker is a well-known personality, we should refrain from listing his entire history or embarrassing him with excessive praise. Even when a person is not well known, we should avoid giving too much detail or saying anything that would put him on the spot. Nor should we steal his thunder and antagonize both him and the audience by making a speech about his subject. We should also resist the temptation to call attention to ourselves by being funny; the one who is introducing should be seen and heard without fanfare. Finally, we should not permit others to steal the show.

This unfortunate situation developed on an occasion when the late Adlai Stevenson spoke in Muskegon, Michigan. Before he was introduced, several politicians spoke at length, apparently hoping to gain audience favor. Instead, people became restless, the politicians and the introducer lost the crowd, and much of the effect of Stevenson's remarks was dampened.

Introducing a speaker calls for caution in our choice of words. Many trite expressions—"It gives me great pleasure," "I am honored to present," "Without further ado," "It is my happy privilege," and "This man needs no introduction,"—dull the introduction. It is little wonder that speakers, as well as audiences, want but a few well-chosen and appropriate comments.

Suggestions for Making Introductions

1.   *Obtain in advance, from the speaker himself—through correspondence or personal interview if feasible—a general idea of his address. Also learn from the speaker's friends or colleagues whether he has written books or magazine articles or been mentioned in such publications.*

2.   *Know your introduction so that you can give it extemporaneously with but very brief references, if any, to notes. Do not read it or memorize word for word; that would tend to make it less warm, friendly, and direct than it should be.*

3.   *In the opening sentence or two, greet your audience, refer briefly to the nature of the occasion and the purpose of the meeting. If the attendance is gratifyingly large, say a word of appreciation.*

4.   *For the body of the speech of introduction, (a) be brief; (b) give factual information about the speaker and his*

subject; *(c) make the speaker feel welcome; (d) point out his qualifications and achievements in his field, where he has been employed, and his present position; (e) relate the content of the forthcoming talk to the interests of the group; (f) mention any timely facts relative to the talk—for example, if the talk is to be about some phase of conservation and the speaker has just returned from a visit to a flooded area, mention this fact.*

5.   *Even if you have announced the speaker's name earlier, be sure to repeat it in the last sentence of your conclusion, along with the title of his talk. Pronounce his name correctly. Speak slowly and with adequate loudness, facing the group, so that your words can be clearly understood.*

6.   *After the talk, express pleasure at hearing it, and thank the speaker. Say nothing further.*

Making an Announcement

The brief bit of speaking that is usually called "making an announcement" is designed to convey information about activities and events or to convince people to attend, assist, cooperate with, or join certain activities.

Since announcements are very much shortened versions of informative, entertaining, or persuasive talks, their preparation will follow the lines discussed in the chapters that dealt with those types of speaking (Chapters 15, 16, and 17).

It is usual for announcements to be heard near the beginning of a program, meeting, or performance; but they may occur near the end, especially if the meeting is conducted according to parliamentary procedure. In that case, members of the group are customarily permitted to make their announcements before the chairman presents his or her own. In reverse of the usual chairman-recognizes-member procedure, the presiding officer may call upon a person who is especially well informed about a matter and concerned with its success to comment briefly.

Because the purpose of an announcement is to give precise information or present reasons for supporting a certain cause, idea, or event, the announcer's chief effort is to make his listeners understand and react favorably.

**Suggestions for Making
Announcements**

1.   Wait until you have the attention of your audience before you start. Don't raise your voice to speak over conversations or other noise. Go to the front of the room where everybody can see and hear you.

2.   Introduce the subject <u>very briefly</u> with a direct or striking statement: "The date has been set for our annual Summerfest."

3.   Give the details or plans of the event concisely and logically. Announce the date, the day of the week, the hours, the place, the admission charge, ticket information, and similar details. Make the details clear, concrete, and interesting.

4.   Use visual aids if they will help to get the message across, such as a poster or an actual object. If you are trying to persuade a group to make contribu-

tions, have a supply of pledge cards, subscription forms, or tickets with you.

5.   Indicate various preferred routes and methods of transportation and tell about available parking facilities. Present such information slowly, using pitch changes and variations in loudness. Or write it on a blackboard.

6.   If the group you are speaking to already knows about the event, condense the information and concentrate on any new features that have been added. Emphasize time and place anyway.

7.   Restate the most important particulars in a very brief summary. Remember that repetition is an important process in understanding. Invite questions to clear up any doubts in the minds of your listeners.

8.   Refer to your notes occasionally in the interest of accuracy.

Words of Welcome

The person who presents "the words of welcome" may be a leader or a member of his organization who expresses pleasure at the presence of a visitor or visitors. There are any number of occasions that require words of welcome from an individual to another individual or from an individual to a group. The purpose of a welcoming talk is, of course, to make the person feel at home, to create a feeling of friendliness and harmony between the visitor and the host. People in organizations need this sense of belonging.

**Suggestions for Making
Welcoming Talks**

1.   *Begin by saying simply that you cordially welcome members and visitors on behalf of your organization. Pronounce names with care, and indicate any official capacities of the visitors. Keep the speech short and speak it extemporaneously.*

2.   *Give the reason for the occasion; say something sincerely complimentary about the guests; and mention any details pertinent to the occasion. If a visitor represents an organization, tell its nature and achievements and point out the relationship between your two organizations.*

3.   *Use simple language, free from flowery words.*

4.   *Adapt both your manner and your material to the occasion, especially in respect to its formality or informality.*

5.   *Mention opportunities and privileges available to the visitors, including specific arrangements for their leisure time and special points of interest in the locality; highlights of the convention—if convention it is. Keep in mind, though, that this is a welcome speech, not an advertising spiel for your organization or city.*

6.   *Try to make each visitor feel at home, and wish all of them an enjoyable and profitable visit.*

Paying Tribute

When the late President Lyndon B. Johnson was Senate Majority Leader, he said that one of his ten rules for making people feel good was never to miss an opportunity to say a word of congratulation upon anyone's achievement, or to express sympathy in sorrow or disappointment. Paying tribute recognizes an individual, an institution, or an organization for admirable conduct, skills, scholastic achievements, attainments, meritorious services, and the like.[1]

---

[1] Tributes develop people and make them feel significant. See Muriel James and Dorothy Jongeward, *Born to Win: Transactional Analysis with Gestalt Experiments* (Reading, Mass.: Addison-Wesley Publishing Co., 1971), pp. 46–50.

Those who give speeches paying tribute must be familiar with the recipient's achievements. However, indulging in ill-contrived or excessive praise will probably embarrass the recipient and perhaps also those who are not being honored. Self-esteem does not always emerge from "buttering people up." Unless words and actions signify the same thing, our listeners detect the discrepancy and don't trust what we say. The following extravagant phrases were used in reference to an official in an organization by one of his staff as he paid him tribute. "His help for others has been outstanding," "He has unconquerable strength of courage," and "His excellent skill in handling people makes him the best administrator in the country." What else could listeners do but wonder about the underlying motive for such exaggeration? It is obvious that such flattery can indicate insincerity and the quest for personal advantage.

Moreover, the dedicatory talk—the unveiling of a plaque, for instance—is closely related to the talk of tribute and should be handled pretty much the same way.

Suggestions for Making Tribute Talks

1.   Open with a reference to the occasion itself. Is it an annual event? Who is sponsoring it?

2.   Speak briefly about the person or persons who are to be honored. Tell about their achievements, concisely and judiciously.

3.   Because there may be aspirants to future honors in the audience, express approval of their interest and their endeavors; encourage them to excel. You will strengthen their confidence and ambition.

4.   Speak cheerfully; the occasion is not a melancholy one. But avoid the use of poorly contrived humor.

5.   Give little time to the award itself, unless it is a trophy with a history or is the gift of a particular donor. Indicate that the gift represents appreciation for work done.

6.   Present the award so that the audience may easily see it, as you offer your congratulations.

Response to a Tribute

In many instances the best course of action in responding to a tribute is for us to say "thank you" and indicate by our behavior that we appreciate it, although under some circumstances appreciation may be spelled out. The most appropriate response is nonjudgmental, containing neither praise nor adverse criticism. Nonverbally, it can identify feelings and acknowledge ideas. When Jane Fonda won an Oscar for her acting in *Klute*, she wisely chose not to express her inner judgments of present-day society. When

© 1964 United Feature Syndicate, Inc.

Marlon Brando failed to appear in person to accept his Oscar award and his substitute expressed some thoughts not related to the award, many Americans were highly critical of this incident. The response to such an honor may be used, also, to establish or strengthen a friendly relationship with those in whose name the tribute is paid.

Ordinarily the acknowledgment of a tribute is an impromptu speech whose content depends upon remarks previously made. However, when advance notice about the occasion for a response has been given, the speech may be prepared.

Suggestions for Responding to a Tribute

1. Speak loudly enough so that all can hear, but also try to be modest as well as thoughtful of others in your behavior and comments.

2. Begin with a sincere statement about what was expressed by the person who paid you the tribute. Perhaps you can expand the accomplishment that won you the tribute to others who were supportive or even equally responsible.

3. If a group is involved with you, speak of the pleasure and satisfaction you have had in associating with it and gratefully recall its efforts and cooperation. Refer to your plans for the coming years, particularly if related to the tribute.

4. If you receive a gift or award, refer to it briefly in your closing sentences. You can say how you will use the gift or where you will display it.

Radio Speaking

As compared to other forms of speaking — except television, of course — radio broadcasting vastly increases the speaker's audience as to size and heterogeneity. In reality, broadcast audiences are not assembled groups collected in a large room — rather they are small gatherings, never larger than several people, in homes or perhaps automobiles. What radio speaking amounts to, then, is conversing with these small groups. The almost infinite range of opinions, attitudes, and prejudices of his unseen listeners makes the speaker's task of putting across his message an especially difficult one. The absence of the stimulation of an audience to provide feedback can be a serious handicap; he needs to be well prepared and experienced as a speaker. In general, radio listeners, especially in small cities and towns, expect to hear (1) the very latest developments in the field, (2) the kind of material that affects local listeners or ties in with their local area, (3) firsthand information from the "expert" concerned, (4) human interest material, and (5) the selection of the most important point for the opening portion of the talk.

Suggestions for Radio Speaking

1. Prepare your material carefully. Usually the broadcast involves being interviewed or participating in a discussion. (See Chapter 20 for assistance with your preparation.)

2. Find out, as far as possible, what kinds of people will be most likely to listen to you—and direct your talk to them.

3. Find out in advance the exact time allotted to you, and prepare your talk with extra paragraphs that can be cut in accordance with the director's signal.

4. Know your message well, thus avoiding hesitations, stumbling over words, or a mechanical manner of speaking. Don't imitate the manner of any well-known radio or television personality. Record your speech in advance to determine this type of shortcoming.

5. Check the correct pronunciations of words, and be careful to enunciate sounds adequately. Mispronunciations, overstressing, and mumbled sounds are quickly noticed by critical listeners.

6. Try to use meaningful vocal variations and enthusiasm. Beginners are often monotonous and lacking in spontaneity.

7. Try to give the radio listener the feeling that you are having an intimate conversation with him. To develop this

style in speaking before a microphone, practice your speech aloud several times and before someone else. If you are using a manuscript, use typed pages with wide margins.

8. Warm up before the broadcast; that is, talk over portions of your material with someone in the studio.

9. On the air, avoid breathing heavily into the microphone, tapping it, coughing into it, or rattling papers near it. Such noises are considerably magnified and annoy the listeners.

10. Begin with an introduction to establish interest—then announce your topic. The restricted radio time will probably force you to make this part very brief.

11. Develop a very few main points with supporting materials to whatever extent time permits.

12. Clarify your ideas by restatement. (See Chapter 6.)

13. Since some of your listeners would probably feel uncomfortable with formal locutions, use contractions, familiar words, and short sentences.

14. Watch the time signals from the production director. Close with a brief conclusion, trying to make it correspond with his final signal.

Television Speaking

With the coming of cable television and other technical breakthroughs that will provide more channels, we can look forward to greatly increased program variety. This will undoubtedly bring a wide range of "experts" discussing a wide variety of subjects—and many of us may be making talks on television. In its plant in Kingston, New York, IBM—for instance—uses closed-circuit television to provide regularly scheduled news, including announcements, recreational news, human interest features, recognition tributes, and community service announcements. This new use of television is certain to develop an exciting and significant impact in mass communication.

The combination of the visual element—the speaker's appearance and behavior and audio-visual effects, together with his audible comments, plays a significant role in communicating information. Hence, the nonverbal, as well as the verbal, aspects of communication discussed in Chapter 14 are especially pertinent here. Let us consider for a moment the dramatic nature of the close-up, which requires the speaker to use a more intimate or personal style, with a different degree of loudness and projection of feeling, than when he or she is addressing a large group. Inasmuch as it compels the speaker to communicate before lights and cameras, as well as before the microphone, televised speaking is not an easy task.

Televised speaking involves any number of visual principles in addition to the audible ones for radio. Here is a list of special reminders:

In Preparation

1. Realize that television is different from radio and requires special plans.

2. Prepare and practice[2] your speech carefully, including your visual aids.

3. Have enough legible copies of the manuscript for the television personnel.

4. Check and doublecheck on all visual aids and properties needed.

5. If you are playing the role of chairman, plan brief introductions of programs and people.

In Your Attitude and Behavior

1. Be cheerful and friendly as you introduce yourself to the TV staff.

2. Be relaxed and informal in the studio.

3. Be cooperative—follow instructions closely.

---

[2] Prior to the Nixon-Kennedy television debates in 1960, John F. Kennedy practiced aloud answers he might need to give on controversial issues of the day.

Suggestions for Television Speaking

1. Refer to the principles of discussion, interviewing, asking and answering questions, listening, and extemporaneous and impromptu speaking, since much of televised speaking depends upon these methods of communicating messages.

2. Participate in a warm-up session, practicing portions of your message or your talk.

3. Come prepared to take responsibility for making the discussion worthwhile; share ideas, questions, and information as well as listen.

4. Follow the directions of your program planner. In "planned interview" shows, participants are expected to follow planned topics and major points outlined in advance, although they speak extemporaneously.

5. Be seated so you can see the members of your group.

6. Speak to these people. Call everyone by name and listen for what the other person is really trying to say.

7. Use simple words in your questions or replies. Avoid complicated language, which is essentially talking down to people.

8. Talk briefly and frankly and to the point. The expression of conflicting viewpoints may lead the listeners to a deeper analysis and understanding of the problem.

9. For the opening of planned talks, use the conventional introduction techniques, being as brief as possible.

10. When planning a television talk, decide on the category into which your message falls (information, advocacy, or entertainment)* and structure your talk accordingly. Use illustrations and other forms of supporting material, as well as visual aids such as objects and pictures, but economize in view of the time limit.

11. To maintain continuity, and to eliminate hesitations and other flaws in delivery of a formal talk, use a manuscript, a key-phrase outline, a Tele-Prompter, or large cards. The manuscript is especially useful to the engineers, the director, and the cameraman because they can set down pertinent camera and microphone directions in the lefthand margin.

12. Speak to the camera or to those about you rather than to your notes. If you read your notes word for word without looking up, you risk losing your listeners to another channel.

13. From the moment your image becomes visible, be sure that it is pleasing, alert, and interested, and that it remains so to the very end. Don't let your facial expression and gestures contradict what you are saying, thus giving your viewers conflicting messages.†

---

* Walter Cronkite, recipient of many awards for outstanding broadcast presentations over CBS, once observed on Kup's Show *that he adheres strictly to an informative broadcast without any intention of advocating change or entertaining viewers.*

† For an extended discussion on communication and bodily movement, see Ray L. Birdwhistell, "Background to Kinesics," ETC.: A Review of General Semantics, *Vol. 13 (1955), pp. 10–18.*

Before the Camera

1. Keep papers from rattling and visual aids or properties noiseless.

2. Remain silent close to "on air" and "off air" times and while others are talking.

3. Allow microphones to remain where they have been placed.

4. Look into the camera with the red light when speaking. Be aware of camera changes. When the change occurs, drop the eyes briefly and naturally to your notes; then look up at the "new" camera.

5. Use close-to-the-body gestures.

6. When using a visual aid, move it into position slowly and hold it there long enough for your viewers to take it in.

7. Watch the timekeeper for signals in order to conclude your remarks on time. Watch the floor manager for other cues.[3]

This chapter has stressed that the occasion, the particular audience, the mass medium used, and the personnel involved in the medium used are among the deciding factors in the preparation of the various special types of speaking. Remember, however, that these special types of speaking should be studied in connection with the principles described in other chapters of this book.

---

[3] We acknowledge our indebtedness to Ruane B. Hill, Director of Radio and Television at the University of Wisconsin-Milwaukee, for a portion of this analysis.

Suggested Assignments

1. Prepare an introduction for a member of your class. Contact this student for the content of his talk and present your introduction prior to his next regularly assigned talk.

2. Welcome some visitor to your class or to an organization of which you are a member.

3. For practice in radio speaking engage in both of the following projects: (a) Obtain a loudspeaking system, or use the loudspeaker of a tape recorder, to practice live presentations. (b) With the use of the tape recorder plan and record a three-minute taped talk. Listen to portions of these classroom talks and write a brief analysis of each.

4. Plan a three-minute informative speech with visual aids for video-tape presentation before your campus television cameras. During the playback of the speeches, note the conversational quality of your voice, your skill in speaking before different cameras, and your ability to get the message across in a brief amount of time.

5. Make an announcement of some worthwhile cultural event soon to come to your campus. Try to deliver this message without notes.

Suggested References

Arnheim, Rudolf, *Radio: An Art of Sound* (New York: Da Capo Press, 1972). Chapter 2, "The World of Sound."

Hilliard, Robert, *Writing For Television and Radio* (New York: Hastings House, 1972). Chapter 6, "Talk Programs."

Lewis, Colby, *The TV Director/Interpreter* (New York: Hastings House, 1968). Chapter 8, "Animation or Liveliness;" Chapter 9, "Expressiveness;" Chapter 10, "Keeping up with the Action."

Miller, Melvin H., *Special Occasion Speeches* (Skokie, Ill.: National Textbook Co., 1964). Pp. 8–12 ("Speeches of Courtesy").

Milton, Ralph, *Radio Programming* (London: Geoffrey Bles, 1968). Project E, "Interviews."

Overstreet, Bonaro, *Understanding Fear* (New York: Harper & Row, 1971). Chapter 16, "Becoming Members One with Another."

Rossiter, Charles M., Jr., "Some Implications of Compressed Speech for Broadcasters," *Journal of Broadcasting*, Vol. 15 (Summer 1971), pp. 303–307.

Samovar, Larry A., and Jack Mills, *Oral Communication*, 2nd ed. (Dubuque, Iowa: Wm. C. Brown Co., 1972). Chapter 11, "Special Occasions."

Schramm, Wilbur (ed.), *The Science of Human Communication* (New York: Basic Books, 1963). Chapter 7, "The Diffusion of New Ideas and Practices" by Elihu Katz.

Skornia, H. J., R. H. Lee, and F. A. Brewer, *Creative Broadcasting* (Englewood Cliffs, N. J.: Prentice-Hall, 1950). Chapter 7, "Working with Scripts."

Swanson, Harold B., "Improving Your Press, Radio, and TV Relations," Information Service Series, The Department of Information and Agricultural Journalism, The University of Minnesota.

Warren, Carl, *Radio News Writing and Editing* (New York: Harper & Row, 1947). Chapter 26, "The Human Interest Touch."

Part Five
Related Speaking Situations

Part Five relates the principles of speaking to problems of leading meetings (Chapter 19) and to the discussion or conference situation (Chapter 20). This part is not intended to replace a full study of these important matters but to assist the student of speaking who encounters leadership or discussion–conference problems as part of his daily activities.

19
Leading a Meeting

"The question has been called for. Are you ready to vote?"

A speaker is generally to be found in the environment of a meeting of some kind — informal or formal, small or large. He has a desire to communicate, he has something to say, and one or more persons are present to receive what he has to say.

Leading a meeting is a highly specialized form of speaking. Knowing how to do it well is important for at least two reasons: (1) virtually every person — especially one who is interested in speaking and has attempted to develop his skills in this area — is likely to be called upon to perform the leadership role in a communication situation, and (2) the principles pertaining to leadership functions are somewhat different from those that are associated with speaking alone.

The leader in any group — fraternity, school government, city council, church organization, private club, staff — is likely to meet at least three kinds of situations that will require an understanding of these leadership principles and methods: (1) *The business meeting,* in which business is conducted according to an agenda. (2) *The program meeting* (like a banquet), in which no business is transacted but in which speeches, testimonials, and announcements are made. (3) *The group discussion, conference, or committee meeting,* where the members discuss and resolve definite problems.

Let us discuss methods of conducting the first two kinds of meetings here and leave the third kind (discussion or conference) to the following chapter because it is basically different.

Business Meetings

For the business meeting, the chairman (or chairperson)[1] usually has at least two major responsibilities: (1) to plan the agenda (order of business) and (2) to conduct the meeting in a fair, orderly, and dignified manner.

---

[1] See footnote 2, page 42.

The chairman should be neither proponent nor opponent of any item of business, and he should not defer to the wishes of anyone beyond the rules of established procedure. If, because of a special interest in an item of business or a special relationship to a member of the group, he cannot conduct the meeting without real or apparent conflict of interests, he should ask somebody else to serve as chairman; or at least he should relinquish the chair until the issue in question has been disposed of by the group. This procedure is usually set forth specifically in the many compilations of rules on conducting business meetings, including *Robert's Rules of Order.*

The chairman has to:

1. Prepare the agenda
2. Call the meeting to order
3. Call for the items of business in the order indicated in the agenda
4. Provide for the introduction of business according to the custom of parliamentary procedure
5. Conduct debate and other features of the consideration of business according to the established rules
6. Conduct voting in a fair and orderly manner
7. Courteously expedite the transaction of business, helping the members of the assembly to participate efficiently and harmoniously
8. Close the meeting according to the established rules

Although there is no pat formula for functioning successfully as a chairman, a thorough understanding of the principles and methods of parliamentary procedure is invaluable. It can help to keep the meeting flowing along smoothly, and it can also save time for the chairman. In fact, to conduct a meeting without an understanding of parliamentary procedure would be foolhardy and ineffectual.

The principles and methods fall into the following categories: (1) the object of parliamentary procedure, (2) the basic principles of parliamentary procedure, (3) some duties and rights of members of an assembly, (4) the usual order of business, (5) the steps in a motion, (6) motions for specific purposes, (7) amendments, (8) committees, and (9) voting.

The Object of Parliamentary Procedure

Parliamentary procedure acts as a guide for conducting business meetings so that the will of the majority can be determined in a just and orderly manner without depriving the minority of the rights customarily accorded to it in a democratic society.

Although parliamentary procedure does provide a somewhat elaborate and comprehensive set of rules for conducting a meeting, it is actually not so complicated and technical as some neophytes believe it to be. The fundamental principles are comparatively few in number, and they represent commonly accepted, commonsense judgments. In most instances, they can be easily grasped and quickly recalled. Furthermore, parliamentary procedure is not a tool to serve the ends of shrewd and devious persons without respect to ethics or the rights of others; it is, rather, a defense against such persons. It provides for free debate in order to assure a fair hearing for all members of the group. *In addition, its basic principles are sufficiently flexible to serve the needs of meetings of every degree of formality.*

The Basic Principles of Parliamentary Procedure

Parliamentary procedure is based on four principles: (1) *the principle of equality,* which holds that every member has an equal right with every other member to introduce, debate, and vote upon business; (2) *the principle of free and full debate,* which holds that unlimited debate is a basic right, that it is to be forbidden only if judged to be irrelevant, and that it is to be curtailed only when the group democratically regards such curtailment to be in its best interest and when it votes to stop it; (3) *the principle of rule of the majority without tyranny to the minority,* which holds that the minority agrees to abide by the decision of the majority in return for the privilege of participation, which privilege the minority enjoys with every procedural right of the majority until the vote is taken; and (4) *the principle of one question or proposal at a time,* which holds that although several proposals may be pending, only one should be immediately subject to vote.

Some Duties and Rights of Members of an Assembly

The Basic Duties   A member has these basic duties:

1. To obtain the floor properly before speaking

2. Not to speak upon a matter until it has been properly brought before the assembly

3. Not to interrupt another member unless the motion he wishes to make permits him to

4. To speak to the issues in debate, avoiding references to personalities (personal remarks pertaining to other members of the group) unless these references are relevant to the matter at hand

5. To abide by the spirit, as well as by the letter, of the principles of parliamentary procedure

The Basic Rights   A member also has certain basic rights:

1.   To offer any motion that he may consider wise, provided he observes the principles and rules governing the phrasing and introduction of motions

2.   To explain or debate upon a motion unless the rules specifically prohibit (certain motions are not open to debate)

3.   To call for "a point of order"—a question concerning the order or propriety of the item being considered

4.   To hold the floor, when it has been legally obtained, until he has finished speaking—unless precise time limits have been determined by the democratic process

The Usual Order of Business

The following activities are usually included in a business meeting (in the order listed). Although the number of steps may vary according to the kind of meeting and to the wishes of the members, the basic order—*because it is chronological*—should be followed as closely as possible. (See also the inset of the "Steps in a Motion," pages 330–331.)

Basic Order of Business

1.   *Call to order*

2.   *Roll call (if necessary)*

3.   *Reading, correction (if necessary), and approval of the minutes*

4.   *Reading and receiving of the treasurer's report*

5.   *Reports of other officers*

6.   *Reports of standing committees*

7.   *Reports of special committees*

8.   *Unfinished (old) business*

9.   *New business*

10. *Adjournment*

Motions for Specific Purposes

Although parliamentary procedure need not be a highly technical body of rules, it does provide for specific means of achieving exactly what a member may wish to have done at almost any point in a business meeting.

Of the proceedings that take place in most business meetings, nine may properly be associated with specific motions:

1.   *To introduce a matter of business;* use a main motion.

2.   *To alter a motion:* (a) amend or (b) refer to a committee.

3.   *To defer action* (motions arrayed in ascending order of "strength" or priority): (a) postpone indefinitely, (b) refer to a committee, (c) postpone to a certain time, (d) lay on the table, (e) make a special order.

4. *To suppress a motion:* (a) object to its consideration, (b) postpone indefinitely, (c) lay on the table, (d) move the previous question and reject the motion.

5. *To suppress or limit debate:* (a) limit debate by motion (set time limits regarding length of speeches, amount of time for each side, or total amount of time for debate), or (b) move the previous question (move to stop debate).

6. *To consider a matter a second time:* (a) take from the table, (b) consider at the time to which it was postponed, (c) consider at the time of the committee report, (d) consider as new business if previously postponed indefinitely, (e) reconsider, (f) rescind, (g) discharge the committee if it fails to make a report.

7. *To reverse a previous decision:* (a) reconsider and defeat the original motion, or (b) rescind.

8. *To set aside a rule:* suspend the rule.

9. *To protect a member from discomfort (and the like):* use the question (motion) of rights and privileges.

Steps in a Motion

The following steps outline the history of a motion from its first proposal to its final resolution, with the exception of motions that do not require a "second" or are not debatable:

1. *The motion is made.* Some member of the assembly must state his wish or point of view in the form of a declaration or "motion." The chairman may call for the motion, or the member may ask for recognition and then introduce the motion by saying "I move . . ."

2. *The motion is seconded.* Because it is assumed that a motion should be considered only if at least two persons support it (or want to have it considered by the assembly), parliamentary procedure provides for the "second." The chairman may ask for a second, or he may merely wait to hear one from the floor. In any event, if a member other than the one who made the motion wishes to second it, he says, "I second the motion," or simply "Second."*

3. *The motion is stated.* After the motion has been seconded, the chairman repeats it word for word so that (1) the member who proposed the motion will know whether the chairman heard it accurately, (2) all members of the assembly can hear the motion, and (3) the secretary can have the time to record it. (If, for reasons of ambiguity or lack of clarity in the wording, the chairman has difficulty in repeating the motion word for word, he will attempt to express the *intent* of the motion and he may assist the member who proposed the motion in formulating a statement that most accurately and clearly expresses the intent.)

4. *The motion is debated.* As soon as the members of the assembly clearly understand the proposal in question, they have an opportunity to present the cases for and against the motion. (Some authorities on parliamentary procedure prescribe rules for the conduct of debate, but such considerations have

Amendments

The motion to amend is a subsidiary motion that can be applied to all motions except those listed as not being subject to amendment. It must be relevant, and it must not have the effect merely of changing the original motion from affirmative to negative. Amendments can be made for four purposes: (1) to add, (2) to insert, (3) to strike out, and (4) to substitute.

An amendment may be amended, but this amendment of an amendment may not be amended. When a motion is under consideration, only one amendment of the first degree is permitted at one time, although any number may be offered in succession.

Committees

The subject of committees can perhaps best be discussed under three headings: (1) types of committees, (2) specific purposes of committees, and (3) means of appointing special committees.

---

no place in this brief review.) At this point the members have the opportunity to speak about the motion, to amend it, to explain it, and to hear all views on it. Discussion is subject only to the limitations which the members themselves impose in the form of time limits, number of participations by each member, and similar special regulations.

5. Debate is stopped. The three ways to stop debate in order to prepare for taking the vote differ largely in degree of formality. A debate or discussion may be stopped (1) by silence, whereby the chairman assumes the absence of further debate to be a sign that the members are ready to vote, in which case he asks, "Are you ready to vote?" and, hearing no dissent, proceeds to the next step; (2) by a "call for the question" by a member whose informal "Question!" indicates that he, at least, wishes the vote to be taken, in which case the chairman says, "The question has been called for. Are you ready to vote?" and,

hearing no dissent, proceeds to the next step; (3) by introduction of the motion called "the previous question" — a motion initiated to stop debate and take the vote; as a motion, it requires a second, and if two thirds of the members voting vote favorably, debate is stopped and the vote is taken, even if the minority wants to continue the debate.

6. The motion is put. At this point the chairman restates the motion as originally stated, or as amended during the discussion period, in order that all members can know the exact details of the motion on which they are about to vote.

7. The vote is taken. The five methods of taking the vote will be presented later in this chapter in the section on "Voting."

8. The vote is announced. The chairman announces the outcome of the voting, usually with the words "The motion is carried" or "The motion is lost." When voting has been recorded, the chairman says, for example, "The motion is carried by a vote of twelve to six."

Types of Committees   Committees may be classified as (1) *special* or *ad hoc* (appointed at a special time for a specific purpose), (2) *standing* (appointed at a regular time to perform regularly designated functions), and (3) *committee of the whole* (the entire assembly acting informally, usually under special circumstances).

Specific Purposes of Committees   Committees are constituted to (1) investigate a matter and report facts, (2) consider and report on a resolution, (3) consider a matter and report recommendations, and (4) perform a specific duty for the assembly (committee with "the power to act").

Means of Appointing Special Committees   Special committees may be appointed by (1) a *statement in the motion* that proposes the committee action, (2) *ballot*, (3) *nominations from the floor*, and (4) *designation from the chairman* as soon as the motion authorizing the committee is passed or at any time before adjournment.

Voting

The subject of voting may be divided into (1) the *forms* of voting and (2) the *place of the chairman* in voting.

Forms of Voting   There are five distinct forms: (1) *ayes and noes* (comparison of volumes of sound), (2) *raising of hands* (division of the assembly by the show of hands), (3) *rising* (division of the assembly by asking each member to stand and be counted, (4) *yeas and nays* (a roll call, with each member responding by saying either "Yea" or "Nay"), (5) *balloting* (the casting of secret ballots).

The Place of the Chairman in Voting   If the chairman is a member of the organization conducting the business, he has the right to vote under certain conditions. In the first three methods of voting described above, the chairman customarily votes only when his vote will affect the result. In roll-call voting, his name is called last. In voting by ballot, he must vote (if he chooses to vote) before the polls are closed.

Selected Parliamentary Motions

Although there are more than fifty motions that may properly be used in the conduct of business, only the ones more commonly encountered in typical situations are given in the table of Selected Parliamentary Motions, based upon *Robert's Rules of Order, Newly Revised* (1970). For each motion, five questions are asked and answered: (1) Does the motion require a second? (2) Is the motion amendable? (3) Is the motion debatable? (4) What vote is required to carry the motion? (5) May another member interrupt the speaker who has the floor in order to make the motion?

Selected Parliamentary Motions

(Based upon Robert's Rules of Order, Newly Revised, 1970 Edition)*

Motions	Second?	Amendable?	Debatable?	Vote?	Interrupt Speaker?
Main or Principal					
1. Original main	Yes	Yes	Yes	Maj.	No
2. Reconsider	Yes	No	Yes[1]	Maj.	Yes[2]
3. Rescind	Yes	Yes	Yes	Maj.[3]	No
4. Take from table	Yes	No	No	Maj.	No
Subsidiary					
1. Postpone indefinitely	Yes	No	Yes	Maj.	No
2. Amend	Yes	Yes	Yes[1]	Maj.	No
3. Refer to committee	Yes	Yes	Yes	Maj.	No
4. Postpone definitely	Yes	Yes	Yes	Maj.	No
5. Limit debate	Yes	Yes	No	2/3	No
6. Previous question	Yes	No	No	2/3	No
7. Lay on table	Yes	No	No	Maj.	No
Incidental					
1. Suspend a rule	Yes	No	No	[4]	No
2. Leave to withdraw a motion	[5]	No	No	Maj.	No
3. Objection to consideration	No	No	No	[6]	Yes
4. Point of order	No	No	No[7]	Chair	Yes
5. Appeal from chair	Yes	No	[8]	Maj.	Yes
6. Division of question[9]	Yes	Yes	No	Maj.	No
Privileged					
1. Make a special order	Yes	Yes	Yes	2/3	No
2. Question of privilege	No[10]	No[10]	No[10]	[11]	Yes
3. Take a recess[12]	Yes	Yes	[13]	Maj.	No
4. Adjourn[14]	Yes	No	No	Maj.	No
5. Fix time for next meeting	Yes	Yes	No	Maj.	No

---

* *Pages cited in footnotes refer to this edition.*

[1] *Undebatable, however, when the motion to be reconsidered or amended is undebatable.*

[2] *Interruption permitted only to make the motion. Consideration has the rank of the motion to be reconsidered.*

[3] *Certain exceptions. See pages 258–260; also, see page 29 of "Charts, Tables, Lists."*

[4] *(a) 2/3 vote required when applied to rules of order; (b) Majority vote required when applied to "ordinary Standing Rules"—those not related to parliamentary procedure as such.*

[5] *(a) "Yes" if motion made by person requesting permission; (b) "No" if made by another member.*

[6] *A 2/3 vote in the negative is necessary to defeat this motion.*

[7] *Unless Chair submits question to the assembly, then rule is as for "Appeal."*

[8] *Undebatable when it relates simply to indecorum, to transgression of the rules of speaking, or to priority of business; or if made during a division of the assembly or while the immediately pending motion is undebatable.*

[9] *Motion refers to propositions relating to the same subject although each part can stand alone.*

[10] *Certain exceptions. See pages 191–196; also, see page 24 of "Charts, Tables, Lists."*

[11] *Chairman decides whether the question is one of privilege, the motion is then made and handled as a main motion.*

[12] *Not always privileged; see pages 196–199; also, see page 26 of "Charts, Tables, Lists."*

[13] *Undebatable if made when another question is before the assembly.*

[14] *Certain exceptions; see pages 200–201; also, see page 8 of "Charts, Tables, Lists."*

It will be noted that the twenty-two motions included in this table are grouped in four categories: (1) main or principal, (2) subsidiary, (3) incidental, and (4) privileged. In general, *main or principal* motions provide for the consideration of business or for means by which business can be brought before the assembly. *Subsidiary* motions provide for the disposition of motions that have been brought before the assembly. *Incidental* motions may arise incidentally in the course of consideration of business—in a sense, they are similar to traffic rules or special regulations. *Privileged* motions represent methods by which special action may be taken or the rights and privileges of members may be protected. (Subsidiary and privileged motions are arranged in this table according to their *increasing strength* or *ascending priority*.)

Program Meetings

A leader in an organization may be called upon to serve as chairman or presiding officer of a program meeting—a dinner meeting, a meeting with one or more speakers, or any other meeting at which business is rarely, if ever, transacted.

Here his or her responsibilities are, necessarily, quite different from those in a business meeting, but they are fully as important. In fact, when such meetings fail, it is often because the chairman has planned the meeting poorly, or decided on no fixed time schedule, neglected the usual amenities or courtesies, or given inadequate introductions to the different portions of the program (including the speakers).

In general, the chairman of a program meeting has the responsibility for (1) planning the program, (2) planning the physical setup (chairs, tables, and seating), (3) considering what amenities and courtesies should be attended to (announcements made and persons recognized or welcomed), and (4) introducing the several features of the program.

Planning the Program

Although there is no typical agenda, or order of events, for program meetings, certain features naturally fit into certain places in the program. For instance, a dinner meeting with a program consisting of a single speech might properly have the following items on its agenda:

1. Invocation (or pledge or song)
2. Dinner
3. Brief remarks by the chairman (to introduce the program and to set the tone for the occasion)

4. Words of welcome by the chairman (or person appointed by him)

5. Announcements

6. Introduction of the speaker by the chairman (or person appointed by him)

7. Open-forum period conducted by the chairman (if such a period is indicated)

8. Adjournment

Whatever the several elements of the program, it is important that the order be determined by a basic principle, that a time schedule be laid out (at least in broad terms), and that the participants be notified of this schedule and their allotment of time. These are clearly the responsibilities of the leader.

Planning the Physical Setup

Certain features of the physical setup will be determined by the nature of the meeting place. However, the chairman usually has the responsibility for making decisions as to (1) whether or not there will be a speakers' table; (2) how the tables (at a dinner meeting) will be arranged; (3) how the chairs and other items of furniture will be arranged; (4) what persons will sit at the speakers' table and in what order; (5) whether there will be a public address system; (6) how the temperature and ventilation will be controlled; (7) how the lighting will be controlled for the speakers or the speakers' table; and (8) how the program (at a dinner meeting) will be coordinated with the food service.

While there is no rigid guide for program arrangement, such considerations as comfort, convenience, and the roles of the persons present should be kept in mind. The chairman should know, for instance, that lights behind a speaker or a speakers' table are likely to cause discomfort to the audience, and he should take steps to have them dimmed or turned out during the program portion of the meeting.

Considering the Amenities and Courtesies

A good chairman will always think of the customs, courtesies, and words of welcome that will do much to make an occasion enjoyable for everyone present. In planning a program meeting—since the guidelines are not arbitrary—the chairman will do well not only to recall what was done at some previous, particularly pleasant meeting but also to anticipate the situation, ask himself what special words and actions would make everybody feel welcome and relaxed.

Introducing the Several Features of the Program

One of the chairman's most important functions is to introduce the different parts of the program and to provide transitions from one part to another. Again, no formula can be cited here, although the special circumstances and the good judgment of the chairman will determine the nature of his handling of these functions. He will win greatest favor, however, if he will *make the introductions brief and to the point*, and, similarly, *make the transitions brief and relevant*. Frequently, chairmen slow down the progress of the meeting and bring in irrelevancies through long introductions and unnecessary (and often "boring") anecdotes. As any experienced listener will tell you, keep the program moving with brief introductions and transitions presented in a spirit of friendliness, warmth, and enthusiasm.

Suggested Assignments

1.   Analyze and evaluate a business meeting in which you have participated. Consider such items as (a) the agenda, (b) the chairman's handling of the business and of the participants, and (c) the nature of any *parliamentary problems*, if any appear.

2.   With respect to the meeting considered in assignment 1, determine the *causes* and the *effects* of the specific situations.

3.   Assume that you are responsible for preparing the agenda for one of the following types of meetings (assume, also, that the rules of the organization do not specify the nature of the agenda): (a) a meeting of a departmental club (History, Philosophy, Speech, etc.); (b) a meeting of a church council or board; (c) a meeting of a high school or college faculty; (d) a meeting of a high school or college student council. Prepare an agenda containing at least ten items.

4.   Be prepared to handle as chairman the following items of business: (a) a secretary's report (minutes); (b) a treasurer's report; (c) a committee report; (d) a main motion from the beginning to the end without the use of subsidiary motions other than "the previous question."

5.   Be prepared to handle as chairman the following items of business: (a) an amendment of the first degree; (b) an amendment of the second degree; (c) a motion "to refer to a committee"; (d) a motion "to postpone definitely" (to a certain time).

6.   Plan a dinner meeting with guests to be introduced, with a speaker or speakers to be introduced, and with announcements to be made.

7.   With respect to the meeting in assignment 6, determine the effects of any un-satisfactory situations. (What were audience reactions to these situations?)

8.   Plan a program meeting with several "platform guests" to be introduced, with a number of announcements to be made, with a speaker to be introduced, and with an open-forum period to be conducted.

9.   With respect to the meeting in assignment 8, perform the operations described there.

10.   Plan the order of events for each of the following meetings: (a) a dinner meeting with guests to be introduced, with two speakers to be introduced, and with an-nouncements to be made; (b) a program meeting with several platform guests to be introduced, with a number of announcements to be made, with a speaker to be introduced, and with an open-forum period to be conducted.

Suggested References

Bosmajian, Haig A., *Readings in Parliamentary Procedures* (New York: Harper & Row, 1968).

Ewbank, Henry L., Jr., *Meeting Management* (Dubuque, Iowa: Wm. C. Brown Co., 1968).

Henry, W. H. F., and Levi Seeley, *How to Organize and Conduct a Meeting* (New York: Noble and Noble, 1938).

Jones, O. Garfield, *Senior Manual for Group Leadership* (New York: Appleton-Cen-tury-Crofts, 1949).

Keesey, Ray E., *Modern Parliamentary Procedure* (Boston: Houghton Mifflin Co., 1973).

O'Brien, Joseph P., *Parliamentary Law for the Layman: Procedures and Strategy for Meetings* (New York: Harper & Row, 1952).

Robert, Henry M. (Sarah Corbin Robert), *Robert's Rules of Order, Newly Revised* (Glenview, Ill.: Scott, Foresman and Co., 1970).

Sturgis, Alice F., *Sturgis Standard Code of Parliamentary Procedure*, 2nd ed. (New York: McGraw-Hill Book Co., 1966).

Wiksell, Wesley, *How to Conduct Meetings* (New York: Harper & Row, 1966).

20
Discussion—Conference

"Can't we talk it over?"

In many instances, oral communication is more than presenting a speech to a group of listeners; it is also an involvement and exchange of ideas. Therefore, no book on speaking would be complete without a treatment of communication *among* the individuals in a group—that is, discussion. Discussion takes place with varying degrees of formality and preparation—from the animated political arguments among a group of friends to the more formal forums. It has also become, through television, a popular spectator sport—witness the success of the televised conferences among prominent journalists and public figures and of the round-table discussions among authorities in various fields.

For a fuller treatment of this phase of communication, we can turn to any of the several complete books on discussion. In this brief survey, we shall touch upon (1) the nature of discussion, (2) problems for discussion (what people discuss), (3) the substance of discussion, (4) some "patterns of thought" in discussion (the structure of profitable progressions of thought in discussion), (5) the forms of discussion, (6) leadership in discussion, and (7) participation in discussion.

This chapter does not include a detailed treatment of the dynamics of the group process, especially with respect to interpersonal relationships, even though such a consideration is pertinent to a complete study of discussion. However, several of these elements have been dealt with in preceding chapters. (See, for example, Chapter 4, where (1) feedback, (2) a profile of listener characteristics (occupations, social conditioning, religious beliefs, interests and hobbies, physical characteristics and actions), (3) classifications of listener attitudes, and (4) classifications regarding listener knowledge were considered. See also Chapter 5, where (1) the attributes, (2) the sources, and (3) the influences of ethos were considered. See also Chapter 7, where (1) motivations for human behavior (preservation, pride, altruism, etc.), and (2) suggestion and types of suggestion were analyzed. Finally, see Chapter 14, where such communication elements as (1) appearance, (2) posture, (3)

movement and gesture, (4) facial expression, (5) eye-contact, and (6) voice—
together with their influence upon listeners—were considered.)

While other personal, nonlogical, extrinsic factors do operate in discussion, as in all other communication situations, let us concentrate in this
chapter on those elements that are unique, or distinctive, with respect to
discussion.

The Nature of Discussion

Discussion usually is associated with, and takes place within, the small
group, although it can be accommodated to large groups. It is concerned with
answering questions or solving problems. It is usually characterized by a
type of speaking other than more-or-less formal speech making; it is more
like committee activity.

For our purposes, discussion may be defined as *thinking through and talking about problems or topics by a relatively small number of persons (usually in
informal circumstances) for purposes of finding solutions or gaining information.*

The relationship between discussion and group dynamics is subtle but
describable. While embracing many of the elements of group dynamics, discussion is much broader. To the extent that both are concerned with the
nature of *persons in groups,* they are essentially the same thing. However,
when discussion is concerned with *the nature of problems for analysis,* with
patterns of thought and organization, with *the reasoning process,* with *methods
of preparation,* and with *forms of discussion groups*—to mention certain factors
—it is much more inclusive than is group dynamics.

As for the relationship of discussion to "brainstorming," the latter
represents, in essence, *one* of the steps in the problem-solving process—the
step subsequently referred to as "the suggestion of solutions or possible
courses of action." To the extent that this is an important step in the process
of analyzing problems and of seeking solutions, brainstorming is most useful. However, to the extent that much more is needed in the attempt to solve
problems (and much more *is* needed), the principles and methods of discussion need to be considered.

The nature of discussion will become clearer when we note some distinctions between it and the other forms of speaking. We can make a comparison as to (1) the number of participants, (2) purpose, and (3) format.

Number of Participants

In the speaking situations described earlier, there is typically only one person speaking to (or with) an audience, whose members participate by listening. Discussion, on the other hand, implies two or more active participants,
whose interaction is the essence of the process.

Purpose

The two primary purposes of speaking to others are to present information and to influence attitudes and behavior. In contrast, the principal purposes of discussion are the solving of problems (personal problems, group problems, institutional problems) and the gaining of information. In discussion, both of these purposes are fulfilled through *interaction* in a spirit of co-operation and awareness of others, plus an attitude of open-mindedness.

Format

Essentially, speaking to others takes place in a more-or-less formal speaker-audience situation, with modifications in formality being largely in degree rather than kind (the speaker stands near his listeners, the speaker is seated while speaking, the listeners are seated informally, the listeners ask questions at any time, and so forth).

However, discussion is normally informal, with the participants seated around, or at, a table and with each person a potential contributor to the discussion at any moment (the round-table, the committee meeting, and the like). Although it is true that in some discussion situations, such as the panel discussion or the symposium, there is an audience, these situations are basically adaptations of the process of discussion to the needs of a group too large for the round-table format.

Problems for Discussion

In discussion, the subjects, or problems, are determined by the purposes, interests, concerns, and needs of the group. Contrary to the widespread notion that some subjects are suitable for discussion and others for speech making, they are actually in no way restricted by the process used. Rather, discussion is a methodology for considering those subjects that normally are—or should be—the business of a group.

For all practical purposes, the three basic kinds of problems *encountered in life* and, therefore, associated with discussion are (1) problems of *fact*, (2) problems of *value*, and (3) problems of *policy*. Some of these are *general* in character, in that they do not suggest any one kind of answer; and some are *specific*, in that they name a particular answer and then inquire whether it is *the* answer or solution.

Problem of Fact

A problem of *fact* is concerned with the existence or occurrence of events, the nature of phenomena, and the nature of concepts or ideas. It has nothing to do with policies, programs, or courses of action; it does not deal with appraisals, evaluations, or judgments about the goodness or adequacy of a person, policy, program, or course of action. The *general* problem might be stated as "What is the Honors College?" or "What is the role of the United Nations in international affairs?" The *specific* problem would be: "Is the Honors College an exemplification of the trend toward acceleration in education?" or "Is the role of the United Nations that of 'policeman' in international affairs?"

Although it might appear that problems of fact are not likely to initiate profitable discussion, we should note that many workshops, study groups, and other bodies do start with this type of problem. Also, because even honest and informed people sometimes do not agree as to what constitutes "fact," they need to explore their concepts and points of view. Furthermore, in considering problems of value and policy, groups may encounter problems of *fact* intrinsic in the total process. For example, the directors of an insurance company would be unable to reach a policy decision regarding premiums and rates, no matter how much discussion they engaged in, without certain facts on which to base their decisions and recommendations. Not only does the problem of fact enter, but also the problem of value, for the data must be interpreted and evaluated as well as reported.

Problem of Value

A problem of *value* is concerned with the goodness or badness, adequacy or inadequacy, strength or weakness of something—an idea, program, institution, or person. It is not concerned with policies, programs, or courses of action to be adopted or recommended by the discussion group; rather, it is concerned with *value judgments* regarding something that is placed under scrutiny. The general consideration might be "How worthwhile is the Honors College?" or "How worthwhile is the United Nations?"; the specific problem might be "Is the Honors College adequate to provide a superior education for the superior student?" or "Is the United Nations to be regarded as a success in its efforts to prevent international tensions?"

Problem of Policy

A problem of *policy* concerns a course of action or a policy to be adopted or rejected. Questions of fact and value may be included in any consideration of policies, but the end product is still a decision regarding a course of action or a policy.

As with fact and value, general problems of policy open up a topic for consideration without indicating any possible answers or limits for consideration. Furthermore, the answers will not be "Yes" or "No" but in the form of statements of policy—for example, "What should be the policy of this university regarding the establishment of an Honors College?" or "What, if anything, should be done to change the basic structure of the United Nations?" Similarly, specific problems of policy are concerned with specific courses of action, with suggested hypotheses, and with "Yes" or "No" answers to alternatives named in the question itself. For example: "Should this university adopt the Honors College plan now in use at X University?" or "Should the basic structure of the United Nations be modified by reducing the power of the large member-powers?"

Even though the specific type of policy problem may seem too restrictive — that is, it may appear to focus consideration upon only the course of action that is named — it need not be restrictive at all. A careful analysis of this type of question should produce alternatives to the one named or designated, and the ultimate decision of "Yes" or "No" should be reached in respect to both its apparent strengths and weaknesses and *those of other possible answers to the question.* Consequently, both the procedure and the end result may be the same as those associated with a general problem of policy. Furthermore, this type of problem needs to be considered here because it actually does arise frequently in human affairs. Do we not often ask "Should this be done?" rather than "What should be done?"

Let us also consider the *best form for the statement of a problem.* Even though a topic or a proposition can be discussed with some measure of profit, the best form ordinarily is a *question.* The major objection to a simply stated topic is that it neither focuses on a problem (does not raise a question) nor delimits the subject. For instance, a topic like "The Honors College" or "The United Nations" does not invite specific, purposeful discussion. Only after issues have been raised and questions have been asked, does a problem seem to evolve. Thus it would be better to begin with a question that has precise meaning and definite limits. The principal objection to a proposition is that it represents a judgment, an answer, a settled opinion regarding the subject at hand. While the proposition is the proper form for phrasing a motion or a statement in a speech of advocacy, it is less likely to invite inquiry than is true of a *question.*

The Substance of Discussion

A charge frequently made against group discussions, conferences, and committee meetings is that they lack real substance — that they are "thin," mere talk sessions based upon hearsay or impromptu personal opinion. While there may be some truth to this charge, it should be noted that (1) not all discussions need to be unprepared and (2) even discussions that arise spontaneously do not have to be "thin" if certain safeguards are observed.

Discussion *can have substance;* and frequently the leader, as well as the other participants, may be able to guarantee this substance. Also, a good organizer and summarizer in a group can help to make the real substance more evident. (See inset, page 351, on "keeping the discussion moving and clear" and "bringing the discussion to a satisfying conclusion.")

Let us briefly consider three topics: (1) sources of materials for discussion; (2) guides to preparation; and (3) methods of using the substance.

Sources of Materials

The sources of materials for discussion (as for any type of oral or written communication) are several: general observation, conversation, general experience, comparable experience, general reading, specific investigation. Some of these sources are inherent in, and arise out of, our everyday activities; others require both guided or controlled experience and investigation through reading or inquiry.

As noted in Chapter 6, the raw materials of reasoning and thinking are basically (1) *facts* and (2) the *opinions* of persons other than the reasoner or speaker himself. Hence, the sources of materials are those that yield facts and opinions. Even *random observation* can provide an almost infinite number of facts about people, institutions, practices, and events—as well as evidences of what people are saying about these phenomena. Similarly, *conversation, general experience, controlled experience,* and *general reading* will yield countless facts as well as judgments made by others. In like manner, specific investigations (involving observation, conversation, inquiry, and reading) produce facts and opinions. Common sources of information are reference books and bibliographies, books, periodicals, newspapers, pamphlets and documents, and guides or other compendia of information prepared for use in the study of various subjects.

Guides to Preparation

Although many discussions develop spontaneously and without the opportunity for specific preparation, others occur under conditions that permit at least *some preparation*. In fact, there are frequently more opportunities for specific preparation than might appear at first thought. Let us consider these two guides to preparation: (1) the exploration sheet or study guide and (2) the discussion plan in outline form.

The Exploration Sheet or Study Guide   This aid to preparation consists of a set of questions organized according to a pattern of thought or plan of development relevant to the problem or question being considered. Ordinarily, the leader composes it to assist the group in its preparation, although on some occasions the participant may profitably construct one for himself.

In either case, the study guide serves to systematize our investigation of a problem by helping us discover what kinds of questions need to be answered in analyzing the subject, what areas of the subject we already know something about, and what areas require specific investigations. It also shapes the investigation as to major points, minor points, types of evidence, and so forth.

The Discussion Plan in Outline Form   This outline is designed to systematize and direct preparation for discussion and to serve as a record of that planning. Ordinarily, both the leader and the members of the group can profitably prepare such a plan together. If it is well done, it can stimulate investigation, clarify thinking, and prepare each person to express himself in discussion more adequately than he could by tossing off his ideas in completely impromptu language.

The discussion plan outline is in no way a speaker's plan, and no one should attempt to speak from it or be bound by it during the discussion. It serves its purpose when it stimulates and systematizes preparation and steers a person toward at least tentative expression of the subject before him. With respect to form, we should keep in mind the customary principles and rules of outlining (see Chapter 10).

Methods of Using the Substance

The substance of discussion consists essentially of (1) the raw materials of *facts and opinions that a person assembles* and (2) the *reasoning or thinking* that he does with them. (This is not to say that the materials are always adequate or that the reasoning process is always valid. This merely says that the process involves reasoning about materials that are possessed by the thinker.) (A review of Chapter 6 will help us to consider the nature and the use of evidence and of reasoning from this evidence.)

Some Patterns of Discussion

In every walk of life a high premium is placed on clear and coherent analysis of subjects and on systematic development of the details suggested by this analysis. In the realm of oral communication, this analysis and development are taken for granted; in speech making, they are demanded. Precisely the same principle applies in discussion, even though it might appear at first glance that problem solving would, by its very nature, be less orderly and coherent than would speeches, reports, and sermons.

Problems of Policy

The theory of scientific method, as well as experiences in problem-solving procedures, indicates that a thorough analysis of a problem of *policy* should include consideration of such questions as these:

1. What is the precise problem before us?

2. What are existing circumstances; what causes them; and what are some of their consequences?

3. What is our yardstick for the measurement (evaluation) of possible solutions?

4. What are the possible solutions (or available alternatives)?

5. What are the relative merits of these possible solutions?

6. What, then, is the solution to the problem?

7. What steps should be taken to implement this solution?

Therefore, it looks as if the ideal analysis of a problem of policy should have a pattern of thought embracing such topics, or units, as these:

1. *Definition and Delimitation of the Problem*   What is the problem? What is the meaning of the terms used to state it? What are the limits of the problem?

2. *Analysis of the Present Situation*   What are the evidences of the problem? What "effects" can be observed? What are the "causes" of the problem? What are some consequences of these conditions?

3. *Analysis of Criteria or Standards of Value*   What are the desires of the person or persons trying to solve this problem? What criteria or values are operating? By what set of principles should the solutions be evaluated? What is the priority of these criteria—the relative weight attached to each?

4. *Suggestion of Possible Solutions*   What are the possible solutions? What are the possible answers to the question? What is the nature of each solution, at least as tentatively conceived? How are the suggested solutions related to each other?

5. *Evaluation of Possible Solutions*   What will be the consequences of the adoption of each proposed solution? To what extent will each proposed solution answer the basic question or solve the problem? What is the relation of each proposed solution to the elements in the present situation? What is the relation of each proposed solution to the criteria?

6. *Determination of the Best Solution*   What are the relative merits of each proposed solution considered quantitatively? How do these relative merits stand up against the relative weight given to the several criteria and the significance of the elements in the present situation? What are the relative merits of possible combinations or modifications of the proposed solutions? What, therefore, appears to be the best solution, and why?

7. *Implementation of This Solution*   What steps should be taken to put this solution into effect?

Problems of Value

Since a problem of *value* is concerned with the appraisal of a person, program, institution, or the like, which is already in existence, a thorough development of such a pattern suggests the following questions:

1. What is our problem?

2. What is the status quo (the circumstances under which we are making the appraisal) — or what is the setting for our appraisal?

3. What are the criteria by which we shall make our appraisal?

4. What is the nature of the subject to be evaluated?

5. What is the evaluation or final judgment based upon the relationships between the criteria and the subject to be evaluated?

This process is very much like that described for the problem of policy, except that in the problem of value we appraise only the subject named.

Problems of Fact

A problem of *fact* concerns events, phenomena, and ideas as they are. Here we are not concerned with evaluation or the determination of policies, but rather with getting at the facts and giving them meaning.

The plans of organization just discussed are not applicable here. On the other hand, several systems of organization may be used, no one of which is the best; each has values under certain conditions. In each instance, the plan of development is selected after thoughtful definition and delimitation of the problem or subject. Five such systems, essentially like some of those described for speech plans (see Chapter 11), follow:

Time Order   After the problem has been defined, the discussion begins at a certain time or date or at a certain step in a process, and moves forward or backward. For example, a discussion on "The Rise and Fall of Empires" might start with a reference to the Egyptians, then the Babylonians, the Greeks, the Romans, through a number of other empires, to the Spanish Empire in the New World, and to modern times.

Space Order   The discussion considers the material by its spatial relationships — such as east to west, north to south, outside to inside, inside to outside, bottom to top, top to bottom, center outward in concentric circles.

Cause-Effect Order   The discussion considers the material from the viewpoint of "causes" and their subsequent "effects," or vice versa. For example, a discussion on "The Rise and Fall of Empires" might begin with a question about any causal relationship between the affluence of the imperial country and its decline in strength.

Journalistic Order   The material is considered by answering such questions as *Who? What? When? Where? Why?*

Special Topical Order   The discussion considers the material as to (1) topical divisions with which the discussants are familiar, or (2) divisions peculiar to the subject, or (3) questions suggested by the subject. Even though the possibilities are almost limitless, it is imperative that some logical or natural sequence be selected and maintained so as to keep the discussion coherent. For instance, the material may be organized as (1) economic, political, social topics, or (2) objectives, underlying principles, general features, and specific details, or (3) such topics as education, theology, church history, and the like.

The Forms of Discussion

Discussions or conferences occur under a variety of circumstances and in groups with different formats and procedures. In the least formal, the *round-table discussion,* a few persons are seated around a table (or in a similarly informal situation). In the *panel discussion,* two, three, four, or perhaps six or eight persons talk informally in the presence of another group of persons (the audience). In the *symposium,* a similar number of persons discusses a subject by means of separate speeches (also in the presence of an audience).

Each of these principal types of discussion groups has its peculiar values, depending on (1) the number of persons participating, and (2) the purpose of the discussion. When there are only ten to fifteen persons, the round-table will provide each one the opportunity for considerable participation. With more than fifteen or twenty, however, it usually works better when a few persons participate quite intensively for a part of the time and the others join in an open-forum period. With this many persons, either the panel discussion or the symposium will probably be more practical.

As for the purpose of the discussion, the round-table will ordinarily be used for the policy-determining committee or similar groups, and sometimes for the small group seeking to learn about the problem. The panel discussion and the symposium will be used by a group that wants to learn about or understand a problem, especially when experts are called upon to discuss the problem for the benefit of the remainder of the group, who constitute the audience.

Round-Table Discussion

The round-table discussion is the typical committee or conference group in which each person may contribute at any moment, in which the thread of the discussion is sustained by the individual and in which (as a result) the stimulus-response pattern is constantly changing as attention is directed from one person to another. To provide the optimum conditions, the person in charge (probably the leader) should arrange the chairs in a circle or around a table, if possible. Accordingly, each person can see and hear the other participants most easily.

The round-table discussion has at least the following characteristics: (1) breadth (as broad as the number of participants), (2) variety, (3) spontaneity, (4) freedom (no restrictions imposed by prepared speeches), (5) participation by all members, and (6) less order and economy of time than with prepared speeches. Therefore, a group of twelve to fifteen persons desiring the first five of these attributes and not objecting to the sixth will choose the *round-table* as its format.

Panel Discussion

In the panel discussion a few persons (the panel) carry on a discussion in front of an audience, which may participate later in a forum period. The members of the panel may be members of the total group, or they may be experts brought in as outside speakers.

The panel discussion has at least the following characteristics: (1) considerable breadth, (2) variety, (3) spontaneity, (4) freedom, (5) provision for a large group (almost any number of persons can constitute the audience), (6) all persons invited to participate (members of the audience may contribute in the forum period), and (7) less order and economy of time than with prepared speeches. If the group wants the benefit of the first five attributes and does not object to limited participation by all members, as well as to less order and economy of time than with prepared speeches, it will choose the panel discussion for a group that is too large for the round-table format.

When planning a panel discussion, it is important to (1) select as panel members persons who have special competence in the subject, (2) seat the panelists so that they can easily be heard and seen by all members of the audience, (3) seat the panelists to secure maximum informality and give-and-take, (4) maintain all features of the round-table discussion that can be adapted to the audience situation, (5) maintain constant adaptation to the audience in content and in speaking, and (6) arrange for a forum period and respect time limits so that this period will not be crowded out.

Symposium

The symposium is a group in which two or more persons, under the direction of a chairman, present in separate speeches the various phases of a problem, with the audience usually participating in a forum period. As in the panel discussion, the speakers may be members of the total group, or they may be experts brought to the discussion.

This more formal type of discussion inherently possesses at least the following attributes: (1) some breadth (the number of speakers); (2) some variety; (3) order, compactness, and economy of time (on the assumption that the contributions are well organized, well phrased, and well developed); (4) provision for a large group; and (5) less spontaneity than in round-table and panel discussion (on the assumption that the speeches have been prepared in advance and that there will be comparatively little give-and-take and development of new ideas beyond those included in the advance preparation). If a group desires a well-organized and carefully phrased analysis of a subject in a format suitable for a large group, and does not object to the absence of the spontaneity that the panel discussion allows, it will choose the symposium. It is also possible to use a combination of the panel discussion or the symposium and the round-table — actually a number of coordinate round-tables — even with a large group.

In conducting a symposium, it is important to (1) select speakers who are competent in both subject matter and delivery; (2) select speakers and assign topics according to a specific plan of development (pattern of reflective thinking, topical subdivisions of the subject, or interests or points of view held by the speakers); (3) arrange for a chairman to introduce the speakers, make necessary transitions, and conduct the forum period; (4) arrange for a forum period and respect the time limits so that this will not be crowded out.

Leadership in Discussion

While opinions vary concerning the need for a designated leader in discussion groups, the most productive discussions usually have one person to lead and direct the flow of ideas among the participants. Since the functions of leadership have to be exercised by one or more members of the group — whether or not anyone is designated as the leader — it is desirable for every participant to have an understanding of the role of the leader and of the basic principles and methods of leadership.

An examination of leadership in discussion may be separated into five topics: (1) conceptions of leadership, (2) qualities of the ideal leader, (3) what the leader should and should not do, (4) methods useful in the normal processes of discussion, and (5) methods useful in handling difficult situations. (Although, of course, leadership does not need to be restricted to a designated leader, we are referring to "a leader" for the sake of simplicity.)

Conceptions of Leadership

Leadership involves at least two important relationships — those to procedure and those to substance. Regarding *procedure*, a leader may, in a sense, exert no leadership at all; he may merely start the meeting and let the discussion proceed as the other members desire. At the other extreme, he may maintain a heavy hand, guiding the group through the several stages of its analysis, clarifying, summarizing, providing transitions, and so on. Or he may exert his leadership at any stage between these extremes.

Regarding the relationship to *substance*, a leader may refrain from any participation as far as the content is concerned (one extreme); or he may act as an authority and pass judgment on all aspects of the subject (the other extreme). Other stages on this continuum might consist, for instance, of a leader's making the same kind of comments as any other member of the group, or of his making final decisions upon certain factors, such as items of evidence.

While much may be said for each of these and related conceptions regarding both procedure and substance, ideally most leaders should be at about the midpoint on the "procedure continuum" and rather near to the nonparticipation point on the "substance continuum." In other words, they will attempt to give direction and guidance, but they will not be authorities on the substance, or participants in the same way as are the other members of the group. While special circumstances may dictate different approaches—and some leaders may wish to participate actively in respect to substance—the problems likely to arise should be carefully weighed in advance.

Some Qualities of the Ideal Leader

Experience has shown that, although there are various types of leaders (and that perhaps similar results are achieved by diverse methods), there are certain qualities that successful leaders have in common. Ideally, a leader should:

1. Be objective—not prejudiced or opinionated
2. Be sensitive to individual and group reactions
3. Know and understand people (their motivations, etc.)
4. Be patient and self-restrained
5. Have, or try to develop, a warm personality
6. Try to exercise a good sense of humor when a light touch may be needed to ease a group over a difficult situation
7. Know the process of problem solving and related patterns of thought that may arise in the discussion of a topic

---

Methods Useful in Normal Situations

Getting the Group Acquainted

1. *Use informal introductions.*
2. *Supply name cards or name tags.*
3. *Stick to informal conversation prior to the actual discussion.*

Getting the Discussion Started

1. *Make a brief statement as to the purpose of the group and the nature of the subject or the problem.*
2. *Present a case, illustration, or incident setting forth the subject or the problem.*
3. *Ask for incidents and experiences of a kind that most of the group have had and about which they can talk freely.*
4. *State the issues of the problem or the subdivisions of the subject.*

5. *In the case of a value or policy problem, in particular, present one or two points of view concerning solutions to the problem.*
6. *In a similar situation, ask some member to present his view about the problem or the solution.*
7. *Ask for suggestions as to the method which the group wishes to adopt in its deliberations.*

Helping All Members Contribute Their Best

1. *Recognize and compliment contributions that are presented in a helpful manner.*
2. *Encourage contributions from all members of the group.*
3. *Recognize—even call upon—different persons from time to time.*

8. Be able to analyze and synthesize

9. Have, or try to develop, skill in oral communication — in phrasing thoughts as well as in voice and manner

What the Leader Should and Should Not Do

Within the context of the principles just set forth, some specific *dos* and *don'ts* may be suggested. In general, when you are a leader, you *should* try to:

1. Secure the process of problem solving or the development of a similar pattern of thought

2. Encourage, without being dogmatic, the group to begin at a specific point and to proceed with as few digressions as possible

3. Develop the most cooperative type of participation

4. Assist the group in introducing information when it is needed

5. Keep the discussion clear

6. Handle conflict constructively — help resolve differences of opinion or sidestep clashes resulting from personality or similar factors

7. Be alert to opportunities for, and means of, sharing your responsibilities and functions with the other members of the group

Keeping the Discussion Moving and Clear

1. *Maintain a happy medium between tedious movement and too-rapid progress — staying too long on one point and allowing shallow and superficial treatment of ideas.*

2. *Recognize the time for movement from one step to another in the thinking process.*

3. *Avoid deadlocks by securing tentative conclusions or an agreement to suspend judgment until further information is secured.*

4. *Encourage every person to speak to the point at hand.*

5. *Supplement oral contributions with chalkboard or similar notations if possible (visual aids are always effective).*

Bringing the Discussion to a Satisfying Conclusion

1. *Give a brief summary based on the steps in problem solving or some other topical pattern.*

2. *Give a summary based on the issues or questions raised in the discussion.*

3. *Give a summary based on the conclusions arrived at by the group.*

4. *Give a summary based on the recommendations a policy-determining group is prepared to present to another group.*

In like vein, when you are a leader, you *should not:*

1. Dominate the group's work

2. Make the "machinery of discussion" superior to spontaneous responses from the participants

3. Talk every time some member contributes

4. Assume the role of an authority in the subject unless you have special qualifications (even then, remember your basic role as a leader)

5. Summarize the progress of the discussion to the point of intruding

6. Present too many points of view on the subject under discussion; rather, be an objective interpreter of contributions from all members of the group

During the course of any discussion or conference, there are at least five situations in which the skillful leader can do much to assist the participants to do their best (see the inset on "Methods Useful in Normal Situations"). In addition, there are certain situations stemming from human frailties and related factors that are likely to arise and to some degree disrupt the smooth, satisfying, and productive course of the deliberations (see the inset on "Methods Useful in Difficult Situations").

Methods Useful in Difficult Situations

Handling the Ready-Talking,
Interrupting Member

1. *Interrupt him as pleasantly as possible, and ask him to state his point briefly.*

2. *Interrupt him pleasantly, sum up his contribution, and turn to other members of the group.*

3. *Ask him to yield to others.*

4. *Help create a situation in which the group pressure makes clear the need for self-restraint.*

5. *As a last resort, request that all members be recognized before speaking.*

Handling the Nonresponsive Member

1. *If he is reticent, do not force him; but eventually and tactfully ask a question of him and finally bring him into the discussion.*

2. *If he seems to be a deliberate, careful thinker, give him time, ultimately directing a question to him.*

3. *Suggest that those who have made contributions turn to the others for comments.*

4. *During a break or recess, converse with this person, trying to warm him up.*

Handling the Too Assertive Member

1. *Ask the person to repeat the statement and to explain it and its implications.*

2. *Feed his statements back to this person in nonemotional terms, and encourage others to do likewise.*

3. *Encourage the group to present supporting material for all points of view that are introduced.*

Participation in Discussion

Participation can be considered from the standpoint of (1) the participant's preparation with respect to content, (2) the participant's attitudes and procedures, and (3) methods of contributing.

Preparation with Respect to Content

A participant's desirable traits in respect to the substance of the discussion may be numerous or few, depending upon the thinking of the person who lists them. For our purposes, the following may be most significant: (1) possession and use of adequate information, (2) ability to think logically, and (3) ability to analyze and synthesize.

With respect to information, it is obvious that one of the essentials of good discussion is substance (adequate content or evidence). So that his contributions can have real substance, the good participant will gather as much information as possible and bring the results of this careful preparation to bear throughout the discussion, making use of the information

---

4. *Provide, if necessary, for the intro-duction of evidence via a reference source, a resource person, or a consult-ant.*

Handling the Person Who Is Overanxious to Settle the Problem

1. *Encourage the person to use the problem-solving or other relevant pattern of thought.*
2. *Ask the person a question or two concerning stages in the thought pattern that he wishes to omit.*
3. *Point out how this group avoided trouble at earlier stages by using a systematic procedure or wherein another group found this methodical procedure to be beneficial.*
4. *As a last resort, handle this person as you would a ready-talking, interrupt-*

ing member—for instance, interrupt him, sum up his contribution, and turn to others in the group.

Handling the Antagonistic, Belligerent Person

1. *Divert any caustic remarks from the other members of the group to yourself— making yourself the butt of the attack.*
2. *Calmly and in less charged language, sum up the antagonistic remarks made by this person.*
3. *In a conciliatory and cooperative manner, comment on the apparent reasons for anger or antagonism.*
4. *Remind the group that frank discussion requires self-control, and that while honest differences of opinion are not only inevitable but actually desirable, they are far different from manifestations of antagonism.*

systematically, logically, and with proper timing. What this implies is that he will be able to reason competently — that is, put together his total knowledge of the subject and give it new meanings.

Clear and coherent sequence of thought constitutes one of the essentials of good discussion. In other words, discussion does not ramble just because it is spontaneous thought-in-process. Consequently, the good participant will place a high premium upon careful analysis of the subject and upon careful development of this subject through clear and coherent thought patterns (synthesis).

Attitudes and Procedures

Experiences in committee meetings and similar discussion groups reinforce the realization that *content alone* is not the essence of such gatherings of people. *People in the discussion* are themselves important; their attitudes, behavior, and methods of contributing will often make a meeting a success or a failure. For our purposes, the following attributes have particular interest: (1) a spirit of cooperation and awareness of others, (2) an attitude of open-mindedness, and (3) adequacy in communication.

Discussion, at its best, is a cooperative activity. Its essence is a *working together to solve a problem or to explore a subject.* To the extent, therefore, that each of us regards our primary duty in discussion as working with others and relating our information and judgments to those of others, the discussion will meet this goal. This does not mean the loss of self; rather, it means cooperation and a realization that other persons and other ideas are present in company with ours and should be constantly kept in mind. It means that while there will, of course, be honest differences in evidence, objectives, and reasoning, there will also be honest attempts to reconcile these differences for the common good.

Growing naturally out of this consideration is the *attitude of open-mindedness.* This is a kind of objectivity through which we recognize and accept the worth of another person's ideas without overlooking the intrinsic worth of our own. The good participant actively values the group achievement as one that is based upon a body of evidence and reasoning broader than solitary thought could produce. Consequently, we come to the discussion anticipating that we will be made aware of new information and that we will be led into new lines of thought by the group. In addition, we acknowledge that this experience will improve our understanding of the problem and of the means of dealing with it.

Adequacy in communication — as represented by a clear, enthusiastic, well-modulated voice; a friendly, lively, direct manner; and clear and meaningful phrasing of ideas — is a requisite in discussion. Such behavior is needed not only to bring out the content to the best advantage but also to satisfy the participants. Clearly, the person who speaks clearly and enthusiastically, and who presents his contributions simply and clearly, with good grammar and

syntax, in as straightforward a manner as possible, will do much to make the total discussion a profitable one.

Methods of Contributing

For effective group work, as represented by good content and by participant-satisfaction, attention to certain attitudes and procedures makes a big difference. Some of these are:

1. *Contribute according to the pattern of thought.* Be aware of, and heed, the underlying pattern of thought that is being developed. Be aware of "where the group is" at any moment—what ground has been covered, what principal ideas are in focus, and where the group is likely to move next. Then be ready to participate at any moment according to this sequence of thought.

2. *Contribute in context.* Contribute by means of a "bridge" to what has just been said by another participant. The thought connection must be real, and the word connection must carry the listeners across. (Examples might be "In line with this, I . . ." or "Extending this idea a bit further, . . ." or "Let's look at this in another light. . . .")

3. *Contribute in the "explanatory manner."* Make completely clear the basis for your contributions toward the development of an idea or the solutions of a problem. In discussion, perhaps more than in other communication situations, the need to foster group understanding stands out. One of the best means of accomplishing this is by presenting the rationale for an idea.

4. *Contribute with tact.* Tactful participation is of great importance in view of the seeming paradox of discussion—cooperation in the face of inevitable differences in evidence, reasoning, criteria, and idiosyncrasies of the participants. Contribute in spirit of thoughtfulness, consideration, polite disagreement, and difference of opinion tempered with avoidance of personalities and with exploitation of elements of agreement and grounds for cooperation.

5. *Contribute clearly and efficiently.* Because communication is the very essence of discussion, try to contribute in a manner that is clear and efficient. Speak clearly and with meaningful inflection; act enthusiastically and with meaningful physical responses. In the area of content, strive for clear, unambiguous, and unequivocal word choice and grammatically correct and easy-to-follow sentence structure.

6. *Listen carefully.* While this admonition may seem unrelated to *contributing* in discussion, it is actually a major factor in good participation. Unfortunately, many participants do not "hear" all that is said *because they have not trained themselves to listen and to interpret meaningfully, because they receive what they want to receive,* or *because they are too busy formulating rejoinders* to listen with care beyond the point of first disagreement. The remedy includes at least three important attitudes and practices: (1) try to get all that is said—listen to everyone and keep your mind focused on and engaged in the problem under discussion; (2) derive meaning from what is being said by carefully making associations and inferences; and (3) resist the temptation to present a rejoinder as soon as a controversial matter is introduced.

7. *Participate in the spirit of "desiring to understand."* This concept represents the epitome of effective activity in discussion. It is the essence of cooperation—the means by which real thought-in-process can be achieved—and perhaps the best means by which member satisfactions can be realized.

This kind of participation consists of (1) an honest desire to understand another person's point of view, (2) an attempt to compare your understanding of another person's contribution with his understanding of it (3) an attempt to find the rationale behind another person's contribution, especially when there appears to be any disagreement, and (4) an attempt to phrase your reaction, together with the rationale for it, in such clear form that the other person clearly understands it. Perhaps the ideal outcome of this combination of *attitude* and *procedure* can be phrased as follows: *A person truly understands another's point of view only when he can state it so perfectly that the other person accepts it without qualification.*

Suggested Assignments

1. Make an inventory of the number and types of discussion situations (as defined and described in this chapter) in which you have participated in recent weeks. What were their purposes? What did they accomplish? What forms did they take?

2. As you reflect upon the experiences considered in assignment 1, what impressions do you have regarding their quality? How satisfactory were they in subject matter? In member satisfactions (a feeling that the experiences were worthwhile)?

3. With respect to the situations considered in assignments 1 and 2, attempt to determine, in general, the reasons for the favorable or unfavorable judgments. Consider (a) the subject matter itself, (b) leadership, and (c) participation.

4. Observe a committee in session. Analyze and evaluate it in regard to both leadership and participation.

5. Analyze and evaluate this same committee meeting in respect to the sequence of ideas—the development of its problems and the development of its solutions to these problems.

6. Observe a panel discussion. Analyze and evaluate it in regard to physical arrangements, selection of participants, leadership, and participation.

7. Observe a symposium. Analyze and evaluate it in regard to the items named in assignment 6.

8. Assume that you are to participate in a round-table discussion or a panel discussion on "What Is the Best Policy for the United States to Follow in Its Relations with the U. S. S. R.?" Prepare a study guide of approximately 35 questions.

9. With respect to the same situation as in assignment 8, prepare a three-page discussion plan.

10. Make a list of the important communication skills that are inherently needed to make a discussion situation satisfactory. Compare and contrast these with those inherently needed in both informal and formal situations associated with the forms of speaking discussed in Part Four of this book.

Suggested References

Barnlund, Dean C., and Franklyn S. Haiman, *The Dynamics of Discussion* (Boston: Houghton Mifflin Co., 1960).

Bormann, Ernest G., *Discussion and Group Methods* (New York: Harper & Row, 1969).

Brack, Harold A., and Kenneth G. Hance, *Public Speaking and Discussion for Religious Leaders* (Englewood Cliffs, N. J.: Prentice-Hall, 1961).

Cartwright, Dorwin, and Alvin Zander (eds.), *Group Dynamics*, 3rd ed. (New York: Harper & Row, 1968).

Crowell, Laura, *Discussion: Method of Democracy* (Glenview, Ill.: Scott, Foresman and Co., 1963).

Gulley, Halbert E., *Discussion, Conference, and Group Process*, 2nd ed. (New York: Holt, Rinehart and Winston, 1968).

Harnack, Victor, and Thorrel B. Fest, *Group Discussion: Theory and Technique* (New York: Appleton-Century-Crofts, 1964).

Jacobson, Wally D., *Power and Interpersonal Relations* (Belmont, Calif.: Wadsworth Publishing Co., 1972).

McBurney, James H., and Kenneth G. Hance, *Discussion in Human Affairs* (New York: Harper & Row, 1950).

Potter, David, and Martin P. Andersen, *Discussion: A Guide to Effective Practice*, 2nd ed. (Belmont, Calif.: Wadsworth Publishing Co., 1970).

Sattler, William M., and N. Edd Miller, *Discussion and Conference*, 2nd ed. (Englewood Cliffs, N. J.: Prentice-Hall, 1968).

Index

Numbers in italics refer to sections of the text set off in boxes, consisting of practical considerations and suggestions for the beginning student.